A Preface to Action

An Introduction to American Politics

Kenneth Smorsten
San Jose State University

with a chapter on public policy by
Larry N. Gerston
San Jose State University

A Preface to Action

An Introduction to American Politics

Second Edition

Goodyear Publishing Company, Inc.
Santa Monica, California

TO THE STUDENT

A study guide has been developed and published to accompany this text. If your bookstore does not have a copy, ask them to order **Study Guide to Accompany A Preface to Action:** *An Introduction to American Politics, Second Edition* by Maurice Waters.

Library of Congress Cataloging in Publication Data

Smorsten, Kenneth.
  A preface to action.

  Includes bibliographies and index.
  1. Political participation—United States.
2. United States—Politics and government.
I. Gerston, Larry N., joint author. II. Title.
JK1764.S56 1980   320.9'73   79-25958

Y–6844–8

Current Printing (last digit):

10 9 8 7 6 5 4 3 2 1

Pp. 11, 122, 221, 444: Doonesbury cartoons copyright © 1971/1972 G. B. Trudeau. Reprinted by permission of Universal Press Syndicate. All rights reserved.

Photo Research: Cynthia Putman and
Susan Caney-Peterson

Printed in the United States of America

Contents

Chapter 3
The Constitutional Setting   43

Chapter 4
Individual Liberties and Civil Rights   71

Part Two
Dilemmas of Citizen Participation   105

Chapter 5
Citizen Politics: Actors and Nonactors   107

Chapter 6
Parties and Elections: The Limits of Participation   135

Preface

The question of whether to engage in or retreat from political action continues to loom as a major issue of our time. It is a question that perplexes students with high ideals and great ambitions who feel frustrated by their own inconclusive attempts at achieving reform. It is a question that confounds members of Congress, state legislators, and other governmental officials who, despite noble intentions, sometimes feel lost in the bureaucracy of the modern political state. And it is a question that challenges those people generally who, with various amounts of political ambition, still strive to have some impact on the political life of this country.

Much controversy has accompanied this question, controversy over whether this nation's political system truly offers meaningful opportunities for citizen participation. While some cling optimistically to the view that the United States remains an open and accessible society, others see an ever-expanding dominance by rich and powerful elites intent on muting the voices of those who might challenge their authority.

Like the original, this second edition offers a unique look at the nature of citizen politics and its accompanying controversies. It presents, for the student's inspection, several popular interpretations of the political power structure and their implications for individual participation. The issues relating to participation have been largely ignored in introductory books on American politics. Rarely has consideration been given to how the nature of American politics affects the opportunities for political action—by ordinary citizens, members of Congress, even presidents. In part, at least, this oversight may explain why some students find political science courses irrelevant or unsatisfying.

Also, the majority of texts espouse a certainty about the nature of political "reality" in the United States, offering readers few tools with which to evaluate and challenge their conclusions. My feeling is that political reality in this country is what one sees it to be. It is merely the sum total of our diverse perspectives, theories, and models. Depending on where we stand in society—as rich man, poor man, beggar, or thief—we will each form our own unique vision of the political landscape.

Understanding that, I have tried as fairly as possible (given my own biases) to present alternative perspectives and theories, encouraging the reader to form a systematic view of American politics that most comfortably conforms with his or her experiences. While this book offers much of the information traditionally covered in introductory government courses, my central goal has been to draw the student into the great controversies and debates concerning the relationship between people and government. To this end, I have tried to maintain a lucid, easy-to-read style of writing—one that, it is hoped, will stimulate, rather than inhibit, creative thinking by the student.

The second edition of the text has been expanded with the addition of several new chapters. These include chapters on the constitutional setting, civil liberties, interest groups, the bureaucracy, and foreign policy. This edition also benefits from a new chapter on public policy, written by Larry N. Gerston of San Jose State University. The public policy chapter features case studies of both President Carter's national tax reform proposals and Howard Jarvis's "citizen-based tax revolt." The remainder of the text has been updated, revised, and, in some sections, completely rewritten in an effort to keep up with the astonishing number of changes that have accompanied this nation's transition into the 1980s.

Acknowledgements

This revision, like the original edition, owes its existence to the combined talents of many people. Perceptive reviewers, supportive friends, and helpful colleagues, as well as a professional editorial and production team at Goodyear Publishing Company, all played an important part in the creation of this book. I am particularly grateful for the comments and suggestions offered by Don Laws (Southern Oregon State College), John McKay (Santa Barbara City College), Ted Neima (Los Angeles Pierce College), T. M. Norton (San Jose State University), Donald T. Rotunda (Executive Office of the President), James R. Soles (University of Delaware), Jack Thomas (San Jose State University), Mary H. Waite (William Rainey Harper College), and Roy E. Young (San Jose State University). I owe special thanks to Maurice Waters (Wayne State University), who critically reviewed the entire manuscript and consented to write the Student Study Guide, and to Roy Christman (San Jose State University), who also reviewed the manuscript and composed perhaps the best Test File in existence. I also must thank Goodyear editors Jim Boyd, for his continued support and guidance on this project, and Laurie Greenstein, for shepherding the book through its various stages of production. Finally, I am indebted to my wife, Sherry, and to all the students who read the first edition and believed what I wrote. My thanks again to all.

We the People

of the United States, in Order to form a more perfect Union, establish Justice, insure domestic Tranquility, provide for the common defence, promote the general Welfare, and secure the Blessings of Liberty to ourselves and our Posterity, do ordain and establish this Constitution for the United States of America.

Article. I.

Section. 1. All legislative Powers herein granted shall be vested in a Congress of the United States, which shall consist of a Senate and House of Representatives.

Section. 2. The House of Representatives shall be composed of Members chosen every second Year by the People of the several States, and the Electors in each State shall have the Qualifications requisite for Electors of the most numerous Branch of the State Legislature.

No Person shall be a Representative who shall not have attained to the Age of twenty five Years, and been seven Years a Citizen of the United States, and who shall not, when elected, be an Inhabitant of that State in which he shall be chosen.

Representatives and direct Taxes shall be apportioned among the several States which may be included within this Union, according to their respective Numbers, which shall be determined by adding to the whole Number of free Persons, including those bound to Service for a Term of Years, and excluding Indians not taxed, three fifths of all other Persons. The actual Enumeration shall be made within three Years after the first Meeting of the Congress of the United States, and within every subsequent Term of ten Years, in such Manner as they shall by Law direct. The Number of Representatives shall not exceed one for every thirty Thousand, but each State shall have at Least one Representative; and until such enumeration shall be made, the State of New Hampshire shall be entitled to chuse three, Massachusetts eight, Rhode Island and Providence Plantations one, Connecticut five, New York six, New Jersey four, Pennsylvania eight, Delaware one, Maryland six, Virginia ten, North Carolina five, South Carolina five, and Georgia three.

When vacancies happen in the Representation from any State, the Executive Authority thereof shall issue Writs of Election to fill such Vacancies.

The House of Representatives shall chuse their Speaker and other Officers; and shall have the sole Power of Impeachment.

Section. 3. The Senate of the United States shall be composed of two Senators from each State, chosen by the Legislature thereof, for six Years; and each Senator shall have one Vote.

Immediately after they shall be assembled in Consequence of the first Election, they shall be divided as equally as may be into three Classes. The Seats of the Senators of the first Class shall be vacated at the Expiration of the second Year, of the second Class at the Expiration of the fourth Year, and of the third Class at the Expiration of the sixth Year, so that one third may be chosen every second Year; and if Vacancies happen by Resignation, or otherwise, during the Recess of the Legislature of any State, the Executive thereof may make temporary Appointments until the next Meeting of the Legislature, which shall then fill such Vacancies.

No Person shall be a Senator who shall not have attained to the Age of thirty Years, and been nine Years a Citizen of the United States, and who shall not, when elected, be an Inhabitant of that State for which he shall be chosen.

The Vice President of the United States shall be President of the Senate, but shall have no Vote, unless they be equally divided.

The Senate shall chuse their other Officers, and also a President pro tempore, in the Absence of the Vice President, or when he shall exercise the Office of President of the United States.

The Senate shall have the sole Power to try all Impeachments. When sitting for that Purpose, they shall be on Oath or Affirmation. When the President of the United States is tried, the Chief Justice shall preside: And no Person shall be convicted without the Concurrence of two thirds of the Members present.

Judgment in Cases of Impeachment shall not extend further than to removal from Office, and disqualification to hold and enjoy any Office of honor, Trust or Profit under the United States: but the Party convicted shall nevertheless be liable and subject to Indictment, Trial, Judgment and Punishment, according to Law.

Section. 4. The Times, Places and Manner of holding Elections for Senators and Representatives, shall be prescribed in each State by the Legislature thereof; but the Congress may at any time by Law make or alter such Regulations, except as to the Places of chusing Senators.

The Congress shall assemble at least once in every Year, and such Meeting shall be on the first Monday in December, unless they shall by Law appoint a different Day.

Section. 5. Each House shall be the Judge of the Elections, Returns and Qualifications of its own Members, and a Majority of each shall constitute a Quorum to do Business; but a smaller Number may adjourn from day to day, and may be authorized to compel the Attendance of absent Members, in such Manner, and under such Penalties as each House may provide.

Each House may determine the Rules of its Proceedings, punish its Members for disorderly Behaviour, and, with the Concurrence of two thirds, expel a Member.

Each House shall keep a Journal of its Proceedings, and from time to time publish the same, excepting such Parts as may in their Judgment require Secrecy; and the Yeas and Nays of the Members of either House on any question shall, at the Desire of one fifth of those Present, be entered on the Journal.

Neither House, during the Session of Congress, shall, without the Consent of the other, adjourn for more than three days, nor to any other Place than that in which the two Houses shall be sitting.

Section. 6. The Senators and Representatives shall receive a Compensation for their Services, to be ascertained by Law, and paid out of the Treasury of the United States. They shall in all Cases, except Treason, Felony and Breach of the Peace, be privileged from Arrest during their Attendance at the Session of their respective Houses, and in going to and returning from the same; and for any Speech or Debate in either House, they shall not be questioned in any other Place.

No Senator or Representative shall, during the Time for which he was elected, be appointed to any civil Office under the Authority of the United States, which shall have been created, or the Emoluments whereof shall have been encreased during such time; and no Person holding any Office under the United States, shall be a Member of either House during his Continuance in Office.

PART ONE

Politics and Government: The Rules of the Game

1

The Political Experience

An introductory course in American politics offers a wonderous opportunity—a chance to see everyday news items dissected, classified, and occasionally made inexplicable. Concepts like "power" and "democracy" suddenly lose their simplicity, turning into solemn and obscure topics for all-night essays.

Perhaps this is inevitable. Studying politics at a distance—whether in the classroom or on television—somehow changes the nature of political experience, making it seem more detached, more abstract, than what we may remember about door-to-door campaigning, demonstrating, or inking in a ballot. Regardless of whether we have engaged in such activities, we sense that studying politics in the classroom is only part of our political education, a step on the way to whatever political experiences are in store for us. At least we can hope that, by reading and talking with others, we will acquire some new perspectives on those experiences.

To ease the reader into the subjects at hand, this chapter reviews the ways many Americans see politics today and how they feel about voicing their concerns. It also presents a brief look at the nature of politics, and, for those curious about the discipline, a peek at political science itself.

Perceptions of Politics

In contrast to many other countries, such as England, where politics is still regarded as a respectable profession, in the United States we often view the political world with suspicion, conjuring up images of shady conduct and under-the-table dealings by astute politicians striving for personal gain. To praise those in public life is to proclaim them as being "above politics."

This jaundiced view is extremely widespread, and has been nurtured even by those active in government. Ronald Reagan, for instance, often remarked during his first campaign for governor of California in 1966 that it was time to save the state from "politicians," time to elect someone like him who had not been tainted by contact with professional politics. When Martha Mitchell, the wife of President Nixon's attorney general, fled Washington in the summer of 1972, she paused to condemn "all those dirty things that go on." And when Jimmy Carter, the political "outsider," thrust himself into the campaign for the presidency in 1976, he took pains to disassociate himself from those "politicians" in Washington.

The disillusionment with politics is, of course, not a new phenomenon; it did not spring entirely from such scandals as *Watergate*. In looking back through the years of polling public attitudes, one finds that politics in this country rarely has been regarded as a respectable occupation. Back in 1945, for example, 68 percent of Americans said they would not want their child to take up a political career. In June 1973, at the height of the Watergate scandal, negative responses stood at 64 percent.[1] The reasons people most commonly gave for not recommending the political life to the young were that politics made it "hard to be honest," involved "too much pressure," and was "too crooked/corrupt."

One apparent effect of the Watergate scandal, however, was to magnify the public's concern over political corruption. Prior to Watergate, Gallup surveys found only a few instances where people considered corruption in government to be among the most pressing issues facing the country. But by May 1973, political corruption was surpassed only by inflation, crime, and drugs as the most important national problem. Moreover, Harris polls revealed that, whereas 46 percent of Americans in 1967 believed that "most politicians are in politics to make money for themselves," in 1973 more than 63 percent believed this statement to be true.

It would be remarkable if, in the wake of Watergate and other scandals—not to mention an unpopular war, spiraling inflation, and an "energy crisis"—some loss of public confidence in our national leaders had not occurred. During the past few years, the Louis Harris polling

organization has asked Americans, "as far as people in charge of running the major institutions are concerned, would you say you have a great deal of confidence, only some confidence, or hardly any confidence at all in them?" It has found that public confidence in the leadership of many of our major institutions has declined since the 1960s. This has been especially true for the executive and legislative branches of the federal government. As Table 1-1 indicates, by September 1978, only 14 percent of Americans showed a "great deal of confidence" in the executive branch, and only 10 percent showed such confidence in Congress. Although confidence in the leadership of these institutions appeared to have recovered somewhat in 1977, by 1978 it had fallen back to the lows recorded soon after Watergate.

Whether government actually suffers from more corruption today than in the past, or whether it deserves less of our confidence, remains debatable. But it seems certain that the evidence of corruption and misuse of governmental power has been presented so persuasively by the news media as to fuel public cynicism and distrust. Indeed, the revelations of governmental improprieties during the past decade have been extraordinary. The revelations began to surface with increasing rapidity in the early 1970s when, as a result of the publication of the *Pentagon Papers*, Americans learned of the deceit by top governmental and military officials intent on prolonging and justifying U.S. military

Table 1-1. Public Confidence in Institutions (Percentage expressing a "great deal of confidence")

	1966	1975	1976	1977	1978
Medicine	73%	43%	42%	55%	42%
Higher education	61	36	31	41	41
U.S. Supreme Court	50	28	22	31	29
The military	62	24	23	31	29
Major companies	55	19	16	23	22
Executive branch	41	13	11	23	14
Congress	42	13	9	15	10

Source: *The Harris Survey*, 25 September 1978 and 14 March 1977.

actions in Southeast Asia. Then came the story of International Telephone and Telegraph's collusion with the Central Intelligence Agency to stage a coup in Chile, the Watergate burglary, and a series of federal indictments of former presidential aides and cabinet officials. By 1975, close to forty of Richard Nixon's White House associates had gone before the courts to face Watergate-related charges. And, if that was not enough to dispel public confidence, Americans witnessed the successive resignations of a vice-president convicted of tax evasion and a president implicated in the Watergate cover-up. They also saw more than a dozen members of Congress indicted for bribery and other illegal activities. Even President Carter, whose campaign of "trust me" politics helped catapult him into the White House, could not prevent one of his closest aides, Bert Lance, from resigning under a shadow of financial impropriety.

Unlike previous scandals and crises in government, such as the Teapot Dome Affair under Warren Harding, news of the more recent scandals was brought "live" into American homes by television, making each viewer feel almost like a participant in the unfolding drama. In fact, some commentators insist that television and other media have helped reinforce feelings of political distrust and alienation not only by disclosing scandals but by commenting repeatedly on the magnitude of public disenchantment with government. The media daily remind the individual that, with cynicism and apathy spreading across the land, he or she is not alone in harboring feelings of disenchantment. Natural suspicions of politicians and government are reinforced and given credence by the media's revealing similar doubts in others.

Because a principal concern of this text is the relationship between people and government, we might wonder how the decline of public confidence in our major institutions has affected people's desire to become involved in the political process. As we will see in the chapters to come, people's political orientations are often greatly influenced by their perceptions of the world around them. If they believe that policy making has fallen into the hands of corrupt and self-serving scoundrels, they may be inclined to take a disheartened view of both the American political system and their own role within it. Indeed, after completing a survey of public attitudes, pollster Louis Harris concluded that a large share of the population views its relationship to government in anything but glowing terms. "America looks to the top of the governmental structure for inspiration," he noted, "and finds it missing. In that unhappy verdict is summed up the broad loss of confidence, the pervasive sense of discontent and the most serious reason for concern about the future course of the American democracy."[2]

To Be or Not To Be in Politics

Many Americans, it is true, still dream of exercising some measure of influence on their political environment. Despite the general decline of confidence in government, people are still out there trying their hand at politics. In newspapers and on television screens we see school teachers parading in front of state capitols and women's rights groups protesting in the streets. We hear about lobbyists courting legislators, while prison inmates negotiate with authorities for changes in the established order. We follow the progress of hardworking reformers, of environmentalists, and of consumer crusaders. And for each American we see struggling to change the status quo, we see another seeking to preserve it. All of these active participants remain optimistic that their efforts are worthwhile, that while their success may be modest, it is still worth striving for.

To many people, the idea of making a mark in the world remains vivid and compelling. The desire for that elusive ingredient called power—which we will examine more closely later—can be one of the most common of human aspirations. It can be a source of ambition as potent and persistent as the quest for security or love. In this society people are often judged and awarded prestige on the basis of their ability to influence the behavior of others, to affect or determine the outcome of events. Obviously, the motivations underlying the pursuit of political power may vary greatly from one person to another. Some people, for example, may envision themselves as potentially great reformers who wish to improve human welfare or reverse the decay of society. Others may seek merely to augment their own self-importance or gratify a lifelong quest for economic gain. Whatever the motivation for political power, the political arena remains, for many, an exciting place in which to shape human events, to make something—anything—happen.

Still, few Americans who dream of exerting a profound influence on the course of political events ever manage to see their dreams come true. In a country with a population exceeding 220 million, it is difficult for any individual—especially one lacking exceptional wealth or political savvy—to be more than just another face in the crowd. A person may vote in every election, join a prominent interest group, write erudite or seething letters to the president, even run for office, and still wonder whether he or she will ever be able to exercise significant political clout.

The reaction of many Americans is simply to stop trying, to forget about politics and avoid the frustrations. They may continue to daydream of personal power, wishing they could change the course of events; but their incentives to act remain weak. As we will see later, the actual proportion of those who become involved in any kind of political activity apart from voting is small. Only a tiny fraction of the voting-age population write letters to their representatives in Washington, join in political campaigns, become active in lobbying, or run for political office. Although a hundred reasons may account for the inaction—including a basic lack of interest in politics (see Chapter 5)—many people abstain out of a deep sense of futility, out of the belief that their involvement would make no significant difference. They feel that, as only one voice among millions, they would be incapable of making government responsive to their desires. In short, they simply do not wish to imitate the proverbial optimist who sits on the pier pushing his feet against the hull of a docked ship, only to find himself, and not the ship, moving under the strain.

In a sense, of course, those who do not participate actively in politics still remain involved in the political drama. Even so-called apathetics find the views and actions of politicians, reformers, and revolutionaries portrayed so vividly by news media intruding on their consciousness. The indignations of Ralph Nader or the surprise revelations by a congressional committee of corruption in industry or government often find their way into people's opinions and attitudes. Even personal views expressed in the presence of close friends—or on bumper stickers, or as graffiti on bathroom walls—can be seen as a response to, and a participation in, the politics of the times.

Some Views of "Politics" and "Power"

What, then, is *politics?* While some would argue that politics refers simply to the activities of government, others view it more broadly as the totality of everyday experience. In former antiwar activist Abbie Hoffman's opinion, politics is "the way you live your life." In fact, a major problem faced by political scientists is how to determine what politics is and what, therefore, they should study. The concept has become so ambiguous and controversial that no universal definition of it exists. As a result of the ambiguity, political scientists have been ridiculed for "riding off in many directions, evidently on the assumption that if you don't know where you are going, any road will take you there."[3]

But, assuming one wants to define and narrow the focus of political study to make it more comprehensible, how may a political act or event be distinguished from other kinds of acts or events? How may one determine when labor union bosses or corporation presidents are engaged in politics and when they are not? Although disagreement is rampant among political scientists, many view politics as the means of settling conflict and distributing scarce benefits. They point out that, in most societies, controversy rages over who should receive the lion's share of whatever happens to be of value, whether it be material possessions, such as money and land, or intangibles, such as prestige and power. People tend to want their own needs and desires satisfied, craving benefits that are likely to be demanded by others. Unless they receive these benefits (or become convinced they cannot have them), disorder and violence may ensue. Consequently, many political scientists see politics as the means of deciding how wealth, power, and other values are to be distributed and how conflicts and disagreements are to be managed. As Harold Lasswell succinctly put it, politics is the process of deciding "who gets what, when, and how."[4]

This means that even many associations not usually regarded as political—such as schools, private clubs, and churches—may become embroiled in internal political conflicts resulting from disputes among rival factions. Casually speaking, even families may become engaged in "politics," as when a mother has to resolve a dispute between her children over which television program to watch, in effect deciding who will receive this "benefit" and who will not. Political scientists do not usually study such family quarrels, however, on the grounds that the outcome does not dramatically affect society as a whole.

It has been said that only when disputes over "who gets what" no longer exist in a society can there be an absence of politics. If benefits could be allocated totally without conflict—without anyone's protesting he or she had "been had"—then even governmental decisions would become merely routine and administrative. Karl Marx, for instance, insisted that, in a true communist society, where all class distinctions have been erased and where each individual receives "according to his need," there would no longer be a basis for conflict and, hence, no need for political machinery to settle it. "Government over persons," he declared, would be replaced by a simple "administration of things."

In a sense, then, as long as conflict exists, it hardly matters how a decision is made in order for that decision to be political. Whether the distribution of wealth and power is decided by a dictator using strong-arm tactics, by a congressional committee compromising on a trade bill, or by citizens voting in a special referendum, a political process is under way to resolve conflict and distribute society's benefits. What is common to most (if not all) political systems, however, is a process of unequal distribution. The "rules of the game" rarely are unbiased: some groups get more of what there is to have, while others get less or nothing at all. When the cake is being sliced, some can expect a larger piece, while others remain outside with their noses pressed against the window.

It should be noted that politics is not necessarily the same as *government*. Government usually refers to the rules and institutions that form the basis for the organization and operation of the political system. While there may be many institutions—including the family, schools, and churches—that help decide how benefits will be distributed, governmental institutions are the principal agencies of social control. They make most of the rules for society and have a virtual monopoly on the use of force (such as the police and the military) to carry them out. In short, if politics is the process of resolving disputes and settling conflict, then government is the principal machinery by which it is done.

Thus, we can see why *power* is such an integral part of the study of politics and government. So long as conflict continues over who gets what, when, and how, there will also be a struggle to see who gets to make this decision. If power is considered the ability to affect the behavior of others (see Chapter 2), then political power is the ability to decide how benefits will be distributed and disputes settled—to determine, for example, whether major oil companies will receive special tax breaks, whether elderly citizens will enjoy an increase in social security benefits, or whether environmentalists will win out over oil refineries in disputes over pollution control. In short, the study of politics leads to an analysis of how power is pursued, achieved, used, and lost. It leads to an examination of political campaigns, backroom deals, voting, manipulation and propaganda, the links between corporate wealth and governmental policy, and even personal motivations and drives—the processes, in other words, that determine who will make the major political decisions affecting society's welfare. As we will see later, the analysis of power has resulted in sharply conflicting views of how important political decisions are made in the United States, and of who makes them.

The Study of Politics

While each discipline no doubt has its own justifications for existence, none makes the claim of providing citizenship training as boldly as does political science. It is said that political science helps prepare students for their roles as productive members of a democratic society. By acquiring better skills of political analysis and improving their understanding of government, they will find it easier to influence the political decisions that affect their lives. As one scholar has put it, "The best reason for improving one's skill in political analysis is this: political analysis helps one to understand the world he lives in, to make more intelligent choices among the alternatives he faces, and to influence the changes, great and small, that are an inherent aspect of all political systems."[5]

At the same time, however, the study of politics, particularly as a profession, carries with it certain limitations. Some students of political science, for example, after having dealt with their subject a number of years, claim to experience a letdown about politics similar to that felt by many other people. As with history and sociology, the study of politics involves examining human behavior, with all its recurring foibles and injustices. One might wonder how many students of the subject have not, at some time, given thought to pursuing some other discipline, such as art history or astronomy. There is a certain appeal to contemplating a Rembrandt painting or sitting alone in a mountaintop observatory viewing stars through a telescope, feeling removed in spirit from the turmoil of human events.

Moreover, some students continuing in the discipline complain that the study of politics does not offer the same "thrills of discovery" found

DOONESBURY

by Garry Trudeau

in disciplines like physics, chemistry, or biology. For them, it does not appear that examining political behavior or philosophy will yield dramatic new information comparable to the discovery of a new subatomic particle, theory of gravitation, or animal species. In a sense they are probably right. Political science continues to inspect many of the same fundamental problems that have confounded political thinkers for thousands of years. And with perhaps only a few notable exceptions, not many new and startling visions have occurred. Over the years the methods and approaches have become more sophisticated, and there certainly has been a proliferation of eager professionals devoted to political research, but the majority of subjects and concepts remain substantially unchanged. It is as if the superstructure of political study has exploded into a thousand little particles, with dozens of academics clumped around each particle, endlessly dissecting it.

This does not imply that new knowledge of political behavior and organization is not being sought. A number of inventive political scientists have been working to expand the discipline, seeking contact with scholars in fields ranging from biology to mathematics. In fact, some political scientists see no outer limits to their research; they are constantly involved with the progress and findings of other areas of study, regardless of labels. As one scholar has concluded, "A political scientist cannot close any doors. He must use the historian's evidence of past human experience; the economist's analysis of wealth, value, and distribution; the sociologist's explanation of status and group interrelations; the geographer's comparative data on natural resources; the psychologist's insights and findings about human behavior; and the philosopher's analysis of political ends."[6]

There is also considerable controversy within the discipline over its true "scientific" capabilities. While some political scientists feel that the study of politics can be both objective and empirical, others insist that politics—whether studied or practiced—cannot, and should not, be divorced from personal values.

The controversy will probably never be resolved, because the nature of "science" is primarily a matter of definition. If science is regarded simply as a way of gathering information through careful and deliberate observation—treating the subject matter with only as much precision as it allows—then perhaps political science can rightly be thought of as a science. But if science implies, instead, an ability to submit the subject matter to controlled experiments that other scholars can duplicate and test under the same conditions, as well as an ability to produce general laws capable of yielding accurate predictions about future behavior, then the label may be less precise.

What we can say for certain is that political science must struggle with its own inherent limitations. Not only do personal values and biases often surface in treatises on politics (and perhaps should not be disguised), but in addition, people tend to be unpredictable subjects of analysis who do not readily adapt to precise laboratory conditions. In fact, there is little overall agreement in political science about the meaning of even the most basic terms, such as *power* or *democracy*. A scholar may select a topic for study and carefully gather data, only to discover that the findings have to be explained using concepts that other political scientists do not accept.

We are, therefore, likely to find in political science a relative paucity of simple and established conclusions. Although political scientists may feel comfortable describing certain features of the political scene, such as the number of people voting in an election or the rules of a committee in Congress, they will have to be a great deal more tentative in offering explanations, such as *why* people vote in a certain way or *how* committee members reach their decisions. As we will discover throughout this volume, political scientists are rarely in harmonious agreement on the major questions of politics, especially on how a citizen may fit into the political scheme of things. We will find that, to arrive at some definite conclusions about our own role in the politics of this country, ultimately we will have to furnish our own explanations.

Key Terms

Watergate	*power*
politics	*democracy*
government	

Notes

1. *Gallup Opinion Index*, July 1973.
2. U.S. Senate, Committee on Government Operations, "Confidence and Concern: Citizens View American Government, A Survey of Public Attitudes," pt. 1 (Washington, D.C.: U.S. Government Printing Office, 1973).
3. Heinz Eulau, "Political Science," in Berthold F. Hoselitz, ed., *A Reader's Guide to the Social Sciences* (New York: Free Press, 1959), p. 91.
4. Harold D. Lasswell, *Politics: Who Gets What, When, and How?* (New York: McGraw-Hill, 1936).
5. Robert A. Dahl, *Modern Political Analysis*, 3rd ed. (Englewood Cliffs, N.J.: Prentice-Hall, 1976), p. 1.
6. Robert E. Murphy, *The Style and Study of Political Science* (Glenview, Ill.: Scott, Foresman, 1970), p. 7.

Recommended Reading

DAHL, ROBERT A. *Modern Political Analysis.* 3rd ed. Englewood Cliffs, N.J.: Prentice-Hall, 1976.

LASSWELL, HAROLD D. *Politics: Who Gets What, When, and How?* New York: McGraw-Hill, 1936.

MURPHY, ROBERT E. *The Style and Study of Political Science.* Glenview, Ill.: Scott, Foresman, 1970.

SORAUF, FRANK J. *Political Science: An Informal Overview.* Columbus, Ohio: Charles E. Merrill, 1965.

WASBY, STEPHEN L. *Political Science: The Discipline and Its Dimensions.* New York: Charles Scribner's Sons, 1970.

2

Political Elites: Who Governs in America?

The question of "who governs" in the United States has probably puzzled most of us at one time or another; and when the issue is raised, it often stirs a flurry of strong opinion. Political scientists have been especially caught up in the controversy and have spent years trying to resolve several pertinent questions: Who makes most of the important political decisions? How widely is political power shared? What impact do economic and other elites have on governmental policies? How accountable are these elites to the general public?

The answers to these questions are obviously crucial to those of us who wonder how we fit into the political system. Clearly our ability to accomplish anything meaningful in the political system depends enormously on how power is distributed and how difficult or easy it is to gain access to that power. Because we will be assessing some popular strategies for influencing policy in the final chapter, we should first look at some opposing theories of "who governs" relevant to citizen action.

Although there has been considerable debate over the question of how power is distributed, the dispute has been most vigorously waged between two currently popular alternatives: the *ruling-elite theory* and the *pluralist theory*. Both theories have been prominently used in studies of community power structures, and have been applied to the national scene. Briefly stated, the ruling-elite theory holds that power is concentrated in the hands of a small group of people subject to little or no control by the rest of society, while the pluralist theory states that power is more widely dispersed among many separate groups held in check by the public and by each other. As we will see, depending on which of these two theories is more plausible, certain implications concerning our own participation and influence become apparent. If the pluralist view is correct, it would seem that most of us can gain meaningful access to, and influence over, decision making. But, if the ruling-elite view comes closer to the truth, then the opportunity for effective action is more limited. As we examine these two conflicting theories, each of us ultimately must decide which one better describes the conditions of American politics and what are its full implications for individual action.

Before proceeding, we should keep in mind that few political scientists accept all the tenets of either complex theory. Nor does either theory necessarily refute point for point all the assumptions of the other. Each is unique in several of its interpretations of the American political scene and should be evaluated on its own merits. And one should not be surprised to discover that disagreements about "who governs" will continue to arise, no matter how persuasive one theory may seem. Despite the elaborate evidence supporting each theory, the problems inherent in defining key terms, such as *elite* and *power*, and in circumventing the long-standing prejudices on each side probably will continue to prevent either theory from becoming universally accepted.

The concept of elite remains especially troublesome, in spite of the many good definitions that have been proposed. Perhaps the most widely accepted definition of an elite is the few who have the most of anything valued in society, whether it happens to be money, fame, status, or power. In political terms, an elite includes those who exercise the most control over the major decisions affecting other people's lives, who determine how desirable goods and values (such as money, security, and even influence) will be distributed. This means that a political elite may comprise not only high governmental officials, such as the president and members of Congress, but also corporation executives and labor union bosses. After all, the decisions of oil companies to raise their prices and unions to strike can affect the distribution of benefits as greatly as can any single governmental policy.

A similar problem of definition arises with the concept of power. At best, we can say that power is *relational:* power is not something that can be possessed in a vacuum or stored, but arises only in relations among people. Thus, social scientists often assert that power is the ability to affect the behavior of others, to compel them to do something they might otherwise not do. This means that, as president of the United States or as corporation executive, a person can compel others to support a policy he or she advocates. It should be understood, of course, that it may be extremely difficult to determine how that individual is able to get his or her own way. A person may succeed in securing compliance from someone by relying on "authority" (where a demand is regarded as legitimate and right, as with a mother to her son), by resorting to "force" (such as putting a gun to another person's head), by using "influence" (such as gentle, reasoned persuasion or monetary rewards), or even by relying on "manipulation" (where subtle, underhanded methods leave the subject unaware of what is taking place). And a person's success in the matter may depend as much on his or her position as on any personal talents or attributes. Consequently, in view of the many alternative forms of power available, it is often difficult to pin down precisely not only *who* wields the power to make major political decisions in this country but also *how* that power is exercised.[1]

The Ruling-Elite Theory

One of the most popular views of who governs in America today is the ruling-elite theory, which holds that power is concentrated in the hands of a relatively small, cohesive group.[2] This theory appeals to those who believe the country is run by a *"military-industrial complex,"* an "establishment," a "ruling class," or a behind-the-scenes "political machine." As one scholar has remarked, "This kind of view . . . is simple, compelling, dramatic, 'realistic.' It gives one standing as an inside-dopester. For individuals with a strong strain of frustrated idealism, it has just the right touch of hardboiled cynicism."[3] Although the ruling-elite theory has several different strains, a number of general observations are made about the structure of American political power.

A Pyramid of Power

First, the ruling-elite theory holds that only a relatively small number of people dominate policy making in American society. According to the late C. Wright Mills, a sociologist and leading proponent of the ruling-elite view, the basic pattern of power in the United States takes the shape of a pyramid (see Figure 2-1). At the apex of this pyramid stand the "power elite," a triumvirate of top corporation executives, military officers in the Joint Chiefs of Staff, and high-ranking politicians, such as the president and his advisors. Together, these three groups control

Figure 2-1. Ruling-Elite Pyramid of Power

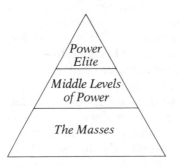

most of the wealth, weapons, and other political resources that underlie the "important" decisions in government and the economy—whether to plunge the nation into war, recognize or trade with other countries, or overhaul current economic policies. Members of the power elite wield this enormous power not because they have seized command by design but primarily because they occupy positions in great and powerful institutions. They get their own way mainly because they serve as chief of staff of the Army, president of General Motors, secretary of state, or chairman of the board of Chase Manhattan Bank.

Beneath this powerful triumvirate is a second layer consisting of judges, interest groups, members of Congress, and media executives who constitute what Mills terms the "middle levels of power." Although they exert a great deal of influence on policies, they cannot usually match the influence of the power elite. At best they can muster limited veto power (for example, through congressional committees) that may temporarily thwart policies of the power elite. But they lack the capacity to initiate or implement major new policies or to block permanently programs enthusiastically favored by the president, large corporations, and the military, especially in economic and foreign affairs.

Finally, at the bottom of the pyramid sit the rest of the population—the "mass society"—who not only have little say on policy but are controlled or dominated from above. They have no direct access to the top decision-making levels of government, except perhaps through elections, which are manipulated anyway by the elite. "The bottom of this society," Mills concluded, "is politically fragmented, and even as a passive fact, increasingly powerless: at the bottom there is emerging a mass society."[4]

A Cohesive Power Elite

A second contention of the ruling-elite view is that an interlocking relationship exists among the top leadership in the United States. Although a balance of power may prevail among interest groups, members of Congress, and judges at the "middle levels of power," the members of the "power elite"—the president, corporation executives, and the military brass—have been drawn together into a fairly cohesive group who know one another and who usually get what they want by pooling their resources. In other words, the top elites are not only more powerful than other groups but they also interlock in several important respects.

In the first place, the career patterns of the elite frequently overlap. Many former military and governmental officials, for example, eventually join major industries as executives and lobbyists, helping their firms win lucrative government contracts, price supports, and other political favors through their ties with former colleagues in these establishments. Senator William Proxmire noted at one point that more than two thousand retired military officers with the rank of colonel or higher were on the payrolls of the top one hundred military defense contractors.[5]

In similar fashion, many top corporation executives and military officials move into important appointive positions in government. Among those who held cabinet-level posts during the Nixon or Ford administrations, for example, were George Romney, former president of American Motors; David Kennedy, chairman of the board of the Continental Illinois National Bank and Trust Company; David Packard, president of Hewlett-Packard Corporation; William Simon, senior partner of Salmon Brothers (a major Wall Street firm); and Bryce Harlow, vice-president of Proctor & Gamble Corporation.

Even Jimmy Carter, the modest Georgia peanut farmer who campaigned for the presidency as an "outsider," continued the practice of filling the executive branch with traditional establishment figures. For secretary of the treasury, he picked Michael Blumenthal, president of Bendix Corporation. For director of the Office of Management and Budget, he chose Bert Lance, president of the National Bank of Georgia. He also tapped four figures from the Johnson administration for prominent posts: Wall Street lawyer Cyrus Vance for secretary of state; Cal Tech President Harold Brown for secretary of defense; former Domestic Advisor Joseph Califano for secretary of Health, Education and Welfare; and former Director of the Office of Management and Budget Charles Schulze for chairman of the Council of Economic Advisors. He even picked James Schlesinger, a familiar face during the Nixon and Ford administrations (as defense secretary and CIA director), to head the new

Department of Energy. And when Schlesinger was sacked in 1979, Carter picked Charles Duncan, former head of Coca-Cola, to replace him. Although Carter's election to the presidency in 1976 seemed, at first, to contradict the ruling-elite scenario, he kept many of the traditional establishment figures out of the unemployment lines.

The cohesion of the power elite is also maintained through a basic overlapping of interests among the military, the government, and many large corporations, especially those seeking defense contracts. A sizable number of major companies—including Lockheed, McDonnell Douglas, Bendix, and Grumman—depend on military contracts for a significant portion of their entire business. In 1977, for instance, the Pentagon awarded military contracts totaling more than $52 billion to major U.S. industries.[6] Lockheed alone accounted for about 3 percent of all defense contracts, doing more than 80 percent of its business with the Pentagon. According to the ruling-elite interpretation, because a major corporation like Lockheed wants lucrative military contracts and the Pentagon needs the hardware the corporation produces, each strives to maintain a high degree of cooperation with the other. Thus, it should be no surprise that the Nixon administration would offer a $250-million loan to Lockheed in 1971. Even though Lockheed's financial troubles stemmed, in part, from its $2-billion cost overrun on the C5A cargo plane, the mutual benefits to the Pentagon and the company were given as justification for providing governmental relief.

But the close partnership between the government and corporations, according to the ruling-elite view, is not based solely on defense contracting. There is a shared conviction that policies benefiting major corporations like General Motors and Exxon will also benefit the government and the economy as a whole. The Nixon administration, for example, openly declared itself a "business administration," a label more than justified, it seemed, by its cozy relationship with International Telephone and Telegraph, its support of the dairy industry in raising milk prices, its backing of oil interests in the Alaskan pipeline controversy, and its effort to push the development of the supersonic transport (SST).

One explanation commonly given for this overlapping of interests between big business and government is that corporations contribute heavily to political campaign funds. Although corporations are prohibited from giving corporate funds directly to candidates, they have continued to do so. As the Watergate investigations revealed, a number of the biggest corporations in America—including Gulf Oil, American Airlines, and Greyhound—admitted to illegally scratching up large sums of money for Richard Nixon's 1972 reelection campaign. Another explanation is that no administration can afford to ignore the views and interests of industry leaders, whose decisions may create jobs and augment private income, making an administration look good in the eyes of the public. As a result, from one administration to another, industries involved in such activities as shipping, oil exploration, sugar production, mining, and farming reap subsidies and special tax breaks in the billions of dollars to enhance their profits and reduce their losses, constituting a blatant form of "welfare for the rich."

For these reasons, according to the ruling-elite view, the ties between government and business are hardly confined to Republican administrations. Corporations will exert a great deal of influence on government regardless of which party controls the White House. As labor boss John L. Lewis once complained, "The only difference between Republicans and Democrats is that the Republicans stay bought. Democrats keep coming back for more."

Concentration of Economic Resources

Complementing the view of a closely knit power elite, then, is the argument that economics and politics are inevitably intertwined. Wealth provides the means to gain access to elected officials, as well as to sustain the lobbyists, lawyers, and experts needed to promote one's special interests. In the opinion of one scholar, "Wealth . . . is doubly powerful, not only for what it can purchase now but for what it can buy in the future. In this double sense, wealth negates, or at least frustrates, other more fleeting power factors that unquestionably are dispersed—ethnic popularity, ingenuity, luck, and others. Men of wealth can afford to wait, to bide their time while maintaining continual pressure on behalf of their interests."[7]

For this reason, advocates of the ruling-elite theory consider it significant that the structure of economic power and resources in America also assumes the shape of a pyramid. As illustrated in Table 2-1, the 1977 census shows that the richest 20 percent of the families in the United States received 41.5 percent of the total private income in the country, while the poorest 20 percent received only 5.2 percent—a distribution that has not changed substantially since the 1940s. In fact, when measured in terms of accumulated wealth instead of just annual income, the economic scales are weighted even more unevenly. According to recent estimates, the top 1 percent of wealthy adults in the United States lay claim to roughly 25 percent of all personal property and financial assets in the country.[8] They own at least 51 percent of all the stock and collect almost 47 percent of all the dividends.[9]

A similar concentration of resources prevails among major corporations. In 1974, the five hundred largest industrial corporations, repre-

Table 2-1. Income Distribution Among American Families

Income Level	Percent of Total National Income			
	1947	*1960*	*1970*	*1977*
Lowest Fifth (under $5,600)	5.1	4.8	5.4	5.2
Second Fifth ($5,600–$9,300)	11.8	12.2	12.2	11.6
Third Fifth ($9,300–$12,900)	16.7	17.8	17.6	17.5
Fourth Fifth ($12,900–$17,800)	23.2	24.0	23.8	24.2
Highest Fifth ($17,800 and more)	43.3	41.3	40.9	41.5

Source: U.S. Bureau of the Census, *Statistical Abstract of the United States*, 1978, p. 455.

senting less than 0.5 percent of all industrials, accounted for 66 percent of the sales of all U.S. industrial companies and 72 percent of the total profits (see Table 2-2).[10] Many of these corporations even interlocked as a result of having some of the same people sitting on their boards of directors. A study of the Rockefeller family by G. William Domhoff and Charles L. Schwartz, presented to Congress in 1974, revealed that fifteen members of the Rockefeller family were directors of forty corporations with total assets of $70 billion. The study also showed that the boards on which the Rockefellers sat had interlocking directorates with ninety-one major U.S. corporations having combined assets of $640 billion.

Moreover, according to a report issued by two Senate Government Operations subcommittees in January 1974, "A few institutional investors, principally six superbanks headquartered in New York," held enough stock in competing corporations to influence entire industries. Of these six, the report stated that the Chase Manhattan bank, headed by David Rockefeller, was the biggest bank stockholder in twenty major corporations. Chase Manhattan held more than 5 percent of the stocks of four airlines and was a substantial stockholder in the firms that own the three major television networks. Altogether the banks held 38.1 percent of the stock of Columbia Broadcasting System, 34.8 percent of the American Broadcasting System, and 6.7 percent of RCA Corporation, parent of the National Broadcasting Corporation. The report concluded that control of even small blocks of stock "by a single or few like-minded financial institutions provides them with disproportionately large powers."[11]

A Sharing of Values

According to the ruling-elite interpretation, the top corporate, governmental, and military elites are fairly united, not only because they

Table 2-2. *The 20 Largest Industrial Corporations (ranked by sales)*

Rank	Company	Sales ($000)	Assets ($000)	Rank	Net Income ($000)	Rank
1	Exxon (New York)	42,061,336	31,332,440	1	3,142,192	1
2	General Motors (Detroit)	31,549,546	20,468,100	2	950,069	8
3	Ford Motor (Dearborn, Mich.)	23,620,600	14,173,600	4	360,900	20
4	Texaco (New York)	23,255,497	17,176,121	3	1,586,441	3
5	Mobil Oil (New York)	18,929,033	14,074,290	5	1,047,446	5
6	Standard Oil of California (San Francisco)	17,191,186	11,639,996	8	970,018	7
7	Gulf Oil (Pittsburgh)	16,458,000	12,503,000	7	1,065,000	4
8	General Electric (Fairfield, Conn.)	13,413,100	9,369,100	10	608,100	12
9	International Business Machines (Armonk, N.Y.)	12,675,292	14,027,108	6	1,837,639	2
10	International Tel. & Tel. (New York)	11,154,401	10,696,544	9	451,070	16
11	Chrysler (Highland Park, Mich.)	10,971,416	6,732,756	13	(52,094)	493
12	U.S. Steel (New York)	9,186,403	7,717,493	12	634,858	9
13	Standard Oil (Ind.) (Chicago)	9,085,415	8,915,190	11	970,266	6
14	Shell Oil (Houston)	7,633,455	6,128,884	16	620,539	11
15	Western Electric (New York)	7,381,728	5,239,551	18	310,633	28
16	Continental Oil (Stamford, Conn.)	7,041,423	4,673,434	22	327,609	23
17	E. I. du Pont de Nemours (Wilmington, Del.)	6,910,100	5,980,300	17	403,500	17
18	Atlantic Richfield (Los Angeles)	6,739,682	6,151,608	15	474,600	15
19	Westinghouse Electric (Pittsburgh)	6,466,112	4,301,804	24	28,132	277
20	Occidental Petroleum (Los Angeles)	5,719,369	3,325,471	32	280,677	32

Source: Fortune magazine, May, 1975.

share common economic interests but also because they subscribe to a number of similar values, including a commitment to private property and capitalism, and a conservative attitude toward change. Though members of the top elite do disagree over policies from time to time, and even compete for power or profits, they agree on the basic "rules of the game," on preserving the capitalist system and their privileged positions within it.

This sharing of values filters down even to the "middle levels of power" among, for example, the Democratic and Republican party leadership. Although the two major parties may reflect somewhat different perspectives on the issues (see Chapter 6), their overall programs tend to be similar and moderate. While Democrats and Republicans may disagree, for example, over the extent to which government should regulate the economy, neither advocates the nationalization of major industries. If either party offered radical policy alternatives, ruling-elite theorists proclaim, it would only alienate voters and undermine the consensus of values shared by prominent officials of both parties and by other elites. As a result, the Democratic and Republican parties offer voters only a narrow range of policy alternatives, a range confined to the interests and values of the ruling elite.

This naturally raises an important question. If a small, cohesive elite with shared values actually governs, why then do significant changes in policy ever see the light of day? Why do policies—such as minimum wage laws, collective bargaining, and environmental restrictions on industry—that appear to conflict with elite interests emerge? Part of the answer, according to the ruling-elite view, is that the elites themselves sponsor and support such changes. Dramatic new policies are occasionally enacted—as in the 1930s under Franklin Roosevelt's New Deal—when a major crisis like the Great Depression threatens the very essence of the economic system. By remaining flexible—by tolerating some regulation of commerce and industry, social security programs, and fair labor practices—members of the elite can incorporate policy changes to satisfy the public while still preserving the system's basic features and their control of it.

Elites Unrepresentative

Supporters of the ruling-elite theory also are quick to point out that top corporate and governmental elites, including the second layer of elites, such as members of Congress, are not representative of the general population. In addition to possessing considerably greater wealth, members of the elite are drawn disproportionately from a certain social background: white, male, Anglo-Saxon, Protestant. Neither the House nor the Senate, for example, truly reflects a cross-section of American society. As noted in Chapter 10, most of the seats in Congress are filled by lawyers, bankers, or businessmen who belong to the white upper-middle class and are overwhelmingly male. Many other groups—including the poor, most minority groups, and women—have a great deal less representation in Congress than might be expected from their percentages in society. Similarly, almost all presidents, vice-presidents, Supreme Court justices, and cabinet officials have been white, male, and Protestant. Many, like Lyndon Johnson and Nelson Rockefeller, have also laid claim to considerable wealth.

These unrepresentative qualities of the top elite convince some scholars, such as G. William Domhoff, that there is a "governing class" in America, composed of people from prominent and wealthy families. A disproportionate number of these people serve as corporate directors, network executives, cabinet officials, and foundation presidents. They are closely knit, says Domhoff, "by such institutions as stock ownership, trust funds, intermarriages, private schools, exclusive city clubs, exclusive summer resorts, debutante parties, fox hunts, charity drives, and, last but not least, corporation boards."[12]

For example, each year over 2,000 of the richest and most powerful men in the country gather at the Bohemian Grove, up the coast from San Francisco. They are all members of the Bohemian Club, an exclusive fraternity of top corporate, social, and governmental elites (all men). The privileged few who received an invitation in 1977 to attend the 99th annual "Summer Encampment" (also known as "the greatest men's party on earth") could play golf and drink expensive bourbon with such luminaries as former President Gerald Ford, Bank of America President A. W. Clausen, former Secretary of State Henry Kissinger, Firestone corporation head Leonard K. Firestone, millionaire entertainers Bing Crosby and Art Linkletter, and columnist William F. Buckley.[13] This and similar gatherings, according to Domhoff, provide an opportunity for members of the elite to exchange views and establish new social ties that, in the long run, help maintain the cohesiveness of the ruling class.

Access Not Open

Supporters of the ruling-elite theory further contend that the ranks of the elite are virtually closed to most members of our society. Although persons with humble origins occasionally do reach elite positions (as Jimmy Carter's meteoric rise from Georgia peanut farmer to president certainly testifies), the occasions are rare, especially in the high corporate and social spheres. They cite sociological studies indicating that the opportunities for social and occupational mobility remain slight for most people, particularly for minority groups and the poor. As one study revealed, most upward mobility occurs within the middle range of society: at both the rich and poor extremes, sons and daughters tend to remain at the same levels as their parents.[14] In other words, those who possess few financial and political resources will not likely be admitted into the ranks of the elite.

And even if they should acquire these resources, only those subscribing to the values of the present elite and willing to play by the rules of the game—to accept compromise, go slowly, and submerge their individuality—will be accepted. "Personal relations," Mills wrote, "have become part of 'public relations,' a sacrifice of selfhood on a personality market, to the sole end of individual success in the corporate way of life . . . the elite careerist must continually persuade others and himself as well that he is the opposite of what he actually is."[15]

Elites Unaccountable

Finally, many supporters of the ruling-elite view strongly criticize the present distribution of political and economic power. They charge that elites are subject to little control by the rest of society and, as the Watergate scandal investigations revealed, can be extremely corrupt and irresponsible. "The men of the higher circles," C. Wright Mills concluded years ago, "are not representative men; their high position is not a result of moral virtue; their fabulous success is not firmly connected with meritorious ability. Those who sit in the seats of the high and mighty are selected and formed by the means of power, the sources of wealth, the mechanics of celebrity which prevail in their society."[16] Although power is supposed to reside ultimately in the people and their elected representatives, in reality it rests with those who control the corporations, bureaucracies, and military. It rests with those who are neither elected by the people nor morally responsible to them.

Indeed, ruling-elite theorists charge, not even elected officials like the president and members of Congress are truly accountable. Although voters are able to choose among alternative party candidates at election time, their choices are narrow and their power is limited almost exclusively to the act of voting itself. Because only a small proportion of the American public participate in other kinds of political activity besides voting or even know what their elected representatives are doing (see Chapter 5), politicians tend to cater to the interests of those few influentials who keep informed and voice their demands. "Policy questions of government," Thomas R. Dye and L. Harmon Ziegler insist, "are seldom decided by the masses through elections or through the presentation of policy alternatives by political parties. For the most part, these 'democratic' institutions—elections and parties—are important only for their symbolic value. They help tie the masses to the political system by giving them a role to play on election day and a political party with which they can identify."[17]

In fact, according to the ruling-elite view, elites not only are unaccountable to the general public but also influence the public more than the public influences them. Corporate executives and politicians, for instance, employ television, radio, and the press to manipulate public opinion through sophisticated advertising and slick public relations techniques. Because elites dominate the mass media, the public has few opportunities to get radically different points of view or to voice their own views and opinions. In fact, the views and opinions of most Americans probably have been conditioned to a significant degree by the media, anyway. As a result, governmental policies and social values do not ultimately reflect the needs and interests of the public as much as they mirror those of the power elite.

Implications for Action

In summary, the ruling-elite theory sees little opportunity for most of us to work effectively within the existing political system, at least not for any significant reform. Although we may believe we can play a major role in the political system (through such processes as elections), our participation remains more symbolic than real. The true source of power rests with a small, fairly cohesive elite drawn from top corporate, military, and governmental circles. Members of this elite share interlocking relationships based on mutal self-interest, overlapping careers, and a commitment to the same basic values. They not only are unrepresentative of the general population but restrict access to those who lack wealth, proper social connections, and a world view similar to their own. And instead of being controlled by public opinion, they usually are in the position to dominate and manipulate that opinion. They, not the public, mark the boundaries of political activity for the majority of society.

One other implication is clear. The ruling-elite theory implies that, to achieve significant political change, it may become necessary to engage in actions more extreme or radical than would be necessary in an open political system. If the system remains closed to large segments of society, justification is offered for resorting to direct action and even to violence. Although not everyone who opposes a ruling-elite system will resort to violence, it is not just coincidental that groups favoring radical means of political action—such as the Weather underground—view the system as hopelessly controlled by an establishment bent on thwarting any kind of major reform. Ironically, however, the ruling-elite theory also offers justification for those deciding not to engage in any political action at all. It gives those who might ordinarily be motivated to work for political change the excuse that such actions would be futile in the face of an indomitable elite.

The Pluralist Theory

Despite widespread support for the ruling-elite theory, many political scientists do not accept its basic tenets. While they agree that elites exist, they believe ruling-elite theorists greatly exaggerate the concentration of political power in the United States.[18] Perhaps the leading critic of the ruling-elite view is political scientist Robert Dahl, who views political power in this country as "pluralistic"—that is, widely dispersed among many separate elites kept in check by numerous social and political forces. The underlying assumption of Dahl and other pluralists is that any theory of who governs must be examined objectively and supported by hard evidence. It must not be assumed that, simply because persons occupy important positions of power, they constitute a single, cohesive ruling-elite whose decisions usually prevail. According to one scholar, "Only if it can be shown that such a group is a cohesive one with a sense of group identity, and that it has a grip on the governmental power in that community approaching a monopoly, can it be argued that it constitutes a 'ruling-elite.' "[19] Nor must it be assumed that those with considerable economic or military resources actually employ those resources to exert great power. Even though the military controls the armaments, for example, it does not employ them to determine defense policy.[20] In other words, one must study the actual decisions made in society and not simply assume that persons in high positions or possessing great wealth actually constitute a single, powerful, ruling group.

In effect, pluralists contend that their examinations of political power are more objective and precise than those of ruling-elite theorists (a view not shared, of course, by the latter), and that their studies paint a considerably more realistic picture of who governs in America. Although, as with the ruling-elite theory, the pluralist theory embraces several different interpretations, certain basic assumptions stand out.

Many Pyramids of Power

First, pluralists reject the idea that a single ruling elite makes most of the "important" decisions in America. (Indeed, they question how we can even determine which decisions are "important" and which are not.) Although they agree with ruling-elite theorists that powerful groups exist, they contend that the power structure is too decentralized and complex to permit such groups to act together in a common design. Whereas ruling-elite proponents see the power structure as a single pyramid dominated by a unified power elite at the top, pluralists see it as a range of pyramids, with shifting coalitions of groups dominating separate areas of policy making (see Figure 2-2). They do not find that the same military, corporate, and governmental leaders determine most major policies but rather that different groups exercise power in different spheres and at different times, depending on the issue.

In studying community power in New Haven, Connecticut, Dahl found that those making the major decisions in the area of urban renewal were not the same as those making the major decisions in education. "Leaders in redevelopment," he reflected, "are with a few exceptions officially, professionally, or financially involved in its fate. Most of the leaders in the public schools have a professional connection of some kind with education ... a leader in one issue-area is not likely to be influential in another."[21]

Part of the reason for this dispersal of power, Dahl and other pluralists contend, is that many different resources of power exist in our society. Whereas ruling-elite theorists assume that economic resources are the key to power, pluralists find that power is based on a variety of factors—wealth, expertise, access to the media, prestige, position in a major institution—each of which may be decisive in different areas. That is, although pluralists do not dispute the fact that most economic resources remain in the hands of a small percentage of society, they do insist that other resources may be equally, if not more, consequential in determining who wields influence. Further, although these other resources may not be equally distributed among the population, no single individual or group can claim a monopoly on any of them.

Competition Among Elites

Adding still more fire to the controversy, most pluralists insist that a great deal of competition prevails among elites. Whereas ruling-elite proponents believe the top elites are unified and mutually supportive—with squabbles occurring mainly at the middle levels of power, such as among interest groups and members of Congress—pluralists find significant competition at all levels. They see power spread widely among many different "veto groups," which balance one another; that is, the ambitions of one group are tamed by the conflicting ambitions of another. Industry, the government, and the military are all fragmented by numerous subgroups having opposing interests and policy goals.

Thus, among major corporations one finds vigorous competition not only among businesses operating within a similar field (such as in

Figure 2-2. Pluralist Pyramids of Power

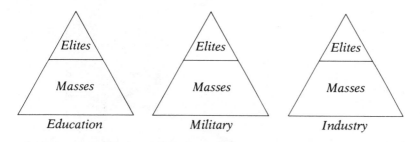

transportation) but also among those having different interests regarding governmental policies. Whereas price supports or import quotas, for example, may be applauded by one industry, they may be condemned as disastrous by another. Even the Vietnam War (which many considered to be economically inspired) revealed a considerable division within industry. While some companies clearly benefited from the defense contracts, other companies suffered, especially those geared to a peacetime, consumer-oriented economy. (Indeed, it may be significant that the *Wall Street Journal* and *Business Week*, which generally reflect business values, were among the first publications to take an editorial stance against the war.)

Similarly, as the evening news keeps demonstrating, conflict frequently erupts among the various branches of government. The president, members of Congress, and the officials of each of the fifty states represent diverse constituencies and do not necessarily share the same policy goals. Indeed, pluralists argue, the competition that occurs in government often thwarts powerful elite interests, as when Congress succeeds in blocking presidential initiatives. In 1970, for example, Congress halted the development of the supersonic transport (SST), which both President Nixon and major corporations like Boeing Aircraft desperately wanted. Although Congress was under great pressure to support the program, it eventually succumbed to the outcries of scientists and environmental groups (such as Friends of the Earth and the Sierra Club), who argued that the plane posed an environmental hazard. As Figure 2-3 shows, presidential success has fluctuated wildly during the past twenty years, reaching the lowest point with Richard Nixon during the Watergate scandal.

Even more dramatically, Congress and the federal courts eventually pressured Nixon into resigning from the White House following repeated probes into the Watergate scandal. Although supporters of the ruling-elite theory point to the scandal as evidence of elite conspiracy

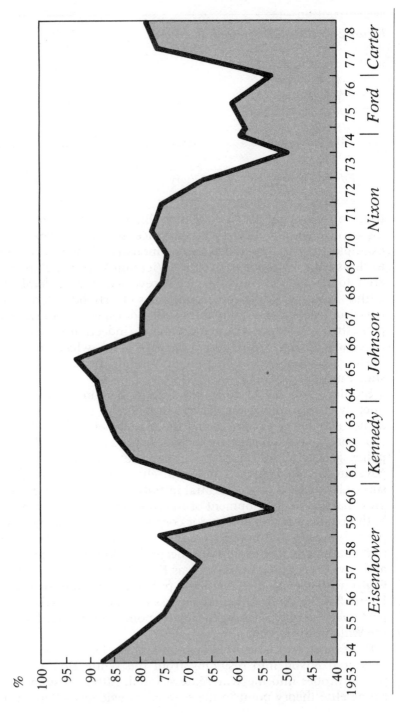

Figure 2-3. *Presidential Success on Votes, 1953–1978 (percentages based on votes on which presidents took a position)*

Source: Congressional Quarterly Weekly Report, 9 December 1978.

and corruption—and, in fact, insist Nixon's demise was hastened by other elites who never fully accepted him—the head-on collision between Nixon and Congress revealed, to pluralists, the presence of true institutional pluralism. Only in a decentralized power structure, they argue, could a president be compelled to resign his office and top cabinet officials and White House aides be carted off to prison. In other words, when viewed in historical perspective, presidents have not been able perpetually to strong-arm either Congress or the courts, or to force unpopular issues and behavior on the American people.

Further, according to the pluralist view, it would be a mistake to interpret presidential actions in terms principally of the benefits accorded the ruling elite. Presidents often find themselves locked in battle with top corporate and military elites, as Jimmy Carter discovered with his energy proposals in 1977. His emphasis on conservation, as opposed to incentives for exploration and production of new oil, resulted in considerable outcry among oil companies and increased lobbying pressure on Congress to reject Carter's energy package. Similarly, Carter hardly could be seen as an instrument of military or corporate interests in the B-1 bomber controversy. Despite appeals from the Air Force, prime contractors like Rockwell International, and even organized labor, Carter decided in 1977 to honor his campaign pledge on defense policy by rejecting the $20-billion bomber project.

What makes this competitive situation significant, according to pluralists, is that, as long as governmental and corporate elites hold each other in check, average citizens have some protection from abuse. As long as corporations must compete for consumers' dollars and as long as presidents and members of Congress must vie for voters' support, the interests of most citizens can be neither ignored nor ultimately repressed.

Distinction Between Elites and Masses Blurred

Pluralists also find the distinction between "elites" and "masses" not as clear as the ruling-elite theory suggests. How is it possible, they ask, to draw precise lines between an elite and a nonelite when groups with wide public membership, such as labor unions, wield such enormous influence on policy? Not only do unions threaten major industries with strikes, but they flex their muscles in Congress and contribute money and organizational skills to political campaigns.

In addition, pluralists suggest, there is really little difference between the social and economic values of elites and those of most other Americans. Although business and governmental leaders may not be truly representative of the general population in terms of education, wealth, and social composition, elites and nonelites alike tend to subscribe to similar values: the sanctity of private property, capitalism, a belief in compromise, and a conservative attitude toward change. These and other shared values, in effect, restrain business and governmental leaders, forcing them to act within the boundaries of society's overall expectations. "How leaders act," Dahl concludes, "what they advocate, what they are likely to believe, are all constrained by the wide adherence to the creed that exists throughout the community."[22] (Ruling-elite theorists, of course, would counter that these values ultimately are propagated by elites, through their control over the mass media and other institutions, and, hence, elites are not constrained at all.)

Access Is Open

Pluralists, furthermore, toss out the ruling-elite thesis that access to decision making is blocked for most members of society. They point out that many persons from relatively poor families and with diverse social and ethnic backgrounds have successfully reached positions of political and economic power. Contrary to the ruling-elite interpretation of sociological studies, pluralists argue that upward mobility has been increasing during the past several decades. According to one study, for example, the proportion of high-level executives who actually "started at the top"—taking into account the board chairmen, presidents, and vice-presidents of the six hundred largest industrial corporations in the United States—has steadily declined, until it is now down to only about 3 percent. Most of the other 97 percent rose through the ranks after twenty or twenty-five years of service to the company; very few of them had any family connections in the firm they now head.[23]

In fact, pluralists feel that access to elite positions probably will continue to improve, especially as more women and members of minority groups are elected to public office and work their way into higher positions in industry and finance. Although women and minority groups are still underrepresented in Congress and the executive branch, they are making significant inroads in other areas. Large cities like Detroit, Los Angeles, Washington, D.C., Oakland, and Atlanta, for example, have been headed in recent years by black mayors. Moreover, such major cities as San Francisco, Chicago, San Jose, and Phoenix have been headed by women mayors, while in Connecticut and Washington women for the first time have been elected governors in their own right.

In any event, continues the argument, if access to elite positions is restricted, society as a whole is to blame, not just the elites. The history of prejudice and low levels of popular support for equal opportunity have set up the roadblocks preventing certain groups from reaching positions of power. The fact that individuals must support certain values and codes to join the ranks of the elite reflects the prevailing ideas of society at large, not just those of elites.

Elites Are Accountable

The proposition that economic and other elites are unaccountable to the rest of society is similarly rejected by pluralists. While they agree that important decisions affecting society are passed down by nonelected, frequently invisible, corporate heads, military brass, and bureaucrats, they believe these elites can be kept in check by elected governmental representatives who are subject to public scrutiny. After all, they contend, elected governmental officials ultimately hold the most powerful positions in America. Only they have the authority and access to the legitimate use of physical force (such as the armed forces and the Justice Department) to make and enforce decisions affecting the whole society. Only the president and members of Congress have the authority to establish the limits of the military budget, set up new regulatory agencies, and (together with the courts) break up monopolistic enterprises.

All of this, according to the pluralist view, means that ordinary citizens ultimately can exert a great deal of influence. Citizen influence can be felt through elected officials who must remain alert to public reaction at the polls. Although corporate and military elites are not directly accountable to the public, their independence is curtailed by governmental elites who are accountable through elections. Presidents and members of Congress often must initiate policies that do not favor prominent corporate executives or military brass—or run the risk of losing public office. Even though presidents and most members of Congress share backgrounds similar to those of other powerful elites, the institutional imperatives of their office—their public reputations and need of voter support—compel them to respond to other influences besides corporate wealth or military lobbying. The necessity of responding to a wider public interest, pluralists argue, accounts for the succession of laws in American history protecting the individual citizen and consumer: truth-in-labeling laws, statutes curbing deceptive advertising, antitrust laws, pollution controls, and regulation of labor practices. Admittedly, such protections often are only poorly enforced or minimally applied, but their existence is, nonetheless, a testament to the frequently opposing interests of corporate and governmental elites. (It should be noted, however, that ruling-elite theorists do not necessarily view elites as unsympathetic to public needs. They argue that elites are capable of being "public-minded" and will support policy changes that benefit society, but only when those changes do not cause their own interests to suffer.)

The fact, therefore, that elites occasionally must "walk the line" to preserve their privileged positions signifies a degree of latent power among the citizenry. Although only a relatively small number of citizens actually throw themselves into the political fray, the voice of the majority is still heard because politicians must remain attentive to opinion polls, votes, and the views of influential community spokesmen. As Dahl puts it, "The leaders who directly control the decisions of political associations are themselves influenced in their own choices of policies by their assumption as to what the voting populace wants."[24]

Elites and Democratic Values

Perhaps the final important area where pluralists and ruling elitists tangle is in their views of public apathy. As we shall discuss later, many Americans turn their backs on politics and are poorly informed about the most rudimentary facts of government. While these findings generally disturb ruling-elite theorists, who fear that nonparticipation and apathy give elites even greater freedom to ignore public needs, a number of pluralists (although certainly not all) conclude that nonparticipation may, to some degree, be beneficial to the political system. First, those who are politically uninvolved and uninformed often have a low commitment to such principles as freedom of speech. It might be a mistake, some pluralists warn, to call for greater participation from people who are relatively uninformed and who reject many of the nation's basic political values. Further, a more politically active populace might only interfere with the work of elected representatives chosen to create policy. A highly active electorate marked by extreme ideological differences might only lead to increased fragmentation of the political system.

In any event, the argument goes, it is the elites, not the general public, who protect and safeguard the American political system. Research on political opinion reveals that leaders in government, education, and industry—those with higher education, social prestige, and positions of power—generally show greater support for freedom of speech, freedom of the press, and equality of opportunity than do most other Americans. (Of course, there may be a distinction between what people say and how they actually feel. Persons in high positions may be under greater pressure to appear more tolerant than those not in the limelight.)[25] Thus, both apathy and rule by elites are regarded, not as a malfunction of the political system, but as a condition for preserving American political values. So long as governmental leaders remain accountable to the public through periodic elections and the people enjoy freedoms of speech and choice, pluralists contend, a political system responsive to the interests of most Americans will prevail.

Implications for Action

We may conclude from this brief view of the pluralist theory that those of us who accept this interpretation of the American political system might be considerably more optimistic about the opportunities for effective citizen action than those of us who adopt the ruling-elite view. According to the pluralist interpretation, the political system in the United States offers a number of ways for persons with motivation and skill to gain access to positions of power and help mold public policy. Because there are many different resources of power besides wealth and social position, a variety of groups and individuals can play major roles in the policy-making process. Under existing conditions, no single power elite can continually restrict access to positions of power. The system is too decentralized and complex for any cohesive group to act in a common design. Rather, many different groups exercise power in separate policy spheres. These groups not only tend to balance one another but are kept in check by a variety of social and political forces.

This does not necessarily imply that political access is wide open under the pluralist interpretation. Obviously, racial and sexual prejudices—not to mention the ever-present obstacles facing the poor—continue to prevent many groups from achieving their political goals. The main difference, however, between the pluralist and ruling-elite views is that pluralists regard the system as considerably more flexible and capable of responding to internal pressures for needed social and political reforms.

Evaluation: The Two Theories

Reviewing the differences between the ruling-elite and pluralist theories gives one the distinct impression that advocates of the two theories do not really speak the same language. Although both groups refer to hierarchy in American society, they disagree about the nature of that hierarchy and about how it affects the chances of ordinary citizens to influence the political process. Although they occasionally depend on the same data and statistics (as when evaluating different groups' degree of access to elite positions), they arrive at entirely different conclusions. Part of the reason for this difference is that each group employs a different research methodology. Whereas those who find a ruling elitism tend to look at the social backgrounds and institutional positions of elites, those who find a pluralist situation emphasize the difficulties inherent in decision making. These differences in methodology result in endless debates on many complex issues, ranging from definitions of power to the value and meaning of vague concepts like "nondecisions."[26]

It is clear, too, that each theory represents an overview of the entire political system in the United States. Each is essentially an ideal or abstract model that attempts to diagram and explain the distribution of political power. Indeed, most texts on American government tend to view political institutions and behavior from the vantage point of one of these two overarching theories. Many conclusions reached in various chapters of this text, for example, reflect assumptions about the distribution and exercise of power that other observers do not accept. Whereas advocates of the pluralist theory probably would feel uneasy about our discussion in Chapter 15 of the frustrations faced by ordinary citizens trying to voice their concerns, supporters of the ruling-elite theory would probably feel just as uneasy about our discussion in Chapter 9 of the pitfalls and frustrations of presidential power.

Actually, both theories are persuasive in some respects. This is particularly true at the community level, where the amounts of pluralism and ruling elitism seem to vary considerably from one city to another.[27] In addition, it is possible to accept one proposition of a theory without necessarily accepting all its other propositions. Even if one adopts the pluralist view, for instance, that separate elites dominate in different policy areas, one need not agree that these elites are restrained by competition among themselves or that they are responsive to the wishes of the community.[28]

Advocates of the two theories even agree on some points, such as the inequality of influence. While differing over the true potentials for citizen action, both groups acknowledge that the ideal of American democracy, in which most citizens wield equal influence over policy making, hardly prevails. Not only are there elites who exert considerably greater influence on government than do most people, but it is also true that many citizens become only minimally involved in the political fabric of society. Many people remain pessimistic about their chances to affect the political process and do not especially care whether a single, cohesive elite or a plurality of elites actually governs.

A Third Theory: The Politics of Bureaucracy

It should be pointed out, finally, that a third, and increasingly popular, theory of power in America holds that ultimately *no one* is in charge. It states that the political system in the United States has become so enveloped in the tentacles of bureaucracy, so divided by a system of internal checks and balances, and so beset by a growing complexity of problems and proposed solutions that effective control over policy making by any group has become virtually impossible. The powerlessness many people feel results neither from the concentration of power in the hands of a few remote elites nor from the dispersal of power among a large number of competing groups and institutions. Rather it results from the fact that no one ultimately has responsibility for policy. The "system" is running by itself, out of control, with no group capable of controlling it.

Some of us probably have suspected as much for quite some time. There is something compelling about this theory, especially in light of the growing use of computers that tolerate no back talk, the pervasive reliance of government and industry on those long, forgettable numbers marking our credit cards, bank accounts, and driver's licenses, and the proliferation of faceless bureaucrats who refuse to budge from "the rules."

Although this theory embraces a variety of concepts and concerns, it is ultimately a response to the seemingly pervasive "bureaucratization" of American society. In government, especially, bureaucracy seems to be everywhere, creating and enforcing rules affecting virtually all aspects of our lives. To those who accept this theory, the most alarming aspect of this sprawling bureaucracy is the power it exerts over the individual. And at no time, they say, is this power more evident than

when federal agencies are engaged in the secret surveillance of people's private lives. The spread of government investigators, computer networks, and data banks has made each citizen subject to the prying eyes of countless civil servants. It has been estimated that at least ten separate dossiers exist in government files on the average American, detailing his or her medical history, financial status, educational achievements, and political activities. Occasionally the existence of such surveillance is revealed in newspaper headlines, as when it was disclosed in early 1975 that the Postal Service had been turning over citizens' letters to the Central Intelligence Agency and that the Federal Bureau of Investigation had been collecting information on the drinking and sexual habits of U.S. presidents, members of Congress, and other high-ranking officials. Former Attorney General Edward Levi testified before a House subcommittee that 883 entries on senators and 722 on House members existed among the FBI's general files on 6.5 million Americans.[29]

The question is: Who is to be held responsible for such acts? Officials who carry out the surveillance claim merely to be obeying orders of superiors who, in turn, similarly claim to be following instructions "from above." In many instances—especially when publicity does not accompany a bureaucratic policy—the maze of specialized departments and the devotion to secrecy make it virtually impossible for an outsider to trace the source of a decision. Although responsibility can always be placed on the president's desk, it is unlikely any chief executive could maintain control over all bureaucratic decisions. Presidents often experience the same frustrations as the rest of us in dealing with bureaucratic obstinacy and red tape. Meanwhile, those responsible for a policy decision—presuming they even know they are responsible—remain hidden in the impenetrable jungle of federal office buildings and executive suites.

Thus, in view of the seemingly ubiquitous presence of bureaucracy in the lives of Americans at all levels of the political system, the alternative theory that ultimately no one can maintain effective control over policy making offers few promises for effective citizen participation. Indeed, the implications of this theory may be even more pessimistic for political action than those of the other two theories we have considered. If no one is in charge—if no one is in control—then no group can be singled out as the target for reform. Those of us who are intent upon influencing the political process will have to wander through a maze of agencies and bureaus simply trying to locate the pressure points. And for each policy decision we wish to affect, we will have to seek an entirely different and obscure locus of power. More will be said about the bureaucracy in Chapter 12.

ruling-elite theory

pluralist theory

elite

military industrial complex

Notes

1. For an excellent discussion of power and its alternatives, see Peter Bachrach and Morton S. Baratz, "Decisions and Nondecisions: An Analytical Framework," *American Political Science Review*, September 1963, pp. 632–642.

2. See, for example, C. Wright Mills, *The Power Elite* (New York: Oxford University Press, Galaxy, 1959); Floyd Hunter, *Community Power Structure* (Chapel Hill: University of North Carolina, 1953); G. William Domhoff, *Who Rules America?* (Englewood Cliffs, N.J.: Prentice-Hall, 1967); Thomas R. Dye and L. Harmon Zeigler, *The Irony of Democracy*, 4th ed. (Belmont, Calif.: Duxbury Press, 1978).

3. Robert Dahl, "A Critique of the Ruling-Elite Model," *American Political Science Review*, June 1958, pp. 463–469.

4. Mills, *The Power Elite*, p. 324.

5. *Congressional Record*, 24 March 1969.

6. U.S. Bureau of the Census, *Statistical Abstract of the United States*, 1978, p. 377.

7. David M. Ricci, *Community Power and Democratic Theory* (New York: Random House, 1971), pp. 168–169.

8. *Business Week*, 5 August 1972, pp. 54–56.

9. *Newsweek*, 23 December 1974, p. 68.

10. *Fortune*, May 1975.

11. *Time*, 21 January 1974, p. 71.

12. Domhoff, *Who Rules America*, p. 4.

13. *San Francisco Examiner*, 14 August 1977.

14. Joseph A. Kahl, *The American Class Structure* (New York: Holt, Rinehart and Winston, 1965), p. 272.

15. Mills, *The Power Elite*, p. 348.

16. Ibid., p. 361.

17. Dye and Zeigler, *The Irony of Democracy*.

18. See, for example, Robert A. Dahl, *Who Governs: Democracy and Power in an American City* (New Haven: Yale University Press, 1961); Nelson Polsby, *Community Power and Political Theory* (New Haven: Yale University Press, 1963); Arnold Rose, *The Power Structure* (New York: Oxford University Press, 1967).

19. Carl Friedrich, *Man and His Government* (New York: McGraw-Hill, 1963), p. 326.

20. See Dahl, "A Critique of the Ruling-Elite Model."

21. Dahl, *Who Governs*, p. 183.

22. Ibid., p. 325.

23. "The Big Business Executive, 1964," *Scientific American*, lithographed report, 1965.

24. Dahl, *Who Governs*, p. 101.

25. See Robert W. Jackman, "Political Elites, Mass Publics, and Support for Democratic Principles," *Journal of Politics*, August 1972, pp. 753–773.

26. See Bachrach and Baratz, op. cit.; Raymond E. Wolfinger, "Nondecisions and the Study of Local Politics," followed by comments, *American Political Science Review*, December 1971, pp. 1063–1104; Geoffrey Debnam, "Nondecisions and Power: The Two Faces of Bachrach and Baratz," followed by comments, *American Political Science Review*, September 1975, pp. 889–907.

27. See, for example, Robert Presthus, *Men at the Top: A Study in Community Power* (New York: Oxford University Press, 1964).

28. See, for example, Wallace S. Sayre and Herbert Kaufman, *Governing New York City* (New York: W. W. Norton, 1965).

29. *Newsweek*, 10 March 1975, p. 16.

Recommended Reading

BACHRACH, PETER. *The Theory of Democratic Elitism.* Boston: Little, Brown, 1967.

DAHL, ROBERT A. *Who Governs: Democracy and Power in an American City.* New Haven: Yale University Press, 1961.

DOMHOFF, G. WILLIAM. *Who Rules America?* Englewood Cliffs, N.J.: Prentice-Hall, 1967.

DOMHOFF, G. WILLIAM, AND HOYT B. BALLARD, eds. *C. Wright Mills and the Power Elite.* Boston: Beacon Press, 1968. 1967.

DYE, THOMAS R. *Who's Running America: Institutional Leadership in the United States.* Englewood Cliffs, N.J.: Prentice-Hall, 1976.

DYE, THOMAS R., AND L. HARMON ZEIGLER. *The Irony of Democracy.* 4th ed. Belmont, Calif.: Duxbury Press, 1978.

HUNTER, FLOYD. *Community Power Structure.* Chapel Hill: University of North Carolina, 1953.

MILLS, C. WRIGHT. *The Power Elite.* New York: Oxford University Press, 1956.

PARRY, GERAINT. *Political Elites.* New York: Praeger, 1969.

POLSBY, NELSON. *Community Power and Political Theory.* New Haven: Yale University Press, 1963.

PREWITT, KENNETH, AND ALAN STONE. *The Ruling Elites.* New York: Harper & Row, 1973.

RICCI, DAVID. *Community Power and Democratic Theory.* New York: Random House, 1971.

ROSE, ARNOLD. *The Power Structure.* New York: Oxford University Press, 1967.

3

The Constitutional Setting

Our understanding of the political power structure and the opportunities for citizen participation cannot be based solely on a grasp of the ruling-elite/pluralist debate. We must also know something about the historical roots of our society and the constitutional arrangements fashioned by a talented band of individuals gathered in Philadelphia almost two centuries ago. Their perceptions of the political world—and of human nature—led to a body of laws and principles that continue to define the boundaries of our political behavior.

By its nature, a *constitution* is something special and unique. It is the principal legal statement of a political system, prescribing the powers and procedures of its governmental institutions. A constitution may be a single document, a group of documents, or even a series of laws and unwritten rules developed over many centuries, as in Great Britain. Although most countries can lay claim to a constitution, not all may be considered a true constitutional state. *Constitutionalism* implies a limited government in which rulers may not arbitrarily do whatever they please. Thus, while a country like the Soviet Union may have a written constitution, it may bear little relation to the powers commanded by Soviet leaders.

In the broadest sense, our own constitution includes more than just the historical document preserved under glass in the National Archives. The Constitution of 1787 is only the original foundation for an entire structure of amendments, Supreme Court rulings, and statutes that form the legal framework of our society. In fact, many vital elements of the political system—such as the political parties and the federal bureaucracy—are not mentioned in the original document, but can be included as part of our "unwritten constitution."

As our political system continues to evolve, so will our Constitution. We will face a constant need to reexamine what the framers had in mind when they drafted the original document and to consider whether we still agree with their intentions. Since it was first drafted in 1787, the Constitution has undergone many important changes in form and interpretation. Scholars and judges over the years have produced a rich literature of judicial analysis based on interpretations of the framers' motives and the changing needs of our society. Let us begin, therefore, with a brief analysis of what the framers had in mind when they assembled to form a constitution.

What the Framers Had in Mind

The Constitution was drafted in Philadelphia during the hot summer of 1787 by a gathering of fifty-five delegates representing twelve of the original thirteen states (Rhode Island did not send delegates). Although seventy-four delegates were named to the Philadelphia Convention, only fifty-five showed up, and only thirty-nine eventually signed the document.

As a group, the delegates embodied the political, intellectual, and commercial elite of American society—"an assembly of demigods," according to Thomas Jefferson. They were not representative of the general population. Most of the delegates were college-educated, had considerable political experience as members of the Continental Congress or as state governors, and were successful lawyers, merchants, landowners, and financiers. There were no women, blacks, or Indians, and few small farmers or tradespeople represented.

Nor were many of the old revolutionary firebrands on hand. Although some of the famous leaders of the Revolution attended—such as George Washington, Benjamin Franklin, James Madison, and Alexander Hamilton—other notables were absent. Thomas Jefferson was serving as a diplomat in Paris, John Adams was in London, and Thomas Paine was busy in Europe spreading the gospel of revolution. Patrick Henry declined to come because he "smelt a rat." In all, only eight of the

THE FOUNDATION OF AMERICAN GOVERNMENT

fifty-six signers of the Declaration of Independence attended the Convention.

The motives of the delegates have inspired considerable scholarly debate. Generations of historians have locked horns over whether the framers were motivated by personal or national interests. Prior to 1910, historians commonly viewed the framers as farsighted statesmen inspired only by the noblest sentiments to produce the best possible system of government. Under the impetus of the Progressive movement, however, scholars began to reevaluate this view, with the most shocking reinterpretation provided by historian Charles Beard in his 1913 classic, *An Economic Interpretation of the Constitution.*[1] Beard unearthed archive information on the delegates' financial holdings, revealing that many owned government bonds issued during the Revolutionary War that had depreciated in value. Beard insisted that the delegates wanted to establish a strong central government that would restore the value of their holdings, protect their property, and preserve their elite status. As he put it, "the members of the Philadelphia Convention which drafted the Constitution were, with few exceptions, immediately, directly, and personally interested in, and derived economic advantage from, the establishment of the new system" so that "the Constitution was essentially an economic document."[2]

Beard's analysis brought on a storm of criticism. Later historians challenged Beard's interpretations, claiming that he overstated the founders' economic motives. Robert E. Brown, for instance, said he found little relation between the delegates' financial holdings and their actions at the Convention. "We would be doing a grave injustice to the political sagacity of the Founding Fathers," Brown wrote, "if we assume that property or personal gain was their only motive."[3]

The debate is by no means ended. Ruling-elite theorists often cite Beard's study when arguing that our elitist political system has deep historical roots, while pluralists and others contend that the framers' economic motives played only an incidental part in the Constitution's creation.

In all likelihood, the framers saw little conflict between their own interests and the well-being of the country. Their desires for personal gain were mixed with practical concerns about the state of society and with broad philosophical views on human nature and the proper role of government. They had to resolve the problems of a new society torn by what they believed were serious sectional and economic cleavages, as well as construct a governmental system capable of safeguarding personal liberties. Indeed, we can gain a better understanding of the Constitution if we consider (1) the political challenges that faced the delegates, and (2) their perspectives on human nature and the problems of factions, as expressed in the writings of James Madison.

Hammering Out Some Compromises

A major reason the delegates gathered in Philadelphia was the failure, in their view, of the existing government to deal with major national problems. *The Articles of Confederation*, drafted ten years earlier during the Revolutionary War, left most governmental power in the hands of the states. After having revolted from the tyranny of centralized British rule, many of the delegates felt the *Confederation* went too far in the opposite direction. The weak central government, embodied in the Continental Congress, lacked the power to tax and regulate interstate commerce, deal effectively with foreign governments, and protect against foreign invasion. It could not prevent the states from coining their own money, setting up tariffs and trade barriers, or violating treaties. And it had no direct authority over the people, who were subject only to the governments of their states. The Confederation, as one scholar has stated, was hardly more than "a league of friendship entered into by sovereign states."[4]

Table 3-1. Chronology of Events

1776	Declaration of Independence
1777	Articles of Confederation drafted
1781	Articles of Confederation adopted
1783	Peace with England
1786	Shays' Rebellion in Massachusetts
1787	Constitutional Convention in Philadelphia
1788	Required nine states have ratified Constitution
1789	George Washington elected president
1790	Last state (Rhode Island) ratifies Constitution
1791	Bill of Rights (first ten amendments) ratified

In addition, the Articles of Confederation provided for only one national branch: a *unicameral* (one-house) Congress. There was no judicial system to settle disputes between states, and no executive branch to enforce the laws. Executive and judicial functions were exercised primarily by committees selected by, and responsible to, Congress.

Clearly, the delegates to the Philadelphia Convention had expected more from the Revolution than a faltering economy and an impotent government. Unless the central government was strengthened, they feared that financial chaos and anarchy would result. This fear was reaffirmed by Shays' Rebellion in 1786, a revolt staged by several thousand poor farmers and laborers in Massachusetts who were unable to pay their taxes and mortgages.

At first, many of the delegates believed they would only be called upon to revise the Articles of Confederation, as they were instructed by the Continental Congress. But it soon became apparent that amending the Articles would not be enough. In their view, an entirely new Constitution was needed. The question then became: What groups and regions would control the new government?

One bitter dispute erupted, for example, over the question of state representation in the new government's legislative body. While the delegates from the larger states like Virginia were anxious to form a strong central government with a legislature they could dominate, the delegates from the smaller states like New Jersey wanted to avoid losing the powers they enjoyed under the Articles of Confederation. In fact, the first proposal placed before the Convention was the *Virginia Plan* introduced by Governor Edmund Randolph. It called for a new structure of national government having three separate branches: legislative, executive, and judicial. The legislature would consist of two houses with representation of the states based on population or the amount of taxes paid. This meant that a state with 600,000 people would have twice as many representatives as a state with 300,000 people. In addition, Congress would appoint both the executive and the judiciary, and could veto any state laws it felt violated the Constitution, thus ensuring national supremacy.

Not surprisingly, the delegates from the smaller states were alarmed at this proposal. They feared that the larger states would band together in Congress and lord it over the smaller states. They backed instead the *New Jersey Plan* introduced by William Paterson, which called for keeping the one-house legislature provided by the Articles of Confederation. Under this plan, each state would continue to be represented equally in Congress so that New Jersey's vote would count the same as Virginia's. And, although Congress would have the expanded power to levy taxes and regulate interstate commerce, it would not appoint the judiciary; judges would be appointed by the president, who would be chosen by Congress.

In a sense, both sides had valid points. Why should a large state like Virginia allow its vote to be counted the same as New Jersey's when it contained more people and thus paid more taxes? At the same time, why should a small state like New Jersey voluntarily hand over the equal status it enjoyed under the Articles and become dominated by the larger states?

Because it appeared that the Convention might break up as the result of hopeless deadlock, the delegates from Connecticut offered a compromise. They suggested a bicameral (*two-house Congress*), allowing for equal representation in the Senate (two senators from each state) and representation by population in the House of Representatives. This would grant a veto power to both large and small states, since any legislation passed by Congress would need the approval of both chambers. In addition, since the larger states would bear the major burden of taxation, all revenue bills would originate in the House, where population determined voting strength. Reluctantly, the delegates agreed to the *Connecticut Compromise*, and it was written into the Constitution. They then proceeded to hammer out compromises concerning the executive and judicial branches, providing for a president to be selected every four years by a "college" of citizens chosen by the states, and a Supreme Court to be appointed by the president.

The sharp dispute over state representation, it should be noted, was coupled with the question of slavery. Northern delegates did not want slaves to be counted in determining representation of southern states in the House. At the same time, southern delegates did not want slaves to be counted in determining their tax burdens. A compromise was eventually reached—incredible from our perspective today—defining each slave as three-fifths of a human being for both purposes. As Article I noted, a state's population would be determined "by adding to the whole number of free persons . . . excluding Indians not taxed, three-fifths of all other Persons." (The term "slave" was not used in the Constitution.) Eighty years later, in 1868, this formula was eliminated by the Fourteenth Amendment.

The Constitution's Philosophical Base

The dispute between the large and small states, and between the northern and southern delegates, should not obscure the important philosophical aspects of the Constitution. Although the document was hammered out by a band of wealthy aristocrats facing serious economic and political problems, it was not solely the product of pragmatic compromise. The Constitution also reflected the framers' perspectives on the nature of human conflict and the values of limited government.

In a sense, the Constitution was partly the product of the eighteenth-century Age of Enlightenment. Many of the delegates were familiar with the writings of English and Continental philosophers, like John Locke, who contended that government should be based on the consent of the governed and that each person has certain natural rights. The framers accepted the idea, for example, of creating a government which, as James Madison stated, is "derived from the great body of the society and not from an inconsiderable proportion or a favored class of it."[5]

Yet, most of the framers were equally certain that the people could not be trusted. Shays' Rebellion had merely reinforced their belief that an unrestrained citizenry could pose as great a threat as any despot to individual liberty, and that government should be carefully designed to impede majority rule. "The evils we experience," Elbridge Gerry of Massachusetts thundered, "flow directly from the excesses of democracy."

Indeed, few of the framers suffered any delusions about human nature. As Alexander Hamilton reportedly exclaimed, "Sir, your people is a great beast." It would be imprudent, they felt, to build a system that depended heavily on the limited virtue and wisdom of the people. "If men were angels," Madison declared, "no government would be necessary. If angels were to govern men, neither external war nor internal controls over government would be necessary. In framing a government which is to be administered by men over men, the great difficulty lies in this: You must first enable the government to control the governed; and in the next place, oblige it to control itself."[6]

The writings of James Madison in *The Federalist* (a series of essays urging the ratification of the Constitution in New York State[7]) provide perhaps the best clue to some of the principles accepted by the delegates. His analysis in *Federalist* No. 10 of "factions" and the need for a mixed government revealed some interesting perspectives on the nature and problems of a political society.

In Madison's view, politics in America was primarily a struggle among competing groups or factions, each pursuing its own selfish goals. He defined a "faction" as any group of citizens whose passions or interests were "adverse to the rights of other citizens, or to the permanent and aggregate interests of the community." Like Karl Marx in the following century, Madison believed that the main divisions in society were between those with property and those without, between those who were creditors and those who were debtors. As he put it, ". . . the most common and durable source of factions is the unequal distribution of property. Those who hold and those who are without property have ever formed distinct interests in society." Unlike Marx, however, he saw more than just two contending classes. There were divisions not only between the "haves" and "have-nots," but also between different sectors of the economy: "a landed interest, a manufacturing interest, a mercantile interest, a moneyed interest," and so forth.

Because factions were based on the pursuit of selfish goals, Madison continued, they were hardly desirable. They divided the society and undermined the public good. More important, there was a danger that one faction might become a permanent majority of society, threatening the liberties of others. "To secure the public good and private rights against the danger of such a faction," Madison stated, "and at the same time to preserve the spirit and form of popular government, is then the great object to which our inquiries are directed."

In short, the problem facing the framers was how to curb the influence of factions without imposing a tyrannical government. What sort of system could be devised capable of insulating individual liberties against both the power of the state and the excesses of "the mob"?

Madison's answer was a masterpiece of political theory. Because factions can be compared to a disease, he contended, either a "cure" or a means of "controlling its effects" would be needed. A cure would be impossible, since there are only "two methods of removing the causes of faction: the one, by destroying the liberty which is essential to its existence; the other, by giving to every citizen the same opinions, the same passions, and the same interests." That is, destroying the liberties that permit factions to flourish would be "a cure worse than the disease." And trying to eliminate factions by sweeping away people's selfish interests would require changing human nature, an impossible task. As Madison put it, "The latent causes of faction are thus sown in the nature of man." Thus, the answer must lie in controlling the *effects* of factions.

James Madison

Because people have to be taken as they are and because the main task of government is to secure order without threatening liberty, good institutional arrangements must be found that will render factions harmless.

One solution would be to combine the thirteen states into a larger nation where many kinds of interests could be contained. In a larger territory, he wrote, "it is less probable that a majority of the whole will have a common motive to invade the rights of other citizens." In fact, it would be difficult for groups even to stay in touch; not only would they be unaware of their common interests, but it would be difficult for them to impose their will on others.

A second solution would be to design a system of staggered elections that would prevent any faction from gaining control of government. If the president and members of the House and Senate were elected for terms of different lengths and by different procedures, no group could dominate all three offices at the same time. Thus, representatives would serve for two years, presidents for four, and senators for six, with a third of the senators elected every two years rather than all at once. In addition, only members of the House would be elected directly by the people. Senators would be elected by state legislatures, while presidents would be chosen by "electors" selected by the states. Justices of the

Supreme Court would be appointed for life terms by the president with the consent of the Senate. (Since Madison's time, of course, several of these arrangements have changed. As we will see, the electoral college has evolved largely into a rubber stamp, while the Seventeenth Amendment in 1913 provided for the popular election of senators.)

It should be noted that the framers' concern over factions were closely tied to their fears of too much popular rule. They deliberately avoided the direct election of senators, for example, in order to mix aristocratic with popular government. As Madison put it, the Senate, comprised of older men with great personal property, would likely proceed with "more coolness, with more system, and with more wisdom, than the popular branch." And although members of the House would be chosen at the polls, it was left up to the states to decide who was qualified to vote. In most states, only white, male property owners were given the franchise; nonwhites, women, and propertyless men were generally excluded. Not until 1870 was the constitutional right to vote extended to nonwhites (Fifteenth Amendment), and not until 1920 was the vote granted to women (Nineteenth Amendment).

Even having a large territory would help limit citizen participation. Millions of people could not possibly squeeze into a town hall to make national policy decisions, as in a direct democracy, but would have to choose the most qualified among them to serve as their representatives. In this way, a representative democracy (a *republic*) would help filter the opinions of the masses. It would "refine and enlarge the public views by passing them through the medium of a chosen body of citizens, whose wisdom may best discern the true interests of their country."

Yet, even these arrangements were not considered sufficient. In addition to a large union, a system of staggered elections, and a representative legislative body, Madison and the other framers insisted on imposing "auxiliary precautions." Indeed, they felt that the most effective way to prevent tyranny—by a majority or a minority—was to scatter power among different levels and institutions of government, with each imposing restraints on the others. As Madison declared, "ambition must be made to counteract ambition."[8]

Our Separated Institutions: Ambition to Check Ambition

One such "auxiliary precaution" was the *separation of powers*. The framers adopted the idea from several sources, especially from the eighteenth-century French philosopher Baron de Montesquieu.[9] Admiring the British political system, Montesquieu mistakenly believed that the secret of its success lay in the separation of powers among the executive (the king), the legislature (the Parliament), and the judiciary (the House of Lords). Unfortunately, Montesquieu was mistaken on a number of points about the British political system, not least of which was the fact that it was based on a fusion—not a separation—of power between the parliament and the cabinet executive.

Despite Montesquieu's errors, however, the framers accepted his notion that the way to avoid tyranny was to divide constitutional authority among three different branches of the national government. "No political truth is certainly of greater intrinsic value, or is stamped with the authority of more enlightened patrons of liberty," Madison wrote, "than that ... the accumulation of all powers, legislative, executive, and judiciary, in the same hands ... may justly be pronounced the very definition of tyranny."[10] Thus, the Constitution declares that the legislative power will be vested in Congress (Article I), the executive power will be in the hands of the president (Article II), and the judicial power will rest with the courts (Article III).

In actuality, of course, the separation of powers is not absolute. The Constitution also provides for a *sharing* of powers. The president, for example, wields the legislative power to propose and veto bills, and the Senate exercises the executive power to confirm or reject presidential appointments and treaties.

In fact, the three branches were not designed to be entirely separate. Because there was always the danger that ambitious politicians in one branch might try to assume command of the government, the framers also provided for a system of *checks and balances*, which would enable each branch to have some say in the operation of the other two. Just as one faction in society would balance another, so would one branch of government prevent another from abusing its powers. Thus, Congress can pass a bill, but the president can veto it. Congress can then override a veto by a two-thirds vote in both houses. The president can negotiate a treaty, but it cannot become effective unless the Senate approves it. And although the president carries out the laws, Congress appropriates the money to keep his administrative apparatus running. The Supreme Court, in turn, can invalidate a law passed by Congress and signed by the president, but the president appoints the justices with the consent of the Senate. In short, each branch balances the others by commanding independent and overlapping powers, and also checks them by limiting their actions.

One point should be noted, however. The checks and balances system devised by the framers was not based solely on abstract principles. It was also the product of political compromise. For example, the appointment of Supreme Court justices by the president with the potential for veto by the Senate was a compromise between those delegates who favored judicial selection by the legislature and those who preferred selection by the executive. While this checks and balances provision might help prevent tyranny, it also provided a convenient compromise between two opposing viewpoints.

Over the years, the fragmentation of political authority has sparked considerable criticism. Many critics have seen the separation of powers as an unwieldy system of governing that encourages needless delay, impedes social reform, and favors the status quo. "In their effort to protect basic rights," one scholar has observed, "what the framers did in effect was to hand out extra chips in the game of politics to people who are already advantaged, while they handicapped the disadvantaged who would like to change the status quo."[11]

Indeed, from the standpoint of citizen action, the fragmentation of power would seem to impose severe limitations on what those seeking social reform are likely to achieve. Even if a group wins the support of the House of Representatives in bringing about a policy change—whether it be handgun controls, tax reform, or improved medical care for the elderly—there is no assurance such support will also come from the Senate or the White House. By scattering power among many centers of decision making, the framers created many potential veto points to frustrate reform.

From another perspective, however, the scattering of power among several institutions has also provided alternative avenues of access to government. Groups unable to penetrate one branch of government have been able to gain access to another branch, where they have won support in bringing about a policy change. In the 1950s and 1960s, for example, the National Association for the Advancement of Colored People (NAACP) found a powerful ally in the Supreme Court in its drive for civil rights, when both Congress and the White House were slow to move. Thus, the separation of powers can both frustrate and encourage opportunities for citizen action, depending on the goals and the circumstances.

Nor has the checks and balances system escaped the notice of critics. Many observers have pointed to periods in history when the president has been dominated by a more powerful Congress (as during the post–Civil War years), or when Congress has been virtually eclipsed by the president (as during the reigns of Lyndon Johnson and Richard Nixon). The Watergate scandal, especially, revealed how one branch of government overstepped its constitutional boundaries and threatened to undermine the principle of checks and balances.

But the scandal also revealed how the checks and balances system could be triggered into action. Congress's drive to impeach Richard Nixon in 1974 brought the checks and balances system into dramatic focus for many Americans. Indeed, let us consider the impeachment process as one illustration of the checks envisioned by the framers.

The Impeachment Process

Perhaps the most awesome power that can be wielded by members of Congress is the *impeachment* and removal from office of all federal officials, from the president on down (only military officers and fellow members of Congress are exempt). The framers provided for impeachment—with the president clearly in mind—after having revolted from an unimpeachable king. They feared that a president who could not be removed from office might become a tyrant. "No point is of more importance," George Mason declared at the Convention, "than that the right of impeachment should be continued. Shall any man be above justice? Above all, shall that man be above it who can commit the most extensive injustice?"

Technically, impeachment is a formal accusation similar to a grand jury indictment. If any member of the House of Representatives accuses a federal official of wrongdoing, the charges go to the Judiciary Committee, which studies the charges and reports its recommendations to the House. After a majority of the House votes to impeach the official, the entire Senate sits as a court hearing the evidence in the case. If two-thirds of the Senate find the official guilty of the charges, he is removed from his post and barred from again holding federal office. In the opinion of most legal experts, there is no appeal.

One of the problems relating to impeachment is the uncertainty regarding what is an impeachable offense. The Constitution states only that an official "shall be removed from office on impeachment for, and conviction of, treason, bribery, or other high crimes and misdemeanors." While the definitions of treason and bribery are clear, the meaning of high crimes and misdemeanors is not. Perhaps the broadest interpretation of the phrase was volunteered by Gerald Ford during his 1970 crusade as a member of the House to impeach Supreme Court Justice William O. Douglas. "An impeachable offense," Ford boasted, "is whatever a majority of the House of Representatives considers it to be at a given moment in history." This suggests that impeachment can be as much a political tactic as a legal decision, and that if Congress becomes intensely opposed to a president or Supreme Court justice, it may initiate impeachment proceedings on what could be questionable legal grounds.

Indeed, there is substantial support for the view that the broadest case for impeachment rests not necessarily on any criminal act, but on an "abuse of the office." "Start with the proposition that impeachment is a removal process," argues Philip B. Kurland. "If a President spent a term fishing, it wouldn't be criminal; but it would be an abuse of office and he would be subject to removal."[12]

Since the ratification of the Constitution, impeachment proceedings have been initiated more than sixty times in the House, although only twelve cases have reached the Senate for trial. And of the twelve persons impeached by the House—including one president (Andrew Johnson in 1868), one Supreme Court justice, one U.S. senator (whose case was dismissed "for lack of jurisdiction"), a secretary of war, and eight lower federal court judges—only four were convicted by the Senate and removed from office. All four were federal judges.

Beginning in the fall of 1973, Richard Nixon clearly faced the strongest call for the impeachment of a president in more than one hundred years. Following a year and a half of Watergate-related revelations in the press and the courts, demands swelled for a congressional investigation into his complicity in the Watergate break-in and cover-up. By January 1974, the House Judiciary Committee had opened its inquiry into the matter, and within six months it had approved three Articles of Impeachment. Article I accused Nixon of "obstruction of justice" on nine counts, including lying to investigators, withholding evidence, and misusing the Central Intelligence Agency. Article II charged him with "abuse of power" for, among other things, employing confidential Internal Revenue Service files against political "enemies," directing the improper surveillance of private citizens, and interfering with the operations of the Justice Department. And Article III accused him of "contempt of Congress" for his refusal to hand over tapes and documents subpoenaed by the Judiciary Committee. Two additional articles—charging him with concealing from Congress the facts about the secret bombing of Cambodia and with misusing government funds to improve his personal property—were rejected by the committee.

Although Nixon's aides tried to undercut the committee as a "kangaroo court," public support for his impeachment grew to the point where two-thirds of those surveyed favored a Senate trial. But a trial never materialized. In August 1974, after confessing he had concealed vital information and after being told by his closest aides that his fate was sealed, Nixon resigned his office, becoming the first president to do so in the history of the Republic.

Federalism: Dispersing Political Power

In addition to splitting the national government into three branches, the framers provided a second "auxiliary precaution" in the form of federalism. *Federalism* can be defined as a dividing of governmental power between a central (national) government and local or regional (state) governments coexisting within the same territory. Unlike the *unitary systems* of Great Britain and France, the local units of government in this country (the states) are more than just administrative branches or departments of a central government. Each of the fifty states boasts its own constitution and judicial system, and can make and enforce its own laws. In effect, all of us possess dual citizenship: we are citizens of both the entire nation and our state, paying taxes to keep the governments of both in operation. As we will see in later chapters, federalism also offers us a number of points of political access—local, state, and national—for affecting governmental policies.

To Madison and the other delegates, the division of powers between the national government and the states offered an additional means to control factions. As Madison put it, "The influence of factious leaders may kindle a flame within their particular states but will be unable to spread a general conflagration through the other states."[13] In addition, federalism was a way to achieve greater national unity and a stronger central government, while preserving the integrity of the states. Most of the people at the time regarded themselves as New Yorkers, Georgians, or Virginians, rather than as Americans, and would not have allowed their states to become totally submissive to a powerful central authority. By dividing powers between the national government and the states, the framers achieved the necessary compromise to win approval for their newly forged document.

The Constitution, therefore, lays out a framework for dividing power between the two levels of government. It assigns the federal government certain *delegated* or *enumerated powers* to be distributed among the three branches. Article I, Section 8, for instance, declares that Congress alone has the power to coin money, establish federal courts, raise armies, make treaties, and declare war. Congress is also granted *concurrent powers* that it shares with the states, such as the right to levy taxes and borrow money.

The powers of the states are not spelled out in the Constitution, but are classified as *reserved powers*. The Tenth Amendment (1791) states that "the powers not delegated to the United States by the Constitution, nor prohibited by it to the states, are reserved to the states respectively, or to the people." Traditionally, those who oppose a strong central government have interpreted this "reserve clause" to mean that the national government can wield *only* those powers granted by the Constitution, and that all other powers belong to the states. In their view, the reserve clause prohibits the national government from stepping into any area not specifically covered in the Constitution.

To a large extent, however, the delegated powers of the national government have been broadened by the famous *necessary and proper clause* at the end of Section 8. This clause (also known as the "elastic clause") allows Congress to "make all laws which shall be necessary and proper for carrying into Execution the foregoing powers, and all other Powers vested . . . in the Government of the United States." This means that, in carrying out a delegated power such as raising armies, Congress may find it "necessary and proper" to draft young men and women into the armed forces, even though the draft is not mentioned in the Constitution. The draft is an *implied power* that may be reasonably inferred from Congress's delegated powers. Section 8 also authorizes Congress to tax and spend for the "general welfare" and to "regulate commerce . . . among the several states." These broad phrases—together with the necessary and proper clause—have been used frequently by Congress to extend its powers beyond those spelled out in the Constitution. It has initiated programs in a wide range of areas on the grounds that they involved interstate commerce or were aimed at the "general welfare."

Generally, whenever the national government and the states have become embroiled in a dispute over the proper boundaries of their authority, the Supreme Court has acted as the "umpire of the federal system." It has wielded its judicial review powers both to strike down acts of Congress that invade the reserved powers of the states and to overturn state laws that are contrary to the Constitution.

Indeed, Supreme Court justices have played a major part in shaping the evolution of federalism through their interpretations of nation-state issues. Although the justices' positions have shifted over time, with support given to the claims of both the states and the national government (see Chapter 11), support for a strong central authority was demonstrated early on in the celebrated case of *McCulloch* v. *Maryland* (1819). The case developed when the state of Maryland tried to tax the politically unpopular Bank of the United States, which had been chartered by Congress. The tax was levied in a thinly disguised attempt to drive the bank out of the state. However, the cashier of the bank's Baltimore branch (James McCulloch) refused to pay the tax, arguing that a state could not tax an instrument of the national government. Maryland countered that the Constitution gave Congress no authority to charter a national bank and, even if it did, a sovereign state could do as it wished within state boundaries.

In a classic statement on the doctrine of implied powers, Chief Justice Marshall supported Congress. In his majority opinion, he stated that the creation of a national bank by Congress was a "necessary and proper" means of carrying out its constitutional powers to borrow money, collect taxes, raise and support armies, and regulate commerce. Chartering a national bank was a power "implied" by other powers listed in the Constitution. In addition, Marshall ruled, the national government is constitutionally superior to the states and in cases of conflict the former must prevail. The states cannot use their reserved powers to hinder the national government's performance of its duties. This ruling echoed the language of Article VI that federal law "shall be the supreme law of the land." The significance of Marshall's opinion was that it affirmed both the supremacy of the national government and the breadth of its "implied" powers, paving the way for countless federal programs—ranging from atomic energy to urban renewal—not anticipated by the framers.

It should be understood, of course, that conflict between the national government and the states has been only one feature of federalism in this country. Despite Madison's calls for divided powers, cooperation between the different levels of government has also been common. Almost from the beginning, the federal government and the states have joined forces in providing essential services in such areas as health, education, law enforcement, and transportation.

Since the Depression of the 1930s, federal *grants-in-aid* to the states and cities have virtually reshaped the concept of federalism. These grants-in-aid (sometimes also called "categorical grants") have been used to assist state and local governments in areas where the federal government has no direct authority. The states are enticed through federal funding to undertake new programs or to beef up existing services. The only major requirement is that states have to cough up matching funds and comply with federal regulations.

Although applauded as a way to improve governmental services in many poor states, the grants-in-aid program also has been widely criticized. Some critics see the program as a means used by the federal government to impose its will on states and local communities. It allows the federal government to earmark funds for certain categories of spending—such as mass transit, housing, and slum clearance—while getting local authorities to operate the programs.

This criticism, in fact, helped convince Congress in the early 1970s to support President Nixon's proposal for a "New Federalism." In 1972, Congress passed a general *revenue sharing* bill entitled the State and Local Fiscal Assistance Act. Under a five-year experimental program, the federal government was instructed to return over $30 billion from federal income taxes to the states and cities. The aim of the program was to do away with the usual strings attached to federal funding by allowing local officials to use the money largely as they wished.

In 1976, Congress extended the revenue sharing program another four years, until 1980. However, the extension included a number of tighter regulations with which the states had to comply. Funds could not be used, for example, to support any program that discriminated against persons because of race or sex. In addition, state and local officials had to supply the federal government with detailed reports on how revenue sharing funds would be used. There were also provisions for enhancing citizen participation in local decision making. Each agency had to hold public hearings to allow citizens to voice their opinions on how the money should be spent.

While revenue sharing has been well received, there also has been some dispute over the program's basic principles. Some observers insist that revenue sharing undermines the national commitment to solving major problems like poverty and poor housing. They argue that national objectives cannot be met unless the federal government has more control over how federal funds should be spent. Supporters of revenue sharing, however, respond that the loss of federal influence also means more local control. Even though money comes from Washington, local governments should be able to respond to local needs in determining priorities of spending. In short, the arguments over revenue sharing echo many of the same arguments that have distinguished American federalism for the past two centuries.

The Ratification Battle

After the delegates had signed the Constitution in September 1787, they faced the difficult task of persuading the states to adopt it, a task that eventually took two and a half years to complete. One formidable obstacle was obtaining the unanimous consent of all thirteen state legislatures, as required by the Articles of Confederation. Because some of the states might veto the newly forged document, the delegates searched for a different scheme.

They decided to appeal to the people over the heads of both the Continental Congress and the twelve state legislatures that had picked the delegates. They provided in Article VII that only nine states—not the entire thirteen—were needed to ratify the Constitution. And because state legislatures might spurn a document that weakened their powers, the delegates proposed using popularly elected state conventions as the ratifying bodies. This scheme would make the Constitution appear as a "compact" among all the people rather than simply an agreement among state politicians.

The delegates knew the Constitution would not be wildly applauded by all segments of society. Many people were satisfied with the Articles of Confederation and were wary of change. Indeed, a debate soon erupted between those who championed the new Constitution (the *Federalists)* and those who opposed it (the *Anti-Federalists)*. Many of the Anti-Federalists were small farmers who feared the Constitution would create a strong central authority that would devour the states and suppress individual rights and local interests. They objected that the president had too much independence, that the Senate was too aristocratic, and that the document lacked a bill of rights to safeguard citizens against governmental tyranny. They even charged a frame-up. They cried that the delegates had met in secrecy to forge a document that was essentially extralegal, exceeding their instructions from Congress merely to patch up the Articles of Confederation. In short, they drew a picture of the Philadelphia Convention similar to that drawn by Charles Beard more than a century later: as a gathering of wealthy aristocrats who secretly fashioned a strong central government designed to protect their own economic interests.

The supporters of the Constitution, however, responded with a well-organized newspaper campaign to whip up support. In New York State, for example, a series of eighty-five essays known collectively as *The Federalist* (or *The Federalist Papers*) were published in local newspapers. Written under the pen name "Publius" by Alexander Hamilton, James Madison, and John Jay, the essays compared the defects of the Articles of Confederation to the virtues of the new government proposed by the Constitution. They emphasized that the new government would be strong enough to meet its obligations and safe enough to respect the liberties of the people. Though strongly partisan, these essays eventually gained recognition as perhaps the most significant contribution to American political thought. They offered a penetrating analysis of the American political system and revealed a great deal about the framers' intentions.

The debate, for the most part, did not involve the general population. Although delegates to the ratifying conventions were popularly elected, only a small percentage of eligible voters turned out to vote. As one historian concluded, "The Constitution was adopted with a great show of indifference."[14]

But it was adopted. Less than three months after the framers departed from Philadelphia, Delaware became the first state to ratify the Constitution, in December 1787. Six months later, New Hampshire became the ninth state to do so, and was soon followed by the two critical states of Virginia and New York. By the summer of 1790, all thirteen states had approved the document (see Table 3-2).

Table 3-2. Ratification of the Constitution

State	Date	Vote in Convention	Rank in Population
1. Delaware	December 7, 1787	unanimous	13
2. Pennsylvania	December 12, 1787	46 to 23	3
3. New Jersey	December 18, 1787	unanimous	9
4. Georgia	January 2, 1788	unanimous	11
5. Connecticut	January 9, 1788	128 to 40	8
6. Massachusetts	February 6, 1788	187 to 168	2
7. Maryland	April 28, 1788	63 to 11	6
8. South Carolina	May 23, 1788	149 to 73	7
9. New Hampshire	June 21, 1788	57 to 46	10
10. Virginia	June 25, 1788	89 to 79	1
11. New York	July 26, 1788	30 to 27	5
12. North Carolina	November 21, 1789	195 to 77	4
13. Rhode Island	May 29, 1790	34 to 32	12

Afterthought: A Bill of Rights

Certainly, the Constitution could not have been ratified without a promise to add a bill of rights once the document had been approved by the states. Although the original text guaranteed trials by jury and protected citizens against being held for crimes without cause (writ of habeas corpus), singled out for punishment (through a bill of attainder), or punished for acts that were not illegal when committed (ex post facto laws), it did not provide for other basic rights. It did not guarantee freedoms of speech, assembly, and religion, or prohibit cruel and unusual punishment or unwarranted searches and seizures. Most of the delegates felt it was unnecessary to draft a bill of rights since the federal government could exercise only those powers granted by the Constitution. In their view, the system of government they fashioned—with its separation of powers and checks and balances—provided adequate safeguards against despotism. Adding a list of rights would only be dangerous, since it would suggest that any rights *not* listed could be denied by the government.

The Anti-Federalists were not persuaded, however. They insisted that without a bill of rights citizens would have no protection against abuses of governmental power. They demanded, as their price for supporting the Constitution, that a bill of rights be attached as soon as a new government was formed. Thus, when the first Congress convened in 1789, over one hundred amendments were considered. Out of this number, ten amendments (mostly the work of James Madison) were finally adopted by the states in 1791, three years after the required nine states had ratified the Constitution (1788) and four years after the delegates had assembled in Philadelphia (1787).

These ten amendments, it should be noted, guarded citizens only against the powers of the national government. They did not specifically guard against the powers of state governments. Only through the Supreme Court's interpretations of the "equal protection" and "due process" clauses of the Fourteenth Amendment (1866) was the protection of the Bill of Rights gradually extended to the states (see Chapter 4).

Table 3-3. Outline of the Constitution

Preamble:	Purpose of the Constitution
Article I:	Legislative branch
Article II:	Executive branch
Article III:	Judicial branch
Article IV:	Intergovernmental relations
Article V:	Amendment procedures
Article VI:	Constitution the supreme law of the land
Article VII:	Ratification procedures

The Bill of Rights (1791)

1. Freedom of religion, speech, press, assembly, and petition
2. Right to bear arms
3. Right of homeowners to refuse to quarter soldiers
4. Protection against unreasonable searches and seizures
5. Rights of accused persons and due process of law
6. Right to a speedy, public, and fair trial
7. Right to a trial by jury in civil cases
8. Prohibition of excessive bail and of cruel and unusual punishment
9. Rights retained by the people
10. Protection of powers reserved to the states

Later Amendments

11. Reduction of judicial power of national courts (1795)
12. Separate election of president and vice-president (1804)
13. Abolition of slavery (1865)
14. Privileges of U.S. citizens, due process, and equal protection of the laws (1868)
15. No prohibition of right to vote because of race (1870)
16. Establishment of federal income tax (1913)
17. Direct popular election of Senators (1913)
18. Prohibition of intoxicating liquors (1919)
19. No prohibition of right to vote because of sex (1920)
20. New dates for terms of president, vice-president, and Congress (1933)
21. Repeal of the Eighteenth Amendment (1933)
22. Limitation of president to two terms (1951)
23. Granting the right to vote in presidential elections to Washington, D.C., residents (1961)
24. Elimination of poll tax as voting prerequisite in federal elections (1964)
25. Regulation of presidential succession and continuity of power in case of disability (1967)
26. Voting age set at eighteen years for federal, state, and local elections (1971)

Where the Constitution Is Silent

In addition to a bill of rights, a number of other key elements of American government were not touched on by the delegates. Many of our most prominent political institutions and processes came into being through custom or congressional legislation. For example, the Constitution makes no mention of political parties. Although parties affect many aspects of our government, they have no written constitutional base. The framers had little experience with parties and probably could not have foreseen the important roles they would play in the future. In fact, as noted in Chapter 6, they abhorred the whole idea of parties, believing they would only encourage factionalism. Not until after the Constitution was drafted did organized parties begin to take shape as different groups clashed over economic issues, foreign policy, and the proper role of the federal government.

Similarly, no provisions are made in the Constitution for the major departments and agencies of the federal bureaucracy. Although the Constitution authorizes the president to "require the Opinion, in writing, of the principal Officer in each of the executive Departments," it is silent about how these departments should be organized and the duties they should perform. All of the agencies of the federal bureaucracy—the Labor Department, the Veterans' Administration, the Central Intelligence Agency, and so on—owe their existence to congressional statutes, not to the intentions of the framers.

Nor does the Constitution provide for the presidential cabinet, the congressional committee system, the civil service system, nominating conventions, or presidential primaries. Not even the Supreme Court's sweeping power of judicial review or the structure of the lower federal courts is specifically provided for in the Constitution. They all evolved in response to changing political needs and circumstances, gradually filling in the gaps left by the original document.

How the Constitution Changes: The Opportunities for Action

The growth of new institutions and procedures should remind us that the process of constitution-making did not end when the delegates packed their bags and departed from Philadelphia in 1787. The document they fashioned was extremely brief (about 7,000 words) and contained statements of broad principles that would require specific application and interpretation.

In fact, the framers did not expect their handiwork to endure without change. They knew, as one scholar put it, that "no amount of drafting skill could be expected to eliminate the necessity of revision and development to adopt the Constitution to the unforeseen and unforeseeable."[15] As Madison stated, "In framing a system which we wish to last for ages, we should not lose sight of the changes which ages will produce." Through a variety of processes, federal court judges, members of Congress, and even ordinary citizens could make their mark on the Constitution.

Let us consider, therefore, three of these important processes, beginning with the role of the courts.

Interpretation by the Courts

One important way the Constitution is changed is through federal court interpretation. Each time a question of the Constitution's meaning is raised—such as in a dispute over the proper authority of Congress—judges must decide what it means in that particular case. In fact, there would be little exaggeration in saying, as former Chief Justice Charles Evans Hughes declared, that "we live under a Constitution, but the Constitution is what the judges say it is."

Through their power of *judicial review* (see Chapter 11 for a fuller discussion), Supreme Court justices can rule on the constitutionality of legislative and executive acts. The nine Court justices can overturn decisions of Congress, the president, and state legislators that, in their opinion, conflict with the Constitution, thereby interpreting the document's meaning. Although this sweeping power is not mentioned in the Constitution, it has been used to overturn more than one hundred national and one thousand state acts, making the Supreme Court one of the most powerful tribunals in the world. Few judges elsewhere wield such power. In Great Britain, for example, a statute passed by Parliament cannot be overturned by the courts, even if it violates long-standing "constitutional" principles such as freedom of speech. Members of Parliament, not judges, have the final say on fundamental law.

But because Supreme Court justices can wield the power of judicial review, they are among the principal agents of constitutional change. As Woodrow Wilson concluded, the Supreme Court represents "a kind of Constitutional Convention in continuous session."

Congressional Statutes

Supreme Court justices are not alone in affecting the Constitution, however. Members of Congress also command the power to amend the document through legislative interpretation. The Constitution grants Congress the authority "to make all laws which shall be necessary and proper" to carry out its enumerated powers, thus giving senators and representatives an opportunity to make changes not anticipated by the framers. As we saw, Congress in 1816 created a national bank, even though the Constitution makes no provision for such an institution.[16] Congress insisted that it was "necessary and proper" for it to charter the bank in order to carry out financial responsibilities—such as coining money and collecting taxes—dictated by the Constitution. Chief Justice Marshall supported Congress's claim, stating that the Constitution was "intended to endure for ages to come and, consequently, to be adapted to the various crises of human affairs."

Since then, members of Congress have affected the structure and powers of the federal government in many ways, for example, by enacting statutes creating the executive departments and federal courts, and determining the order of succession to the presidency. Presidents also have contributed to constitutional change over the years, for example, by developing executive agreements as an instrument of foreign policy making (see Chapter 9).

Constitutional Amendments

But the most dramatic means of changing the Constitution has been through constitutional amendment. Because the Founding Fathers believed that no Constitution could remain unchanged for all time, they provided four amending procedures (two ways to propose and two ways to ratify) for modifying the original document (see Article V).

A constitutional amendment can be proposed either by a two-thirds vote of both houses of Congress, or by a national convention called by Congress at the request of two-thirds of the states. All existing amendments were proposed by Congress, although there have been movements to propose amendments by the convention method. By 1980, for instance, a number of states had passed resolutions calling for a constitutional amendment to balance the federal budget.

Once passed, an amendment must then be approved either by three-fourths of the state legislatures, or by special ratifying conventions in three-fourths of the states. Only the Twenty-first Amendment, repealing prohibition, was ratified (in 1933) by the convention method.

A striking aspect of this amending procedure is that the president has no legal power to veto. In fact, not even the Supreme Court can overturn an amendment. An amendment ratified by the states becomes part of the Constitution, and in no way can the Court declare part of the document itself "unconstitutional." This means that members of Congress can use the amending power to reverse a Supreme Court ruling. For example, Congress proposed the Sixteenth Amendment, establishing the federal income tax, after the Court in 1895 had declared such a tax unconstitutional.

Two additional amendments have been proposed by Congress, but as of this writing are still making the rounds of the states. In 1978, Congress passed an amendment giving full voting rights and congressional representation to the residents of the District of Columbia (seat of the federal government). Although the district has an elected mayor, a city council, and one nonvoting delegate in the House of Representatives, its residents cannot vote in congressional elections and have no representation in the Senate. The amendment, if approved by the required thirty-eight states, would deliver full voting rights to district residents and entitle them to two U.S. senators and one or two representatives.[17]

A second amendment, banning discrimination on the basis of sex, was proposed by Congress in 1972. The amendment declares that "equality of rights under the law shall not be denied or abridged by the United States or by any state on account of sex." It was proposed to ensure continued progress toward equality of the sexes by overturning federal and state laws that discriminate against women (as well as men).

The struggle to ratify the Equal Rights Amendment (ERA) illustrates the kinds of obstacles new amendments may face. After whizzing through thirty-five state legislatures (twenty-two in 1972 alone), the amendment stalled three states short of ratification. Because of a surge of strength by stop-ERA forces, it appeared as though the amendment would fail to be ratified before the March 1979 deadline. A resolution accompanying the amendment had set the usual seven-year deadline for ratification by three-fourths of the states. (Although the Constitution says nothing about how long the process should take, Congress in 1917 set a seven-year time limit for ratification of all new amendments. In 1921, the Supreme Court ruled that approval should come "within some reasonable time after the proposal."[18])

However, ERA supporters persuaded Congress in 1978 to take an unprecedented step: to add thirty-nine months to the original seven-year period. The extension resolution set a new deadline of June 1982, thus keeping the amendment alive for several more years. Although disagreements flared among constitutional experts over the legality of the extension, few expected it to be rescinded.[19] As Senator Birch Bayh declared, "It has been clear in every court decision and in every action by the U.S. Congress that Congress has the authority to determine what is a reasonable time for ratification of a constitutional amendment. . . . Ten years is a reasonable time for the ERA. This is no ordinary constitu-

tional amendment. We are dealing with the rights of over half the people in this country."[20]

The push by women's rights organizations to win ratification of the ERA illustrates the kind of role that can be played by ordinary citizens in stimulating constitutional change. In fact, many Americans have tended to see the amendment process as a means of last resort in achieving policy goals. When pleas to legislators and judges have been exhausted, citizen groups have tried to persuade Congress (and state legislatures) to support a constitutional amendment. In recent years, amendments have been proposed that would abolish the income tax, outlaw abortions, permit prayers in public schools, require a balanced federal budget, and elect Supreme Court justices by popular vote.

The prognosis for most such proposals, however, is not good. Amending the Constitution remains difficult not only because of the reluctance of members of Congress to take such a bold step, but also because of the need to secure the approval of three-fourths of the states. Apart from the first ten amendments (the Bill of Rights), which were tacked on as part of the politics of ratification, only sixteen amendments have been passed and ratified during the past two hundred years. While the Constitution is constantly undergoing change, it will not easily be rewritten to accommodate the passing concerns and passions of the times.

constitution

constitutionalism

Articles of Confederation

confederation

unicamera

bicameral

Virginia Plan

New Jersey Plan

Connecticut Compromise

republic

separation of powers

checks and balances

impeachment

unitary system

delegated (or enumerated) powers

concurrent powers

reserved powers

necessary and proper clause

implied power

grants-in-aid

revenue sharing

Federalists

Anti-Federalists

Federalist Papers

judicial review

Federalism

Notes

1. Charles Beard, *An Economic Interpretation of the Constitution* (New York: Macmillan, 1954). First published in 1913.

2. Ibid., p. 324.

3. Robert E. Brown, *Charles Beard and the Constitution of the United States* (Princeton, N.J.: Princeton University Press, 1956), p. 198.

4. C. Herman Pritchett, *The American Constitution*, 2nd ed. (New York: McGraw-Hill, 1968), p. 11.

5. *The Federalist*, No. 39.

6. *The Federalist*, No. 51.

7. James Madison, Alexander Hamilton, and John Jay, *The Federalist Papers*, 1788.

8. *The Federalist*, No. 51.

9. Baron de Montesquieu, *The Spirit of the Laws*, 1748.

10. *The Federalist*, No. 47.

11. Samuel Hendel, "Separation of Powers Revisited in Light of Watergate," *Western Political Quarterly*, December 1974, pp. 575–588.

12. Philip B. Kurland, quoted in *Time*, 4 February 1974, pp. 30–31.

13. *The Federalist*, No. 10.

14. Brown, *Charles Beard and the Constitution of the United States*, p. 170.

15. Pritchett, *The American Constitution*, p. 33.

16. *McCulloch* v. *Maryland* (1819).

17. See *Congressional Quarterly Weekly Report*, 26 August 1978, pp. 2277–2278.

18. *Dillon* v. *Gloss* (1921). See also *Coleman* v. *Miller* (1939).

19. See *Congressional Quarterly Weekly Report*, 26 November 1977, pp. 2493–2495.

20. *Associated Press*, 12 October 1978.

Recommended Reading

BEARD, CHARLES A. *An Economic Interpretation of the Constitution*. New York: Macmillan, 1954. First published in 1913.

BROWN, ROBERT E. *Charles Beard and the Constitution of the United States*. Princeton, N.J.: Princeton University Press, 1956.

CORWIN, EDWARD S. *The Constitution and What It Means Today*, revised by Harold Chase and Craig Ducat. Princeton, N.J.: Princeton University Press, 1974.

CORWIN, EDWARD S., AND J. W. PELTASON. *Understanding the Constitution*. 7th ed. New York: Holt, Rinehart and Winston, 1976.

ELAZAR, DANIEL J. *American Federalism: A View from the States*. 2nd ed. New York: Crowell, 1972.

FISHER, LOUIS. *The Constitution Between Friends: Congress, the President, and the Law*. New York: St. Martin's Press, 1978.

FARRAND, MAX. *The Framing of the Constitution of the United States*. New Haven, Conn.: Yale University Press, 1913.

The Federalist Papers. 1788. Various editions.

GRODZINS, MORTON. *The American System*. Chicago: Rand McNally, 1966.

PRITCHETT, C. HERMAN. *The American Constitution*. 3rd ed. New York: McGraw-Hill, 1976.

4

Individual Liberties and Civil Rights

Our ability to influence governmental decision making obviously depends on whether we can freely communicate our political views and question governmental decisions. Without freedom of expression and the right to organize into groups, we would enjoy few opportunities to voice our objections to governmental policies and to work actively against them.

Yet, as we saw in Chapter 3, the Constitution framed in Philadelphia in 1787 did not contain any specific provisions guaranteeing freedom of expression or most other basic rights. In fact, the lack of such provisions was one of the major criticisms lodged against the document by the Anti-Federalists, who demanded that a *bill of rights* be added as their price for supporting the Constitution. The original document did impose certain restraints on government, such as prohibiting Congress from suspending the writ of *habeas corpus,* or enacting *bills of attainder* or *ex post facto laws.* It also guaranteed the right of trial by jury in criminal cases and imposed limits on punishments for treason. But the principal foundation of American civil liberties came with the addition of the first ten amendments (especially the first eight) in 1791 and the passage of the Thirteenth, Fourteenth, and Fifteenth Amendments shortly after the Civil War.

For the most part, these amendments are couched in *negative* terms. They are aimed at restricting government from interfering with the rights of the individual. Congress is prohibited, for example, from abridging a person's freedom of speech or religion, and from depriving a citizen of his life, liberty, or property without *due process of law*. These amendments protect not only the individual's right to participate *in* government—such as through freedom of speech and assembly—but also, to some extent, the individual's freedom *from* intrusion by government into his or her private affairs.

Moreover, the Bill of Rights was drafted principally to restrain the actions of the federal government and not those of the states. The First Amendment declares that *"Congress* shall make no law . . . respecting an establishment of religion . . . or abridging the freedom of speech, or of the press . . . ."* It says nothing about the states. At the time the amendments were drafted, most people tended to fear the power of the federal government more than that of the states, believing state governments were closer to the people and thus easier to control. In addition, many state constitutions already included a bill of rights limiting the actions of state officials. In fact, in *Barron* v. *Baltimore* (1833), the Supreme Court rejected the idea that the Bill of Rights applied to the states. If the framers had intended the states to be covered by the Bill of Rights, Chief Justice Marshall stated, "they would have declared this purpose in plain and intelligible language."

The result was that for years there was no consistent national policy regarding civil liberties. Some states imposed severe limits on individual rights, denying their citizens the right of legal counsel and jury trial and even tolerating such brutal practices as mob lynchings.

However, a change was made possible with the adoption in 1868 of the Fourteenth Amendment, which proclaims that no state shall deprive any person of "life, liberty, or property, without due process of law" or deny any person "the equal protection of the laws." Following World War I, the Court gradually began to use the language of the Fourteenth Amendment to make the Bill of Rights binding on the states. The major turning point came in *Gitlow* v. *New York* (1925), in which the Court ruled that a state which denied a person's First Amendment rights of freedom of speech or freedom of the press would be depriving him of "liberty" without due process of law, an action barred by the Fourteenth Amendment. Freedom of speech and of the press are such fundamental rights, the Court stated, that they should be "incorporated" into the Fourteenth Amendment and protected from impairment by the states. During the next four decades, the Court applied the protections of most the Bill of Rights to the states, including the First Amendment freedoms of assembly, petition, and religion, the right to legal counsel in criminal cases, protection against unlawful search and seizure, and the prohibition of "cruel and unusual punishment."

The impact of the Supreme Court on our civil liberties should not be underestimated. Basically, the amount of freedom we enjoy is determined not only by the Bill of Rights but by how the nine justices of the Supreme Court interpret them. With their power of "judicial review" to overturn laws that, in their opinion, conflict with the Constitution, Supreme Court justices serve as the final arbiters on questions of civil liberties. Indeed, to understand American civil liberties one must trace their evolution through a history of Court rulings and interpretations, a history marked by both enlightened and repressive judicial decisions.

Political Participation and the First Amendment

The First Amendment states that "Congress shall make no law respecting an establishment of religion, or prohibiting the free exercise thereof; or abridging the freedom of speech, or of the press; or the right of the people peaceably to assemble, and to petition the Government for a redress of grievances." No other amendment is as central to the operation of our democratic society. Freedom of speech, the press, assembly, religion, and petition are all vital elements of effective citizen action and are closely intertwined. Freedom of speech, for example, would be nothing but the right to talk to oneself without freedom of assembly. Likewise, the right to petition government would be meaningless without a free press to provide information on what government is doing. And without freedom of religion, as a form of personal expression and conscience, freedom of speech and assembly would, for many people, be hollow.

At the same time, none of these freedoms is absolute. The rights of the individual have to be properly balanced against the rights of others. As Justice Oliver Wendell Holmes once observed, "The right to swing my fist ends where the other man's nose begins." Finding that balance, of course, has been the Court's major problem.

Let us consider, then, the nature and evolution of these freedoms, beginning with the cornerstone of our political system: freedom of speech.

Freedom of Speech

Throughout history, it has been observed that no democratic society can exist without freedom of expression. For people to press their demands on government, they must be able to voice their political views. They must be able to engage in free and open discussion with others and to criticize the actions and policies of their leaders.

In fact, justification for freedom of speech goes even beyond the requirements of a democracy. The English philosopher John Stuart Mill, in his essay *On Liberty* (1859), argued that, without a free exchange of ideas, individuals cannot reach their full potential and society as a whole cannot advance. "The worth of a state in the long run," he declared, "is the worth of the individuals composing it; and a state which ... dwarfs its men, in order that they may be more docile instruments in its hands even for beneficial purposes, will find that with small men no great thing can be accomplished." In fact, Mill argued, because it is often difficult to distinguish "good" ideas from "bad" ones, all views need to be expressed. Even if an idea turns out to be false, it can at least help make the truth easier to see by comparison. The only way progress can be achieved is for all ideas to be considered, no matter how unpopular or "wrong" they may be.

It is largely for these reasons that the American Civil Liberties Union (ACLU) and other strong advocates of free speech have backed the rights of all members of our society to express their views. Freedom of speech, they point out, benefits not merely the speaker but those who wish to hear what he has to say. Even a would-be tyrant should be allowed to speak, not because he necessarily deserves to exercise that right, but because others need to be aware of his position. By denying someone his freedom of speech, one also denies the rights of others to understand the meaning and implications of his views.

Do these justifications mean there should be no limits on expression? According to former justices Hugo Black and William O. Douglas, when the Constitution says "Congress shall make no law ... abridging the freedom of speech," it literally means *no law*. In their view, freedom of speech is such an important and basic right it should not be curbed in any way.

The Supreme Court generally, however, has tended to take a less absolutist position. It has held that while free speech is important, it may have to yield to other interests. If certain kinds of speeches lead directly to actions that threaten society, for example, then society has both a right and a duty to restrict them. The problem has been in deciding where the line should be drawn between the rights of the individual and those of society. At what point should a person be compelled to step down off the soapbox and be silent?

One answer was offered by the Court in the famous case of *Schenck* v. *United States* (1919). During World War I, a pacifist named Charles Schenck was convicted and sent to prison under the Espionage Act of 1917 for distributing leaflets urging potential draftees not to serve in the armed forces. Schenck appealed his conviction to the Supreme Court, arguing that the Espionage Act was unconstitutional because it stripped him of his First Amendment rights of freedom of speech and of the press. The Court disagreed, ruling that his actions presented a "clear and present danger" to national security and thus his conviction was valid. "The question in every case," Justice Oliver Wendell Holmes proclaimed, "is whether the words are used in such circumstances and are of such a nature as to create a clear and present danger that they will bring about substantive evils that Congress has a right to prevent." As an analogy, Holmes noted that even "the most stringent protection of free speech would not protect a man in falsely shouting fire in a theater and causing a panic."

Obviously, this "clear and present danger" test tends to be highly subjective. Unlike the dubious analogy of a man falsely shouting fire in a crowded theater (which can likely be proved one way or the other), how does one determine when a political speech or pamphlet presents a "danger" to society? Is it not possible that governmental officials could use the clear and present danger test to suppress opinions with which they disagree? During the Vietnam War, students and others who protested administration policies were sometimes accused of giving "aid and comfort" to the "enemy" and even committing "treason." Should protestors against the war have been thrown in jail because some high-ranking officials regarded their criticisms as a danger to America's war effort? Still, many scholars insist that the clear and present danger test actually helps bolster freedom of expression because it places the burden on government to prove that curbs are needed to prevent some identifiable evil from occurring.

In 1925, in *Gitlow* v. *New York*, the Court once again grappled with the question of where to draw the line between the rights of the individual and those of society. In this case, the Court seemed to come down harder against the individual's right of free speech with the "bad tendency" rule. Benjamin Gitlow had been convicted in New York State for publishing a pamphlet calling for the violent overthrow of the U.S. government. In upholding Gitlow's conviction, the Court ruled that the government could ban speeches or publications that merely had a *tendency* to pose a danger to society. In other words, despite lack of evidence that Gitlow's tract had any adverse effects, government could take steps to protect society even before an act occurred.

Nor did the court stop there. As the fear of communism began to take a firmer hold on government in the 1940s and 1950s, the criteria for curtailing speech became even broader. In 1948, Eugene Dennis and ten other leaders of the homegrown American Communist party were convicted and sent to prison for violating the Smith Act. Passed by Congress in 1940, the Smith Act made it a crime to advocate overthrow of the government or to belong to any group advocating such action. The Court upheld the group's convictions, arguing that the criteria for restricting speech was not only its possible effects but the "gravity of the evil" to be avoided.[1] The fact that Dennis and the other members of the Communist party advocated the use of force to overthrow the government was justification enough, the Court stated, to curtail their activities. (Six years later, the Court modified this formula by noting that people could be convicted under the Smith Act only for promoting illegal *action* against the government, not for their political beliefs alone.[2])

Since the 1950s, the Court has continued to apply these and other formulas in interpreting the constitutionality of restrictions on speech. However, as the fear of internal communism has ebbed, the Court has shown less willingness to accept restraints on the rights of communists or other groups. It has, for example, overturned laws denying passports to American Communist party members[3] and requiring them to register with the government.[4] It has also struck down laws requiring private citizens to take loyalty oaths in certain cases.[5] Nevertheless, the Court has not denied in any sweeping fashion the right of government to curtail speech on national security grounds.

In recent years different kinds of free speech issues have occupied the Court's attention. Protests against the Vietnam War, for example, raised the question of whether the Constitution protects "symbolic speech" (the expression of political views through actions rather than words). In one case, the Court upheld the right of students to protest the war by wearing black armbands in school.[6] But, in another case, it contended that burning draft cards was not a legitimate exercise of symbolic speech.[7] The Court even has become involved in controversies involving "commercial speech." During the 1970s, for example, it overturned state laws that barred pharmacies from advertising their prices for prescription drugs and lawyers from advertising their services and rates.[8]

One free speech issue that has generated considerable emotion has been that of "obscenity." The balance between the freedom of individual expression and the rights of society has taken on new meaning as the Court has tried—somewhat unsuccessfully—to define the constitutional status of obscene material. For years, people have contended that material depicting sex or violence offends public morality or leads to criminal behavior and thus should be permanently banned. But because material that appears obscene to one person may not appear so to another, judges have had a difficult time defining obscenity in precise terms. As one judge cracked, "To come to grips with the question of obscenity is like coming to grips with a greased pig."[9]

In 1957, in *Roth* v. *United States,* the Supreme Court tried to tackle the obscenity issue head on, stating that "obscene" material did not enjoy the protection of the First Amendment. However, the definition of obscenity offered by the Court proved to be slippery. It defined obscenity as material that appeals to the "prurient interests" of the "average person" and that lacks any "redeeming social importance"—concepts almost as vague, and therefore as difficult to apply, as the word obscenity itself. The Court clouded the issue even more by ruling in 1966 that "the constitutional status of an alleged obscene work must be determined on the basis of a national standard."[10] Moreover, it said, no work could be judged obscene unless it was "utterly without redeeming social value." Because opinions varied on what this "national standard" meant and because nothing could be banned unless it appeared to be *utterly* without social value, obscenity laws became almost impossible to enforce. "Adult" bookstores flourished, while producers of X-rated movies and sex magazines raced to see who could offer the public the most explicit details of human anatomy or violence.

In 1973, however, the Court tried a different approach. It abandoned the idea of a national standard in favor of local standards, giving each community the discretion to define for itself what is obscene. "It is neither realistic nor constitutionally sound," the Court ruled in *Miller* v.

California, "to read the First Admendment as requiring that the people of Maine or Mississippi accept public depiction of conduct found tolerable in Las Vegas or New York City." The Court also changed its earlier position by saying that a questionable work might be adjudged obscene if it lacked "serious literary, artistic, political, or scientific value." Because it is easier to demonstrate that a work has no "serious" value than it is to establish that it is entirely without value, convictions became somewhat easier to obtain. Thus, in 1977, Larry Flynt, publisher of *Hustler* magazine, was convicted by an Indianapolis jury for offending local community standards.

The fear among civil libertarians, however, that local prudes would ban everything in sight was partly relieved by the Court in 1974. When a Georgia theater owner was convicted for showing the film *Carnal Knowledge* the Court overturned the conviction, saying that it did not find the film "patently offensive" and that local juries could not use "unbridled discretion" in defining obscenity.[11] Thus, local communities and judges alike would have to continue to wrestle with the definition of obscenity on a case-by-case basis.

On a final note, whatever one's position may be on the issue of obscenity, one must still face the difficult question of deciding who should set the standards. Should anyone be handed the authority to determine what other adults may read or see? Civil libertarians argue that a distinction should be drawn between "private" and "public" activities. People should not be forced to confront obscenity in public places (such as on highway billboards), but they should be free to read or watch anything they wish in the relative privacy of a home or theater. (Whether the charging of admission makes entering a theater a "private" or "public" activity remains a matter of definition.) Considering, however, the ongoing controversy surrounding obscenity, the issue will hardly be resolved by any Supreme Court decision.

Freedom of the Press

"One of the most powerful hopes advanced by theories of representative government," two scholars noted recently, "is that news media remain free so they may educate the public in making political choices. Ignorance condemns people to sway with the most available rhetoric."[12]

A free press has always been considered indispensable to the public's "right to know." Without a press free to criticize government officials and to provide information on their activities, citizens could not determine whether to keep them in office or to throw them out. Freedom of the press means that government may not censor what is published. It means that government may not exercise *prior restraint* on what a journalist reports, even though he or she may have to answer for what is written afterwards.

The issue of prior restraint gained national attention in 1971 when the government tried to block publication of the *Pentagon Papers* by the *New York Times* and *Washington Post*. The papers were copies of classified documents smuggled out of the Pentagon by defense analyst Daniel Ellsberg, that showed how successive administrations had withheld information from the public on the conduct of the Vietnam War. The Nixon Administration tried to prevent their publication, claiming they would cause "injury to the defense interests of the United States." The Supreme Court, however, ruled six to three against the government, arguing that national security would not be threatened and that the press could not be muzzled except to prevent "direct, immediate, and irreparable" damage to the nation.

The issue of prior restraint also arose in March 1979, when the government obtained a court order preventing *The Progressive* monthly from publishing an article describing how an H-bomb is built ("The H-Bomb Secret: How We Got It, Why We're Telling It"). Government lawyers argued that the article violated sections of the 1954 Atomic Energy Act prohibiting disclosure of secret detailed information about atomic weapons. The article, they said, could be used to help other countries develop the bomb, thus causing "irreparable damage" to the nation. Press champions feared, however, that a permanent ban on the article would set a dangerous precedent. As a *Washington Post* editorial noted, "Once the door is open to advance judicial scrutiny of what the press may publish, it will never close." (Following publication of similar information by other papers, the federal government abandoned efforts to stop *The Progressive* from publishing the article.)

Press freedom, of course, has never been absolute. It has not protected journalists, for example, from damaging a private citizen's reputation with irresponsible accusations. Only when the press has commented on public figures or government officials has it enjoyed substantial protection against *libel* suits. The Supreme Court ruled in 1964 that public figures must prove "actual malice" as well as falsehood in libel cases.[13] This was to prevent libel laws from being used to shield politicians and other public figures from criticism.

In early 1979, however, the Supreme Court eroded some of the protection given the press. It ruled that a public official, in trying to prove actual malice by a reporter, can ask the court to evaluate the reporter's "state of mind," that is, can demand to know what the reporter was thinking while preparing the story.[14] By declaring that a reporter can be hauled into court and questioned about his or her thought processes, the Supreme Court appeared to open the door wider to possible libel suits and intimidation of the press. As James Goodale of the *New York Times* put it, the decision will hamper investigative reporting because reporters now know they "are going to have to stand naked in front of the courts with respect to all their thought processes."[15]

Journalists have been dismayed, in fact, by a series of recent court rulings against the press. In the summer of 1979, for example, the Court ruled that a judge may close a pretrial hearing to the press and the public if the defendant and prosecutor feel the publicity will harm the defendant's chances of a fair trial.[16] Neither the press nor the public, the Court stated, has a constitutional right under the "public trial" guarantee of the Sixth Amendment to attend criminal trials. To many journalists and legal scholars, this ruling was a serious contradiction of the First Amendment, which guarantees freedom of the press so that the public may be informed on what is going on.

Moreover, in 1978, the Court held that police, after obtaining an ordinary search warrant, could conduct unannounced searches of newsrooms, including reporters' notebooks and phone records.[17] It also held in 1972 that reporters could not withhold information from grand juries looking into potential crimes.[18] In 1978, *New York Times* reporter Myron Farber was sentenced to jail, and his paper fined $5,000 a day, for refusing to surrender his notes for possible use in a New Jersey murder case he helped uncover. While the defense attorney argued that Farber's notes might help clear his client, Farber insisted that the confidentiality of his sources had to be protected. If he complied with the court, he said, he would become an investigative arm of the government and would jeopardize his ability to gather news. The New Jersey Supreme Court, however, upheld Farber's conviction, stating that the First Amendment guarantee of a free press is superseded by a defendant's Sixth Amendment right to a fair trial.

It should be noted that radio and television tend to be more closely regulated by the government than the print media. Radio and television stations, for example, must obtain a federal license to use one of the limited number of frequencies or channels on the "public airwaves." These licenses are granted by the Federal Communications Commission (FCC) and must be renewed at regular intervals. Although the FCC may not censor political messages, it does require stations to operate in the "public interest." Stations must, for instance, honor the *fairness doctrine* by providing opportunities for conflicting views to be aired on important issues. They must also provide equal time to candidates seeking public office, and must set aside a certain amount of broadcast time for news programs and community messages. The FCC can revoke the licenses of stations that ignore the "public interest," although it rarely has done so. More will be said about the media in Chapter 8.

Freedom of Assembly and Petition

As we will see in later chapters, the most promising way to affect public policy is through concerted group action. Groups, not single individuals, have become the basic units of influence in our society. Thus, our ability to influence government requires not only freedom of expression, but also the right to organize into groups and exchange political views—that is, the right "peaceably to assemble, and to petition the Government for a redress of grievances."

Over the years, the Supreme Court has tended to give substantial protection to freedom of assembly and petition. It has upheld the right of groups and individuals not only to petition government directly (see Chapter 7) but also to engage in peaceful protests and demonstrations. In the early 1960s, for example, a group of about two hundred black students assembled on the South Carolina state capitol grounds to protest discrimination. As a crowd of several hundred onlookers gathered, some threatening violence, the police ordered the students to disperse. When the students failed to comply, they were arrested and convicted of breach of the peace. The Supreme Court reversed their convictions, stating that "the Fourteenth Amendment does not permit a state to make criminal the peaceful expression of unpopular views."[19] When violence may be sparked because of audience hostility, the Court declared, the police must try to control the crowd rather than disperse the demonstrators.

At the same time, the Court has recognized that the right to assemble may conflict with the needs of local governments to prevent violence or maintain the free flow of traffic. It has upheld the right of local officials to regulate public meetings and demonstrations in the streets, parks, and other public places through use of parade permits and other restrictive devices. Such devices are constitutional, the Court has held, so long as they are "reasonable" and applied equally to all groups.

The problem, of course, is in defining what is "reasonable." It is sometimes difficult to determine the motives of local officials who refuse to permit certain groups to express their views. Groups on both the political left and the political right have been denied permission to stage local marches or demonstrations on the grounds that violence might ensue. Although concern over violence has often been genuine, there have also been instances when groups have been denied the right to assemble simply because local officials disapproved of their views.

In recent years, the Supreme Court has recognized a related freedom—that of association—even though it is not specifically mentioned in the First Amendment. In 1958, the Court overturned an Alabama state law requiring the local chapter of the National Association for the Advancement of Colored People (NAACP) to reveal the names of its members. The Court said it could find no legitimate reason Alabama would need the names of its members, except perhaps as a way to harass the association and impede its activities. "Freedom to engage in association for the advancement of beliefs and ideas," the Court stated, "is an inseparable aspect of the 'liberty' assured by . . . the Fourteenth Amendment which embraces freedom of speech."[20]

Freedom of Religion

The same First Amendment provisions that protect speech, press, and assembly also protect religious freedom. Religious belief, as a form of personal expression, was so important to the authors of the Bill of Rights that it was listed first. They knew that deep religious feelings can sometimes spark intolerance in others and that people have been persecuted for their religious beliefs. In fact, the desire to escape religious persecution was a major reason many of the early settlers fled Europe and came to America. Even today, we can see in other countries how religion and politics have become intertwined. The civil strife in Northern Ireland stems largely from the long-standing hostility between Catholics and Protestants, while in Iran the Ayatollah Khomeini's Islamic government imposes its religious views as a matter of civil law.

The First Amendment deals with two aspects of religion. It states that "Congress shall make no law respecting an establishment of religion, or prohibiting the free exercise thereof . . . ." The first provision — prohibiting the establishment of religion—has been interpreted by the courts to mean not only that government may not set up a state religion but also that it may not favor any religious sect. Thus, the Supreme Court has struck down some government attempts to give financial aid to religious schools[21] and has banned Bible study and prayer in public school classrooms.[22]

This does not mean that church and state have been kept entirely separate, however. The Supreme Court has allowed states, for example, to provide free bus transportation, textbooks, and equipment to parochial school children, arguing that such aid benefits the children, and not the schools. In fact, government has even tended to encourage religious practices in a number of ways: religious organizations have been exempted from taxation; our coins and paper money carry the motto "In God We Trust"; sessions of Congress open with prayers; the Pledge of Allegiance contains the phrase "one nation, under God"; and court witnesses sometimes are asked to swear on the Bible.

In addition to prohibiting the establishment of religion, the First Amendment also prohibits the government from interfering with religious observances. This means that an individual is free to believe or disbelieve as he or she chooses. But like all other rights, religious freedom is not absolute. A person may not engage freely in human sacrifice, for instance, just because his or her religion demands it. The Supreme Court has consistently ruled that government may prohibit religious groups from practicing their beliefs if those practices are harmful or offensive to others. Thus, in 1879 the Court upheld laws banning polygamy (the practice of having more than one mate at a time), even though it was part of the Mormon faith.[23] Mormons had the right to believe that God allows plural marriages, the Court ruled, but they could not practice that belief because it was "in violation of social duties or subversive of good order."

Still, the Court has tended to give religious groups broad support in pursuing their religious convictions. It has backed the right of Jehovah's Witnesses, for instance, to distribute and sell their religious literature without a city permit or payment of a license fee. It has also upheld the right of Witnesses' children to refuse to salute the flag because of their belief that the pledge violates the biblical injunction against worshiping graven images.[24] It has upheld the right of Amish parents to keep their children from attending high school, and has supported the right of conscientious objectors to avoid military service for religious reasons.[25]

Hare Krishnas

The most heated controversy in recent years has centered on the proliferation of religious cults like the People's Temple and the Reverend Sun Myung Moon's Unification Church. The Jonestown tragedy in 1978, in which more than nine hundred members of the People's Temple died in a mass ritual of suicide and murder in Guyana, triggered national debate over whether cults can—and should—be curbed. Many argued that for society to grand special status and privileges to any group calling itself a religion is to invite additional tragedies like Jonestown. Various legislative proposals were offered designed to forbid cults from using "mind control" techniques and to force cult recruiters to reveal their affiliations and goals to potential converts at an early stage.

Civil libertarians responded, however, that such proposals would be hard to reconcile with the First Amendment. How could government, they argue, define what is and what is not a true "religion" or determine which recruiting practices are good and which are bad? In their view, it would be better to remove the status and privileges given to all religious groups than to single out certain ones for punishment. Perhaps society, they contend, should address the underlying problems that allow cults to flourish in the first place: the breakdown of traditional family ties, the spread of public cynicism toward governmental and social institutions, the pervasiveness of corruption that fuels that cynicism, and even the willingness of so many people to shirk responsibility for their own lives. The controversy surrounding cults exemplifies the traditional problem facing government: how to balance society's right to be protected from harmful religious practices and the individual's right to exercise his or her religious beliefs.

Due Process: the Rights of the Accused

The Bill of Rights affords other protections besides those covered in the First Amendment. Scholars traditionally have defined freedom of speech and other First Amendment rights as *substantive rights*, as ends in themselves which may not be taken away by government. In contrast are the *procedural rights* found in the Fourth through Eighth Amendments. These are the rights that government must honor in its dealings with individuals, that protect those who run afoul of the law.

Procedural rights are not just the rights of criminal suspects: they are also society's assurance that prosecutors and judges will act in a fair and proper manner. Although society has a right to protect itself against those who disobey its laws, the citizen also has a right to be protected against government harassment in the name of "law and order." Without such protection, no person could feel secure against threats of imprisonment or even death at the hands of the state. A person who criticizes governmental policies could find himself carted off to jail for committing unspecified "crimes against the state" and for an unspecified prison term—a fate encountered by political dissidents in many parts of the world.

Although the application of procedural rights in this country has been spotty at best, with local officials and judges sometimes ignoring them with impunity, the Constitution gives considerable attention to procedural safeguards. The Fourth through Eight Amendments guarantee, for example, the right to legal counsel, to have a "speedy and public trial" by an impartial jury, to cross-examine hostile witnesses, to call friendly witnesses on one's own behalf, and to be protected against self-incrimination and *double jeopardy* (being tried twice for the same crime). They also guarantee protection against "cruel and unusual punishment" and "excessive bail" (see Table 4-1). These rights have gradually been incorporated into the due process clause of the Fourteenth Amendment and applied to the states as well as to the federal government.

Table 4-1. Procedural Rights

Article 1, Sections 9 and 10	Guarantee writ of habeas corpus; forbid bills of attainder and ex post facto laws.
Article 3, Section 3	Regulates trial and punishment for crimes of treason; requires jury trial in criminal cases.
Fourth Amendment	Prohibits unreasonable searches and seizures; requires search warrants.
Fifth Amendment	Guarantees right to a grand jury hearing in criminal cases; protects against double jeopardy and self-incrimination; requires due process of law and compensation for seized property.
Sixth Amendment	Guarantees right to a speedy and public trial by jury, to be informed of accusations, to be confronted with witnesses, to obtain witnesses on one's own behalf, and to have legal counsel.
Seventh Amendment	Guarantees trial by jury in civil suits.
Eighth Amendment	Protects against excessive bail or fines and against cruel and unusual punishment.
Fourteenth Amendment	Requires states to guarantee similar procedural rights through the due process clause.

In this section, let us briefly consider several of these important procedural safeguards, beginning with the protection against unreasonable searches and seizures.

Protection Against Unreasonable Searches and Seizures

Throughout history, one of the most feared uses of governmental power has been the sudden midnight rapping at the door and the forced entry into one's home by agents of the state. Such forced entry has been a common tool of authoritarian regimes, used to terrorize their subjects and force their compliance. Indeed, such a fear was well understood by the framers of the Bill of Rights. The Fourth Amendment guarantees "the right of the people to be secure in their persons, houses, papers, and effects, against unreasonable searches and seizures." In the event of intrusion, warrants must be issued upon "probable cause," describing "the place to be searched, and the persons or things to be seized."

The framers of the Fourth Amendment did not ban all warrantless searches and seizures: they banned only "unreasonable" ones. They knew that in some situations there would be probable cause for a search to be carried out without a search warrant. The courts have ruled, for instance, that a police officer making a lawful arrest does not need a warrant to search a suspect for weapons or evidence. Moreover, if an officer hears someone scream for help inside a house, he would likely have probable cause to suspect a crime and thus enter the building without waiting for a warrant. In a borderline case, an officer may believe there is probable cause, but the judge may disagree and let the suspect go.

In *Mapp* v. *Ohio* (1961), the Supreme Court applied the so-called exclusionary rule to both the states and the federal government. This rule bars improperly seized evidence from being used against a suspect (although some exceptions were noted by the Burger Court in the 1970s[26]). The purpose of the rule was to protect suspects against the sometimes excessive zeal of the police. In 1952, for example, the Court overturned the conviction of a man who was charged with drug possession after having his stomach pumped to recover some morphine capsules he had swallowed.[27] The Court realized that the only way to discourage the police from engaging in such practices—from making illegal searches and seizures—was to bar evidence obtained in this manner from being admitted at a trial.

But what about electronic means of surveillance, like wiretapping? Does electronic eavesdropping on people's private conversations represent "unreasonable search and seizure"? In 1928, the Court said no. It

James McCord demonstrating a bugging device.

stated that wiretapping someone's telephone does not violate the Fourth Amendment because it does not involve actual physical entry into a person's home.[28] However, forty years later, in 1967, the Court reversed itself. It held that the Fourth Amendment "protects people, not places," and thus electronic snooping without a proper warrant does represent an unlawful form of search and seizure.[29]

It should be noted, of course, that the Court did not actually prohibit electronic spying: it said only that a valid warrant authorizing such spying had to be obtained. Thus, following the Court's ruling, Congress enacted the Omnibus Crime Control and Safe Streets Act of 1968. The act authorizes court-approved wiretaps and other forms of electronic snooping. It also allows governmental officials to proceed without a warrant in cases involving possible threats to "national security," provided that a warrant is obtained within forty-eight hours after the surveillance has begun. In the years since the act's passage, the government has tapped the phones, opened the mail, and bugged the homes and offices of thousands of American citizens, ranging from suspected gangsters to political "radicals." And, as the Watergate and other investigations have revealed, not all of these activities have been lawful.

There is clearly a relationship between protection against unreasonable searches and seizures and a right to privacy. As technology has become more sophisticated, with listening devices that can be concealed in a martini olive or implanted under a person's skin, the potential for unlawful invasion of privacy has become increasingly more frightening. At the time the Constitution was drafted, there was little reason to be concerned about invasion of privacy. Since there were no phones to tap or computer files to fill, about the only real threat to privacy was the local town gossip. In fact, the Constitution does not specifically mention a "right to privacy." Instead, it has been up to the Court gradually to recognize such a right as one of the "penumbras" of the Constitution. The general right to privacy , it has said, is implied not only by the Fourth Amendment's protection against government searches and seizures, but also the First Amendment's protection of freedom of religion and association, the Third's restrictions on quartering soldiers in private homes, the Fifth's ban against self-incrimination, and the Ninth's assertion that the rights listed in the preceding eight do not exhaust all other existing rights. In recent years, the Court has extended the right to privacy to cover a variety of personal activities, ranging from the use of birth control devices[30] to having an abortion.[31]

Self-Incrimination and the Right to Counsel

Closely related to the protection against unreasonable searches and seizures is the Fifth Amendment guarantee that no one "shall be compelled in any criminal case to be a witness against himself . . . ." A person may "take the Fifth" when being interrogated by police officers, prosecutors, or even legislative committees. This right has been vigorously defended to discourage the use of coercion (the "third degree") in wringing confessions or other incriminating statements from suspects, some of whom may be innocent of the charges.

Moreover, since most people are ignorant of the technicalities of the law, they also have a right to legal counsel, a right guaranteed by the Sixth Amendment. Until the 1960s, however, this right applied almost exclusively to cases tried in the federal courts. Even though the bulk of criminal laws (from auto theft to murder) are enacted by the states and applied in state courts, suspects in many states have not always been provided with an attorney. In *Gideon* v. *Wainright* (1963), the Court finally held that states must furnish counsel to all persons facing serious criminal charges. It also ruled, in *Escobedo* v. *Illinois* (1964), that legal counsel must be provided by the states at the time a suspect is arrested, not just at the time of trial.

One of the most important—and controversial—decisions handed down by the Supreme Court was that of *Miranda* v. *Arizona* (1966). Ernesto Miranda was arrested in 1963 for kidnapping and raping and eighteen-year-old girl near Phoenix. After being interrogated by the police for two hours, he confessed to the crimes and was convicted. The Supreme Court, however, overturned his conviction on the grounds that Miranda confessed without being told of his right to remain silent and to see a lawyer. The Court declared that a person arrested must be informed that anything he says may be used against him, that he has a right to remain silent, that he has a right to have a lawyer present, and that a lawyer will be provided if he cannot afford one.

Some people denounced the Miranda ruling, accusing the Court of "handcuffing" the police. They claimed the Court misread the Constitution by putting the rights of criminals above those of their victims. Because the majority of criminal convictions stem from confessions, they charged, curbs on police interrogation procedures limit the police's ability to bring dangerous criminals to justice.

Under the direction of Chief Justice Warren Burger, the Court during the 1970s began to whittle away at the Miranda decision. In 1971, for

---

DEFENDANT	LOCATION

SPECIFIC WARNING REGARDING INTERROGATIONS

1. YOU HAVE THE RIGHT TO REMAIN SILENT.

2. ANYTHING YOU SAY CAN AND WILL BE USED AGAINST YOU IN A COURT OF LAW.

3. YOU HAVE THE RIGHT TO TALK TO A LAWYER AND HAVE HIM PRESENT WITH YOU WHILE YOU ARE BEING QUESTIONED.

4. IF YOU CANNOT AFFORD TO HIRE A LAWYER ONE WILL BE APPOINTED TO REPRESENT YOU BEFORE ANY QUESTIONING, IF YOU WISH ONE.

SIGNATURE OF DEFENDANT	DATE
WITNESS	TIME

☐ REFUSED SIGNATURE   SAN FRANCISCO POLICE DEPARTMENT   PR.9.1.4

The "Miranda Card" is used to inform suspects of their rights at the time of arrest.

example, the Court held that statements made by a suspect before police warned him of his rights could be used later to discredit his testimony on the witness stand.[32] In 1975, the Court also ruled that incriminating statements made by a suspect after he asked for an attorney (but before the attorney arrived) could be used to cast doubt on his credibility.[33] Generally, however, the Miranda decision has been upheld and continues to guide police when making arrests.

Protection Against Cruel and Unusual Punishment

After a person is convicted of a crime, there must also be some protection against "cruel and unusual punishment." The framers provided such protection in the Eighth Amendment in order to bar such practices as torture, maiming, and lingering death. Although the amendment has rarely been invoked, a few cases have attracted the Court's attention. In one case, for example, the Court held that a state law sending drug addicts to prison, rather than to the hospital for treatment, was cruel and unusual punishment.[34]

The principal focus of controversy has been on the death penalty. Movements to abolish the death penalty have existed for centuries, based on arguments that it is immoral, cruel, and does not serve as a deterrent. In *Furman* v. *Georgia* (1972), the Court struck down the death penalty laws used by the states, declaring that they were often applied "wantonly and freakishly" and exercised mainly against poor and uneducated defendants.

A number of states, however, responded to the ruling by passing new death penalty laws. In 1976, the Court heard five related cases involving the constitutionality of the death penalty and upheld the laws of three states.[35] The Court ruled that the death penalty was not inherently cruel and unusual punishment so long as it was not mandatory and that judges and juries considered the character and record of the defendant and the mitigating circumstances of the case. Thus, in January 1977, Gary Gilmore, convicted of murdering two people, faced a Utah firing squad, becoming the first person to be executed in the United States in almost ten years.

The Struggle for Equal Rights

A crucial element of constitutional rights, of course, is that they be applied equally to all. Guarantees of free speech or due process would mean little if government could arbitrarily exclude certain groups from the protection of the law. If one group can be denied the rights enjoyed by others—because of skin color, sex, religion, or even physical handicaps—then no group can consider itself safe from discrimination. Denying basic rights to one group increases the potential for denying them to all.

Over time, the struggle for equal rights has expanded to include demands for social, economic, political, and legal equality. When Thomas Jefferson noted in the Declaration of Independence that "all men were created equal," he was referring mainly to equality before the law. This concept of legal equality was later coupled with the idea of political equality, an idea best expressed by the concept of "one person, one vote." In recent decades, the concept of equal rights has also included the notion of equal opportunity. This notion implies that each person has a right not only to equal treatment before the law, but to equality of opportunity in education, employment, and housing.

There is perhaps no more meaningful purpose for political action than trying to remove the sting of prejudice and discrimination. Achieving equality has long been a struggle for black Americans, who were deprived of their constitutional rights and liberties first as slaves and then as second-class citizens. On paper, black Americans appeared to have achieved political and social equality immediately after the Civil War. The Thirteenth Amendment (1865) abolished slavery. The Fourteenth Amendment (1868) guaranteed to all citizens "due process of the law" and "equal protection of the laws." And the Fifteenth Amendment (1870) ensured that the right to vote "shall not be denied or abridged by the United States or by any State on account of race, color, or previous condition of servitude." In addition, a series of civil rights acts were enacted by Congress in the 1860s and 1870s. The Civil Rights Act of 1875, for example, prohibited any operator of a hotel, theater, or other public facility from discriminating against someone on the basis of race or color.

But hopes for equality soon evaporated. In 1883, the Supreme Court struck down the Civil Rights Act of 1875 on the ground that Congress had no authority to prohibit one citizen from discriminating against another. The Fourteenth Amendment, the Court stated, applied only to the actions of states and not to those of private individuals. This ruling was followed a decade later by the infamous case of *Plessy v. Ferguson* (1896), in which the Court upheld a state law requiring separate accommodations in railroad coaches for black and white passengers. Separate accommodations, the Court ruled, were not inherently a denial of equality. For more than half a century, this "separate but equal" rule was used to justify segregation in virtually all areas of southern life, from restaurants and theaters to restrooms and water fountains. Many southern states also employed such discriminatory devices as "literacy" tests and poll taxes to deny black citizens their voting rights.

It was not until 1954 that the Supreme Court finally overturned the separate but equal doctrine. In the landmark case of *Brown* v. *Board of Education,* the Court held that separate facilities for black and white school children were inherently unequal. A year later, the Court demanded that desegregation in all public schools be achieved "with all deliberate speed." Congress also got into the act by passing the Civil Rights Act of 1957. The Act created a permanent Commission on Civil Rights to investigate charges of discrimination, as well as a new Civil Rights Division in the Justice Department to enforce federal civil rights laws.

These actions, however, were hardly sufficient to abolish segregation. Resistance to change in the South and elsewhere were marked. In fact, many of the same local officials who supported segregation were handed the responsibility of enforcing the Court's rulings. Thus, it became increasingly apparent that citizens themselves had to work to erase the discriminatory practices that flourished throughout most of the South and in other parts of the country. A major step came in December 1955 when a black woman named Rosa Parks was arrested in Montgomery, Alabama, for refusing to move to the rear of the bus. Under the leadership of Martin Luther King, Jr., a year-long boycott of the bus company resulted, which led to a court order ending segregation on Montgomery city buses. Soon strategies of nonviolent direct action—marches, sit-ins, and "freedom rides"—were launched throughout the South. With national television focused on the spreading protests by black and white Americans alike, the struggle for equality was

brought to the attention of people everywhere. An emotional climax was reached in the summer of 1963 when a quarter of a million people gathered in Washington, D.C., to demand an end to policies of discrimination.

The impact of the civil rights movement was registered in a series of congressional laws passed between 1960 and 1975 (see Table 4-2). The most significant of these laws, the 1964 Civil Rights Act and the 1965 Voting Rights Act, were major steps toward achieving equality for all Americans. The 1964 Civil Rights Act, among other things, barred discrimination in public accommodations, authorized the attorney general to file suits in civil rights cases, and outlawed discrimination in any program receiving federal money. The 1965 Voting Rights Act banned the use of voter-qualification tests in a number of southern states where black voter turnout was markedly low, making it easier for black adults to register and vote (see Table 4-3). One major impact of the Voting Rights Act was to expand the number of black Americans

---

Table 4-2. Major Provisions of Recent Civil Rights Laws

Civil Rights Act of 1960
Provided federal referees to help register black voters in southern states; strengthened provisions against obstructing voting.

Civil Rights Act of 1964
Barred discrimination in restaurants, hotels, theaters, and other public accommodations; outlawed discrimination in employment on account of race, sex, religion, or national origin; created the Equal Employment Opportunity Commission to administer these provisions; authorized the attorney general to file civil rights lawsuits; authorized the cutoff of federal funds for programs that practiced discrimination.

Voting Rights Act of 1965
Authorized federal examiners to register voters in counties where patterns of discrimination were present; suspended the use of literacy tests for voting in a number of southern states.

Civil Rights Act of 1968
Prohibited discrimination in the sale or rental of housing; made it a crime to interfere with the legal activities of civil rights workers.

Voting Rights Act of 1970
Extended the life of the 1965 Voting Rights Act for another five years and broadened its provisions to include states in the North as well as in the South.

Equal Employment Opportunity Act of 1972
Applied employment provisions of the 1964 Civil Rights Act to the states; gave the Equal Employment Opportunity Commission power to file suits to end discriminatory practices in the private sector.

Voting Rights Act of 1975
Extended the provisions of the 1965 Voting Rights Act until 1982 and broadened its provisions to cover "language minorities," such as the Spanish-speaking.

---

holding elected office. The number of black officeholders grew from fewer than 500 in 1965 to more than 4,500 in 1978. By 1980, more than 150 cities, including Atlanta, Detroit, Oakland, Washington, D.C., and Los Angeles, were governed by black mayors.

Yet, the combination of civil rights acts and growing number of black officeholders has not retarded the spread of *de facto segregation*, where predominantly black ghettos continue to breed unemployment, crime, and other evils that, in turn, foster frustration and anger. Nor have black Americans achieved economic equality with whites. The vicious circle of poverty and unemployment that has afflicted black people for generations remains to be broken. As one civil rights worker stated, "What good is a seat in the front of the bus if you don't have the money for the fare?" For example, the unemployment rate for black adults—double that for whites—has remained virtually unchanged since the early 1960s. Moreover, according to 1975 Census Bureau statistics, the median income for black families in the United States is only 58 percent of that earned by white families—only 7 percent higher than that estimated for 1947. This gap in income and employment between whites and blacks leaves the civil rights movement with major unfinished work in the 1980s.

Black Americans, of course, are not the only citizens who have been struggling to achieve their constitutional rights. Other groups, including American Indians, people of Asian ancestry, Spanish-speaking Americans, and women, have also been victims of discrimination in varying degrees. They have been denied equal opportunity in education,

Table 4-3. Voter Registration in Eleven Southern States, 1960 and 1976

	Percent of Voting-Age Population			
	1960		1976	
	White	*Black*	*White*	*Black*
Alabama	64	14	79	58
Arkansas	61	38	63	94
Florida	69	39	61	61
Georgia	57	29	66	75
Louisiana	77	31	78	63
Mississippi	64	5	80	61
North Carolina	92	39	69	55
South Carolina	57	14	58	56
Tennessee	73	59	74	66
Texas	42	35	69	65
Virginia	46	23	62	55

Source: U.S. Bureau of the Census, *Statistical Abstract of the United States,* 1978, p. 519.

employment, and other aspects of their economic and social lives. American Indians, for example, did not win the right to vote until 1924. They have the highest unemployment rates, the lowest income levels, and the lowest life expectancy of any major ethnic group. Like black Americans, Indians and other groups have had to rely on a variety of tactics, ranging from court litigation to protest demonstrations, to try to remove legal and social obstacles to equality.

The largest "minority" group in America is the majority of the population: women. Although women represent more than 51 percent of the population, they have held, as Table 4-4 shows, less than 1 percent of all major governmental positions since 1789. Even today, they comprise only 4 percent of the state governors, 3 percent of the members of Congress, and less than 10 percent of the nation's doctors, lawyers, and college teachers. They are also often paid less than men who do similar work and rarely wind up in high corporate and management positions. One estimate is that 75 percent of all working women are still in low-level clerical and service occupations. In recent years, groups like the National Organization of Women (NOW) and the National Women's Political Caucus (NWPC) have been formed to press for women's rights. Building on the achievements of black civil rights activists, these and

Table 4-4. Numbers of Persons Who Have Held Major Governmental Positions in the United States, by Sex, 1789–1978.

	Men	Women	Percent Women
President and Vice-President	66	0	0.0
Cabinet	507	5	1.0
Supreme Court	101	0	0.0
Senate	1,715	11	0.6
House of Representatives	9,591	87	0.9

Source: Women's Campaign Fund.

other groups have won a variety of legislative battles, ranging from the passage of the Equal Credit Opportunity Act of 1974 to revisions in state laws dealing with rape. Less success, however, has been achieved with the Equal Rights Amendment (ERA), which as of this writing has stalled several states short of the two-thirds needed for ratification (see Chapters 3 and 13).

Inspired in part by the black civil rights and women's movements, still other groups, such as homosexuals, the physically handicapped, and older people, have organized to combat discriminatory laws and practices. One of the latest groups to attract national attention to its cause has been the physically handicapped. In 1977, disabled Americans staged protest demonstrations in cities throughout the country in a successful effort to force the kederal government to implement the Rehabilitation Act of 1973. Among other things, the act prohibits employers from refusing to hire the disabled and mandates that all schools, hospitals, and other institutions receiving federal funds make their buildings accessible with ramps, elevators, and other conveniences. As the American Coalition of Citizens with Disabilities noted, the implementation of the act represented an important first step toward bringing the physically disabled into the mainstream of American life.

A major question facing our society, of course, is how far government should go to ensure equality of opportunity. How far should it go to help minorities and women succeed in a society dominated by white males? Just as the courts have faced the difficult problem in free speech and criminal justice cases of balancing the rights of the individual against those of society, so the courts have faced the problem in civil rights cases of balancing the demands of one group against those of another.

In recent years, schools and businesses have employed quota systems and *affirmative action* programs designed to improve educational and job opportunities for disadvantaged persons. While these policies have been touted as an important means of remedying past discrimination, they have also raised charges of "reverse discrimination" against whites. In the mid-1970s, a white engineer named Allan Bakke sued the Regents of the University of California after he was refused admission to medical school at that school's Davis campus. Bakke charged the school with reverse discrimination because his test scores were higher than those of sixteen minority students admitted under a special admissions program. In June 1978, the Supreme Court ruled five to four in favor of Bakke, stating that Davis's admissions program was unfairly biased against white applicants. The use of rigid quotas, the Court ruled, violated the Civil Rights Act of 1964, which outlaws racial discrimination by institutions receiving federal funds (as the Davis medical school did). At the same time, however, the Court held that affirmative action programs for minority applicants were legal, so long as race was not the only criterion used.

Obviously, this decision left the issue of reverse discrimination—and the future of affirmative action—far from settled. It was not until June 1979 that the Court spoke again on the issue. In *United Steelworkers of America* v. *Weber*, the Court held that private companies can legally give

Allan Bakke

special preferences to minority workers in hiring, training, and promotion. Specifically, the Court ruled that a white worker, Brian Weber, was not the victim of illegal racial bias when two black co-workers with less seniority were picked ahead of him for an on-the-job training program, in which half the positions were reserved for minorities and women. Voluntary affirmative action plans, the Court held, even those containing quotas, do not automatically violate Title VII of the 1964 Civil Rights Act, which bars racial discrimination in employment. "It would be ironic," Justice William Brennan wrote in his majority opinion, "if a law triggered by a nation's concern over centuries of racial injustice . . . constituted the first legislative prohibition of all voluntary, private, race-conscious efforts to abolish traditional patterns of racial segregation and hierarchy." Thus, the Supreme Court not only upheld the principle of affirmative action, but also supported the use of quotas in certain instances to eliminate "manifest racial imbalances" in traditionally white-only jobs.

Perhaps some day our society will overcome prejudice and discrimination and thus have no need for affirmative action. As Justice Harry Blackmun remarked, "At some time . . . the United States must and will reach a stage of maturity where (such) action is no longer necessary. Then persons will be regarded as persons, and discrimination of the type we address today will be an ugly feature of history that is instructive but that is behind us."

Public Opinion and Individual Rights: Where We Stand Today

A fundamental aspect of a democratic society is that the people themselves, and not just the government, support its underlying principles. After all, curbs on individual freedoms can be just as readily imposed by one's neighbors as by governmental officials. It would seem, therefore, that a serious problem exists for this country since many people appear to display little tolerance for individual rights, although evidence does suggest that the tolerance is increasing. While many say they believe in the right of free speech, for example, they do not always endorse the right when applied to specific groups and situations.

In the early 1950s, political scientists began to examine the public's views toward individual rights to find out how many Americans supported or rejected the constitutional "rules of the game." One of the first to undertake such a study was Samuel Stouffer, who found in 1954 that most Americans would not permit certain groups to exercise their right of free speech. He discovered, as Table 4-5 shows, that 60 percent would

Table 4-5. *Free Speech for Whom? (1954)*

	Yes	No	Don't Know
If a person wanted to make a speech in your community against churches and religion, should he be allowed to speak, or not?	37%	60%	3%
If a person wanted to make a speech in your community favoring government ownership of all the railroads and big industries, should he be allowed to speak, or not?	58	31	11
Consider a man whose loyalty has been questioned before a congressional committee, but who swears under oath he has never been a communist. Should he be allowed to make a speech in your community, or not?	70	21	9
Suppose an admitted communist wanted to make a speech in your community. Should he be allowed to speak, or not?	27	68	5

Source: Samuel A. Stouffer, *Communism, Conformity, and Civil Liberties* (New York: Doubleday, 1955), pp. 28–41.

not permit an individual to speak in their community against churches and religion. He also found that 31 percent would not permit a socialist to speak; 68 percent would not permit a communist to speak; and 21 percent would not allow an individual to speak whose loyalty has only been *questioned* before a congressional committee. The people in this sample were not asked to support any criminal activity; they were asked only whether an individual with generally unpopular beliefs should be allowed to express an opinion.

Stouffer's findings were validated by later studies that revealed a similar lack of support for individual rights. In 1964, Herbert McClosky found that, although a favorable consensus emerged on most general statements concerning civil liberties and procedural justice, the consensus evaporated when specific examples were given. He found, as Table 4-6 indicates, that freedom of speech was generally supported as a concept, but not necessarily when applied to school teachers. Similarly, legal rights were strongly defended in principle, but not always for those who "hide behind the laws" when questioned about their activities.

One interpretation of these findings was that people often react positively to such popular phrases as "free speech" and "legal rights and protections" and negatively to such loaded concepts as "foreign ideas"

Table 4-6. Consistency in Political Values?

	Percent Agreeing
1. No matter what a person's political beliefs are, he is entitled to the same legal rights and protections as anyone else.	94.3
Any person who hides behind the laws when he is questioned about his activities doesn't deserve much consideration.	75.7
2. I believe in free speech for all no matter what their views might be.	88.9
Freedom does not give anyone the right to teach foreign ideas in our schools.	56.7
3. Nobody has a right to tell another person what he should and should not read.	80.7
A book that contains wrong political views cannot be a good book and does not deserve to be published.	50.3

Source: Adapted from Herbert McClosky, "Consensus and Ideology in American Politics," *American Political Science Review*, June 1964, pp. 361–382.

and "wrong political views." If the persons questioned had a real commitment to the principles of civil liberties and procedural justice, they would have been more consistent in their responses, no matter what emotional phrases were given. In McClosky's view, the evidence clearly indicated that "a large proportion of the electorate has failed to grasp certain of the underlying ideas and principles on which the American political system is based."[36]

More recent studies indicate, interestingly, a gradual shift toward greater tolerance of individual rights. In 1977, the National Opinion Research Center at the University of Chicago asked a national sample of Americans some of the same questions Stouffer had asked in 1954 and obtained somewhat different results. For instance, whereas in 1954 only 27 percent would allow a communist to speak in their community, 55 percent would do so in 1977 (see Table 4-7). Similarly, when asked whether a person who wants "to make a speech in your community against churches and religion should be allowed to speak," 62 percent said yes in 1977, as compared with only 37 percent in 1954. Apparently, either pressures to appear more tolerant toward such persons have increased during the past two decades, or more Americans generally feel unthreatened by these persons' views and opinions. However, it should

Table 4-7. Free Speech for Whom? (1977)

	Yes	No	Don't Know
If a person wanted to make a speech in your community against churches and religion, should he be allowed to speak, or not?	62%	37%	1%
Consider a person who advocates doing away with elections and letting the military run the country. Should he be allowed to speak, or not?	50	48	2
Suppose an admitted communist wanted to make a speech in your community. Should he be allowed to speak, or not?	55	42	3
Suppose an admitted homosexual wanted to make a speech in your community. Should he be allowed to speak, or not?	62	34	4

Source: National Opinion Research Center, University of Chicago, 1977.

be noted that, despite the rise in tolerance, a significantly high percentage of Americans in 1977—42 percent in situations involving communists, and 34 percent involving atheists or homosexuals—did not support specific applications of individual rights.

A final illustration also suggests how unwillingness to support individual rights relates to lack of knowledge about our system of government. In Fairfield, California, a number of years ago, high school students in an American Studies class made a door-to-door survey in a residential neighborhood to ask support for what they described as "a possible amendment to the Constitution." After reading the proposed amendment, one resident exclaimed it was "unconstitutional"; another said it was "gibberish"; and a third was afraid it "would increase the sale of marijuana." Out of a total of 850 Fairfield residents surveyed, only 290 agreed that the proposed amendment should be added to the Constitution and only 64 (8 percent) recognized it as being, in fact, a verbatim copy of the First Amendment: "Congress shall make no law respecting an establishment of religion, or prohibiting the free exercise thereof; or abridging the freedom of speech, or of the press; or the right of the people peaceably to assemble, and to petition the Government for a redress of grievances."[37]

Key Terms

Bill of Rights

habeas corpus

bill of attainder

ex post facto law

due process

prior restraint

libel

fairness doctrine

substantive rights

procedural rights

double jeopardy

de facto segregation

affirmative action

Notes

1. *Dennis* v. *United States* (1951).
2. *Yates* v. *United States* (1957).
3. *Aptheker* v. *Secretary of State* (1964).
4. *Albertson* v. *Subversive Activities Control Board* (1965).
5. *Elfbrandt* v. *Russell* (1966); *Whitehall* v. *Elkins* (1967).
6. *Tinker* v. *Des Moines Independent Community School District* (1968).
7. *United States* v. *O'Brien* (1968)
8. See, for example, *Virginia State Board of Pharmacy* v. *Virginia Citizens Consumer Council* (1976).
9. Paul Blanchard, *The Right to Read: The Battle Against Censorship* (Boston: Beacon Press, 1955), p. 148.
10. *Memoirs* v. *Attorney General of Massachusetts* (1966).
11. *Jenkins* v. *Georgia* (1974).
12. Peter Clarke and Eric Fredin, "Newspapers, Television, and Political Reasoning," *Public Opinion Quarterly*, Summer 1978, p. 143.
13. *New York Times* v. *Sullivan* (1964).
14. *Herbert* v. *Lando* (1979).
15. Associated Press, 20 April 1979.
16. *Gannett Co.* v. *De Pasquale* (1979).
17. *Zurcher* v. *Stanford Daily* (1978).
18. *Branzburg* v. *Hayes* (1972).
19. *Edwards* v. *South Carolina* (1963).
20. *NAACP* v. *Alabama* (1958).
21. *Lemon* v. *Kurtzman* (1971).
22. *Abbington School District* v. *Schempp* (1963); *Engel* v. *Vitale* (1962).
23. *Reynolds* v. *United States* (1879).

24. *West Virginia State Board of Education* v. *Barnette* (1943).
25. *United States* v. *Seeger* (1965).
26. See, for example, *United States* v. *Calandra* (1974) and *Stone* v. *Powell* (1976).
27. *Rochin* v. *California* (1952).
28. *Olmstead* v. *United States* (1928).
29. *Katz* v. *United States* (1967).
30. *Griswold* v. *Connecticut* (1965); *Eisenstadt* v. *Baird* (1972).
31. *Roe* v. *Wade* (1973).
32. *Harris* v. *New York* (1971).
33. *Oregon* v. *Hass* (1975).
34. *Robinson* v. *California* (1962).
35. See, for example, *Gregg* v. *Georgia* (1976).
36. Herbert McClosky, "Consensus and Ideology in American Politics," *American Political Science Review*, June 1964, p. 365.
37. Herb Caen, *San Francisco Chronicle*, 16 December 1969.

Recommended Reading

ABERNATHY, GLEN M. *Civil Liberties Under the Constitution.* 3rd ed. New York: Harper & Row, 1977.

ABRAHAM, HENRY J. *Freedom and the Court: Civil Rights and Liberties in the United States.* 3rd ed. New York: Oxford University Press, 1977.

BARKER, LUCIUS J., and TWILEY BARKER. *Civil Liberties and the Constitution: Cases and Commentaries,* 2nd ed. Englewood Cliffs, N.J.: Prentice-Hall, 1975.

CASPER, JONATHAN. *The Politics of Civil Liberties.* New York: Harper & Row, 1972.

EMERSON, THOMAS. *The System of Freedom of Expression.* New York: Random House, 1970.

LEWIS, ANTHONY. *Gideon's Trumpet.* New York: Random House, 1964.

MILL, JOHN STUART. *On Liberty.* New York: W. W. Norton, 1975. Originally published in 1859.

SCHAPIRO, MARTIN. *Freedom of Speech: The Supreme Court and Judicial Review.* Englewood Cliffs, N.J.: Prentice-Hall, 1966.

WESTIN, ALAN F. *Privacy and Freedom.* New York: Atheneum, 1967.

PART TWO

Dilemmas
of
Citizen
Participation

5

Citizen Politics:
Actors and Nonactors

There is no denying that few of us see eye to eye on politics. While some of us adhere to a "liberal" point of view, others cling to "conservatism"; while some of us cry loudly for expanded federal regulation of industry, others clearly do not. But *why* do we hold such different views? Why do some of us accept the idea, for example, that powerful elites keep a tight grip on the political system, whereas others see the system as open and unrepressed?

Since the 1920s, political scientists have been studying how people behave—how they vote, perceive current issues, and communicate their political views. More recently, political scientists have joined with sociologists and psychologists to investigate how and when people acquire their political views. By turning to opinion surveys and personality profiles, they have tried to gain insight into how family upbringing, encounters with friends, and experiences in school, on the job, and in front of the television set mold attitudes and opinions.

Although not all the information gathered by political scientists can be considered provocative or surprising, it does offer a picture of the way many Americans relate to the political system and how they feel about becoming involved in—or avoiding—the political world. Some of the research into the origins of political attitudes and opinions has been especially revealing, suggesting that people's willingness, desire, or refusal to immerse themselves in politics depends enormously on their environment, upbringing, and education. Since we will focus later on the popular strategies for political action, we should look first at the social base and character of political behavior in this country. After all, strategies for political action will be relevant only if people intend to use them, and that intention will largely depend on how they acquire a "political self."

The Social Base: Learning about Politics

A "political self" is made, not born. As infants, we do not emerge from the womb with a preconceived view of the political world, no matter how opinionated our mothers may be. We possess no inherent allegiance to one political party over another, no loyalty to any government or ideology. All such things must be acquired and learned through a lifelong process known as *political socialization.* As the authors of one study explain, "Acquiring a political self is a natural corollary to general social maturation. As with all social learning, political learning is gradual and incremental. . . . Each citizen's political views result from lifelong experiences."[1]

Even our perceptions of the world around us are thought to be the end products of our experiences. What we see—and *how* we see it—reflects what we have learned. Naturally, each of us tends to believe that he or she is unique, that what he or she perceives is objectively real and not just subjective. Yet, it is difficult to imagine how any of us can distinguish between our perceptions and any other reality; our own view of the world is the only reality most of us understand.

Let us consider a vivid illustration of this point. Anthropologist Colin Turnbull, in his book *The Forest People,*[2] offers an interesting example of how one's perceptions even of physical dimensions—something most of us take for granted—are affected by upbringing and environment. When a Pygmy friend of his named Kenge was led for the first time to a vast open plain uncluttered by the dense forests in which he had spent his life, he was unable to grasp its immense expanse. Noting a herd of wild buffalo grazing on the plain several miles away, Kenge concluded they were very unusual looking "insects." His lack of experience with great distances would not allow him to be persuaded that the buffalo appeared small only because they were so far away. His range of vision in the forest had been so restricted that he was unaccustomed to allowing for distance when judging size.

We might say that our perceptions of politics are similarly conditioned by our experiences and environment. If we have been taught the virtues of only one ideology or political party, we will not easily be persuaded that our values or loyalties are purely relative. Although the influences on our lives are virtually boundless, political scientists have tried to identify the socializing agents that share the major responsibility for inculcating our political values and opinions. Apart from the overall culture of American society itself (which we will consider briefly later), the first and most fundamental of these agents has been the family.

The Family

In both political science and folklore ("As the twig is bent so grows the tree"; "The hand that rocks the cradle . . . "; "Like father, like son"), the family is regarded as an important influence on the development of attitudes and values. In the nineteenth century, the French writer Alexis de Tocqueville stressed the importance of the family in the early stages of political learning. To understand the adult, he said, "We must begin higher up; we must watch the infant in his mother's arms; we must see the first images which the external world casts upon the dark mirror of his mind, the first occurrences which he witnesses; we must hear the first words which awaken the sleeping powers of thought, and stand by his earliest efforts, if we would understand the prejudices, the habits, and the passions which will rule his life."[3]

When most of us first come into contact with the political world, it is with a set of social values acquired from our family. Depending on the family we are born into, we are given at birth a race, a sex, a religion, and an economic background, all of which may strongly influence our political actions in later life. According to one scholar, by the time a child enters "kindergarten—where many adults naively think his learning is about to start—this new semisocial being has already acquired the equivalent of 350 college courses, enough for an A.B. degree more than eight times over, in learning the values, customs, and attitudes that are sanctioned by his own unique family."[4]

Although many changes have been taking place in the American family, it continues to play a vital role in the development of political attitudes. One reason is that the family tends to have almost exclusive influence over the child during the preschool years, a period many psychologists believe is the most emotionally critical part of a child's life. During this early period, even when parents are not consciously trying to teach their children certain values and attitudes, children are picking them up anyway, just as they are picking up their parents' habits and expressions.

Studies have revealed, for example, that when both parents support the same political party, a child often acquires a way of ordering the political world that will continue for much of his or her life. The child will learn to separate the good guys from the bad by party labels, long before party differences are understood. One political scientist found in his interviews with fourth-graders in New Haven that many referred to a political party as a family trait. As one ten-year-old girl put it, "All I know is *we're* not Republicans."[5] Only a few of the children said their party preferences differed from those of their parents.

However, if family influences tend to be so exclusive at an early age, how do we explain those individuals—apparently one out of every three—whose party preferences eventually differ from those of their parents? How do we account for those "radical" sons and daughters whose conservative parents voted for Richard Nixon in 1972 or Gerald Ford in 1976?

As children grow older, they do not remain political carbon copies of their parents. While many fundamental attitudes and values shaped early on by the family (perspectives toward authority, social prejudices, and so on) will endure in some form, specific views and opinions on political issues will change in response to new influences. The family will eventually yield much of its authority to other socializing agents, such as the schools, peer groups, and the mass media.

The Schools

A seven-year-old child, when asked in school why American presidents are the most important persons, replied, "They do much more work and they're much importanter."[6] Similarly, a ten-year-old child, when asked what communism means, answered, "Well, communism is sort of—it's a different way of people; well, sort of like . . . to me it's *bad*."[7]

While other social forces may greatly affect a person's way of thinking about politics, no institutions are handed as much responsibility for spreading the basic symbols of the political system as are the schools. Most of us probably can recall sitting in elementary school learning about the country's early political heroes and celebrating our national holidays. We can recall solemnly saluting the flag, raising our squeaky voices to the chords of the "Star-Spangled Banner," and perhaps identifying with the rowdy young George Washington and his infamous cherry tree. And, as we advanced into junior high and high school, we can remember being herded into American history and civics classes.

Yet, despite these political symbols and civics classes, the role of the schools in political socialization is not really clear. Controversy continues over what the schools are actually teaching children about politics and how they are teaching it. Research collected in the 1960s, for example, suggested that the schools were reinforcing most children's loyalties to the political system. A study of Boston high school students revealed that although the curriculum inspired few of them to immerse themselves in political activities, it did tend to reinforce patriotic feelings and to encourage acceptance of the political values being taught.[8] Similarly, other studies of elementary school children found that most of them expressed great esteem for and confidence in such governmental figures as the president of the United States. Most of the fourth-graders in New Haven, for example, felt a personal attachment to the president, regarding him as wise and worthy of great trust. As one child volunteered, "The President is doing a very good job of making people be safe."[9]

However, studies completed in the 1970s offered a somewhat different perspective on the role of the schools. Whereas the earlier studies focused primarily on white, suburban school children, the later research also examined black, Mexican-American, and poor white children. Generally, this research revealed far less support for and faith in the political system, especially among poor and black children.[10] It reminded us that, for many youngsters, the lessons in school are undermined by personal experience and conflicting family attitudes. Children living in city slums, for instance, often find that their own experiences contrast sharply with the idealistic views of society and government touted in the school curriculum. Children whose parents are distrustful and disapproving of the political system often develop similar doubts and negative feelings.

Moreover, this later research raised strong doubts about the ability of the schools to instill a positive view of governmental figures and the political system, especially when outside political events, such as the Vietnam War and Watergate scandals, contradicted the schools' lessons. A 1973 study of elementary school children in Boston found that most of the children had come to reject the image of the president as a benevolent leader.[11] Comparing them with a similar group interviewed in the early 1960s, the study found that the number of youngsters who felt the president "was not one of my favorites" had jumped from 17 percent to 75 percent. Under the impact of Watergate, the study noted, politicians as a group were cynically viewed by the children in 1973 as "more selfish, less intelligent, more dishonest and less likely to keep their promises." Later research found similar declines in children's esteem for the president, although not as great as while Nixon was in office.[12] As Vietnam and Watergate recede into the past, confidence in the president may recover.

A persistent finding, however—and one that is of special relevance to our discussion of political influence in Chapter 15—is that people's perceptions of their place in the political system correspond to the amount of formal education they acquire. As their educational level advances, so does their level of participation and interest in politics. Education appears to have some correlation with their confidence in being able to understand the political world and play an effective role within it.

But it is not only the amount of education or the formal curriculum that is of relevance to political learning. The informal lessons of the classroom and playground should also be evaluated for their impact on children's political views. One social scientist, for example, made the following observations about his visit to a third-grade class:

As I was sitting in the back of the classroom shortly after school started, three boys larger than those in the class came in and asked for Mike Smith. The teacher asked the boys what he had done, and she was told that he had pushed in line. She called Mike to the front, made disapproving sounds, and commanded Mike to leave the room with the boys. The leader of the three placed one monitor in front of Mike and one behind, and, with the leader directing, Mike was marched from the room. As an observer I felt very uneasy and a bit like it must have felt to watch the Gestapo come for an enemy of the state. . . .

A little later this same morning, after the lesson on current events, which was notable for the vapidity of the items discussed, mass movement began in the class. Soon I discovered that all the boys had—at some unseen signal—lined themselves up on the opposing side of the room from the girls and both groups stood patiently waiting for the teacher to do something. I became alarmed at this bizarre behavior until I realized that they were preparing to march to the bathrooms simultaneously. No one was allowed to remain behind. . . . I found this regimentation as disconcerting as the fact that earlier mere accusation had been enough to establish Mike's guilt in the teacher's mind. Relating the two events, I thought the children were being well trained for a life of regimentation.[13]

He also concluded from his classroom visit that the accused child "learns that punishment is capricious, not judicious. He learns that it depends on factors over which he has no control and little understanding, that accusation is more important than investigation, and that, in the distribution of punishments, some are privileged, some are not." Consequently, what the school teaches in theory about democracy and justice may or may not conform with the informal lessons children learn in dealing with teachers, classmates, and school administrators.

Peer Groups

While our initial views on politics may stem from our family environment, these views often are affected later by our *peers:* friends, classmates, co-workers, and neighbors. Although peers may become influential at almost any time in our lives, they tend to assume special importance in early adolescence when most of us first become involved in activities away from the family. At this early stage, the family rapidly yields its exclusive influence and may become less significant in providing daily guidance.

It is not difficult to understand why peers can be influential. The opinions and views of people one sees face to face each day are usually harder to ignore than those voiced by distant and formal acquaintances or expressed, as we will see later, through the mass media. One's spouse, close friends, roommates, and especially those who seem better informed and more articulate than we are enjoy a unique influence not shared by other social forces. Should a close friend or roommate suddenly launch into a tirade against the evils of government, one might find it awkward to slip out of the room.

In fact, if people very close to us voice strong party preferences different from those of our parents, they may succeed in drawing us away from our previous partisan loyalties. One study found that "when the majority of a voter's peers do not support the party favored by his family, the conditional probability is high (over 80 percent) that he will abandon the family's voting tradition and shift his support to the opposition."[14]

Although the influence of peers is usually casual and reciprocal, pressures to conform also can augment the importance of peer groups. Psychologists have found that people often will support a group's views even when those views conflict with their own judgments. This tendency has been most strikingly illustrated by experiments in which people yield to group pressure in their perceptions of inanimate objects and shapes. For example, one experiment revealed that when a group of college students is told to state incorrectly that one of several unequal lines is shortest (even though it clearly is not), other unsuspecting students often will repudiate the evidence before their eyes and echo the group's false response.[15] It has been hypothesized that the students' desires to be accepted by their peers is stronger than the clues supplied by their senses. They echo the group's false reply because they fear ridicule and rejection if they do not. This suggests that if people willingly respond to group pressure by ignoring their own perceptions of inanimate objects and shapes, they may also conform by altering their views of less concrete political and social issues, especially if they are not strongly committed to a certain viewpoint. Clearly, one's peers can have a strong effect on political opinion, competing with and sometimes even surpassing that of family and school.

Mass Media

Many scholars contend that the *mass media*—television, radio, films, books, newspapers, and magazines—now compete with the family, schools, and other institutions in shaping our political views and attitudes. It has been estimated, for instance, that American families spend an average of six hours a day watching television and that the television set babysits for the average child more hours of the week than he or she spends in school. Indeed, most of us pass a great part of our lives tranquilized by television, absorbed in magazines, newspapers, and books, and listening to the radio.

Yet, controversy continues over the nature and degree of the media's influence on political views. On the one hand, the media's ability to change specific opinions on current issues appears to be severely limited. Studies indicate that the media tend more to reinforce political opinions acquired from the family and other social agents than to create new ones. Part of the reason is that most people are inclined to pay attention to news programs, editorial opinions, and political ads that conform to their present views and tune out those that contradict them. This does not mean that people can completely avoid information that conflicts with their views, any more than they can avoid repetitious television commercials that peddle toothpaste and deodorants. It just means that "the audiences of the mass media," as one scholar reflects, "tend toward a selectivity that supports rather than weakens their pre-existing outlooks."[16]

Moreover, much of the information provided by the media goes through a "two-step flow." Rather than persuading people directly, the information often is interpreted by a small number of opinion leaders who pass on their views. Whether these opinion leaders happen to be school teachers, union officials, or just friends and neighbors, their views on the information conveyed by the media may have greater impact than the original information. Thus, the television program watched on Monday may have less effect on a person's opinions than what someone he or she respects says about the program on Tuesday.

Other observers insist, however, that the important question is not whether the media change specific opinions on current issues; rather, it is whether the media portray certain social and political "realities" that indirectly affect political perceptions over the long term. Children may be especially susceptible to the messages of television and other media because their world views and values are rarely as well developed as those of adults.

Indeed, studies suggest that the media can teach as well as reinforce certain kinds of social values.[17] Children are constantly exposed to lessons of social importance in comic books, television dramas and commercials, magazines, and films. All of these popular means of communication promote, whether intentionally or not, certain social concepts and stereotypes, such as that violence is a simple and masculine way to settle disputes, or that a woman's place is in the home.

School children, for example, are likely to be assigned books with certain social messages, in effect, combining the influences of the schools and the media. David Riesman and his colleagues illustrated this point with a once-popular volume in the Little Golden Books series called *Tootle the Engine*.[18] In this tale, Tootle is a young train locomotive who attends engine school where he learns that, to become a big stream-liner, he must obey two important lessons: stop at a red flag and "always stay on the track no matter what." Despite repeated warnings, however, Tootle continues to wander off the track to look for flowers. To stop him from doing so, the town in which his school is located decides to play a trick on him. The next time Tootle leaves the track, red flags suddenly pop up wherever he goes. He turns and twists but can find no spot of grass on which a red flag does not appear. Confused, he returns to the track where he feels relieved to be able to speed back and forth unhindered. He then promises the town never again to leave the track and to grow up to be a streamliner.

The obvious moral of the tale is that it is bad to leave the track and that success and approval—and even freedom—can be found only by conforming to the expectations of the community. The child reading this tale may apply its lessons to relations with peers: adopt the views and behavior of the group to avoid disapproval. More will be said about the media in Chapter 8.

Additional Influences

Ultimately, it is difficult to determine the precise impact that each of these four major influences has on political attitudes and opinions. Because each person is a unique product of many social forces, no one influence will apply equally to all. In fact, other social forces can also play important parts in political learning.

Considering, for example, the potential impact of a job on a person's income, choice of residence, and exposure to other people, one's occupation can significantly influence political orientations. As we will see later, a person's desire to participate in politics and pay attention to current issues can often be related to such occupational factors as income and personal contacts. The same is true for party preferences. Although no universal rule applies to any occupational group, there has been a tendency for well-paid professional people, such as doctors and corporate executives, to vote Republican and for factory workers and teachers to vote Democratic. Obviously, related factors, such as education and family upbringing, also influence party tendencies.

A person's political orientations may be affected also by whether he or she is brought up in a large city, a suburb, or a rural area: each may have its own traditions and social customs that can affect long-term political views.

Sometimes, political events and social crises can create pressures for adjustments in political thinking. History is made up of major events that have produced dramatic breaks with the past. The Great Depression in the 1930s, the Vietnam War and civil rights protests in the 1960s, and the Watergate scandal in the 1970s have all led to changes in many people's political orientations.

The same can be said for a personal crisis, such as the loss of a job or the death of a spouse. One's normal interest in and perspectives on the political world can change abruptly in the face of a personal problem or tragedy.

Finally, people's broad political orientations are affected by the social and cultural traditions of their society. They learn not only the specific values of their families and friends but also the general values that make their culture (or subculture) unique. It has been said, for instance, that Americans as a group are inclined to view politics as more of a private than a public matter. They tend to believe that political opinions, like religious views, should not be discussed openly at the dinner table but instead should be hidden behind the protective curtain of the voting booth. It has also been said that, in contrast to many other nationalities, Americans tend to be competitive and materialistic, religion-oriented, and infatuated with violence. Whether or not any of these generalizations is true, our society undoubtedly propagates—with the aid of the schools, the mass media, and the family—its own special demands, expectations, and traditions that sustain the unique quality of American political life.

A Portrait of the American Voter

Having considered some of the social factors that influence political opinions and attitudes, we may wonder how these opinions and attitudes are expressed: how attentive are people to politics and to what extent do they actively participate? Some classic political writers, like John Locke and John Stuart Mill, thought that the citizens of a democracy should ideally sense a responsibility toward their society: they should keep abreast of current issues; they should participate actively in political affairs; and they should carefully weigh alternatives before lending their support to any policy. Similarly, a common hope today is that most Americans, although not necessarily highly educated about politics, still try to keep reasonably informed about political issues and carefully consider the facts before stepping into the voting booth.

Yet, despite evidence suggesting that people today are somewhat better informed and more issue-oriented than in the past, the ideal state of an attentive, active citizenry hardly exists. Political scientists continue to find that a great number of Americans not only are ignorant about politics but rarely try to make their voices heard. Let us consider each of these findings in turn.

Political Awareness

One discovery is that many Americans appear to be poorly informed about even the most rudimentary elements of government. A 1973 Harris survey, conducted for a Senate subcommittee, revealed that only 46 percent of those questioned could correctly name their representative in Congress, and only 41 percent could identify the representative's party.[19] Even among those with some college education, only 55 percent could name their representative, and no more than 49 percent could identify the representative's party. The survey also found that only 39 percent knew the names of both U.S. senators from their state, and that 20 percent believed Congress includes the U.S. Supreme Court. A few years back, voters in one part of Illinois even renominated a man for Congress who had died three months earlier. His name on the ballot apparently was sufficient recommendation for his reelection.

Widespread lack of knowledge also is revealed in surveys of public opinion on current issues and events. When the Supreme Court ruled in 1971, for example, that the *New York Times* and *Washington Post* could publish articles based on a secret Pentagon study of Vietnam policy, 45 percent admitted they had not heard of the *Pentagon Papers*.[20] Moreover, in March 1979, a Gallup poll found that only 58 percent of Americans had heard or read about SALT II, the proposed strategic arms limitation treaty being negotiated between the United States and the Soviet Union (see Chapter 14).

Political Awareness of Young People

How well informed are young people just out of high school? A Gallup survey conducted in 1978 for the National Municipal League found that 17–18 year olds had difficulty answering some basic questions on American politics and history. The survey found, for example, that only 42 percent had heard of absentee ballots, only 38 percent realized a voter can split his party choice between President and other offices, and only 29 percent were aware that national conventions make the final choice of presidential nominees. The study also found that only 3 percent of the nation's 17–18 year olds could correctly identify Alaska and Hawaii as the last two states to join the union, and only 4 percent could name the three men who served as President immediately before Gerald Ford. When compared to young people surveyed in similar tests in sixteen other countries, young Americans ranked near the bottom (although they did score high in reading, writing, and math skills).

Source: The Washington Post, 16 February 1979.

It should be noted that the level of most people's awareness of political affairs corresponds roughly to the amount of formal education they have acquired. Even though in 1973 only 55 percent of those with some college education could correctly name their representative, this was still considerably higher than the 35 percent of those whose schooling stopped at the eighth grade.[21] Persons with more formal education also are more likely to scan the newspaper and search the dial for the few public affairs programs on television to become better informed about current events.

Still, how can we account for these dismaying statistics? Why are so many people unaware of even who represents them in Washington? Essentially, we can interpret these findings in a number of ways. We can assume, for example, that Americans are a bunch of inveterate "know nothings" who simply lack curiosity about politics. This view has been commonly shared among political observers for years, supported by opinion polls suggesting that large segments of the population show little or no interest in political affairs.[22]

Another interpretation, however, is that the levels of ignorance may reflect not just lack of interest but also the paucity of information the public is given. If meaningless campaign slogans, empty political rhetoric, and superficial news accounts are as common as some critics insist, we must place at least as much of the blame on the transmitters of information as on the receiving public.

Television especially can be criticized for rarely fulfilling its potential to stimulate and educate. Although most people report television to be their main source of news (see Chapter 8), the actual proportion of broadcast time given to public affairs programming is considerably less than that devoted to soap operas, game shows, and commercials. Except for coverage of unusual and dramatic events, such as the Watergate scandals, there is little sophisticated presentation of current political and social issues. The nature and quality of programming reflect instead a commercial desire to reach the largest number of viewers, to sell programs that, as one scholar sarcastically observed, "arouse no controversy, irritate no sensitivity, irritate no gray cells."[23]

Furthermore, low levels of political awareness do not necessarily imply lack of concern about issues. Recent studies suggest that Americans are becoming more sensitive to political issues and are more likely to be guided on election day by how candidates stand on the issues, especially when enough information is made available.[24] One study, for example, found that, as a result of extensive televised coverage of the House Judiciary Committee's 1974 hearings on Nixon's role in Watergate, constituents back home became increasingly aware of committee members' positions on the impeachment issue.[25] The study pointed out that, whereas only one member of the committee who favored impeachment was defeated in the following election, four of those who were openly loyal to him lost their congressional seats. Their decision to support Nixon on the impeachment issue had an independently damaging effect, even taking other factors like campaign strategy into account. "Our analysis suggests," the authors of the study concluded, "that in those circumstances where voters do have meaningful information about candidates, issue voting is both possible and probable in congressional elections."

In the final analysis, the reasons so many people show little awareness of political matters are difficult to sort out. Whether one blames the transmitters of information, or the public for not seeking it out, depends in large part on one's view of fellow citizens as either helpless victims or lazy drones. Perhaps the safest conclusion is that the motivation to become informed may coincide with a variety of other factors, including the expectation of participating in—or avoiding—the political arena. Let us turn then to the question of how many people actually become involved in political activities.

Political Participation

A consistent finding about American political behavior is that most people do not participate actively in politics. The most conspicuous example of this lack of participation is the low voter turnout during elections. As Figure 5-1 shows, turnout in presidential elections since 1960 has not exceeded 63 percent, and has actually declined each year since 1960, with only about 54 percent voting in 1976. This means that out of a potential electorate of 150 million, only 81 million registered voters marched to the polls in 1976 to choose between Jimmy Carter, Gerald Ford, and assorted third-party candidates; 69 million others stayed home.

Turnout is usually even lower in midterm congressional elections, when the entire House of Representatives and one-third of the Senate is chosen. In the five congressional elections between 1960 and 1978, an average of only about 41 percent voted; in 1978, turnout was only 36 percent. And in statewide and local elections involving the choosing of governors and mayors, turnout frequently dips below 30 percent.

These figures compare unfavorably with those of other countries, such as Italy, France, Denmark, and Japan, where turnout is commonly about 80 to 90 percent. Although turnout is often computed differently in these countries, the figures tend to reflect a higher voting rate than in the United States.

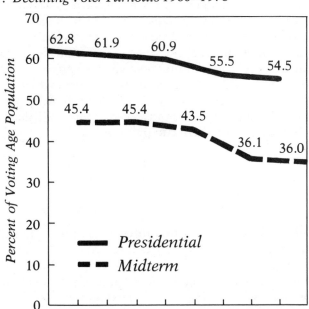

Figure 5-1. Declining Voter Turnouts 1960–1978

Percent of Voting Age Population

- 62.8
- 61.9
- 60.9
- 55.5
- 54.5
- 45.4
- 45.4
- 43.5
- 36.1
- 36.0

——— *Presidential*

■ ■ *Midterm*

1960 62 64 66 68 70 72 74 76 78

Source: Statistical Abstract of the United States, 1977, p. 508.

Those Americans who go beyond voting to engage in other kinds of political activity represent an even smaller fraction of the voting-age population. One political scientist, Lester Milbrath, stratified the population into three basic types: "gladiators" (who become active in party politics or run for office); "spectators" (who seek information and vote); and "apathetics" (who either minimally participate or abstain altogether). According to Milbrath, those "gladiators" who engage in one active form of political participation, such as raising campaign funds, tend to be active in other ways as well. "This division," Milbrath reflected, "is reminiscent of the roles played at a Roman gladiatorial contest. A small band of gladiators battle fiercely to please the spectators, who have the power to decide their fate. The spectators in the stands cheer, transmit messages of advice and encouragement, and, at given periods, vote to decide who has won a particular battle (election). The apathetics do not bother to come to the stadium to watch the show."[26]

Thus, although most Americans have made at least an effort to vote and express a political opinion, only about 15 percent have written letters to an elected official; fewer than 5 percent have volunteered their services in a campaign; and only 12 percent have contributed money to a candidate or party.[27] It has been estimated that the number of Americans who have done anything political other than vote is less than those who have participated in amateur stage shows. And, contrary to expectations, relatively few college students ever take an active part in campaigns. Following the 1970 congressional elections, when student antiwar protest was at its peak, a Gallup poll found that 91 percent of the students interviewed had not been involved at all in political campaigning, in deciding who would help run the country.[28]

Obstacles to Participation

Although there has been sustained interest in unraveling the reasons many people *do* participate in politics (see Chapter 15), political scientists have been greatly interested in discovering the factors that inhibit participation. Because voting is a particularly important ritual in American politics, scholars have tried to explain why millions of people stay home on election day. Even though they do not yet have a definitive answer to this question, a few explanations have been offered.

Registration Requirements

First of all, the low turnout of voters may be partly explained by institutional barriers, such as state registration requirements. In 1976, 38 percent of those interviewed by the Gallup organization claimed not to

DOONESBURY   by Garry Trudeau

have voted because they failed to register.[29] State laws usually require voters to register in person and to renew their eligibility whenever they move or miss a major election. Sometimes these registration procedures are seen as awkward or burdensome, or are too far removed from the election itself; someone who normally is interested in the outcome of an election may not feel sufficiently excited a month before it to register. In contrast, voters in European countries are registered automatically when they come of age and are thus spared having to take the extra step in order to vote.

In 1977, President Carter handed Congress an "instant registration" proposal that would have allowed any citizen to vote in a federal election by merely walking up to the polling place on election day and flashing a driver's license or other acceptable identification. In the few states already using such a system—Maine, Minnesota, and Wisconsin—voter turnout has tended to be higher than the national average, even taking other factors into account. However, many members of Congress opposed the plan, fearing it would lead to widespread voter fraud (despite little evidence of fraud in the states already using such a plan). Republican members were especially unhappy with the idea, insisting that instant registration would only swell the ranks of Democratic voters, who are less likely to register than Republicans. As a result, despite the continuing decline in voter turnout, the proposal was rejected.

Still, the reasons many people fail to register in the first place remains puzzling. Also, even after accounting for those who were sick or away from home on election day, we find that at least 20 million other eligible voters did not turn out in 1976; and a much larger number ignored other kinds of political activity. To account for these no-shows, we must consider some additional factors.

Group Differences

Political scientists have found that certain groups or categories of people tend to participate less than others. Although many potential group differences have been noted, those relating to age, income, and education have been found to be the most important (see Table 5-1). The younger people are, the less formal schooling they have, and the less income they draw, the more likely they are to abstain from voting. Thus, those under twenty years of age tend to show their faces at the polls less often than the middle-aged; those with only grade school education tend to show up less than those with college degrees; and those who are unemployed tend to show up less than those who are employed.

Table 5-1. Percent of Persons Reporting They Voted, 1972 and 1976

	1972	1976
Male	64.1	59.6
Female	62.0	58.8
White	64.5	60.9
Black	52.1	48.7
65 years and over	63.5	62.0
45-64 years old	70.8	68.7
18-20 years old	48.3	38.0
North and West	66.4	61.2
South	55.4	54.9
Metropolitan	64.3	59.2
Nonmetropolitan	59.4	59.1
College-educated	78.8	73.5
High-school-educated	65.4	59.4
Grade-school-educated	47.4	44.1
Employed	66.0	62.0
Unemployed	49.0	43.7

Source: U.S. Bureau of the Census, *Statistical Abstract of the United States,* 1977, p. 508.

These group differences appear to result from a variety of personal and social factors that contribute to noninvolvement. Studies suggest, for instance, that those under twenty years of age probably vote less than those of middle age in part because they are more unsettled and are less exposed to political information. Similarly, those without high school diplomas or who are out of work probably vote less than those with college degrees or who are drawing good salaries because they have fewer resources (including knowledge and confidence) to deal with the political world. Indeed, it is not hard to understand why someone under twenty years of age struggling to find even a low-paying job is likely to suffer special hardships and disillusions that will dampen his or her political interest.

The differences in group turnout also reflect a disturbing fact: those who are most likely to benefit from governmental assistance, such as the poor and less educated, participate less than those who already enjoy considerable advantages, such as the wealthy and well educated. The same lack of resources that deprives many people of a decent standard of living also contributes to their failure to vote or their inability to participate in campaigns, contribute money to candidates, or attend political conventions. And by not participating, the poor and less educated are less effective in communicating their needs and exerting pressures on politicians to implement policies directly benefiting them.

Attitudes and Perceptions

There is also a relationship between participation and people's political attitudes and perceptions. In 1976, for example, 10 percent of those interviewed cited lack of interest as their reason for not voting. Another 14 percent said they did not like the candidates, while 10 percent gave no special reason at all.[30]

Such responses frequently hide a variety of more specific attitudes toward politics, ranging from general boredom or contentment to a lack of faith in the political process. These attitudes often are shaped early by family or friends, and may be affected by the social factors we just discussed, such as education and income.

Some people, for example, simply see no meaningful connection between politics and their personal lives. While the political world may occasionally be viewed with some interest, it still remains distant from the more immediate concerns of day-to-day living. A hardworking father with four children may spend more time worrying about automobile repairs and the high cost of food for his family than about the country's balance-of-payments problems or who will win the next election for county supervisor. His neighbor, meanwhile, may simply be too busy following the progress of the Oakland Raiders football team or driving his new Volkswagen Rabbit to regard politics as worthy of his attention. One study even suggested that this lack of interest can be reinforced by the behavior of others. Those who initially feel some guilt about their inactivity lose it when they see how common apathy is among their friends and neighbors.[31]

Other people (although perhaps not as many as we might expect) abstain from voting as a form of political expression. This includes those who scorn politics because it appears to be dishonest or self-serving, or who are disgusted by a lack of meaningful choice between the parties.[32] We might sympathize with the elderly lady who, when asked which candidates she was going to vote for, replied, "I never vote. It only encourages 'em."[33]

Some people even find politics socially distasteful. They carry images of themselves as agreeable, likable individuals who do not wish to create conflicts with their friends, families, or co-workers by having political disagreements—at the dinner table or anywhere else. As a result, they will impose a self-censorship even on their political opinions. In one study, a person admitted she does not discuss politics with her husband "because when we do, we are likely to disagree violently. Right now I want to avoid friction—we were just married last June—so we try not to get into political discussions." Another person wished to avoid conflict with friends and neighbors: "We don't discuss politics much. I think it's sort of like religion. It's personal, and I don't like to get into arguments. When politics comes up in conversation, I always say, 'Let's talk about something else.' "[34]

Voter interest can even be affected by the type and nature of the election. As we have seen, more people show up in presidential elections, when media coverage of the candidates and issues is more intense, than in congressional or state elections. Also, in contests where one party has no more than a slim chance of defeating the other, feelings of futility may halt further political involvement. Some people may decide that, even with their participation, their party's candidate will fail at the polls anyway (or, conversely, that their candidate will coast to an easy victory and does not need their support). This situation is most likely to occur in regions, such as the South, where one party traditionally dominates most congressional and state elections (see Chapter 6). Persons favoring the minority party may prefer to stay at home rather than experience again the frustrations of defeat.

But perhaps the most common and serious reason given for nonparticipation is a feeling of futility that reaches beyond the outcome of any single election. Many people are deterred from participating in politics by the belief that their involvement would not make a significant difference.[35] The air around them is being poisoned, prices continue to rise unchecked, and their neighborhoods seem unsafe and increasingly filled with violence. Yet they feel lost among the millions of other voters and sense that those who make the major political decisions—politicians, corporate executives, and bureaucrats—will not pay any attention. As we will see in the final chapter, many even accept the ruling-elite view that elections are just "rituals" anyway, which do not communicate people's real wants and needs. Consequently, they see little point in doing anything, least of all voting.

A feeling of powerlessness may derive to some degree, of course, from the enormous size and complexity of modern society. In a large country where government can seem remote and out of reach, people may see little chance of personally influencing the decision-making process. In fact, one of the most dramatic problems facing the country is the overwhelming lack of public confidence in government's responsiveness to the individual. Many Americans have come to believe not that they can control and regulate government but that government controls and regulates them. They sense that much of government has fallen into the hands of corrupt and self-serving scoundrels who pursue their own selfish interests with little regard for the welfare of the nation as a whole. According to opinion surveys conducted by the Louis Harris polling organization, a growing number of Americans take a disheartened view of both the American political process and their own roles within it (see Table 5-2). They feel ineffective against the wishes of powerful interests and believe governmental officials are largely unresponsive to their needs.

Table 5-2. Do You Make a Difference?

	Percent Agreeing		
	1966	1972	1976
The rich get richer and the poor get poorer.	45	68	77
The people running the country don't really care what happens to you.	26	50	61
What you think doesn't count much anymore.	37	53	64
You feel left out of things going on around you.	9	25	42

Source: Louis Harris Survey, 25 March 1976.

It is hardly surprising that such feelings of inefficacy tend to be most pronounced among certain minority groups and the poor. People in these groups are more likely to feel estranged from government and to believe they have little control over their political environment.[36] Nor is this pessimism necessarily unrealistic. The poor especially have been served badly by the political system. They have experienced a long history of futility in trying to draw some kind of governmental response to their needs. American political institutions have been notable for being slow to help those who lack organized or meaningful representation of their interests. If one accepts the ruling-elite view that "money talks" in politics, then one can understand why a poor person may feel his or her political actions would be futile.

We may ask, therefore, whether nonparticipation is not, in some ways, an understandable response to frustration in dealing with the political system. In view of the fact that government can often seem remote and unresponsive, the desire to avoid the disappointments of politics becomes an understandable psychological defense. Similarly, the tendency to remain unaware of public issues may stem from a desire to veil oneself from the oppressive nature of current events. Through the news media, the outside world can impose a despairing reality on people—political kidnappings, payoff scandals, and murders—over which they have no control. Although awareness of current issues may be a positive goal, it may be unreasonable to expect people to feel guilty about screening out events that increase their sense of helplessness and despair.

Still, we may also hope that the political world never becomes so oppressive that we are forced into a permanent cocoon of apathy. As anthropologist Margaret Mead warned many years ago, "We must never see the government as something other than ourselves, for then automatically we become children; and not real honest children, but adults dwarfed to childhood again in weakness and ineffectiveness."[37]

The Consequences of Indifference

What, then, are some of the likely consequences of nonparticipation and lack of awareness? Many of us assume that if public opinion and elections are to control politicians, most people must be aware of what these characters are doing, if only to decide at election time whether to keep them in office or throw them out. Although, as we saw in Chapter 2, there are different interpretations of the relationship between people and government, we are still likely to believe that public opinion and elections can provide some checks on elected officials.

Yet we might wonder how elected representatives can be held accountable when so many Americans are politically inactive and poorly informed. How can people control their representatives when they know so little about their legislative stands and, in many instances, do not even know their names? Indeed, how serious are the low levels of participation and awareness? Do they suggest a fundamental impairment of the political system? Let us take a brief look at two sides of this issue.

The Positive Side

The pluralist perspective discussed in Chapter 2 offers some comfort by noting that we do not rely merely on something called "the public" to keep elected officials in line. The whole concept of the public is deceptive, because our population is comprised of many "publics," or different opinion groups. There are always some attentive citizens who remain sufficiently interested in an issue to keep informed and politically active. They write letters to their representatives and to the local newspapers, follow political events on television, and most important, inform others of the issues. In the words of one member of Congress, "While the rank and file don't attach much importance to your committee assignment and your effectiveness, there are a handful of people in almost every community who will attach importance to them, and they are the ones who have considerable influence on public opinion."[38] In other words, politicians know they are being observed and must consider constituents' possible responses to their policy decisions if they wish to avoid falling from favor.

Further, we are told, it may not be crucial whether most citizens are attentive as long as politicians *believe* people are aware of their activities. Even though members of Congress may suspect a general apathy among constituents, they nevertheless prefer to overestimate rather than underestimate their public visibility. In some measure, this caution reflects the difficulties politicians encounter in learning what their constituents want or feel. Elected officials know constituents mostly from dealing with organized groups and individuals who *do* write letters, who *will* contribute campaign money, and who *have* expressed an interest in their legislative activities. Moreover, they know they can win or lose an election by only a small fraction of the popular vote. If the number of informed voters is large enough, it can have considerable impact on their chances of survival. They know some people back home will abandon them at the polls if their legislative efforts fail to conform to expectations. Of course, constituents who are the most visible to their representative will probably reap the most benefits, a fact that may not comfort either the apathetic majority or the poor and disorganized.

Elected officials also are aware there are limits to how far they can pursue a policy without suffering popular repudiation. Following severe inflation, a scandal, or an unpopular war, public consciousness may increase and result in pressure for the removal of those considered responsible.

The Watergate scandal is particularly illuminating. As the story came together piecemeal in the most damaging ways—in newspaper headlines and televised committee hearings—the strain on the reputation of Richard Nixon and on the Republican party became more and more intense. Shattering the initial assumption that most Americans were indifferent to the Watergate issue, the *Wall Street Journal* in April 1973 published a poll showing that, even at that early stage of the scandal, 91 percent of those questioned were aware of it, and that one in five Independent voters and two in eleven Republicans said it might turn them against the *GOP*. A few weeks later, a Harris poll showed that 63 percent of those surveyed did not believe the official White House version of Watergate, while only 9 percent accepted its account. As we know, the publicity stemming from Watergate and its aftermath compelled Nixon to dump most of his closest associates in an effort to contain the damage. Among those purged were two successive attorneys general, his chief of staff, chief domestic advisor, private lawyer, and staff counsel. And, ultimately, facing the specter of his own impeachment and removal from office, he resigned in disgrace.

Finally, as we saw earlier, some supporters of the pluralist theory feel that universal participation may not even be desirable.[39] They see little value in encouraging those who are relatively uninformed and uninterested to participate more actively in politics. In their view, many of these people are incapable of making rational political choices and are likely to be swayed by dangerous propaganda and the tirades of demagogues. Thus, encouraging them to participate may bring only disaster to the democratic process.

The Negative Side

Other observers, however, remain disturbed by the low level of participation and awareness. They worry that politicians take advantage of the fact that most people do not know or care what they are doing. As one member of Congress admitted, "In my district, they think I am a fighter. I can do anything I want down here and they will say, 'He is the greatest fighter we have ever had down there.' No one pays attention to the votes."[40]

Also, people who are not actively involved in politics tend to be underrepresented. It is most often the poor and less educated who are left out of the decision-making process. The lower the level of income and education, the more likely are people to abstain from voting, to be uninformed, and to be neglected by the political system.

As to the argument that heightened participation could pose a danger to the democratic process, they counter that, considering the urban riots of the 1960s, noninvolvement in the ongoing political process may be far more dangerous. When people feel excluded from traditional political channels and are estranged from government, the potential for disruption and violence can become explosive. After all, not everyone who feels slighted by the system will remain inactive. The danger is always present that frustration may promote the extreme forms of action that apologists for nonparticipation wish to avoid.

Finally, and most important, a basic tenet of democracy is that people who are affected by a decision deserve to have a say about what that decision will be. To assert that the political system could be threatened by an increase in participation is to reject the democratic ideal of providing everyone who wants it a role in the decision-making process.

The solution, therefore, may not be to moralize about the need for more citizen involvement or to force people to vote. Because nonparticipation is often tied to certain social conditions, it may be more worthwhile to work for needed institutional and social reforms: raise the quality of education and economic well-being; make the choices between the political parties more meaningful; and, most significant of all, find ways to open up the decision-making process to more people.

Key Terms

political socialization

peers

mass media

opinion leader

Notes

1. Richard E. Dawson and Kenneth Prewitt, *Political Socialization* (Boston: Little, Brown, 1969), p. 19.

2. Colin M. Turnbull, *The Forest People* (New York: Simon and Schuster, 1961).

3. Alexis de Tocqueville, *Democracy in America*, vol. 1 (New York: Schocken Books, 1961), p. 12.

4. David Wallace, *First Tuesday: A Study of Rationality in Voting (New York: Doubleday, 1964), p. 231.*

5. Fred I. Greenstein, *Children and Politics* (New Haven: Yale University Press, 1965), p. 23.

6. Ibid., p. 34.

7. Ibid., p. 26.

8. Edgar Litt, "Civic Education, Community Norms, and Political Indoctrination," *American Sociological Review*, February 1963, pp. 69–75.

9. Greenstein, *Children and Politics*, p. 39.

10. See, for example, Edward S. Greenberg, "Black Children and the Political System," *Public Opinion Quarterly*, Fall 1970, pp. 333–345; Harrell R. Rodgers, Jr., "Toward Explanation of the Political Efficacy and Political Cynicism of Black Adolescents: An Exploratory Study," *American Journal of Political Science*, May 1974, pp. 257–282; John S. Jackson, "Alienation and Black Political Participation," *Journal of Politics*, November 1973, pp. 849–885.

11. F. Christopher Arterton, "The Impact of Watergate on Children's Attitudes Toward Political Authority," *Political Science Quarterly*, June 1974, pp. 269–288.

12. See, for example, F. Christopher Arterton, "Watergate and Children's Attitudes Toward Political Authority Revisited," *Political Science Quarterly*, Fall 1975, pp. 477–496; Marjorie Randon Hershey and David B. Hill, "Watergate and Preadults' Attitudes Toward the President," *American Journal of Political Science*, November 1975, pp. 703–726.

13. From *The Learning of Political Behavior*, edited by Norman Adler and Charles Harrington (Scott, Foresman, 1970), p. 190.

14. Herbert McClosky and Harold E. Dahlgren, "Primary Group Influences on Party Loyalty," *American Political Science Review*, 1959, p. 772.

15. S. E. Asch, "Effects of Group Pressure upon the Modification and Distortion of Judgments," pp. 151–162 in *Group Dynamics: Research and Theory*, edited by Dorwin Cartwright and Alvin Zander (New York: Harper & Row, 1960).

16. V. O. Key, Jr., *Public Opinion and American Democracy* (New York: Alfred A. Knopf, 1961), p. 355.

17. For a brief review (and bibliography) of studies on television, see Douglass Cater and Richard Adler, eds., *Television as a Social Force* (New York: Praeger, 1975).

18. David Riesman et al., *The Lonely Crowd* (New Haven: Yale University Press, 1961).

19. U.S. Senate, Committee on Government Operations, "Confidence and Concern: Citizens View American Government, A Survey of Public Attitudes," pt. 1 (Washington, D.C.: U.S. Government Printing Office, 1973).

20. *Gallup Opinion Index*, August 1971.

21. U.S. Senate, Committee on Government Operations, pt. 1.

22. *Gallup Opinion Index*, December 1972.

23. Key, *Public Opinion*, p. 386.

24. Norman H. Nie, Sidney Verba, John R. Petrocik, *The Changing American Voter* (Cambridge: Harvard University Press, 1976). See also discussion in the *American Political Science Review*, September 1976, pp. 753–849.

25. Gerald C. Wright, "Constituency Response to Congressional Behavior: The Impact of the House Judiciary Committee Impeachment Votes," *Western Political Quarterly*, September 1977, pp. 401–410.

26. Lester W. Milbrath, *Political Participation* (Chicago: Rand McNally, 1965), p. 20.

27. Survey Research Center, University of Michigan.

28. *Gallup Opinion Index*, February 1972.

29. *Gallup Opinion Index*, December 1976.

30. Ibid.

31. Morris Rosenberg, "Some Determinants of Political Apathy," *Public Opinion Quarterly*, Winter 1954, pp. 349–366.

32. For a discussion of the relationship between cynicism and participation, see Arthur H. Miller, "Political Issues and Trust in Government: 1964–1970," followed by comments, *American Political Science Review*, September 1974, pp. 951–1001.

33. Quoted in Robert Sherrill, *Why They Call It Politics*, 2nd ed. (New York: Harcourt Brace Jovanovich, 1974), p. 316.

34. Rosenberg, *Political Apathy*, pp. 349–366.

35. Angus Campbell et al., *The American Voter* (New York: Wiley, 1960).

36. Milbrath, *Political Participation*; Jack Citrin et al., "Personal and Political Sources of Political Alienation," *British Journal of Political Science*, January 1975, pp. 1–32.

37. Margaret Mead, *And Keep Your Powder Dry: An Anthropologist Looks at America* (New York: William Morrow, 1942), pp. 165–166.

38. Quoted in Charles L. Clapp, *The Congressman: His Work As He Sees It* (Washington, D.C.: Brookings Institution, 1963), p. 108.

39. See, for example, Bernard Berelson et al., *Voting: A Study of Opinion Formation in a Presidential Campaign* (Chicago: University of Chicago Press, 1954).

40. Clapp, *The Congressman*, p. 373.

Recommended Reading

Best, James J. *Public Opinion: Micro and Macro.* Homewood, Ill.: Dorsey Press, 1973.

Dawson, Richard E., and Kenneth Prewitt. *Political Socialization.* 2nd ed. Boston: Little, Brown, 1977.

DENNIS, JACK, ed., *Socialization to Politics*. New York: Wiley, 1973.

ERIKSON, ROBERT, and NORMAN LUTTBEG. *American Public Opinion: Its Origins, Content, and Impact*. New York: Wiley, 1973.

FLANIGAN, WILLIAM H., and NANCY ZINGALE. *Political Behavior of the American Electorate*. 3rd ed. Boston: Allyn and Bacon, 1975.

JENNINGS, M. KENT, and RICHARD NIEMI. *The Political Character of Adolescence: The Influence of Families and Schools*. Princeton: Princeton University Press, 1974.

MILBRATH, LESTER W. *Political Participation*. 2nd ed. Chicago: Rand McNally, 1977.

MILLER, WARREN E., and TERESA E. LEVITIN. *Leadership and Change: The New Politics of the American Electorate*. Cambridge: Winthrop, 1976.

NIE, NORMAN H., SIDNEY VERBA, and JOHN R. PETROCIK. *The Changing American Voter*. Cambridge: Harvard University Press, 1976.

NIEMI, RICHARD, and HERBERT WEISSBERG. *Controversies in American Voting Behavior*. San Francisco: W. H. Freeman, 1976.

POMPER, GERALD. *Voters' Choice: Varieties of American Electoral Behavior*. New York: Dodd, Mead, 1975.

VERBA, SIDNEY, and NORMAN H. NIE. *Participation in America*. New York: Harper & Row, 1972.

6

Parties and Elections: The Limits of Participation

Among the institutions offering a route to power, political parties have traditionally attracted the most attention. Throughout our history, parties have given hope to countless ambitious power seekers that they would be selected as candidates for such high public office as Congress or the presidency and provided with the funds and organization needed to achieve victory. As in many other countries, parties in the United States have served as major links between citizens and government, and have figured prominently in the personal strategies for political influence among many successful brokers of power. Parties have represented an important source of access to government—as well as a source of frustration—even to those intending to engage only minimally in political activities.

Yet, one of the most interesting features of political parties in this country is that they have no written constitutional base. Although the Constitution spells out many of the duties of Congress, the president, and the Supreme Court, it does not even mention political parties. The Founding Fathers had little experience with parties and probably could not have foreseen the important roles they would play in the future. In fact, the Founding Fathers abhorred the whole idea of parties, on the grounds that they would undermine a legislator's independence and encourage undesirable divisions and factionalism. George Washington, in his famous farewell address in 1796, cautioned against "the baneful effects of the spirit of party." He feared that parties, in encouraging the pursuit of selfish partisan goals, might destroy national unity at a time when the new country was struggling to survive. John Adams, his vice-president, agreed with him, saying, "There is nothing I dread so much as the division of the Republic into two great parties. . . . This, in my humble opinion, is to be feared as the greatest political evil under our Constitution." Even Thomas Jefferson, who later became a key figure in the creation of strong rival parties, declared in 1789, "If I could not go to heaven but with a party, I would not go there at all."

Needless to say, parties developed anyway. Even though the Founding Fathers considered a party system to be, as Frank Sorauf puts it, "an extra-constitutional excrescence not to be dignified by mention in the constitutional document," parties began to take shape as different groups clashed over economic issues, foreign policy, and the proper role of the federal government. As the eighteenth century came to a close, there were two national parties: the Jeffersonian-Republicans and the Federalists. The political campaign became the common route to political office, and candidates who previously had boasted of their independence now supported a party line.

But the antipathy toward parties, surprisingly, has not disappeared. Many Americans today share the Founding Fathers' distrust of political parties. Among college students, for example, the performance of parties has received the lowest "favorable" rating of nine major American institutions, well below that of high schools, police, the courts, and business.[1] Moreover, according to a study published in 1975, a majority of Americans agree with the statements that "political parties more often than not create conflicts where none really exist," that "parties do more to confuse the issues than to provide a clear choice on them," and that "it would be better if, in all elections, we put no party labels on the ballot."[2]

The reasons parties rank so low in popular esteem is not entirely clear. Perhaps a tradition of bad feelings toward them has been perpetuated since colonial times. Or perhaps parties have been sullied by their close association with politics, which, as indicated in the preceding chapters, many Americans perceive as dirty business. One poll taken early in the Watergate scandal found that, while 31 percent of Americans regarded the affair as "a serious matter," 53 percent dismissed it as "just politics—the kind of thing both parties engage in."[3]

Whatever the reasons for the antipathy toward parties, evidence indicates that party loyalties are on the decline.[4] As Table 6-1 shows, the number of Americans who claim a party affiliation has been dropping

"Your mother and I think you are old enough now to know that we are Republicans!"

almost steadily since the 1950s. In fact, there are more people today who consider themselves *independents* than who identify themselves as Republicans. Although many of these independents admit leaning to one of the two parties when pressed by interviewers, they still resist being labeled a Democrat or a Republican.

One sign of this decline in party affiliation has been the tendency of voters to split their votes during elections. For example, of the twelve states in 1972 in which voters chose candidates for president, governor, and U.S. senator, only in North Carolina did they support the same party (Republican) for all three offices.[5] In 1976, more than one-fourth of all congressional districts were carried by a presidential candidate of one party and a House candidate of the other.[6] As one study noted, "Party affiliation, once the central thread connecting the citizen and the political process, is a thread that has certainly been frayed."[7]

To make matters even worse for the parties, they have also been declining in organizational strength. As we will see in the section on nominations, the parties have become less and less important in the

Table 6-1. Party Affiliation, 1950–1979.

| | Percent Claiming Affiliation | | |
	Republican	Democrat	Independent
1979	24	38	33
1978	22	42	31
1977	20	49	31
1972	28	43	29
1968	27	46	27
1960	30	47	23
1950	33	45	22

Sources: Gallup Opinion Index, December 1977; *ABC News-Harris Survey,* 18 June 1979.

selection and support of candidates for public office, one of their most traditional functions. The spread of primaries, the growing use of the media in campaigns, and the decline in party loyalties have all helped erode traditional party power bases. Candidates have been able with increasing frequency to build their own bases of electoral support with little more than token reference to the wishes of the party organizations. Jimmy Carter's election in 1976 provides only one dramatic example of how an "outsider" has been able to grab a party's nomination from the "regulars" who used to run the show.

The Trademark of a "Party"

But what exactly is a *political party*? How do we distinguish between a party and, say, an interest group or political movement? As is true of many other concepts in political science, a party is difficult to define. "As there are many roads to Rome and many ways to skin a cat," one scholar has quipped, "there are also many ways to look at a political party."[8]

One traditional way of distinguishing a party from another kind of political group is to examine its *purpose*. According to most political scientists, the unique goal of a party is to capture public office, to wield the powers of government. An interest group, in contrast, strives merely to influence governmental policy on specific issues. It does not attempt to assume responsibility for running the government itself. The American Medical Association, for instance, may try to affect policies relating to medical practices, but it is not interested in determining foreign policy as well.

While this distinction is a valid one, it fails to take into account those parties that have little hope of taking command of government, or that even attempt to do so. Members of the Prohibition and Libertarian parties, for instance, often assert they have little realistic chance of gaining political control and are more interested in using elections to publicize their cause and sway public opinion. They reason that, even though they have little hope of winning elections, they can attract more attention by fielding candidates for office than by working behind the scenes as an interest group. As John Hospers, the 1972 presidential candidate of the Libertarian party confessed, "We're not even going to watch the votes very closely. But as a mouthpiece for ideas, I happily consented to run."[9]

Perhaps then we also need to differentiate between parties and other groups by their *method* of satisfying their objectives: only parties run candidates for public office under their own banners. Although other kinds of political organizations, such as interest groups, may try to mobilize public support for their views, they do not do so by nominating candidates for public office. No one runs for Congress, for example, under the banner of the National Rifle Association or the United Brotherhood of Carpenters.

But besides running candidates for office and trying to gain control of government, parties also serve a number of other functions for both the political system and the individual citizen. They offer information on current issues, help organize the creation of policy, serve as watchdogs on those in power, and provide a channel for political action. Most of these functions, in fact, bear directly on the opportunities for participation at various levels of the political system, not only for political elites but for ordinary citizens as well.

For example, one of the most important functions of parties is to provide a channel for those trying to affect policy making in some direct way. Several important party activities, including the political campaign and the nomination of candidates for office, draw upon the resources of ordinary citizens. Those who seek expanded opportunities for political action may serve as delegates to county and state party conventions, sit on local party platform and policy committees, or help recruit candidates for local offices. In fact, those willing to spend the time learning how the party in their state chooses delegates to its quadrennial national convention may even help decide who will be their party's nominee for president. As we will see later, pressures have been mounting on both major parties to encourage greater grass-roots participation in the presidential nomination process.

Moreover, for political action to carry any significance, it must be based on some understanding of current issues and problems. Even voting would be largely meaningless if one knew nothing about what was at stake, about what the policy proposals touted by the various candidates would mean for the country. In this respect, parties are also looked to for information. People will rely on party platforms, press releases, and the speeches of party candidates for information on current issues and solutions to national problems. They will depend on their party spokesmen to point out the errors of the opposition and to acquaint them with alternative policy ideas. Naturally, the parties do not always provide the kind of information voters need. Some critics charge that, although the parties do occasionally focus public attention on issues, party candidates rely too heavily on emotional speech making and simplistic media campaigns that exploit voters' needs and insecurities. "The claim that parties 'educate the public,'" scoffs one scholar, "is open to serious reservation if education means mobilizing facts ... and impartially appraising problems and solutions. Hyperbole, exaggeration, the oversimple solution, and demagoguery too often characterize the educational efforts of party activists."[10] (More will be said about the style of political campaigns in Chapter 8.)

Going a step further, party support is also regarded as an important asset for many of those who seek an expanded political role by running for public office. Although the role of parties in political campaigns has declined over the years, candidates still rely on the party label to gain the support of voters who habitually champion that party. By running on the Democratic party ticket, they may hope to capture many Democratic votes regardless of their own personal views and positions. In addition, candidates will knock on the door of the local party headquarters seeking campaign workers and party volunteers eager to ring doorbells, lick stamps, and encourage potential supporters to register and vote.

And, finally, parties assist those who presumably have made it to the summits of power. At the national, state, and local levels, party organizations are looked to for help in creating public policy. Members of Congress, for example, often rely on the party leadership to steer a program over the various legislative hurdles and to help staff committees, define responsibilities, and select presiding officers (such as the Speaker of the House). The parties additionally are viewed as a bridge between Congress and the White House. The president will frequently appeal to fellow party members in the House and Senate to support his prized legislative proposals. He knows their common party ties and mutual desire to fashion an effective party program can provide an incentive for cooperation between the two branches of government.

In stating these functions of parties, it should be kept in mind that neither the Democratic nor the Republican party has performed these tasks in a particularly effective manner. As we will see, each party has fallen short in terms of organization and discipline to be dependable in coordinating the policy-making activities of government. It cannot even be said that the two parties, by supporting candidates and espousing certain views, have adequately represented voters' interests, translating their needs into public policies. As ruling-elite theorists contend, the Democratic and Republican parties have been too similar and moderate to represent all segments of our society. Many Americans—especially among the poor, the alienated youth, and the members of some minority and ideological groups—do not believe either party articulates their interests. And since third parties have been too weak to take control of government, a climate of dissatisfaction and tension has persisted in some areas of our society that neither major party can resolve.

Democrats and Republicans: Group Support and Ideology

Before turning to the major features of American parties, we might consider a matter perhaps more laden with myths and shrouded in emotion than any other in American politics, namely the differences between Democrats and Republicans. Those who continue to identify with one of the two parties undoubtedly believe their party embodies the country's major virtues. Although they may be confused at times about the essential differences between the two parties—if indeed such differences exist—they most likely subscribe to some popular notion about what distinguishes Democrats from Republicans. One observer, for example, irreverently summed up the differences this way: "A gathering of Democrats is more sweaty, disorderly, offhand, and rowdy than a gathering of Republicans; it is also more likely to be more cheerful, imaginative, tolerant of dissent, and skillful at the game of give-and-take. A gathering of Republicans is more respectable, sober, purposeful, and businesslike than a gathering of Democrats; it is also more likely to be more self-righteous, pompous, cut-and-dried, and just plain boring."[11]

Before we can even consider the validity of this stereotyped view of the two parties, we must ask ourselves what we mean by "Republican" and "Democrat." Do these terms refer to all of those people who simply call themselves Republicans and Democrats? Do they refer only to the active members who consistently vote for and support these parties? Or do they refer exclusively to the inner circle of leaders who hold an official party post or an elective office? The distinctions between the two parties will likely seem quite different, depending on which of these categories we consider.

Perhaps the differences between the parties can best be illustrated by the kinds of people each party attracts on election day and by the levels of support the active members and voters of each party give to major political and social issues.

Group Support

Surveys reveal, first of all, that the two parties differ in terms of the occupational, ethnic, and other social groups each attracts for relatively long periods of time. As we can see in Table 6-2, Democratic presidential candidates have tended to draw greater support from nonwhites, younger voters, Catholics, union members, and manual workers, whereas Republican candidates have tended to attract the college-educated, members of professional and business groups, older voters, and Protestants.

Obviously, these are only tendencies. Neither party commands the exclusive support of any group. Many Democrats are college-educated, attend a Protestant church, or own a business. Likewise, many Republicans are Catholic, young, or belong to a union. Nor does either party historically draw support always from the same groups. Prior to the 1930s, for instance, Jewish and black voters tended to be predominantly Republican.

Although defections to the other party are common among all of these groups (as was especially true in 1972), some groups within each party provide a significant basis of continuing support. This is most clearly illustrated by the overwhelming support black voters have given to the Democratic party. As the authors of one recent study point out, "The Democratic party now draws almost a fifth of its support from blacks. They are crucial to Democratic dominance in general; and in some states they are the segment of the electorate that keeps the party competitive."[12]

This crucial support has not escaped the notice of either black leaders or Democratic politicians. Jimmy Carter, for example, quickly discovered that presidential support for black needs and aspirations was expected in return for the overwhelming support he won from black voters in 1976. As Vernon Jordan of the National Urban League commented, "Much has been made of regional loyalties that gave Carter a solid south, but without black voters the Republican ticket would have cracked Carter's southern bloc, with devastating results for his candidacy. . . . It was a heavier than expected black vote that put Carter over

Table 6.2 Vote by Groups in Presidential Elections Since 1952

	1952		1956		1960		1964		1968			1972		1976[a]		
	Steven-son	Eisen-hower	Steven-son	Eisen-hower	Ken-nedy	Nixon	John-son	Gold-water	Hum-phrey	Nixon	Wal-lace	McGov-ern	Nixon	Carter	Ford	McCar-thy
National	44.6%	55.4%	42.2%	57.8%	50.1%	49.9%	61.3%	38.7%	43.0%	43.4%	13.6%	38%	62%	50%	48%	1%
Sex																
Male	47	53	45	55	52	48	60	40	41	43	16	37	63	53	45	1
Female	42	58	39	61	49	51	62	38	45	43	12	38	62	48	51	—[b]
Race																
White	43	57	41	59	49	51	59	41	38	47	15	32	68	46	52	1
Nonwhite	79	21	61	39	68	32	94	6	85	12	3	87	13	85	15	—
Education																
College	34	66	31	69	39	61	52	48	37	54	9	37	63	42	55	2
High school	45	55	42	58	52	48	62	38	42	43	15	34	66	54	46	—
Grade school	52	48	50	50	55	45	66	34	52	33	15	49	51	58	41	1
Occupation																
Prof.-business	36	64	32	68	42	58	54	46	34	56	10	31	69	42	56	1
White collar	40	60	37	63	48	52	57	43	41	47	12	36	64	50	48	2
Manual	55	45	50	50	60	40	71	29	50	35	15	43	57	58	41	1
Age																
Under 30 years	51	49	43	57	54	46	64	36	47	38	15	48	52	53	45	1
30–49 years	47	53	45	55	54	46	63	37	44	41	15	33	67	48	29	2
50 years and over	39	61	39	61	46	54	59	41	41	47	12	36	64	52	48	—
Religion																
Protestants	37	63	37	63	38	62	55	45	35	49	16	30	70	46	53	—
Catholics	56	44	51	49	78	22	76	24	59	33	8	48	52	57	42	1
Politics																
Republicans	8	92	4	96	5	95	20	80	9	86	5	5	95	9	91	—
Democrats	77	23	85	15	84	16	87	13	74	12	14	67	33	82	18	—
Independents	35	65	30	70	43	57	56	44	31	44	25	31	69	38	57	4
Region																
East	45	55	40	60	53	47	68	32	50	43	7	42	58	51	47	1
Midwest	42	58	41	59	48	52	61	39	44	47	9	40	60	48	50	1
South	51	49	49	51	51	49	52	48	31	36	33	29	71	54	45	—
West	42	58	43	57	49	51	60	40	44	49	7	41	59	46	51	1
Members of labor union families	61	39	57	43	65	35	73	27	56	29	15	46	54	63	36	1

a. Figures for some groups do not add to 100 percent because of the vote for other third-party candidates. b. Less than 1 percent.
Source: Gallup Opinion Index, December 1976.

Jimmy Carter and Rep. Ronald Dellums.

the top in some key states he needed to win. That's something Jimmy Carter should not forget, nor should black people allow him to forget it."[13]

Ideology

In addition to group support, the two parties also differ in their ideological tendencies. Political observers have found that Democratic leaders and activists (such as governors, members of Congress, and campaign workers) tend to take a more liberal or progressive stand on many political issues than their Republican counterparts. Democrats are more inclined than Republicans to experiment with new governmental programs, to favor expanded regulation of the economy, and to support more extensive health and welfare programs. This greater inclination is due, at least in part, to the kind of group support the Democrats have maintained. "The fact that the Democratic party has built a national coalition of urban, lower socio-economic and minority groups," Frank Sorauf argues, "lies beneath its espousal of a wider social-welfare program than the Republicans have favored."[14]

One way to determine the ideological differences between Democratic and Republican leaders is to examine the voting records of Congress members. For some years now, the self-proclaimed *conservative* Americans for Constitutional Action (ACA) and the *liberal* Americans for Democratic Action (ADA) have been doing just that—rating the votes of Democratic and Republican members of Congress on key legislation. Generally speaking, the conservative ACA awards its highest ratings to members who seem committed to a strong defense posture, a competitive market system, and states' rights. The liberal ADA, on the other hand, awards its top marks to members who favor lower defense spending, welfare reform, civil rights, and environmental protection. Thus, for the 1977 congressional session, seventy-six Republicans and only ten Democrats in the House received positive scores of 80 percent or better from the conservative ACA. At the same time, seventy-one Democrats and only one Republican received positive scores of 80 percent or better from the liberal ADA.[15]

What then about the voters? Are there ideological differences also among the rank and file? There do appear to be such differences, although they are not as marked as among policy makers. As we can see in Table 6-3, only one-third as many Republicans as Democrats identify themselves as "liberal." In fact, Republican voters identify their political views as "conservative" about five-to-one over "liberal," whereas Democratic voters are split almost evenly between the two positions.

Moreover, evidence suggests that Democratic and Republican voters are tending to express increasingly different degrees of support for certain political and social issues. Voters with strong Democratic party ties now give at least twice as much support as Republican voters to such issues as increased aid to education, governmental guarantees of fair employment, and school integration.[16] The stronger the identification with the parties and the more active the support, the greater are the differences in opinion. "People who vote Republican and those who vote Democratic," one study has concluded, "are separated by greater opin-

Table 6-3. Party Identification and Ideology

| | Percent Identifying Themselves As | | | |
	Conservative	Middle of Road	Liberal	No Opinion
Republican	57	30	11	2
Democrat	31	29	33	7
Independent	41	31	25	3

Source: Gallup Opinion Index, August 1972.

ion distance than those who simply think of themselves as Republicans and Democrats."[17]

Party Characteristics and Citizen Confusion

Yet, despite these apparent differences in ideology and group support, many Americans are still confused about what the two parties represent. They cannot easily distinguish between the Democratic and Republican parties on many controversial issues, and some are even unclear about which one is more "conservative" or "liberal."[18] Nor is this a recent phenomenon. British writer James Bryce, after visiting this country in the late nineteenth century, observed that a European is always asking Americans to explain the differences between the two parties. "He is always asking," Bryce quipped, "because he never gets an answer."[19]

Although many reasons may account for this confusion, some observers believe several features of the parties themselves are to blame. They contend that the parties' decentralized character, their ideological potpourri, and their overlapping programs prevent many people from seeing any clear distinctions between them. Let us take a look at each of these features in turn.

Our Fragmented Parties

Certainly one factor contributing to the confusion has been the fragmentation of party leadership. Although most of us may regard the Democratic and Republican parties as national bodies, they are little more than loose alliances of state and local parties that converge every four years at a national convention to select a nominee for president. For most of American history, each of the states—and not any national body—has directed party operations. This reflects the federal system in this country, in which power is constitutionally divided between the national government and the states. Each state boasts its own constitution and its own rules concerning elections and the operations of parties. As a result, the Democratic and Republican parties differ in form and membership from one state to another, with each local party responding to its own rules, policy needs, and constituencies.

Naturally, this does not mean that the Democratic and Republican parties have operated without any national organization (see Table 6-4). But in each major party the national organization has focused primarily

Table 6-4. National Party Organization

The National Convention
On paper, the supreme authority in both parties is the national convention, which meets only a few days every four years to select a presidential candidate, settle disputes, and write a party platform. During the rest of the time, the direction of the party is turned over to the national committee and its chairperson.

The National Committee
The national committee is composed of representatives from each state and the territories (in the Democratic party, added representation is given to the larger states), who are commonly selected by state delegations to the national convention. The committee meets only rarely, mainly to assist in the presidential campaign and to arrange for the next national convention.

The National Committee Chairperson
Most of the committee's responsibilities are assumed by the committee leader and staff. Usually chosen by the party's presidential candidate after the convention, the chairperson's main functions are public relations, administration, and fund raising for the presidential campaign. Otherwise, his or her powers may be marginal.

The Congressional Campaign Committees
Composed of members of the House and the Senate, these committees solicit speakers and money for candidates who face serious opposition. In both parties, friction prevails frequently between the committees and the national committee.

on the election of the presidential candidate and has not intruded into state and local campaigns. It has not chosen the party's candidates for Congress or for state political offices. With virtually no exceptions, one observer has noted, the state and local party organizations "pick their own officers, nominate their own candidates, take their own stands on issues, raise and spend their own funds."[20]

This decentralization has been criticized not only for confusing voters but also for making it difficult for either party to maintain unity on the issues. The Democrats and Republicans have been unable to forge their diverse state and local organizations into unified party machines capable of implementing policies desired by voters. Voters have had no assurances that the party they support would carry out even the vague policies they were promised. Hence, their incentive to remain loyal to either party has often been low.

Consider, for example, the situation in Congress. Because members of Congress have tended to draw most of their campaign support from local organizations or special-interest groups, they often have succeeded in building their own bases of power independent of the congressional party leadership. They have realized that the leadership can do little to help or hurt their chances for reelection. As one member of Congress boasted, "They can't do a thing to me as long as they don't have any patronage to dish out. They don't give me any campaign money so they can't take that away."[21] Thus, a prevailing feature of

Congress has been that members often ignore pleas for party unity when voting on issues. In the Senate during 1978, for instance, the average Democrat voted with his party only 66 percent of the time, while the average Republican stuck with his party only 59 percent of the time.[22]

Concern about disunity, in fact, prompted the Democratic party to hold midterm conventions in 1974 and 1978. The 1974 convention, held in Kansas City, marked the first time in American history that a major party tried to incorporate its disparate elements under a binding national charter. In three days of seminars and debates, the delegates fashioned a formal party constitution and proposed a legislative agenda to be taken up by the Democrats in Congress. Although neither convention brought an end to party squabbling, important new rules were established giving the national party the power to impose stricter criteria on the state parties in their methods of selecting delegates to the presidential nominating conventions (see the discussion on nominations).

Not all party reformers, however, wish to see the parties become more centralized. Some contend that party decentralization actually encourages citizen participation in party affairs. Because many important party decisions, including the choosing of candidates for local offices, are made at the local and state levels, citizens remain relatively close to the real power centers of their party. If all major decisions were centralized at the national level, most citizens would find it more difficult to have an impact on party policy.

A Potpourri of Ideology

In addition to sharing a tradition of disunity, the Democratic and Republican parties have tended to be ideologically mixed. Both parties have continued to elect members to office who span the spectrum of liberal and conservative philosophy. In fact, there are perhaps as many ideological differences *within* each party as there are between them. The Democratic party, for instance, attracts not only "liberals" like Edward Kennedy and George McGovern, but also "conservatives" such as Herman Talmadge and Russell Long. Similarly, the Republican party embraces not only "conservatives" like Ronald Reagan and Barry Goldwater, but also moderate "liberals" such as Jacob Javits and Charles Percy. Obviously, the decentralized tradition of the two parties has a great deal to do with this ideological potpourri. As long as state and local party organizations maintain some autonomy, politicians will tend to reflect the unique values and interests of their own local power bases.

What then holds the members of the Democratic and Republican parties together? Aside from sharing a common party tradition, most members of a party also share some common views. Although Edward Kennedy and Jimmy Carter, for example, have hardly seen eye to eye on policies like national health insurance and tax reform, both have subscribed in principle to a number of basic concepts, such as an active governmental role in the economy, that distinguish them from most Republicans. Shared views and a mutual desire to see the party come out on top in elections have helped to hold members of a party together despite policy differences.

Just the same, the tensions have sometimes reached the breaking point, as in 1968 when George Wallace bolted from the Democratic party to form his own American Independent party. Similar defections occurred in 1948 when Henry A. Wallace left the Democratic party to run for president on the Progressive party platform, and when in the same year southern Democrats stormed out of the Democratic national convention over the civil rights issue to support Strom Thurmond as their "States' Rights" candidate for president. (Thurmond later switched to the Republican party.) Even the generally less turbulent Republican party has suffered major defections, as in 1912 when the followers of former President Theodore Roosevelt bolted to support his Progressive party candidacy for another White House term.

A Blurring of Differences

A third characteristic of the two major parties—and one subject to many criticisms—is that they do not seem very different from each other. George Wallace used to complain in his 1968 presidential campaign that "there's not a dime's worth of difference" between Democrats and Republicans. Similarly, James Bryce once charged that "the two major parties are like two bottles, identical in size, shape, color, bearing different labels, but both empty."[23]

These are, of course, exaggerations. As we have seen, the two parties do express somewhat different viewpoints and draw support from different social groups. In fact, a person's perceptions of the differences will likely depend on his or her political views. A Marxist writer, for example, will perhaps perceive less of a significant difference between the two parties than a Republican politician. Still, when compared with the range of political parties in other countries, where the spectrum may run from the extreme left to the extreme right, the Democratic and Republican parties do seem similar and moderate. Although they may differ, for example, over how much government should regulate business, neither party promotes the nationalization of industry. And, although they may differ over the merits of governmental economic assistance, few Democrats or Republicans advocate the abolition of social security or the graduated income tax. In fact, Democratic and Republican politicians tend to espouse many of the same values: free public education, a strong military defense, law and order, governmental subsidies for key industries, and so forth.

This similarity and moderation stems not only from their mutual support of certain traditions (like capitalism), but also from the pressures of two-party competition. With only the Democratic and Republican parties having a likely chance to gain control of government (for reasons we will discuss shortly), each party must attract a wide spectrum of the population to win an electoral majority. Each must offer programs and candidates having as broad-based an appeal as possible. As a result, the two parties tend to sound and look alike. "In some important respects," one scholar concludes, "there is and can be no real difference between the Democrats and Republicans, because the unwritten laws of American politics demand that the parties overlap substantially in principle, policy, character, appeal, and purpose—or cease to be parties with any hope of winning a national election."[24]

Moreover, because both parties must draw support from a wide spectrum of the population, they cannot afford to be ideologically extreme. A party that proposes drastic changes in current policies or that caters only to a small segment of society risks alienating more voters than it attracts. The dramatic failures of both George McGovern in 1972 and Barry Goldwater in 1964 suggest that strong policy statements can be a handicap in presidential elections.

The similarity between the parties carries interesting implications for citizen action. If the two major parties fail to offer clear policy alternatives, then access to party decision making (when one can get it) may not seem very meaningful. After all, if the pressures of two-party competition demand a bland policy approach, efforts to use the parties as channels for political action may accomplish little in the way of significant policy reform. As long as both parties try to attract as many people as possible—without simultaneously alienating their own partisan loyalists—they will remain low-keyed and equivocal. Both parties (and their candidates) will continue to indulge in what some cynically describe as "verbal exercises in calculated ambiguity."

One-Party Dominance

An additional feature of the American party system has been the tendency of each major party to eclipse the other in certain regions and for certain historical periods. Although this feature may not contribute to citizen confusion, it contradicts the notion that the two parties have been closely competitive. In most local congressional districts, for example, one of the two parties has been able to maintain the upper hand for considerable periods of time. This means that, in cities like Berkeley and Boston, Democratic candidates have tended to be swept into Congress without stiff opposition from Republican candidates. In fact, it has been estimated that about 75 percent of all congressional districts have generally been safe for one party or the other; the changes in party strength that have occurred in Congress have resulted mainly from the defeat of incumbents in the other 25 percent of the districts where the two parties have been closely competitive.[25]

Such one-party dominance has also been seen in statewide elections for senator and governor, especially in the South and parts of the Midwest. As Figure 6-1 indicates, although in most states the Democrats and Republicans have been closely competitive, in some states (like Louisiana, Alabama, North Dakota, and Kansas), one of the two parties has managed to win a vast majority of elections at the state and local levels.

There has been evidence, however, of a trend away from one-party control of statewide and congressional elections, especially as traditional ties between parties and voters have loosened. For example, during the past two decades, Republicans have made significant inroads into the South. In the 96th Congress (1979–1981), five of the twenty-two southern senators were Republicans, as were more than one-fourth of the southern representatives in the House. Still, the Democratic party tradition in the South has been so strong historically that it is likely to prevent the two parties from becoming fully competitive there for some time to come.

Moreover, when we look back in history, we find few times when the Democratic and Republican parties have been evenly matched at the national level with control of the federal government alternating frequently between them. Instead, the usual pattern has been for one of the two parties to dominate the White House and Congress for long stretches of time. "Our political solar system," one writer reflects, "has been characterized not by two equally competing suns, but by a sun and a moon. It is within the majority party that the issues of any particular period are fought out; while the minority party shines in reflected radiance of the heat thus generated."[26] As we can see in Table 6-5, since 1800 there have been at least three periods in American history when either the Democrats or the Republicans virtually "owned" the White House.

The first period, from 1800 to 1860, was dominated by the Democrats. During this entire sixty-year period, the opposition Whig party (which had replaced the Federalists) managed to win only two contests for

Figure 6-1. State Party Systems

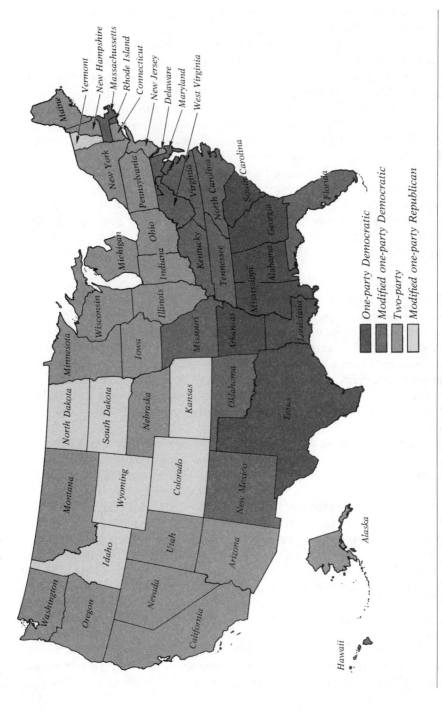

One-party Democratic

Modified one-party Democratic

Two-party

Modified one-party Republican

Source: Austin Ranney, "Parties in State Politics," p. 62 in Herbert Jacob and Kenneth Vines, *Politics in the American States*, 3rd ed. (Boston: Little, Brown, 1976).

Table 6-5. Party Domination of the White House

DEMOCRATIC PERIOD

	Federalist, Whig	Jeffersonian-Republican Democrat
1800		Jefferson
1804		Jefferson
1808		Madison
1812		Madison
1816		Monroe
1820		Monroe
1824		J. Q. Adams
1828		Jackson
1832		Jackson
1836		Van Buren
1840	Harrison-Tyler	
1844		Polk
1848	Taylor-Fillmore	
1852		Pierce
1856		Buchanan

REPUBLICAN PERIOD

	Republican	Democrat
1860	Lincoln	
1864	Lincoln-Johnson	
1868	Grant	
1872	Grant	
1876	Hayes	
1880	Garfield-Arthur	
1884		Cleveland
1888	Harrison	
1892		Cleveland
1896	McKinley	
1900	McKinley-T. Roosevelt	
1904	T. Roosevelt	
1908	Taft	
1912		Wilson
1916		Wilson
1920	Harding-Coolidge	
1924	Coolidge	
1928	Hoover	

DEMOCRATIC PERIOD

	Republican	Democrat
1932		F. Roosevelt
1936		F. Roosevelt
1940		F. Roosevelt
1944		F. Roosevelt-Truman
1948		Truman
1952	Eisenhower	
1956	Eisenhower	
1960		Kennedy-Johnson
1964		Johnson
1968	Nixon	
1972	Nixon-Ford	
1976		Carter

president, electing William Henry Harrison in 1840 and Zachary Taylor in 1848. All of the other thirteen presidential contests were won by Democrats.

The second period, from 1860 to 1932, largely belonged to the Republicans. During this long stretch, only two Democrats were elected president, each for two terms: Grover Cleveland (1884 and 1892) and Woodrow Wilson (1912 and 1916). The Republicans won all of the other fourteen presidential elections and were able to dominate Congress most of the time as well. One reason given for the rise to prominence of the Republican party (formed in 1854 by Whigs, antislavery Democrats, and third parties) was that, by the end of the Civil War, the Democrats had to bear the burden of being the party of the defeated South; the Republicans, on the other hand, were lauded as the party of Lincoln, the party that had "preserved the union." This, together with other factors, permitted the Republicans to enjoy for many decades the same mass support previously given the Democrats.

But during the third great period, beginning in 1932, the Democrats returned to prominence. They gained control of the White House that year with the election of Franklin Roosevelt, and have since yielded it to the Republicans for only eight years under Dwight Eisenhower (1952 to 1960) and eight more under Richard Nixon and Gerald Ford (1968 to 1976). And, except for the years 1946–1948 and 1952–1954, the Democrats have also held a majority of seats in Congress. Apparently, just as the Civil War dealt a severe blow to the Democrats, the stock market crash in 1929 and the Great Depression undermined the Republicans. By the mid-1930s, the Democratic party had largely shed its image as the party of the Confederate South and was able to attract widespread support as the party of reform under Franklin Roosevelt.

In 1968, the Republicans appeared to have a strong chance of bouncing back. They reclaimed the White House that year with the election of Richard Nixon as president, and subsequently saw him win a landslide victory over George McGovern in 1972, a victory that prompted some observers to herald the "bankruptcy" of the Democratic party. Then, in 1974, Nixon resigned the presidency. Although Gerald Ford kept the White House briefly in Republican hands, the Watergate burglary and its aftermath shattered Republican hopes of renewed glory.

In 1976, the Democrats took possession of the White House again with the election of Jimmy Carter and continued to dominate both houses of Congress and the state capitals. Following the 1978 congressional elections, the Democrats held a solid majority of seats in the Senate (59 to 41), strongly outnumbered Republicans in the House of Representatives (276 to 143), and controlled most of the statehouses (32 to 18). On top of that, recent Harris polls have indicated the lowest public support for the Republican party in more than thirty years of measurement. While 38 percent of those surveyed in 1979, for example, classified themselves as Democrats, only 24 percent said they were Republicans.

Yet, despite this long period of dominance, the Democratic party has had little to cheer about. Not only was the race between Ford and Carter in 1976 extremely close, but the party has seen its own ranks decline. It has had to face the fact that many Democrats are only weakly affiliated with the party, ready to desert it for the first attractive Republican candidate who shows his or her face. The largest actual gain has been registered among independents, who now account for about one-third of the electorate. This increase in the number of independents, coupled with a growing incidence of crossover voting, has revealed a growing disenchantment with both major parties, making their futures uncertain.

Third-Party Alternatives

Some Americans who have become fed up with the similar and moderate traits of the Democratic and Republican parties have put their faith in third parties. They have given their support to and worked within alternative parties that favor policies neither of the two major parties has been willing to support. In doing so, however, they have had to accept the enormous difficulties third parties have faced in trying to carry out their programs. For most of American history, only two parties at any given time have had sufficient strength to compete for the control of national government with any chance of success.

Variety of Third Parties

Third parties have, of course, played an active role throughout the nation's history. Since the Constitution permits any native-born American over thirty-five years of age to become president, elections in this country have brought out an abundance of eager competitors for the job. In 1976, voters had an opportunity to vote for a score of presidential aspirants other than Jimmy Carter and Gerald Ford. Among the most prominent of these candidates were Eugene McCarthy (Independent); Lester Maddox (American Independent party); Roger MacBride (Libertarian party); Gus Hall (Communist party); Peter Camejo (Socialist Workers party); and Benjamin Buber (Prohibition party). None of these candidates, however, came close to receiving the 13.5 percent captured by

Wallace claimed there was "not a dime's worth of difference" between the two major parties and in 1968 ran for president as a third-party candidate.

George Wallace in 1968. Combined, they garnered only 1.6 million votes of the more than 80 million cast in 1976, a total of about 2 percent.

In the past, there have been many kinds of third parties, each with a different reason for existence. Some, like the American Communist party, have been highly doctrinaire, demanding the overhaul of the entire economic and political system. Others, like the Progressives in 1912 and the States' Rights party in 1948, have been basically "splinter parties," that broke off in protest from the Democratic or Republican party. Still others, like the Prohibitionists and the Vegetarians, have been primarily "educational parties," using the electoral process to gain publicity for their ideas. Other third parties have included: the Anti-Masons in the 1830s, who contested only one presidential election and then disappeared; the Know-Nothings in the 1850s, an anti-Catholic, anti-Irish Native American party, so secretive its members pretended to have heard nothing about it (hence the name); and the Mugwumps, Republicans who bolted from their party in 1884 in protest against the presidential nomination of James C. Blaine and who were once jokingly described: "I am a mugwump . . . my mug is on one side of the fence and my wump is on the other."

Some third parties even have attained sufficient strength to affect the outcome of a presidential election or to elect members to Congress. One of the most successful, although short-lived, parties was the Populists, a coalition of agricultural and labor interests that gained prominence in the 1890s. Although it failed to attract a national following, it was able in 1894 to win the election of six senators and seven representatives to Congress. In this century, the most impressive third-party showing was by Teddy Roosevelt's "Bull Moose" Progressive party, a group of liberal Republicans who left the party in 1912. The Progressives captured 27 percent of the popular vote that year—more than the Republican incumbent William H. Taft—and thus brought victory to the Democratic candidate Woodrow Wilson.

Third parties have also enjoyed some success in state and local politics. The Socialist party, for example, has elected mayors in Bridgeport and Hartford, Connecticut, and in Milwaukee, Wisconsin. In Minnesota during the 1920s and 1930s, the Farmer-Labor party—not the Democratic party—provided the main opposition to the Republican party in most state and congressional elections; in the 1940s, the Farmer-Labor party even won the governorship. Similarly, in New York State, the Conservative party in 1970 sent James Buckley to the U.S. Senate, where he served for one six-year term.

Reasons for Failure

The main pattern, however, has been for third parties in both state and national elections to suffer a common fate of few victories at the polls. No third party has ever captured the presidency, and only a few have occupied more than a handful of seats in Congress. As Table 6-6 shows, only five third parties since 1832 have collected more than 10 percent of the popular vote in a presidential election.

In a sense, the absence of powerful third parties seems rather surprising in view of the many regional, economic, and social differences in this country. We might expect many parties to flourish in Congress and in the state legislatures, each representing a different segment of our society. Yet, the United States is one of the few democracies in the world where strong third parties have not been able to thrive. Norway, Italy, West Germany, and Switzerland, for example, have all had several competitive parties.

Although political scientists have been unable to agree on any overall explanation for the persistence of only two major parties in this country, several hypotheses have been offered. Easily the most popular is that the system of electing candidates reinforces two-party competition.[27] In this country, the *single-member district system* is used in all federal elections, meaning that only one representative may be elected from a congressional district regardless of how many candidates are

Table 6-6. Third-Party History

Year	Party	Percent Popular Vote
1832	Anti-Masonic	8.0
1844	Liberty	2.3
1848	Free Soil	10.1
1852	Free Soil	4.9
1860	Constitutional-Union	12.6
1880	Greenback	3.4
1884	Greenback	1.7
1888	Prohibition	2.2
1892	Populist	8.5
1904	Socialist	3.0
	Prohibition	1.9
1908	Socialist	2.8
	Prohibition	1.7
1912	Progressive	27.4
	Socialist	6.0
1916	Socialist	3.2
1920	Socialist	3.4
1924	Progressive	16.6
1932	Socialist	2.2
1936	Union	2.0
1948	States' Rights	2.4
	Progressive	2.4
1968	American Independent	13.5
1972	American	1.4
1976	American Independent	.2

running: it is simply a case of winner-take-all. (The same applies to the presidential election, where the candidate who receives the most popular votes in a state receives all its electoral votes.) This means that even if a third party wins 20 or 30 percent of the votes all over the country, it may still not be rewarded with a single seat in Congress.

In such countries as West Germany, Norway, and Sweden, a different system of *proportional representation* is used. Under this system, a number of candidates can be elected from each district and parties are assigned seats in the legislature in proportion to their percentages of the popular vote. This means that parties failing to win a majority of votes can still be represented in the legislature: their campaign efforts are not entirely wasted.

Consider, then, what might happen if the United States converted to a system of proportional representation. A party like the American Independent, winning 20 percent of the popular vote, might control 20 percent of the seats in Congress. In 1936, New York City actually approved such a system, deciding it would be more responsive to the true divisions of opinion among the electorate. As a result, the voters in 1945 elected to the city council not only fourteen Democrats and three Republicans but also two American Labor party candidates, two Liberals, and two Communists. But the presence of the two Communists met such stiff opposition that in 1947 the city reinstated the tradition of one member per district. Thus, during the next election in 1949, only Democratic and Republican candidates won seats on the city council.[28]

Nevertheless, the election of only one member per district does not fully explain Democratic and Republican party supremacy. It does not explain why third parties have been unable to gain enough support to displace either of these two parties. Another popular hypothesis is that the United States has simply had a historical tradition of two-party competition, first inherited from the split between the Whigs and Tories in England and then reinforced by the division between the Federalists and Anti-Federalists over ratification of the Constitution. The pattern of two dominant, competitive parties became entrenched at this early stage and has been perpetuated ever since.

Moreover, the traditional allegiances of voters to the two dominant parties have been difficult for third parties to break. After more than a century of Democratic and Republican supremacy, most voters have become used to supporting one of these two parties. Because partisan loyalties tend to pass from generation to generation, the Democratic and Republican parties have enjoyed a tremendous historical and psychological advantage over smaller and more sporadic third parties.

It is also possible that many third parties are too ideologically extreme or specialized to gain widespread support. In contrast to France and Italy, where both socialist and communist parties flourish, this country has never given much support to parties outside the mainstream of capitalist ideology. Beyond that, the programs of many third parties are too narrow and specialized to appeal to a broad spectrum of voters. Not enough people feel strongly about single issues, such as prohibition or vegetarianism, to cast their votes for special-interest third parties, especially when the tradition of electing only one member per district may discourage them from "wasting" their votes. When people do feel strongly about single issues, they are more likely to pursue these issues through interest groups, which unlike parties, do not have to compromise across a broad political spectrum to achieve their goals (see Chapter 7).

Third parties also face tremendous financial obstacles, especially in presidential elections. As we will see later, the new Federal Election Campaign Act provides public funds for Democratic and Republican presidential candidates in the general election. Third-party candidates, however, are eligible for such support only if their party obtained 5 percent of the total vote cast in the preceding election—a high percentage for most third parties. Thus, without funds, third-party hopefuls cannot gain publicity; and without publicity, they cannot hope to win enough support to carry out a credible campaign.

Finally, the failure of third parties often results from the ability of the Democrats and Republicans to steal their thunder. A third party sometimes proposes a promising idea—such as the direct election of senators, the progressive income tax, or the regulation of banks—only to have the two major parties appropriate the idea when it becomes popular. The unique appeal of the third party is thus undercut, and it loses whatever support it had started to gain.

Value of Third Parties

So what contributions do third parties make to the political system? Despite their inability to gain mass public support or play a major role in policy making, these parties do provide some important services.

In the first place, third parties often express the views and demands of those who are disgusted with the Democratic and Republican parties. Although third parties normally are unable to translate these views and demands into concrete policies, they do provide a forum for alternative viewpoints. Without third parties, in other words, many more persons might abstain from voicing their political concerns.

In addition, third parties sometimes draw public attention to controversial issues ignored by the two major parties. Whether it is because third-party candidates tend to be more ideological or because they see little hope of gaining control of government anyway, they have tended to be more outspoken on the issues. Third-party candidates in the past, for example, called for the primary election, old-age pensions, universal and compulsory education, women's suffrage, and the initiative and referendum well in advance of their acceptance by Democratic and Republican candidates.

But, besides drawing attention to controversial issues, third parties sometimes directly affect the programs of the two major parties. By threatening to steal votes away from the Democrats and Republicans with a popular campaign issue—as George Wallace attempted with the "law and order" issue in 1968—third parties sometimes compel the other two parties to alter their long-term policy orientations and to adopt ideas endorsed by third-party candidates. This occurred, for example, in the 1890s when the Democratic party absorbed the Populists and in 1924 when the Democratic party adopted many of the Progressive programs of Robert La Follette. "The evidence seems to suggest," one scholar has concluded, "that the rather large-scale, episodic, nonrecurring minor-party movements must be regarded . . . as integral elements of the so-called two-party system. They spring from the center of the political melee, and in turn affect the nature of the major parties and the relationship between them as they cumbersomely make their way from election to election."[29]

Parties and the Road to Nomination

As stated earlier, one of the most important tasks of political parties has been to nominate candidates for public office and to provide money and other means of support for their campaigns. In recent years, however, control by party officials over the selection and support of nominees has been on the decline. As a result of the growing number of primary elections, campaign financing laws, and other reforms, not to mention the decline of party identification among the voters, state and national party organizations have become less and less important in the electoral process. With growing frequency, candidates like Jimmy Carter have emerged who have not been tied to any regular party organizations.

Let us consider, therefore, some of the major features of the nomination process and the changes that have occurred. In addition to the spread of primary elections and the role of presidential nominating conventions, we might take a look at the implications of recent reforms in campaign financing and the continuing controversy surrounding the role and impact of the electoral college.

The Direct Primary

The method of selecting candidates for public office has gone through a long evolution, with a trend toward expanding citizen participation at the expense of party professionals. During the early 1800s, candidates were usually chosen in legislative *caucuses*, or closed meetings of party leaders. Presidential candidates, for example, were selected in caucuses attended by influential party members of the Senate and the House of

Representatives. The problem with the caucus system, however, was that it failed to represent all party elements and excluded the participation of those at the grass-roots level. It even appeared to violate the separation of powers principle by having legislators pick candidates for executive offices.

By the 1830s, a more representative method of selecting candidates—the *convention* system—began to be adopted by the parties. Delegates chosen by local party members would gather at state or national conventions (as they still do today) to nominate slates of candidates. But while it was an improvement over the caucus method, the convention system still tended to exclude most rank-and-file members from the nomination process. Generally, only the most active of the party faithful turned out to select convention delegates, while the conventions themselves were frequently dominated by party bosses. Thus, an alternative method of choosing nominees that would be even more responsive to the party rank and file was sought. The result was the *direct primary* election.

The direct primary came into being in the early 1900s as part of the Progressive movement, which also brought about the popular election of senators and the use of the initiative process (see Chapter 15). In contrast to the convention system, in which delegates pick the party's candidates, the primary election allows the voters to select the candidates themselves. Most states today use the *closed primary*, where voters may cast ballots only for the candidates of their own party. Only a few states maintain an *open primary*, where citizens are free to vote for the candidates of either party.

In several respects, the direct primary has caused problems for the parties. Although it allows more rank-and-file participation in the nomination process, usually fewer than 30 percent of the eligible voters turn out. And those who do are generally not representative of the party membership as a whole. Voters in primary elections tend to be more well-to-do, better educated, and more ideological than those who participate in general elections. This sometimes favors candidates with sharp ideological views who are difficult to elect in November. Some observers noted, for instance, that George McGovern's primary victories in 1972 helped him capture the Democratic presidential nomination even though he did not enjoy widespread support among the electorate. Primaries also can lead to divisiveness within a party. Following a bitter primary fight, supporters of the losing candidate may refuse to support the primary victor in the general election. In 1976, for example, some of Ronald Reagan's supporters refused to back Gerald Ford's presidential bid in the wake of the Republican primaries. And, finally, primaries have tended to erode party unity. Candidates do not need to be loyal to the party to get on the primary ballot: they usually need only to file a petition or declaration of candidacy. This means that candidates with a great deal of money or name-recognition may succeed in winning the party's nomination without much party support and with little obligation to follow the "party line" once elected.

In recent years, more and more states have adopted the primary as a means of choosing delegates to the national presidential conventions. In 1968, fewer than half of the delegates to the Democratic and Republican national conventions were chosen in primaries. Most of the states continued to select delegates in state caucuses or conventions. As a result, Hubert Humphrey was able to garner enough delegates to win the Democratic presidential nomination even though he did not enter a single primary.

But in 1976, more than three-fourths of the delegates, from thirty states, were picked in primary elections scattered from February until June. With little doubt, this spurt in the number of primaries greatly affected the nomination contests in both the Democratic and Republican parties. Because most of the delegates were chosen in primary elections, none of the major candidates could hope to win the nomination through state party conventions alone. Ronald Reagan, for instance, took advantage of the primaries to mount a strong challenge to incumbent President Gerald Ford. Faced with possible defeat by the former movie star and California Republican governor, Ford was forced to enter the primaries in order to win the Republican party nomination.

Even more significant, Jimmy Carter's victories in the early primaries transformed him from a relative unknown into a successful contender for the Democratic party nomination. By entering most of the primaries, he was able to attract national attention and demonstrate his popularity with the voters. In 1976, the Democratic party had scrapped "winner-take-all" primaries, in which candidates with the most votes would win all of a state's convention delegates, and encouraged instead a system of proportional representation. This meant that although Carter did not win all of the primaries he entered, he collected enough delegates to impress party leaders that he could not be stopped and that he offered the party's best chance of defeating the Republican candidate (Ford) in November. Ironically, with another increase in the number of primaries in 1980, Carter faced challenges from prominent politicians in his own party who sought to wrest the party's nomination from him.

The National Conventions

The climax of the nomination process, of course, is the national convention in July or August. As most of us learn from watching the proceedings on television, not until after the delegates have voted in the carnival atmosphere of the national convention will a party's presidential nominee be officially chosen. It is here that the supporters of each candidate will make their final attempts to persuade wavering delegates that their candidate is the one most likely to capture the White House.

The number of convention delegates may range anywhere from 1,200 to more than 3,000, depending on the party and the year. Both parties apportion delegates on the basis of population and party strength within each state. In recent years, both major parties have encouraged greater grass-roots participation in the presidential nomination process. In the Democratic party, especially, there have been sustained efforts to wrest control of the selection of delegates from local party bosses meeting in smoke-filled back rooms and to hand it over to a broader segment of the voting population. Following the turmoil at the 1968 Democratic Convention in Chicago, a reform-minded commission, headed by Rep. Don Fraser and Sen. George McGovern, set new guidelines for nominating candidates. One was to require state party organizations to select delegates the same year as the convention and to encourage the participation of more Democratic voters in the selection

The Republican National Convention, 1976.

process. Another was to increase the number of women, minorities, and young people in state delegations "in reasonable relationship to their presence in the population of the state." As a result of these guidelines, the 1972 Democratic Convention included more women, young people, blacks, and Chicanos and fewer party regulars than ever before. However, the proportion of these groups dipped in 1976 as a result of rule changes adopted at the 1974 midterm convention. New rules for the 1980 Democratic Convention partly reinstated the quota system by requiring state delegations to be equally divided between men and women.

In addition to selecting a presidential nominee, the convention also selects a vice-presidential candidate and adopts a party platform. In the past, platforms tended to be vague and largely indistinguishable from one party to the other. The platforms would be hammered out by delegates meeting in back rooms, carefully phrasing the planks to attract as many voters as possible without alienating regular supporters. But in recent years, the platforms of the two parties have tended to reflect different views on many controversial issues. On matters ranging from abortion to gay rights, party platforms have stressed what the more issue-oriented groups within each party wish to see translated into policy. This change has come about in large part because of the increased participation of women, young people, and minority groups. Thus, the 1976 Democratic platform demanded greater use of the government's powers to relieve poverty and achieve equal rights, while the Republican platform stressed the need for reduced federal spending and less government involvement in the economy. In the words of one observer, a party's platform planks have begun to provide "reasonably meaningful indications of the party's intentions in the years ahead."[30]

The Electoral College

In addition to the increased number of primaries, another potential party-weakening measure has frequently been discussed: the abolition of the *electoral college*. In a message to Congress in 1977, President Carter recommended that Congress draft a constitutional amendment providing for the direct popular election of the president and the vice-president. His recommendation, although coolly received in Congress, was favored by more than a five-to-one margin among American voters, according to opinion polls.[31] If passed, such an amendment would reduce the role of state parties by making state boundaries largely irrelevant to election outcomes. Candidates would become even freer to wage campaigns independent of state party organizations.

Although most people believe that a president is elected directly by the voters in November, such is not the case. Rather than choosing between the candidates, voters in each state are actually casting their ballots for rival slates of presidential electors (usually loyal party workers) selected by state party organizations. Not until the electors vote in December is a president officially chosen.

As we may recall from Chapter 3, direct election of the president was opposed by most of the Founding Fathers, who believed the people were not competent to make informed decisions. "It would be as rational to refer the choice of a proper character for Chief Magistrate to the people," George Mason declared, "as it would be to refer a trial of colors to a blind man." As a result, during the early part of American history state legislatures picked the electors, who, in turn, voted for the President; ordinary citizens had no direct say over who would be the chief executive. Only with the passage of time have the state legislatures allowed citizens to vote directly for members of the electoral college, who now reflect the voters' preferences. (In most states voters are unaware that they are voting for electors because their names do not appear on the ballot.) Although highly unlikely, state legislatures could legally change the rules again and discontinue popular election of electors.

Over the years, the electoral college has played a significant role in presidential selection, focusing the attention of candidates on the most populous states. The Constitution grants each state as many electoral votes as it has senators and representatives, with the most populous states being given the most representatives. Since all of a state's electoral votes go to the candidate who captures the most popular votes (a custom, not a constitutional requirement), it is to the candidate's benefit to win the largest states.

The fear, of course, is that the electoral outcome could frustrate the popular will. A candidate who wins enough large states by even narrow margins could beat an opponent with more popular votes. Indeed, in three elections (1824, 1876 and 1888), the popular-vote winner failed to obtain an electoral-vote majority and lost the presidency. Although there has been no such upset in this century, a small shift in the popular vote in 1976 could have given the election to Ford instead of Carter. A change of only 9,000 votes in Ohio and Hawaii would have given Ford more electoral votes than Carter, even though Carter beat Ford by 1.7 million votes nationwide. Moreover, in the event no candidate wins a majority in the electoral college (perhaps as the result of a strong showing by a third-party candidate), the election would be thrown into the House of Representatives. The House members would choose from among the top three candidates, with each state delegation having a single vote. The possibility would then exist that a candidate with less popular support could be named president.

Yet, despite these drawbacks, the abolition of the electoral college has been vigorously opposed by many party officials. In their view, such an action would deprive them of their ability to swing a state and all its electoral votes to one candidate or another. They also insist that the change could further weaken the two major parties by encouraging the growth of third parties. Most proposals for the direct popular election of the president provide that the winning candidate must receive more than 40 percent of the popular vote, or a runoff election has to be held. This means that a third-party candidate could amass enough popular votes to bargain for favors and affect the electoral outcome—a prospect, of course, that many third parties would welcome.

The Campaign and Its Funding

Finally, a traditional role of political parties has been to provide money and other means of support for candidates. In the 1970s, however, parties became less important in this role as campaign finance reform swept through Congress. In 1974 and 1976, Congress passed landmark legislation radically overhauling the traditional ways of funding federal election campaigns. For the first time in history, both major presidential candidates in 1976 financed their general-election campaigns exclusively with federal money. Jimmy Carter and Gerald Ford each spent approximately $22 million in federal funds in their fall campaigns for the White House, for a combined total of $44 million—about half the amount spent in the 1972 presidential campaigns. However, before we look at the specifics of this legislation, we should consider some of the problems of campaign financing that prompted the drive toward reform.

For one thing, campaigns for national political office have become extraordinarily expensive. In most states, candidates may spend as much as $200,000 to run for the U.S. House of Representatives. To run for the U.S. Senate, candidates may dole out close to $2 million, especially in large states like New York and California. In fact, in 1978, Senator Jesse Helms of North Carolina raised a record $6 million to finance his reelection campaign.

In addition to inflation and the toilsome length of campaigns, television and other media expenses have contributed greatly to the escalation in campaign costs. This escalation can be seen both in the soaring costs of television and radio time (a half-hour of prime time on network television may cost more than $200,000) and in the practice of employ-

"I bet if I had a million dollars I could hire an image-maker and make you vote for me."

ing professional advertising firms (see Chapter 8). Many candidates believe that office seekers who cannot afford such media expenses (and this applies particularly to most third-party hopefuls) remain at a considerable disadvantage.

Although laws have been enacted over the years that place a ceiling on campaign expenditures, they have been either ignored or repealed. The Corrupt Practices Act of 1925, for example, was intended to limit spending by congressional candidates to three cents per eligible voter, with a maximum expenditure of $5,000 by candidates for the House and $25,000 by candidates for the Senate. But this legal limit was never enforced. Because the limit applied only to expenditures made with the "knowledge and consent" of the candidate, funds simply could be channeled through campaign committees that were not required to file reports.

A major concern of reformers has been that the large sums of money required to meet the exorbitant costs of campaigns have increased the influence of a relatively few contributors or "fat cats," to the detriment of average citizens. In 1972, for example, Richard Nixon's reelection campaign reaped more than $7 million from just twenty-seven individuals, nine of whom each contributed $250,000 or more. W. Clement Stone, a Chicago insurance baron, alone shelled out $2 million to the Nixon campaign. The Hatch Act of 1940 was supposed to prohibit any person from contributing more than $5,000 to a candidate for federal office, but loopholes rendered it largely ineffective. A person who wished to part with more than $5,000 could simply contribute to a variety of separate party committees or make the contributions in the names of relatives. And in the absence of any serious intention to enforce the law, even blatant violations went unpunished. As a result, when compared with $250,000 donations, $5 or $10 contributions from ordinary citizens have tended to be virtually meaningless: these citizens simply have been priced out of the political system. As each election has ended, "fat cat" contributors have enjoyed an access to legislators that other citizens simply cannot match.

Furthermore, the pumping of large sums of money into campaigns has often been associated with corruption. In 1972, a number of corporations, including American Airlines and Gulf Oil, admitted making illegal contributions running into hundreds of thousands of dollars to Nixon's reelection campaign, often in response to pressures from the White House itself. Some of these contributions were "laundered" through foreign subsidies and Swiss banks and turned up in the cash accounts of Watergate burglars and conspirators. As former New York Mayor John Lindsay remarked, "The contributions of Vesco, ITT, milk producers, airlines and others financed this kind of thing, whether they knew it or not. And most of them did know that, in return, they were buying some kind of political protection—an air-route franchise, immunity from SEC or antitrust protection, or license to engage in political pot-boiling in some Latin American country. Watergate was made possible by the use of political money raised under the umbrella of an election campaign—just as the bugging, house-breaking and other crimes occurred under the umbrella of national security."[32]

Moreover, many reformers have realized that without a way to open the books on all contributions to candidates, voters cannot know how much candidates are indebted to special interests. Voters have no way of finding out how money is being spent, or how much money candidates have received from particular groups.

Consequently, legislation passed by Congress in recent years has been extremely significant. In 1971, for instance, Congress enacted the Federal Election Campaign Act, the first noteworthy campaign reform bill since the Corrupt Practices Act of 1925. Among its provisions, the new law required candidates for federal office to file detailed reports on all donations and expenditures exceeding $100. It also set limits on the amounts candidates could spend on media advertising (although these limits were later removed by new legislation and Supreme Court rulings).

By ironic coincidence, in the same year the new Federal Election Campaign Act became law, the Watergate scandal became public. In fact, the revelations of the scandal may have been aided by the law's disclosure provisions. For example, the General Accounting Office issued a series of reports citing apparent violations of the 1971 Act by the Committee for the Reelection of the President (CREEP). These reports led to the indictment of the committee by the Justice Department on eight separate counts of campaign spending violation. Federal investigators charged that the Nixon Reelection Committee had raised $10 million more than it reported, that top Nixon hands had skimmed campaign money for their personal use, and that campaign funds had been converted into Watergate "hush money."

Thus, spawned by Watergate and a desire to limit the influence of big-money contributors, pressures increased on Congress to pass even more comprehensive reform legislation. Finally, in 1974, Congress enacted the most far-reaching campaign finance legislation in American history, amending the 1971 Federal Election Campaign Act. The new legislation, making its initial impact on the 1976 presidential election, set new limits on the amount of money that could be contributed by individuals or groups to congressional and presidential races and established an independent Federal Election Commission to administer the law (see Table 6-7). It also gave presidential candidates of the two major parties the choice of either accepting public financing of their general election campaigns or raising their own funds, without limits. If they decided to accept public funds—as both Jimmy Carter and Gerald Ford did in 1976—they could accept no private contributions. According to the Center for Public Financing of Elections, which had lobbied actively for the measure, the 1974 Federal Election Campaign Act (also known as the Campaign Reform Act) represented "the only decent legacy of Watergate."

Originally, the law also set limits on the amounts candidates could spend on their campaigns. But this provision provoked considerable opposition and resulted in a court challenge by Senator James Buckley, Eugene McCarthy, and others who felt that spending limits violated the constitutional right of free expression. They insisted that ceilings on campaign spending would give an unfair advantage to incumbents, who usually enjoy greater public recognition than challengers. The use of large sums of money, they argued, frequently has been the only way for

Table 6-7. Major Provisions of the 1974 Federal Election Campaign Act (as amended in 1976)

1. No individual can give more than $1,000 to any presidential or congressional candidate in any primary or general election, and not more than $25,000 to all candidates for federal office during one campaign season.

2. No group or organization can give more than $5,000 to any congressional or presidential candidate in any one election.

3. Candidates in presidential primaries raising a minimum $100,000 in amounts of $5,000 in each of at least twenty states (through gifts not exceeding $250) will receive matching federal funds up to $5.5 million.

4. In the general election, each major-party candidate for president is entitled to federal funds (in 1976 it was $21.8 million) on the condition that no private contributions will be accepted.

5. Each major party is entitled to $2 million in federal funds to finance its national convention.

6. Third-party candidates will be eligible for federal funding if their party obtained at least 5 percent of the total vote cast in the preceding election.

7. A six-member bipartisan Federal Election Commission will administer the law. Criminal violations of the law will be handled by the Justice Department.

---

unknown challengers, particularly third-party candidates, to compete with incumbents.

As a result, the law came under the scrutiny of the Supreme Court, which used its judicial review power in 1976 to strike down some of its provisions.[33] Although most of the law was upheld by the Court, the tight squeeze on campaign spending was loosened. The Court ruled that candidates could spend any amount they wished in seeking public office (although presidential candidates accepting federal funds had to remain within the bounds set by the 1974 law). Moreover, a freer rein was given to individual citizens and "fat cats." Although limits on direct contributions to candidates were upheld, individuals and groups were free to spend extravagantly *on behalf* of a candidate, such as by paying for television spots and billboard ads. The Court also temporarily undercut the Federal Election Commission by ruling that the commission could not wield the powers of an enforcement agency because most of its members were appointed by congressional leaders instead of by the president. Congress was thus forced in 1976 to enact new legislation, giving the appointive power to the president.

But, the constitutional issues aside, the new law seemed likely to reduce party influence on campaigns. As one political scientist noted, "When we went to public financing of presidential campaigns, we didn't vest those funds in the party; we vested them in the candidates. That tends to emancipate candidates even further from national party organizations."[34] At the same time, the Court's ruling kept alive the old worries about the link between money and politics. With spending ceilings removed, candidates who could raise substantial sums on their own would continue to enjoy a political advantage over their less well-financed opponents. Money would still talk in politics, particularly in the struggle to achieve recognition through political advertising and other media blitzes, a concern to which we will turn in Chapter 8.

Key Terms

independent voter	*caucus*
political party	*convention*
conservative	*direct primary*
liberal	*closed primary*
single-member district system	*open primary*
proportional representation	*electoral college*

Notes

1. See *Newsweek*, 29 December 1969, p. 43.

2. Jack Dennis, "Trends in Public Support for the American Party System," *British Journal of Political Science*, April 1975, pp. 187–230.

3. *Gallup Opinion Index*, May 1973.

4. See, for example, Norman H. Nie, Sidney Verba, and John R. Petrocik, *The Changing American Voter* (Cambridge: Harvard University Press, 1976).

5. *Congressional Quarterly Almanac*, 1972.

6. *Congressional Quarterly Weekly Report*, 22 April 1978.

7. Nie et al., *The Changing American Voter*, p. 73.

8. Frank J. Sorauf, *Political Parties in the American System* (Boston: Little, Brown, 1964), p. 1.

9. John Hospers, quoted in *Newsweek*, 23 October 1972, p. 47.

10. Hugh A. Bone and Austin Ranney, *American Politics and the Party System*, 3rd ed. (New York: McGraw-Hill, 1965), p. 662.

11. Clinton Rossiter, *Parties and Politics in America* (Ithaca, N.Y.: Cornell University Press, 1960), p. 117.

12. Nie et al., *The Changing American Voter*, p. 242.

13. *Newsweek*, 22 November 1976, p. 15.

14. Sorauf, *Political Parties*, p. 63.

15. *Congressional Quarterly Weekly Report*, 15 April 1978.

16. Gerald M. Pomper, "From Confusion to Clarity," *American Political Science Review*, June 1972, p. 417.

17. Everett Carll Ladd, Jr., and Charles D. Hadley, "Party Definition and Party Differentiation," *Public Opinion Quarterly*, Spring 1973, pp. 31–32.

18. Pomper, "From Confusion to Clarity," pp. 415–428.

19. James Bryce, *The American Commonwealth*, 1893.

20. Frank J. Sorauf, *Party Politics in America* (Boston: Little, Brown, 1968), p. 113.

21. Quoted in Charles L. Clapp, *The Congressman: His Work As He Sees It* (Washington, D.C.: Brookings Institution, 1963), p. 358.

22. *Congressional Quarterly Weekly Report*, 16 December 1978.

23. Bryce, *American Commonwealth*.

24. Rossiter, *Parties and Politics*, p. 108.

25. William J. Keefe and Morris S. Ogul, *The American Legislative Process and the States* (Englewood Cliffs, N.J.: Prentice-Hall, 1968), pp. 109–114.

26. Samuel Lubell, *The Future of American Politics* (Garden City, N.Y.: Doubleday, 1956), p. 212.

27. See, for example, Maurice Duverger, *Political Parties* (New York: Wiley, 1955).

28. Belle Zeller and Hugh A. Bone, "The Repeal of P.R. in New York City—Ten Years in Retrospect," *American Political Science Review*, December 1948, pp. 1127–1148.

29. V. O. Key, Jr., *Parties, Politics, and Pressure Groups*, 5th ed. (New York: Thomas Y. Crowell, 1964), p. 279.

30. Gerald M. Pomper, *Elections in America* (New York: Dodd, Mead, 1971), p. 178.

31. *Gallup Opinion Index*, April 1977.

32. John V. Lindsay, "Let's Get the Money Out of Politics," *Newsweek*, 20 May 1974, p. 18.

33. *Buckley* v. *Valeo*, 1976.

34. Jeane Kirkpatrick, quoted in *U.S. News & World Report*, 18 September 1978, p. 56.

Recommended Reading

CHAMBERS, WILLIAM NISBET, and WALTER DEAN BURNHAM, eds. *The American Party Systems: Stages of Political Development*. 2nd ed. New York: Oxford University Press, 1975.

DE VRIES, WALTER, and LANCE TORRANCE, JR. *The Ticket-Splitter*. Grand Rapids, Mich.: William B. Eerdmans, 1972.

Gelb, Joyce, and Marian Lief Palley. *Tradition and Change in American Party Politics.* New York: Crowell, 1975.

Keefe, William J. *Parties, Politics, and Public Policy in America.* New York: Holt, Rinehart and Winston, 1972.

Ladd, Everett Carll, Jr., and Charles D. Hadley. *Transformations of the American Party System.* 2nd ed. New York: W. W. Norton, 1978.

Mazmanian, Daniel A. *Third Parties in Presidential Elections.* Washington, D.C.: Brookings Institution, 1974.

Ranney, Austin. *Curing the Mischiefs of Faction: Party Reform in America.* Berkeley: University of California Press, 1975.

Saloma, John S., and Frederick H. Sontag. *Parties: The Real Opportunity for Effective Citizen Politics.* New York: Alfred A. Knopf, 1972.

Sorauf, Frank J. *Party Politics in America.* 3rd ed. Boston: Little, Brown, 1976.

7

Interest Groups: The Promises of Collective Action

Because laboring alone to achieve a political goal can be lonely and exasperating, an alternative for some people is to join an interest group working toward similar goals. Politicians and social scientists alike have noted that collective, rather than individual, action offers the greatest promise for affecting governmental policy. By joining and working in concert with a large group having similar goals, an individual may be able to overcome his or her feelings of political isolation and impotency.

Yet, of all the political institutions in our society, interest groups probably have had the worst press. Just mention the term "lobbyist" or "pressure group" and many people conjure up images of shady characters with suitcases stuffed with cash skulking in and out of doorways buying up politicians' votes. Members of the "third house," as lobbyists are sometimes called, have won a reputation for corruption and shady dealing that, while occasionally deserved, tends to obscure the important ways interest groups help link citizens with the governmental process.

In several respects, the activities of interest groups lie at the heart of the American political system. They reflect the enormous diversity of opinion in our society, representing a wide range of interests at virtually every stage of the policy-making process. Although interest groups are not mentioned in the Constitution, the right to influence government through collective action is based firmly on the First Amendment freedoms of speech and assembly, and the people's right "to petition the Government for a redress of grievances." As we saw in Chapter 3, James Madison and some of the other Founding Fathers viewed the division of society into many competing groups (or "factions") as a natural outcome of economic and social differences. Even though they were worried about the potential dangers posed by many self-serving and competing groups, they also recognized the value of providing these groups with access to governmental decision making.

What the Founding Fathers could not foresee was the phenomenal growth in the number and variety of groups pressing their claims on government. During the past two centuries, as the federal government has ballooned into a bureaucratic colossus touching the lives of all Americans, lobbyists have flocked to Washington by the thousands to influence legislation on behalf of their clients. One estimate is that there are now more than twenty active lobbyists for every member of Congress, and that they represent more than ten thousand organizations—ranging from the American Petroleum Institute to the National Association of Wine Bottlers. In fact, Congressional studies indicate that interest groups now collectively spend more than $1 billion annually to influence Washington policy makers and a comparable sum to sway public opinion.

One result of this enormous influx of interest groups has been to fragment the political system even further. With political parties declining in strength (see Chapter 6), policy makers have faced increased pressures from interest groups that tend to judge political performance on the basis of single issues, ranging from gun control to abortion. Without the parties to achieve compromise among many competing factions, policy makers have found themselves supported or rejected by groups on the basis of a single roll-call vote, with little attention paid to their overall voting records or party affiliations. Thus, when Sen. Wendell Anderson of Minnesota failed to oppose tuition tax-credits for private-school pupils, he lost the endorsement of the influential Minnesota Education Association. Anderson's six-year record as a former governor who expanded state support for public education was largely ignored.

In this chapter, we will take a close look at interest groups in an effort to understand more about their activities and the controversy that surrounds them. We will explore a number of questions, including: What are interest groups? What do they do to affect governmental policy?

What are the benefits and limitations of joining an interest group? And whose "interest" do they tend to represent?

The Trademark of an Interest Group

What is an *interest group?* In the broadest sense, an interest group can be defined as a collection of people with shared attitudes and goals who band together to influence governmental policy. Although one often hears people refer to "pressure group" as well, the term is somewhat more limited since "pressure" carries a strong negative connotation and is only one of many techniques employed to influence policy. The same is true for the term "lobby." Although it is also used to describe an interest group, lobbying usually refers to making direct contacts with policy makers and is only one kind of activity engaged in by organized groups. The word *lobbyist* can be traced back more than a century when it was first used to identify those who tried to buttonhole legislators in a corridor or lobby outside the legislative chambers.

Interest groups differ widely, of course, in their goals, organizations, and activities. While some pursue a broad range of political objectives, others specialize and become only marginally entangled in legislative conflicts. And while some interest groups can draw on considerable financial resources, skilled leaders, and large memberships, others are not much more than "letterhead" groups with little money, organization, or permanence.

In fact, the variety of goals and interests represented by organized groups today defies any simple scheme of classification. There are many types of groups operating on the political scene, each expressing a different need or concern. Some groups, for example, like the National Association of Manufacturers (NAM) and the Teamsters Union, are primarily economically motivated, set up to represent the economic interests of their members. Others, like the Americans for Democratic Action (ADA) and the John Birch Society, are more ideologicaly inspired, concentrating on policy issues that reflect their members' political beliefs. Still others, like the National Education Association (NEA) and the American Medical Association (AMA), represent the interests of professional groups and may voice their members' political as well as economic concerns. There are also groups, like the National Association for the Advancement of Colored People (NAACP) and the American Israel Public Affairs Committee (AIPAC), that articulate the interests of identifiable ethnic groups. And then there are the "citizens' lobbies," like Common Cause and Ralph Nader's Public Citizen, that claim to champion not the specific interests of their supporters, but the general public good.

Influencing the System: Tactics and Resources

The targets and tactics of interest-group influence are almost as varied as the organizations themselves. Given the many ways government touches the lives of citizens, interest groups will be found at virtually every stage of the political process exploiting every available opportunity to shape public policy. They will lobby members of Congress and state legislators, appeal to presidents and judges, and become chummy with bureaucrats. They will even try to mobilize the public, employing sophisticated propaganda techniques to gain sympathy and rally support.

In this section, we will take a look at some of the common tactics and targets of interest groups and consider what resources are most likely to make a group politically effective.

Lobbying Congress

The term lobbyist usually refers to someone who seeks to influence the passage or defeat of legislation through direct contact with policy makers. There are essentially two kinds of lobbyists operating on Capitol Hill: (1) full-time employees of single organizations, who roam the halls of Congress drumming up support for their organizations' interests; and (2) the lobbyists-for-hire, who may represent several organizations at once. A prominent example of the latter is Charls E. Walker, a former undersecretary of the treasury during the Nixon administration, who set up his own "economic consulting" firm in 1973. He has represented a score of corporate clients, including such blue-chip companies as General Electric, U.S. Steel, General Motors, and Allied Chemical.

Most lobbyists are highly skilled (and highly paid) professionals whose backgrounds in law, business, and/or government are useful to the organizations they represent. Some of the most influential lobbyists, in fact, are former members of Congress who, after leaving office, have been hired to represent private lobbying groups. For example, when Joseph Tydings of Maryland lost his Senate seat in 1970, he was quickly snatched up by a Washington lobbying firm representing a prominent electric power company. To the lobbying firm, the advantages of having a former Senator on the payroll were clear: Tydings had extensive experience with congressional procedures and could help the firm gain access to members of Congress who were personal friends and former colleagues.

The tactics used by lobbyists vary, depending on the issue and the interest group. As we might suspect, some lobbyists succeed in winning the support of senators and representatives through bribes, lavish entertainment, and promises of future employment. The Korean lobby scandal during the late 1970s, for example, in which over a dozen members of Congress were accused of illegally accepting cash or gifts from a South Korean businessman named Tongsun Park, clearly demonstrates the kind of corruption that can seep into relations between lobbyists and lawmakers.

Yet, it is not money that wins votes, as much as it is information and statistics provided for committee members. Indeed, one of the most common tactics employed by lobbyists is to focus on the committees where policy decisions are likely to be made. As we will see in Chapter 10, most legislative craftsmanship in Congress takes place in committee. Each bill introduced on Capitol Hill is referred to a committee for consideration; and it is in the committee, not on the floor, that its fate usually is determined. Lobbying groups know that busy committee members are often hungry for information, especially on how pending legislation may affect their districts. By supplying members with detailed information through committee testimony, personal discussions, or even suggested drafts of bills, lobbying groups can often incorporate their own ideas into the final version of the law.

Lobbying groups also know that, in fights over specific bills, it is easier to influence a handful of committee members than the entire Senate or House and that a committee's recommendations tend to be accepted by other senators and representatives. Rather than wasting their time on legislators strongly opposed to their views, lobbyists will focus instead on wavering members who may tip the balance in their favor and carefully nurture the friendships of members who have supported their concerns in the past.

Some lobbyists insist that their jobs have become tougher as a result of recent changes in Congress (see Chapter 10). The diffusion of power among subcommittees, for example, has forced them to cover more bases. They can no longer just cozy up to a few powerful committee chairmen, but must take into account the whims and wishes of any number of legislators. They can never be sure which member may cast the deciding vote in passing or defeating a piece of legislation.

One interesting development in recent years has been the growing tendency of lobbying groups to pool their resources by forming temporary coalitions. Even large organizations like the AFL-CIO and the

Chamber of Commerce have aligned themselves on occasion with other groups sharing similar legislative goals. They have found that, by swapping information and coordinating strategies, they can accumulate enough collective strength to expand their political influence. Dramatic examples of such coalition efforts can be seen in the alliance of environmental groups and scientists in 1970 against the supersonic transport (SST), the joining of auto companies and labor unions in 1977 against the Clean Air Act, and the alliance of civil rights organizations, labor unions, and northern liberal groups in 1969 against the nomination of Clement Haynesworth to the Supreme Court. Although coalitions are usually temporary, they have been instrumental in obtaining or preventing passage of major legislation.

Lobbying the Executive Branch

Interest groups do not, of course, direct their lobbying energies exclusively at Congress. Once bills are passed by the House and Senate, interest groups must also make sure that the president signs them into law and that the bureaucracy carries them out (or, conversely, that the bills are vetoed, or buried through administrative inaction).

As noted in Chapter 12, laws passed by Congress often leave considerable room for interpretation. Bureaucrats are given great discretion in deciding how laws are to be put into practice. Congress may pass legislation restricting the emission of pollutants by factories, for example, but the actual standards and applications of the law will likely be defined by administrators. As a result, interest groups will try to develop friendly ties with bureaucrats whose decisions may advance or subvert their interests. Trucking companies will cozy up to the Interstate Commerce Commission, airlines to the Civil Aeronautics Board, and labor unions to the Department of Labor. And administrators will honor those ties because they value the information interest groups can supply and because they may need interest-group support in lobbying Congress for adequate budgets for their programs. Executive agencies and departments, after all, often become lobbying groups in their own right, trying to cement long-term friendly relations with members of Congress who regulate the flow of funds.

How do interest groups lobby executive officials? They employ many of the same tactics used to influence members of Congress. They testify at hearings, provide detailed information on complex issues, and even bombard officials with telegrams, letters, and special appeals.

Litigation

Interest groups also have found that they can achieve results by resorting to *litigation*. If pressures on members of Congress or on bureaucrats prove to be ineffective, they can always try to challenge a law or executive action in the courts. In 1976, for instance, the Ford administration recommended sweeping cutbacks in the federal food-stamp program. Supporters of the program lobbied members of Congress to resist such a move, but without success. So they went to court and won a judicial ruling prohibiting the cutbacks. In this way, they were able to block a presidential decision that would have adversely affected more than eight million people.

Some groups have discovered that the courts are sometimes more sympathetic to their cause than Congress or the president. Civil rights organizations, environmental groups, and consumer interests have all looked to the courts in recent years for support in contesting governmental and corporate practices. The NAACP has been especially successful in gaining the support of the Supreme Court in overturning discriminatory laws at both the federal and state levels. And the Court has made it clear that litigation is a legitimate and useful tactic for influencing public policy. "In the context of NAACP objectives," it has ruled, "litigation . . . is a means for achieving the lawful objectives of equality of treatment. . . . It is thus a form of political expression. Groups which find themselves unable to achieve their objectives through the ballot turn to the courts. . . . And under conditions of modern government, litigation may well be the sole practical avenue open to a minority to petition for redress of grievances."[1]

This is not to say, however, that litigation is a tactic available equally to all groups. Initiating litigation can prove to be a costly and time-consuming undertaking, especially if a case goes all the way to the Supreme Court. Groups that have the money to pay for high-powered attorneys and are willing to endure the long delays of the judicial process usually enjoy a great advantage over groups struggling to make ends meet.

Partly for this reason, some interest groups prefer to become involved in court actions as an *amicus curiae* ("friend of the court"). Instead of participating as a direct litigant, they will submit written arguments known as amicus briefs, outlining their own legal views on an issue. For example, in the 1970s, women's rights organizations joined forces to submit amicus briefs on a number of court cases involving women. In one case, the Women's Law Project (WLP), the Women's Legal Defense Fund (WLDF), the National Organization of Women (NOW), and others filed a joint amicus brief in support of a petition challenging the constitutionality of the death penalty for rape. The law, they stated, "is part of the fabric of laws and enforcement practices which in fact hamper prosecution and convictions for that crime, thus leaving women with little real protection against rape."[2] In another case, the Women's Law Project (WLP) joined forces with the American Civil Liberties Union (ACLU) to file an amicus brief in a case involving the denial of pregnancy disability payments to women workers. By submitting amicus briefs, these groups were able to demonstrate group solidarity on the issues, as well as to appraise the Court of new moral arguments and points of law not addressed by those who originally filed the suits. (For more on litigation as a tactic, see Chapter 15.)

Mobilizing the Public

In recent years, interest groups have also placed increased emphasis on generating grass-roots support for their aims. They have learned a great deal from advertising and public relations specialists about how to sway public opinion, and they have become convinced that legislators will often respond to constituent pressures when other means of influence fail.

Essentially, two kinds of grass-roots tactics are used. An intensive letter-writing campaign may be waged to whip up citizen support for, or opposition to, a particular policy. Groups will use their mailing lists to alert members and supporters to pending legislation and to spur them to express their views. The National Rifle Association, for example, operating on the premise that nothing shakes a politician like a pile of angry letters from home, has been using its large mailing lists to turn aside gun laws since the 1930s.

In contrast to letter-writing campaigns directed at single policies are tactics designed to create a favorable public attitude toward a group's fundamental goals. Many large corporations, for instance, launch elaborate public relations campaigns to sell their political views as well as commercial products to the public. Illustrative of such campaigns are the television commercials sponsored by oil companies like Texaco and Chevron. While Texaco soothingly promises that "we're working to keep your trust," Chevron uses cartoons to assure us that it does not reap enormous profits from the soaring price of gasoline and that the search for oil must continue, environmental protests notwithstanding.

The aim of such campaigns is not only to attract consumers, but also to gain public acceptance of a company's fundamental goals and thus to bolster its influence over lawmakers. Most company officials are aware

A word to nonsmokers
(about smokers)

A great jazz musician once said of his art, "If you don't understand it, I can't explain it."

That's the way it is with smoking.

If you've never smoked, it just *looks* puzzling — the whole ritual of lighting, puffing. What's the point?

There's really no way to explain it.

We've all heard from the people who think the 60 million American smokers ought to be, like you, nonsmokers. But even those people know there's *something* going on that smokers like.

Maybe that's the key to the whole tobacco thing from the beginning. It's a small ritual that welcomes strangers, provides companionship in solitude, fills "empty" time, marks the significance of certain occasions and expresses personal style.

For *some* people. And by personal choice, not for you. That's the way it ought to be. Whether your preference is carrot juice or bottled water, beach buggies or foreign cars, tobacco smoking or chewing gum or none of the above. Personal style.

What we're saying is that, like jazz or chamber music, some people like it and some don't.

And most of you nonsmokers understand that. It would be a dull world if everybody liked the same things.

The trouble is that some people (*anti*-smokers, as distinguished from *non*smokers) don't like those who march to the sound of the different drummer, and want to harass smokers and, if possible, to separate them from your company in just about everything.

And the further trouble is that even the tolerant *non*smokers, and that's most of you, are honestly annoyed by the occasional sniff of tobacco smoke that's a little too pervasive.

It annoys us smokers equally.

But it would be a shame if we allowed a tiny handful of intolerant anti-smokers, and a small group of discourteous smokers, to break up the enjoyable harmony we find in each other's personal style.

Maybe if we ignore them both, they'll go away and leave the rest of us to go on playing together.

THE TOBACCO INSTITUTE
1776 K St. N.W., Washington, D.C. 20006

Freedom of choice is the best choice.

An excerpt from a media campaign by the tobacco industry to gain support for its cause. Reprinted by permission of The Tobacco Institute.

of people's tendency to view the world according to their own predispositions. To win public support, a company's goals must be couched in terms that most people will want to accept. It is not by chance that companies selling gasoline, automobiles, and other products with potential environmental hazards will run television commercials featuring patriotic slogans and catchy titles. After all, Exxon's tune, "Energy for a Strong America" is not merely a Madison Avenue jingle: it is a political and economic rallying cry as well.

Influencing Elections

Finally, interest groups often throw themselves directly into the political fray by aiding candidates for public office. While interest groups (unlike parties) do not run candidates for office under their own banners, they do contribute money and other means of political support.

In the 1978 elections, interest groups poured a record $31.1 million into House and Senate campaigns.[3] As Table 7-1 shows, corporations contributed about $9.8 million, while labor unions coughed up $10.3 million. Most of the remaining contributions came from health and professional organizations like the American Medical Association and from agricultural interests like the dairy industry. The main recipients of this cash were incumbents who sat on key committees, such as House Ways and Means, and Senate Finance, which decide the fate of many bills relevant to these groups.

Although corporations and labor unions are barred from making direct contributions to candidates for federal office, the restrictions are so loosely worded that they can easily be sidestepped. The Federal Elec-

Table 7-1. Congressional Campaign Contributions, 1976 and 1978 (in millions of dollars)

Interest Group	1976	1978
Labor	$8.2	$10.3
Corporations	7.1	9.8
Health	2.7	2.1
Agriculture	1.5	0.9
Realtors	0.6	1.1
Lawyers	0.2	0.3

Source: Common Cause, "Report to the American People on the Financing of Congressional Election Campaigns," May 1977; *Congressional Quarterly Weekly Report*, 2 June 1979.

tion Commission has stated that corporations may form political action committees (PACs) to collect "voluntary" contributions from employees, while labor unions can set up separate political organs, such as the AFL-CIO's Committee on Political Education (COPE), to round up donations from union members. In addition, corporations and unions are free to supply campaign volunteers, help with voter registration drives, and buy television, radio, and newspaper ads on a candidate's behalf.

The potential for corruption is always present. There is always the temptation to hand over bundles of cash in exchange for political favors, especially when the likelihood of severe penalties seems remote. As Carol Greenwald points out, "in 1972 nineteen corporations and two dairy cooperatives were caught contributing $1.5 million in corporate funds to Nixon's reelection campaign. The total fines paid by the companies and individuals involved amounted to $149,000, or less than 4 percent of their total campaign contributions. In terms of personal penalties, the twenty-one individuals involved fared equally well: only two were discharged from their jobs; the rest are still drawing six-figure salaries and living the comfortable, corporate good life."[4]

What most interest groups are trying to buy, of course, is access. When legislation affecting their interests comes up in Congress, they want to be sure they will receive a warm reception when they come to lobby. They see a campaign contribution not so much as a bribe for support on a particular policy, but as a downpayment on a long-term friendly relationship—a relationship the member of Congress will not easily let dissolve if he or she desires future campaign support.

Some interest groups are even cagey enough (or unprincipled enough, depending on one's viewpoint) to hedge their bets by contributing to candidates of both parties; regardless of which candidate loses, the interest group still wins. But the most widespread and effective strategy is helping candidates who are already sympathetic to the group's cause. Thus, in 1968, oil industry officials doled out over $1.2 million to help Richard Nixon win the presidency not because they expected to buy his support on tax provisions like the oil depletion allowance, but because they knew he already favored such provisions. Helping a friend gain public office may be less dramatic than converting an enemy, but over the long run it is likely to prove more beneficial.

The Basis of Group Influence

It might be asked what separates a truly effective interest group from the rest of the pack. The answer is difficult to state precisely because the relations between groups and policy makers are often hard to define.

Ruling-elite theorists and pluralists, for example, continue to debate whether economic resources are the key to power, or whether such resources as expertise, organization, or even status can be equally, if not more, important in determining who wields influence. Does a member of Congress, for instance, respond to an interest group because it promises future campaign support, because it commands his or her respect, or simply because the member and the group share the same goals? Unless we are present, how do we determine the precise basis for agreement between them? Do we ask the Congress member? The principal lobbyist? And will they tell us the truth? The nature of power and influence remains one of the foggiest areas of study in political science and will not clear up simply because we desire easy explanations of why one group wins out over another. Our understanding of group influence will likely be tied to our overall perspective of the political power structure and to the specific policy area we examine.

Despite these limitations, however, scholars have tried to draw some conclusions about the resources used to influence public policy, based on actual case studies. They have suggested that certain kinds of resources are desired for a group to compete effectively in the political system. Certainly one desirable resource in any lobbying arsenal is money. While most groups may not approach politicians with direct illegal bribes, they do need money to contribute to campaigns and to hire able lobbyists, attorneys, and public relations experts. It is not entirely coincidental that some of the nation's most active and prominent interest groups, such as the American Petroleum Institute, the American Bankers Association, and the Teamsters Union, all command considerable financial resources. But money alone does not guarantee success. Even though the American Medical Association in 1965 reportedly doled out more than $1 million to block passage of Medicare, the act was signed into law (albeit with features that bore the AMA stamp).

Access to reliable information is also regarded as an important source of influence. The ability to provide policy makers with accurate data and statistics on complex policy questions can be a decisive factor in winning or losing a legislative battle. The success of environmental groups and scientists in stopping production of the supersonic transport (SST) in 1970 was largely attributed to the data they presented on the plane's potentially harmful impact on the environment.

Another valuable asset is a large membership. Many successful organizations, including labor unions and veterans' groups, marshall the resources of large segments of the population to influence lawmakers. As stated earlier, the National Rifle Association has been using its large mailing lists to turn aside gun laws since the 1930s. But even size has limitations. Although the National Congress of Parents and Teachers represents one of the largest groups in the country, it has little lasting impact on educational policies. Its members are only loosely associated and share little in common except the broadest goals.

Thus, in addition to money and size, other desirable resources might include prestige, unity, and good leadership. These three attributes have been especially important for professional organizations like the American Medical Association and the American Bar Association, whose impact on policies has been largely traced to the skills and respect commanded by their leadership. Even psychological factors, like hope and confidence, can be important, as can broad public support and the absence of any powerful countervailing group.

The Defeat of an Antismoking Measure

At the state level, corporations are generally not barred from using corporate funds to influence election campaigns. In 1978, for example, the five major tobacco companies spent more than $3.2 million to defeat a California state proposition (Proposition 5) that would have limited smoking in certain public places. R. J. Reynolds Corporation alone paid out more than $1.2 million. Most of the money was spent on radio and television ads that played upon public resentment of excessive government regulation and compared the proposed smoking controls to the prohibition of liquor. In contrast, backers of the measure (including the American Cancer Society and the California Lung Association) raised only $290,000. Although a strong majority of California voters early in the campaign had indicated support for the antismoking proposition, it eventually went down to defeat. According to many analysts, the heavy advertising campaign mounted by the tobacco companies succeeded in shifting voter opinion against the measure.

In Whose Interest?

Despite the enormous number and variety of interest groups in this country, there is some question whether most Americans are well-represented in interest group politics. Indeed, one of the major controversies relating to interest groups is whether they express the needs and concerns of a broad spectrum of our society, or whether they serve instead to advance the goals of powerful elites.

As we saw in Chapter 2, supporters of the pluralist theory insist that power in America is widely dispersed among many different groups whose competing ambitions help keep them in check. In their view, American politics is principally "interest group politics." They argue that, on any given issue, there will likely be rival groups representing a variety of alternative views. For each auto company trying to relax emission standards, for example, there will also be an environmental group pressing for stricter pollution controls. For each oil company trying to gain rights for offshore drilling, there will also be a coalition of citizen groups trying to keep it out. Over the long run, pluralists believe, the policies emerging out of this group competition will reflect the diversity of opinions in our society, with each group taking its turn winning or losing in the struggle for political influence.

Pluralists also contend that membership in interest groups is spread widely among the population, providing many Americans with an opportunity to participate more fully in political activities. As Table 7-2 indicates, 62 percent of Americans say they belong to some kind of organization. Of this number, 31 percent say they belong to an organization that engages in political discussion, and 44 percent say they belong to one that is active in community affairs. Interest group membership, pluralists insist, provides an important channel of influence for many citizens who wish to express their political views. It provides a way for citizens to feel more effective in influencing policy by bringing them into contact with like-minded individuals who share the same goals.

Indeed, pluralists point out, an interest group often can represent an individual in ways that a political party or an elected representative cannot. As noted in Chapter 6, the Democratic and Republican parties are not strictly issue-oriented. Both parties offer only the broadest and vaguest programs in an effort to harvest votes. Furthermore, members of Congress and state legislators are elected on a geographical basis and are forced to represent districts comprising hundreds of conflicting

---

Table 7-2. Organization Membership in the United States

Percent of Sample Reporting

That they belong to an organization	62
That they belong to more than one organization	39
That they are active in an organization	40
That they belong to an organization in which political discussion takes place	31
That they belong to an organization active in community affairs	44

Source: Sidney Verba and Norman H. Nie, *Participation in America* (New York: Harper & Row, 1972), p. 176.

---

groups. Under these circumstances, it is difficult to imagine how any individual can feel adequately represented as part of a large, mixed constituency. Interest groups, on the other hand, provide supplementary representation for specific groups by serving their unique occupational or other interests. The American Medical Association, for example, can speak for the interests of doctors in ways that a party or a legislator alone cannot.

Ruling-elite theorists, however, challenge many of these claims made for interest groups. They reply that interest groups do not serve a broad spectrum of our society. With the exception of such prominent associations as the National Welfare Rights Organization, most interest groups speak primarily for middle- or upper-class interests. "The flaw in the pluralist heaven," one scholar has quipped, "is that the heavenly chorus sings with a strong upper-class accent."[5] Many people such as the elderly poor, who greatly depend on governmental assistance, do not belong to, and are unable to benefit from, any effective organization that speaks on their behalf. They possess neither the financial resources nor the leadership to pressure the government for policies directly benefiting them.

The memberships of most organizations, ruling-elite theorists point out, confirm their middle- and upper-class bias. Just as people with higher education and income are more likely to vote and write letters to the editor, they are also more prone to become active in voluntary associations. The same study cited by pluralists, for example, indicates that people with a college education are twice as likely to belong to such associations as those with only a grade-school education.[6] And, contrary to the belief that many Americans take part in political groups, studies show that only about 8 percent belong to organizations, such as Common Cause or the NAACP, whose energies are directed mainly toward influencing governmental policy.[7]

Advocates of the ruling-elite view also reject the notion that group competition leads to a general equality and balance among interests. They see no guarantees that "ambition will counteract ambition." Although consumer groups and other so-called public interest lobbies may win an occasional battle, they cannot, over the long run, effectively compete against powerful corporate interests. Industry groups, such as the oil and utility lobbies, tend to be the most well organized and well financed of all organizations operating on the national scene. They have large budgets with which to court legislators and bureaucrats and to build up public support for their policy goals. What is more significant, they enjoy the support of many top governmental officials who share their economic concerns and who have held, or hope to hold, managerial positions in industrial and financial institutions. And there is little indication that the influence of corporate lobbies will wane. According to recent estimates, over 80 percent of the nation's one thousand largest companies support an organized lobbying effort in Washington.

But perhaps the most significant aspect of interest group representation, ruling-elite theorists insist, is that it tends to favor the status quo. Although interest-group goals may vary, few organizations that acquire a stake in the existing order will be likely to push for major social and political change. "Interest group conflict," one pair of scholars conclude, "reflects merely the most visible disputes between factions within the established elite. Business and labor may contest over the raising of the minimum wage, but both unite to keep demands for radical reform out of the pressure system."[8]

Which of these two conflicting views of interest groups is right? Is it possible interest groups can provide ordinary citizens with added opportunities to participate effectively in politics and can also serve as the tools of powerful elites? Like other political issues, the role played by interest groups in our society will be perceived by people in different ways, depending on their views of, and experience with, the political order. What is certain is that the kind of collective action engaged in by interest groups will continue to be seen by most activists as the most promising way to affect public policy. Even if ruling-elite theorists are right in perceiving an imbalance in group representation—and their arguments are persuasive—groups, not single individuals, will continue to be the basic units of influence in our society. Membership in an organization will enhance the prospects that an individual will be able to influence government and will make an effort to do so.

Joining with Lobbyists: The Benefits and Limitations

Considering the advantages of engaging in collective action, we might wonder why some people, and not others, decide to join an interest group. Why do some people spend the time and money to belong to a civic organization, labor union, or citizens' lobby, while others who share similar interests and goals do not? Are those who join an interest group more politically motivated than the rest of society, or do they expect to receive benefits having little to do with politics?

The question is an intriguing one, in part because observers sometimes wonder whether the disadvantages of joining an interest group outweigh its advantages. Despite the appeal of engaging in collective action, there are certain limitations to interest group membership. Because many interest groups, for example, have evolved into large organizations with thousands of members, the individual member may become only a small cog in a large machine. Few exciting opportunities for political action may be offered, even in a public interest group like Common Cause, which claims to be a "citizens' lobby." Apart from paying dues and receiving information on its activities, the individual may regard his or her contribution as insignificant compared with the efforts of those working directly to influence policy makers. Even volunteer activities often entail doing menial chores, such as stuffing envelopes, which are not likely to satisfy the desire to be directly involved in policy making.

In addition, many interest groups tend to be led by a small cadre of active elites. The members of a large interest group often elect their leaders from among candidates sanctioned by a dominant or ruling clique, a clique that, year after year, represents the group in its relations with governmental officials. While some organizations may place great emphasis on democratic controls over internal policy making, questions continue to arise in others over whether the ruling clique accurately reflects the policy views of the membership. An individual may contribute money and other means of support to an organization with only limited knowledge—or approval—of the group's day-to-day operations and policies. While the person may obtain satisfaction from belonging to a large organization, he or she will be unlikely to have a strong personal influence on its policies and tactics.

Still another limitation—especially for those who are dissatisfied with present governmental policies—is that most powerful interest groups do not press for creative reform. While some do seek major changes in existing policies, the majority of large, successful organizations, such as the American Medical Association and the National Rifle Association, are better known for their ability to delay and obstruct policies than to force the enactment of new ones. This is not simply because they desire stagnation, but because, as we will see in Chapter 10, the legislative process is strewn with obstacles. It is easier to persuade a few prominent committee members to block an undesirable bill than it is to effect reform by running the gauntlet of numerous centers of decision making. Studies of lobbying techniques reveal that lobbying tends to be most effective when used to reinforce or sway the opinions of a few committee members than to convert a majority of both the House and Senate into taking a new path.

What then are the advantages in belonging to an interest group? Why do many Americans initially join, and then continue to maintain their membership in, a large organized group?

One of the most intriguing explanations for why people belong to interest groups is offered by economist Mancur Olson.[9] Olson argues that it would be irrational for people to join a large organization where their influence will probably not be felt, especially if they can benefit from its activities without having to pay dues or other costs. Why should a college professor, for example, join a union pressing for higher teacher salaries and smaller classes if she will gain these benefits whether or not she is a dues-paying member? Unless she is forced to join through peer pressure or other means, why not simply sit back and reap the rewards of other people's labors?

Olson maintains that people will join an interest group like a labor union or professional association only if their individual participation is considered significant (thus, the size of the group becomes a relevant factor), if they are coerced into joining (for example, through a "union shop"), or if they expect to receive *selective benefits* available only to members. The college professor will join the union, not necessarily because the union will press for higher wages, but because it may provide her with new professional contacts, low-cost health insurance, and perhaps even cheap charter flights to Europe.

In effect, Olson contradicts the pluralist view that interest groups arise out of common political interests and serve primarily to translate people's political dreams into reality. He insists that, on the contrary, most large economic groups arise—and succeed—by also supplying members with selective benefits that are essentially nonpolitical. "The common characteristic which distinguishes all of the large economic groups with significant lobbying organizations," he writes, "is that these groups are also organized for some *other* purpose. The large and powerful economic lobbies are in fact the by-products of organizations that obtain their strength and support because they perform some function in addition to lobbying for collective goods."[10]

Olson's view also suggests why many people will remain part of an interest group despite the absence of internal democratic controls. As long as the organization does a good job in providing benefits and achieving its goals, the individual member may not care about the nature of its internal operations or its responsiveness to the membership.

Is Olson correct in his assumptions about why people join interest groups? Do people tend to join for nonpolitical reasons? It seems certain, as we will see in the final chapter, that many people will engage in political activities for reasons other than wanting to influence policy. They may desire the social contacts stemming from their membership in a political organization, or indeed expect to gain material or other benefits. However, it is also possible that Olson exaggerates people's tendency to ignore political motivations and to weigh costs and benefits in an informed (and material) way. In fact, many of those who join an interest group may not see their dues or time spent as significant costs at all. Their commitment to certain political goals or ideals may provide sufficient motivation to bear the minimum demands of membership. (When one considers that interest group membership is more common among those with higher income and education, how much significance can be attached to a membership fee?)

Olson does concede that certain kinds of interest groups, notably "public interest" groups like Common Cause and the Sierra Club, do not fit his general assumptions. Those who contribute money or volunteer their time to a worthy cause, such as the protection of the environment or the advancement of human rights, usually do not require any material benefits or services in return for their support. Public interest groups represent a rather unique kind of political force in government, a force to which we will now turn our attention.

The Rise of Citizens' Lobbies

One of the most interesting developments in recent years has been the spread of *public interest groups* or *citizens' lobbies* organized to promote the "public interest." Many desiring reform and wishing to extend interest-group representation to a broader segment of society have put their faith in such groups as the National Committee for an Effective Congress, Ralph Nader's Public Citizen, the Environmental Defense Fund, and Common Cause. These and other citizens' lobbies purport to represent the interests of society as a whole rather than just their own membership. They claim to provide a necessary counterbalance to vested interests, such as the corporate and labor lobbies, which have tended to dominate the Washington political scene.

Common Cause is perhaps the best known of these organizations and is certainly the most well financed. As Table 7-3 shows, it has for several years headed the list of the top declared spenders among all registered groups. Since its inception in 1970, more than half a million people have paid membership dues of $15 or more a year to join its ranks. Common Cause was founded by John Gardner, a former secretary of Health, Education and Welfare, to press for what it regards as common public goals, with an emphasis on structural and procedural reforms: a more equitable tax system, the scrapping of the seniority rule in Congress, a more open system for financing political campaigns, and the like. Its members are regularly polled to learn which national and local issues require the most immediate attention.

And it has achieved some notable legislative and legal victories. By filing suits in federal courts and by employing the same professional lobbying techniques used by other interest groups, it spearheaded the

Table 7.3. Twenty-five Top Spenders

The top twenty-five spenders of the organizations that filed lobby spending reports for 1973 are listed below with the amounts they reported spending in 1973 and 1972.

Organization	1973	1972
Common Cause	$934,835	$558,839
International Union, United Automobile, Aerospace and Agricultural Implement Workers	460,992	no spending record
American Postal Workers Union (AFL-CIO)	393,399	208,767
American Federation of Labor-Congress of Industrial Organizations (AFL-CIO)	240,800	216,294
American Trucking Associations, Inc.	226,157	137,804
American Nurses Association, Inc.	218,354	109,642
United States Savings and Loan League	204,221	191,726
Gas Supply Committee	195,537	11,263
Disabled American Veterans	193,168	159,431
The Committee of Publicly Owned Companies	180,493	no spending record
American Farm Bureau Federation	170,472	180,678
National Education Association	162,755	no spending record
National Association of Letter Carriers	160,597	154,187
National Association of Home Builders of the United States	152,177	99,031
Recording Industry Association of America, Inc.	141,111	88,396
National Council of Farmer Cooperatives	140,560	184,346
American Insurance Association	139,395	82,395
The Farmers' Educational and Co-operative Union of America	138,403	113,156
Committee of Copyright Owners	135,095	no spending record
National Housing Conference, Inc.	125,726	77,906
American Petroleum Institute	121,276	38,656
American Medical Association	114,859	96,145
Citizens for Control of Federal Spending	113,659	no spending record
American Civil Liberties Union	102,595	73,131
National Association of Insurance Agents, Inc.	87,422	50,924

Source: *Congressional Quarterly Weekly Report,* 27 July 1974.

effort to ratify the Twenty-Sixth Amendment lowering the legal voting age to eighteen, worked successfully with environmental groups to defeat the supersonic transport (SST), and helped force the enactment of the 1974 Federal Election Campaign Act (see Chapter 6).

Also prominent is Ralph Nader's group, Public Citizen, an umbrella organization that raises and distributes funds for a variety of affiliated groups, such as the Tax Reform Research Group, the Health Research

Group, Congress Watch, the Litigation Group, and the Citizen Action Group. Although not strictly a membership-based organization like Common Cause, Public Citizen is supported by an estimated 150,000 contributors annually, as well as by foundation grants, book sales, and Nader's own lecturing and writing fees. With dozens of paid professionals on its staff and hundreds of volunteers, Public Citizen pursues a broad range of consumer, environmental, legal, and economic issues.

The techniques employed by Nader's Raiders, as they have come to be called, are similar.to those used by other interest group advocates. While they may not ply members of Congress with liquor or make campaign contributions, they do prepare testimony for committee hearings, help draft legislation, stimulate grass-roots lobbying campaigns, and file lawsuits in federal courts. And they have been able to claim a number of successes. They helped force the repeal of the oil depletion allowance, effectively petitioned the Food and Drug Administration to ban hazardous products like red dye no. 2, prevented states from prohibiting advertising of prescription drugs, and helped form dozens of independent, student-run Public Interest Research Groups around the country.

As the founder and principal spokesman for the group, Ralph Nader has commanded the kind of media attention no ordinary lobbyist can match. With his rumpled suits and drooping socks, Nader has become a folk hero to millions, a crusader who has been able to rise above personal interest and to work for the well-being of society as a whole. He first gained national attention in 1965 with the publication of his book, *Unsafe at Any Speed*,[11] charging that the Chevrolet Corvair had such fundamental safety defects that it was dangerous to drive. (The Corvair has since been scrapped.) After winning an out-of-court settlement against General Motors for invasion of privacy (the company had tried to discredit him by prying into his sex life and attempting to lure him with a prostitute), Nader used the funds to institutionalize his activities by forming the Center for the Study of Responsive Law in 1969 and Public Citizen in 1973. Naturally, not all of his actions have proved to be popular. He has been criticized both for his intentions and for his methods. While some have attacked him for supposedly undermining the free enterprise system, others have scolded him for battling too long on too wide a range of issues.

The most persistent criticism hurled against Nader's organization and other public interest groups, however, is the use of the term "public interest." Citizen groups often imply that their interests deserve special attention because they are looking out for the general good of society. Some critics argue, however, that public interest groups are almost invariably liberal and Democratic in character, and thus cannot claim

Ralph Nader

to represent all major elements of American public opinion. In fact, they argue, many policies favored by public interest groups are detrimental to large segments of society. As one scholar puts it, "There are those who argue that consumer, environmental, and other so-called 'public interest' issues are in reality middle and upper-middle class concerns which are addressed for the most part at the expense of the poor, the aged, and urban and ethnic minorities. Environmentalists often advocate strict zoning laws and growth curbs on city development, while others argue that these policies discriminate against the less affluent and translate directly into loss of jobs and local economic growth."[12]

Public interest group representatives, however, respond that the term "public interest" does not apply strictly to middle-class or liberal concerns, because consumer, health, and environmental issues affect everyone. The prospect that some jobs may be lost over the short term does not contradict the fact that all segments of our society—not just one social or economic group—will benefit from safer drugs, cleaner air, a fairer tax system, and more responsive government. Moreover, they argue, no single citizens' lobby tries to lay exclusive claim to the "public interest" label. As Common Cause President David Cohen remarked, "We are *a* citizens' lobby, *a* public interest group. The difference between 'a' and 'the' is very important. We don't define 'the public interest' in the sense that one group represents it while others don't."[13]

But whether or not the term "public interest" can legitimately be used by any group, citizens' lobbies have had an impact on policy making. Few sectors of our society and government have escaped the probes and challenges of consumer advocates, environmentalists, civil rights leaders, and others who claim to champion the public good. As one student of public interest groups concludes, "these organizations are slowly changing the overall environment within which governmental officials formulate public policy. . . . The opinion they can arouse, the bad publicity they can generate, the law suits they can file, are all factors that are relevant to the deliberations of those who must make policy decisions."[14]

Regulating Interest Groups

The impact interest groups have on government can be considered either good or bad, depending on their purposes and the methods they use to achieve their goals. Some take the extreme view that the activities of interest groups are inconsistent with democratic government. They believe interest groups represent narrow concerns that are antithetical to the general welfare of society and, therefore, should be suppressed.

Others insist, however, that the problems and dangers surrounding interest groups stem mainly from secrecy and the excessive amounts of money lobbyists may throw around. They contend that most abuses can be prevented if interest group activities are given greater visibility and if lobby spending by individuals or groups is restricted and fully reported.

The history of interest-group regulation in this country hardly inspires confidence in Congress's commitment to scandal-free government. Despite periodic revelations of bribery and outright criminal corruption during the past two centuries, drives by Congress to wipe out shady practices have usually collapsed under the weight of apathy, or resulted in weak and toothless laws.

Not until the 1930s, in fact, did Congress begin passing even limited legislation regulating interest-group lobbying. In 1935 and 1936, it passed laws requiring the registration of lobbyists for public utility companies and shipping firms who appeared before congressional committees or certain regulatory agencies.[15] This was followed by the Foreign Agents Registration Act of 1938, requiring lobbyists for foreign governments to register with the Justice Department.

Finally, in 1946, Congress passed the Federal Regulation of Lobbying Act, designed not to restrict the activities of interest groups but merely to disclose them. Enacted as part of a general scheme to reorganize Congress, this law requires the registration of any group which "solicits, collects, or receives money or any other thing of value to be used principally to aid . . . the passage or defeat of any legislation by the Congress of the United States." Lobbyists are required to register with the House and the Senate, and to file quarterly financial reports with the House.

The problem with the law, however, is that it is riddled with loopholes and essentially unenforceable. Under the language of the law, only those groups whose "principal purpose" is influencing Congress need to register and report their lobbying expenses. Many large lobbying groups, such as the American Trial Lawyers' Association and the National Association of Manufacturers, have been able for years to avoid the law's reporting requirements by merely claiming that lobbying is only an incidental part of their overall program, not their principal purpose. Even though the American Trial Lawyers' Association, for example, spent thousands of dollars lobbying against no-fault auto insurance legislation in 1974, it did not register as a lobbying group. Moreover, the law applies only to lobbying directed at Congress; it does not apply to lobbying of the White House or regulatory agencies. In fact, the Supreme Court in 1954 further weakened the law by ruling that only direct contacts with members of Congress were subject to control.[16] Indirect "lobbying," such as bringing public pressure to bear on Congress through letter-writing campaigns, was not subject to the law's restrictions. And, although the law provides for penalties, it does not designate anyone to check for reporting inaccuracies or to enforce its provisions. As a result, few violators have had even their wrists slapped since its enactment.

Reformers have not been idle, however. Since the Federal Regulation of Lobbying Act was first passed in 1946, Congress has been deluged with proposals to replace it with tighter regulations. Despite disagreements over details, most reformers contend that a good lobby disclosure law should contain at least four provisions: (1) coverage of the executive branch as well as Congress; (2) a broader definition of lobbying groups to include all organizations that attempt to influence legislation; (3) comprehensive reporting of all major lobbying expenditures and activities, including those aimed at the grass-roots level; and (4) strict enforcement provisions.

The strongest push for reform in recent years came in 1976 when the Senate passed legislation requiring most lobbying groups to register annually with the General Accounting Office and to file detailed quarterly reports of their activities, including how much they spend, the names of their lobbyists, and the issues in which they are interested. It also provided for stiff fines and possible prison sentences for violators. However, the bill failed to clear the House, and for more than two years was bounced from committee to committee. Then, in 1978, the House passed its own version of the bill ("The Public Disclosure of Lobbying Act"), sending it back again to the Senate. Along the way, the bill ran into opposition from virtually every major lobbying organization in Washington, including such "reform-minded" public interest groups as Ralph Nader's Congress Watch and the American Civil Liberties Union (ACLU).

The question might be raised: Why would public interest groups like Congress Watch and the ACLU oppose legislation aimed at curtailing lobbying abuses? Why would they try to stop a bill designed to educate the public about how much is spent to influence Congress, who spends it, and for what purposes?

Their voices were raised against the bill, they claimed, because its disclosure requirements would place a monumental record-keeping burden on smaller lobbying groups. It would impose a barrier of regulations and red tape against groups new to the Washington political scene, and have, as David Landau of the ACLU testified, a "general chilling effect" on people's inclination to lobby Congress. And by imposing such a barrier, the bill would abridge First Amendment rights of free speech, association, and petition. Rather than encouraging citizens to speak up about the issues that concern them, the bill would impose unfair and unnecessary restraints on those wishing to become more directly involved in the policy-making process through collective action.

Clearly, the need for regulation must be balanced against the desires of smaller organizations to influence public policy. The goal of regulation should be to illuminate the activities of interest groups, not restrict them. If current reform proposals do indeed result in a "general chilling effect" on citizen access to government, then one kind of "abuse" will only be replaced by another.

Key Terms

interest group

public interest group

lobbyist

citizens' lobbies

litigation

amicus curiae brief

selective benefits

Notes

1. *NAACP* v. *Button*, 1963.
2. Brief submitted in *Coker* v. *Georgia*, 1977.
3. *Congressional Quarterly Weekly Report*, 2 June 1979, p. 1043.
4. Carol S. Greenwald, *Group Power: Lobbying and Public Policy* (New York: Praeger, 1977), p. 140.
5. E. E. Schattschneider, *The Semisovereign People* (New York: Holt, Rinehart and Winston, 1960), p. 35.
6. Sidney Verba and Norman H. Nie, *Participation in America* (New York: Harper & Row, 1972), chap. 11.
7. Ibid.
8. Thomas R. Dye and L. Harmon Zeigler, *The Irony of Democracy*, 4th ed. (Belmont, Calif.: Wadsworth, 1978), p. 214.
9. Mancur Olson, Jr., *The Logic of Collective Action*, rev. ed. (Cambridge, Mass: Harvard University Press, 1971).
10. Ibid., p. 132.
11. Ralph Nader, *Unsafe at any Speed* (New York: Grossman, 1965).
12. D. Stephen Cupps, "Emerging Problems of Citizen Participation," *Public Administration Review*, Sept./Oct. 1977, p. 481.
13. Quoted in *Congressional Quarterly Weekly Report*, 15 May 1976, p. 1197.
14. Jeffrey M. Berry, *Lobbying for the People* (Princeton, N.J.: Princeton University Press, 1977), p. 289.
15. The Utilities Holding Company Act of 1935; the Merchant Marine Act of 1936.
16. *United States* v. *Harriss*, 1954.

Recommended Reading

BERRY, JEFFREY M. *Lobbying for the People: The Political Behavior of Public Interest Groups.* Princeton, N.J.: Princeton University Press, 1977.

CONGRESSIONAL QUARTERLY SERVICE. *The Washington Lobby.* 2nd ed. Washington, D.C.: Congressional Quarterly, Inc., 1974.

DEXTER, LEWIS A. *How Organizations are Represented in Washington.* Indianapolis: Bobbs-Merrill, 1969.

GREENWALD, CAROL S. *Group Power: Lobbying and Public Policy.* New York: Praeger, 1977.

LOWI, THEODORE J. *The End of Liberalism.* New York: W. W. Norton, 1969.

MILBRATH, LESTER W. *The Washington Lobbyists.* Chicago: Rand McNally, 1963.

OLSON, MANCUR, JR. *The Logic of Collective Action.* Rev. ed. Cambridge, Mass: Harvard University Press, 1971.

ORNSTEIN, NORMAN J., and SHIRLEY ELDER. *Interest Groups, Lobbying and Policy Making.* Washington, D.C.: Congressional Quarterly Press, 1978.

SALISBURY, ROBERT H., ed. *Interest Groups in American Politics.* New York: Harper & Row, 1970.

TRUMAN, DAVID B. *The Governmental Process.* 2nd ed. New York: Knopf, 1971.

WILSON, JAMES Q., *Political Organizations.* New York: Basic Books, 1973.

ZEIGLER, L. HARMON, and G. WAYNE PEAK. *Interest Groups In American Society.* 2nd ed. Englewood Cliffs, N.J.: Prentice-Hall, 1972.

8

Television and Other Media: Information and Images

Most of us pass a great part of our lives watching television, reading newspapers, books, and magazines, and listening to the radio. Watching television is especially popular, as shown by the fact that, besides sleeping and working, it is what most of us spend the greatest amount of time doing. It has been estimated that in most homes the television set is turned on an average of six hours a day and that by the time the average student graduates from high school, he or she has spent more hours in front of the television set than in school.

Because of their commanding presence, television and other *mass media* have great relevance to those of us concerned about our relationship to the political system. The media, after all, supply much of the information on which we must base our political actions. Because most of us have few alternative sources of information, we are enormously dependent on the media for our awareness of current issues, political candidates, and changes in the ongoing struggles for power. We know that unless we can acquire such awareness, we are not likely to gain easy access to, or effective influence over, the policy-making process.

Moreover, as we will see in the final chapter, the media have great relevance as instruments and avenues for political action. Those of us who can employ the media to communicate our ideas will enjoy a considerable advantage over others in stimulating new policy ideas. As long as television and other media spread information on politics, they must be considered essential tools for political influence by those intent on contributing to the information process.

But whether or not we intend to use the media to expand our influence or obtain information for purposes of political action, it is a safe bet that the media have played a major role in our education. Television especially has become so pervasive that it not only provides the bulk of family entertainment but has become the main source of information about world events. According to studies by the Roper polling organization, an increasing number of Americans claim to receive most of their news about what is happening in the world from television (see Table 8-1). In fact, television not only has become the public's main source of news; it has been accepted, as Table 8-2 indicates, increasingly as the most reliable source, apparently supporting the popular maxim that "seeing is believing."

These findings lead some observers to fear that those who control television may be able to manipulate our views and opinions. If we do indeed receive most of our information about world events from television—and are not very critical about what we receive—those who dominate the medium may have inordinate power to mold our perspectives on politics.

We need to consider, therefore, not only whether our opinions and perspectives are at the mercy of television and other media, but whether the media have supplied the information we need to undertake effective political action. We also need to consider the media's potential impact on our perceptions of government, as well as their effect, if any, on our interest in and awareness of current issues. These questions are obvi-

Table 8-1. Where People Get Their News

Source of Most News	1959	1963	1967	1971	1976
Television	51%	55%	64%	60%	64%
Newspapers	57	53	55	48	49
Radio	34	29	28	23	19
Magazines	8	6	7	5	7
Don't know or no answer	1	3	2	1	—

Source: The Roper Organization, "Trends in Attitudes Toward Television and Other Media: An Eighteen-Year Review," May 1977. Figures add to more than 100 percent because of multiple responses.

Table 8-2. What Sources They Most Believe

Most Believable	1959	1963	1967	1971	1976
Television	29%	36%	41%	49%	51%
Newspapers	32	24	24	20	22
Radio	12	12	7	10	7
Magazines	10	10	8	9	9
Don't know or no answer	17	18	20	12	11

Source: The Roper Organization, "Trends in Attitudes Toward Television and Other Media: An Eighteen-Year Review," May 1977.

ously related, for if the media present only inadequate, one-sided, or distorted information, then probably we can expect our political awareness and behavior to be correspondingly affected.

Consider the vote. As we will discuss further in Chapter 15, one of the most basic forms of political action is voting for candidates in an election. Because our choices are based not only on our party preferences but also on information supplied by the media, such information should ideally be as useful and accurate as possible. But if it should turn out that the media, especially television, have been employed in political campaigns primarily to sell slogans and manufactured images of candidates, then one of our most fundamental acts of political expression will have been based on distorted information. Thus, in evaluating the relationship between the media and our political behavior, we can begin with the charge that our votes have been corrupted by the use of Madison Avenue selling techniques in political campaigns.

Campaign Advertising: The Political Image Makers

As we are aware, it is virtually impossible to enjoy our favorite television shows without facing endless commercials imploring us to buy this or that hair spray, chewing gum, or deodorant. Commercials are as much a part of our viewing entertainment as the programs they interrupt. What we are not always aware of is that these commercials sell more than just nonessential products. They also sell inflated promises of beauty and youth, social acceptance, and heightened sexual prowess, frequently exploiting people's personal insecurities and social values. They make exaggerated claims that, by dousing oneself with Old Spice cologne or Charlie perfume, or by driving a Datsun 280Z, one can magically transform his or her sexual image. A team of psychologists suggest that consumers are being sold the "Cinderella effect." "Cinderella," they write, "was a rejected girl until she acquired a beautiful gown and a coach. . . . The adjusted American hopes that the goods he acquires will transform him in similar fashion into an exciting, desirable person. When he gets a new convertible (or she gets a new dress or a mink coat) there is an exhilarating period in which he imagines that such a transformation has taken place."[1]

In this way, television commercials serve as powerful formulators of public opinion, teaching people to define their needs and desires according to the profit goals of advertisers. They create new images—often false and absurd—with which the viewer is expected to compare. By this comparison, he or she is made to feel insecure, and this insecurity is then exploited. (After all, who used to believe that temporary "static cling" in socks, barely discernible spots on glassware, or even the sometimes pleasant odors of food cooking in the kitchen could inspire such personal trauma or social disapproval?)

What about advertising in political campaigns? Can commercials similarly "sell" candidates for public office by compelling voters to buy exaggerated claims and promises? Can presidential and congressional hopefuls be packaged on television like shiny automobiles and sweet-tasting mouthwashes—making them consumable by exploiting people's values and insecurities?

During every major election, television screens throughout the country become showcases for the modern wizards of American politics, the creators of political commercials. In many expensive campaigns, the same technical experts who peddle cat food, cosmetics, and hair sprays are employed to sell aspiring politicians to voters. Jack Tinker and Partners, for instance—the firm responsible for many of the popular Alka-Seltzer commercials—was hired in the late 1960s to create ads for Nelson Rockefeller's reelection campaign for governor of New York, in large part because the Alka-Seltzer ads were so clever. And the firm accepted the challenge because, as Managing Partner Myron McDonald unabashedly put it, "We looked at the Governor almost as though he were a product like Alka-Seltzer."[2]

Indeed, when advertising specialists are employed to direct media campaigns for candidates, we can expect them to rely on the same marketing strategies used in commercial advertising. Just as they try to determine what will appeal to consumers before marketing a new product, advertising specialists survey voters to discover what qualities they are seeking in presidential and congressional candidates. They examine different regional and social groups to find out where certain slogans and messages will be effective—and where they will be wasted. In both commercial and political advertising, the same consideration often applies: find out what people want and then give it to them in the most glittering package possible.

Usually, such a package comes in the form of a *spot commercial*, a short one-minute political advertisement that typically projects a single dramatic theme. It is commonly employed to build a favorable image of a candidate or to present an unfavorable view of an opponent, sometimes by exploiting public fears and anxieties. One of the most controversial one-minute spots was used briefly by the Democrats in 1964 against Sen. Barry Goldwater. To discredit Goldwater's support for the above-ground testing of nuclear weapons, the film showed a little girl standing innocently in a meadow, picking petals from a daisy. As she finished counting the petals, the scene dissolved into a countdown of an atomic test, concluding with a billowing mushroom cloud. "The stakes," a voice warned, "are too high for you to stay home."

Similarly, in the 1972 elections, commercials presented by Richard Nixon's supporters attacked George McGovern's welfare and defense proposals through the use of symbolic devices. In one such ad, a voice somberly announced: "The McGovern defense plan: He would cut the Marines by one-half. He would cut Air Force personnel by one-third and interceptor planes by one-fourth. . . ." With each statement, a hand swept away portions of toy soldiers, miniature warships and planes. The voice then concluded: "President Nixon doesn't believe we should play games with our national security."

In 1976, however, both Jimmy Carter and Gerald Ford relied less on this kind of emotional advertising than on documentary-style commercials portraying the candidates as just plain folks. Consultants for both candidates believed voters would be swayed more by low-keyed, upbeat commercials than by negative, opponent-baiting advertising. Ford's ads, for example, showed him delivering his State of the Union message to Congress or working at the White House, emphasizing the traditional virtues of the incumbent: "President Ford is your President. Keep him." Similarly, the Carter spots featured him on his Georgia farm sifting peanuts through his fingers, proclaiming that government should be as "good and honest and decent and truthful . . . and as filled with love as the American people."

Some observers believe this simple documentary approach probably will be used increasingly in future campaigns. It avoids the negativism of the older-style commercials and is particularly suited to portraying candidates in the most favorable light possible. Advertising specialists can shoot hours of film, splicing together thirty-second and one-minute spots of candidates at their best and disposing of the remainder showing

Senator Birch Bayh

them as they are normally. In short, the documentary approach provides a means of exposing candidates under controlled conditions, while suggesting to voters that the presentations are natural and unrehearsed.

But whatever style of political commercials are employed in future campaigns, candidates probably will continue to take advantage of one-minute spots. The reasons are easy to understand. Apart from being less expensive than longer ads, short political commercials can be tucked conveniently into popular television shows like *Love Boat* or *M*A*S*H*, to reach those voters who happen to be watching. Spot commercials can catch voters unaware, exposing them to the messages before they can turn them off. Indeed, as some campaign managers see it, the only effective way to reach many voters is to sneak up on them, surprising them with a political message while they sit before their sets complacently enjoying something else.

Moreover, one-minute spots can grab the attention of voters by projecting single dramatic themes using graphic visual effects similar to those found in commercial ads. Candidates have found that viewers are not as irritated by and bored with short commercials as they are with longer ones, especially if the commercials do not preempt their favorite shows. Adlai Stevenson once made the mistake in the 1950s of replacing an *I Love Lucy* show with a campaign address. As a result of this "unforgivable act," Stevenson later received a letter from an irate viewer who wrote: "I Like Ike and I Love Lucy. Drop Dead."

It appears, therefore, that instead of using television to illuminate the issues and to acquaint voters with their qualifications, candidates have frequently allowed themselves to be merchandized for public consumption like boxes of detergent. When Joe McGinniss, in his book *The Selling of the President 1968*,[3] revealed the premium that campaign managers place on good lighting, makeup, and a format tailored to the expectations of viewers, he demonstrated how carefully packaged many campaigns have become. He showed that a campaign manager's task is not so much to reveal a candidate's stand on the issues as to display whatever images are most likely to win votes. In this respect, political advertising raises even more objections than commercial advertising. "If a television commercial," one observer contends, "makes you like the image of one kind of toothpaste enough to buy a tube, it is no great matter if you find you don't like the stuff after all. You can quickly revert to the brand you like. If a television commercial makes you like the image of a politician, it may be six years before you can change him and he is next to impossible to throw away."[4]

Indeed, criticism of political advertising has been sufficiently severe to spark a number of proposals for reform. There has been a growing demand for more "structured" formats similar to the Ford-Carter presidential debates in 1976 and for improved press coverage of political campaigns. But before we look at these proposals, we should consider whether political advertising really changes people's minds. In view of the efforts of Madison Avenue advertising specialists to "sell" political candidates, are people actually persuaded by media campaigns?

The Media and Political Opinion

Probably, as we will see, the media do have considerable impact on political perceptions over the long run, especially in affecting people's views of government, social issues, and political events. But evidence indicates that, for the relatively short duration of a typical political campaign, television and other media rarely have the powerful impact on people's opinions that many have assumed. While the information spread during campaigns may be distorted, it tends to be interpreted in ways that reinforce the political opinions acquired from the family, school, and friends.

Several hypotheses have been offered to account for this.[5] One is that many people *selectively expose* themselves to television programs, magazines, and campaign speeches with which they already agree. They seek out information sources that reinforce their opinions rather than those that contradict them. Democrats, for example, are likely to listen more attentively to speeches of Democratic candidates than to those of Republican opponents. Apparently, it is often psychologically easier for people to absorb information that bolsters their present views than to confront new information that challenges them.

This does not mean that people can always avoid information that conflicts with their opinions. Television spot commercials, for instance, usually can attract viewers' attention before they can change the channel. And when debates between opposing candidates are aired, it is difficult for viewers to ignore one candidate entirely and pay attention only to the other.

Moreover, changes in opinion sometimes occur when there are strong cross-pressures or when people confront potentially dissonant situations that require adjustments in their thinking. This may happen when they see a politician they respect courting the favor of one they dislike, thus forcing a change of opinion toward one or possibly even both. One can only speculate how conservative Republicans initially reacted to the televised coverage of Richard Nixon's amiable conversations with Mao Tse-tung on his 1972 visit to China.

The media's impact during campaigns, however, depends not only on the sort of messages sent, but on how messages are construed. People not only select the messages they wish to hear; they selectively *interpret* them as well. Instead of merely absorbing information from the media like human sponges, voters color and shape it according to their own predispositions. Thus, a Democrat may see a Republican candidate in a political commercial without ever getting the message that was intended. The voter may interpret the commercial to mean what he wants it to mean, not what the candidate was trying to say.

The tendency to perceive information selectively has been noted even in people's reactions to physical phenomena. Psychologists have found in several intriguing experiments that people's perceptions of moving lights, shapes of objects, and even sizes of other people are determined, in part, by what they are used to seeing—or wish to see. If people suddenly are confronted with an unusual phenomenon, it often will be altered to fit their normal expectations.[6]

Moreover, as we discussed in an earlier chapter, messages carried by the media frequently go through a "two-step flow." Rather than persuading people directly, the messages are often interpreted by a smaller number of "opinion leaders" who pass on their interpretations to others. A televised campaign speech or a debate may not affect viewers' opinions as much as what someone they respect says about the event later on. And in the process, the opinion leader may alter the information to conform to his or her own views.

One final point. Some observers suspect that the reinforcement effect may also include a cynicism or skepticism toward much that is advertised, including politicians. Children, for example, often find that the toys they buy break down easily in spite of their advertised quality. Adults, too, find that products are often less reliable than alleged. Skepticism results. The same is true of political advertising; despite all the claims made in a political ad, voters know that more is usually promised than achieved.

"With a Little Help from My Friends"

If these selective processes reduce the likelihood that media campaigns will change political views, why do candidates continue to rely heavily on the media in their efforts to become elected? Most of them certainly are aware that voters reinforce their existing opinions and are not totally susceptible to political messages. Consequently, candidates must derive advantages from using television and other media that take account of and offset the limitations implied.

Reinforce Partisan Support

One reason for using the media is to bolster weak support and persuade loyalists to trek to the polls rather than stay at home. Because almost two-thirds of all American voters still tend to identify with one of the two major parties, Democratic and Republican candidates alike must broaden their party base and persuade as many potential supporters as possible to vote. Indeed, many elections can be won just by ensuring the turnout of partisans who are inclined to vote along party lines.

But this is often a difficult task. Many potential supporters are affiliated only weakly with a party and, for a variety of reasons, seldom vote. Consequently, the candidate must rely on media campaigns to reach these people and persuade them to lend their support. He must identify his views with theirs and convince them—as though peddling a popular brand of deodorant soap—that, unless they support his candidacy, they will suffer the consequences. Thus, although media campaigns may not change the minds of voters who cling loyally to the opposition party, they can reinforce the support of partisan voters, whom the candidate needs to win.

Attract Independents

A second, and increasingly more important, reason for using the media is to attract the support of the growing number of independent and undecided voters (see Chapter 6). These people remain uncommitted to any party candidate and may be susceptible to the right kind of media campaign. Because their party bonds are weak, they may not be as subject to the same selective processes—exposure and perception especially—that insulate other voters from the emotional pitches of partisan politics. And, in a close election, the uncommitted voters can swing the election either way. "It seems clear," one scholar concludes, "that professional politicians drive themselves and their organizations to influence every remaining undecided voter in the hope and expectation that they are providing or maintaining a winning margin."[7]

An intriguing question thus arises. If the number of independent voters continues to climb, does this mean that television and other media will play an ever-expanding role in political campaigns? It would seem that, as more voters split their tickets, politicians will find it less valuable to identify closely with a party. Instead, they will be tempted to lean even more heavily on the media to display their independent qualifications and personal attractiveness. The role of party labels will thus be weakened even further, with television and other media displacing parties as the primary basis for deciding which politicians to support. In addition, as the importance of the media increases, so will the importance of having the money to pay for media campaigns, whether privately or publicly provided. (For more on campaign financing, see Chapter 6.)

Publicity for Unknown Candidates

Certainly a third, even more basic, reason to rely on media campaigns is to gain added visibility. An unknown candidate running against a popular incumbent especially needs television and other media to attract attention to himself and overcome the traditional support favoring the incumbent. "Because the newcomer is unknown," one scholar suggests, "his managers know that voters will not come to his public appearances, peruse his literature, note his displays, or read about him in newspapers. He must therefore wage his campaign in the voters' homes when residents settle down to be entertained."[8]

Indeed, in many statewide and national elections, television can be the crucial factor in assuring a victory at the polls. By using television, a candidate can display his charms to millions of potential voters with no more effort than that needed to reach hundreds in a speech before a town-hall gathering. With an extensive television campaign of spot commercials and speeches, a relatively obscure candidate can become known quickly to millions of party loyalists, independents, and opinion leaders whose support he needs for an electoral victory.

Our Window on the Political World

In considering the relationship between the media and our political opinions and behavior, we should keep in mind that the media can have significant long-term effects other than just possibly influencing our votes during campaigns. Because our relationship to the media is a lifetime experience, the media undoubtedly present images of government and the world that indirectly affect our social and political views. Our attitudes toward violence, sex, and authority are very likely influenced by the television programs, films, books, and magazines to which we are exposed during our lives.

Recent research, for example, suggests that people who watch violent programs on television see the world outside as a more dangerous and frightening place than those who watch very little. Heavy viewers consistently overestimate the crime rate, the number of police officers in the United States, and their own chances of encountering violence. They are less trustful of other people and more fearful of their environment. Some researchers speculate that such fear may actually contribute to the current flight from our cities and bring increased demands for the election of law-and-order candidates.[9]

Still, if we review studies on the long-term influences of television and other media, we will encounter an abundance of contradictory findings. We will learn that social scientists have experienced considerable difficulty in agreeing on the precise long-term impact of the media, in part because they must take into account millions of messages—from the media and other sources—to which we are exposed. Even those within the media offer contradictory evaluations of the media's impact on behavior. The three television networks, for example, sell billions of dollars worth of advertising time to major corporations on the assumption that viewers' buying habits will be influenced by repetitive ads. Yet, when the same networks are chided for presenting violent crime shows or airing commercials peddling sugar-coated cereals to children, they insist their programming has no harmful effects on behavior.

For the purposes of this chapter, however, we might consider ways in which the media may have affected our perceptions of government and politics, keeping in mind that several interpretations are possible. Because the media play such important roles in providing us with information, we might want to know whether such information has been reliable, how it has influenced our views of government, and whether it has increased our awareness of and interest in political issues.

Information on Government

To begin with, much of the information we receive—information on which we must base our actions—has been provided by media often tied to powerful economic interests. In this country many television stations, publishing houses, and newspapers are multimillion-dollar enterprises owned and controlled by large corporations like Westinghouse, ITT, and RCA. These enterprises rely heavily for their profits on advertising by other large corporations and often share the same values as other economic elites.

As we noted earlier, advocates of the ruling-elite theory regard television and other media as instruments of powerful elite interests. They see the economic and political controls over the content of the media as a means by which elites can perpetuate their own values and self-interests. By controlling the media, elites not only determine the flow of information to the public but give the public few opportunities to obtain radically different or critical viewpoints.

Although the charges of ruling-elite theorists are somewhat exaggerated (certainly neither the chairman of General Motors nor the Joint Chiefs of Staff of the military regard magazines like *Playboy*, *Ms*, or *Mother Jones* as the best vehicles for expressing their interests), the media, over the long run, do not give "equal time" to all points of view. Most television stations and newspapers in the United States are fundamentally commercial enterprises that cater to a mass audience and are not prone to emphasize political perspectives that have not yet become fashionable or "newsworthy." Radical political ideas are rarely presented with much enthusiasm by most of the media and tend to be limited to a few magazines and newspapers with relatively small distribution. (Of course, this situation may reflect the public's own narrow selective orientations, as well as the economic and political realities of media ownership.)

The lack of diversity is also aided by the steady decline of competing voices, especially among newspapers. Even in the larger cities like New York and Chicago, there are fewer and fewer competing dailies. It has been estimated that only about 3 percent of American cities have more than one daily paper. In fact, in many cities the same people who run

"So much for *my* version of the news. And now over to my colleague for the same news but with a different set of biases, hangups, and axes to grind."

Source: Drawing by Donald Reilly; © *1970 The New Yorker Magazine, Inc.*

the newspaper also own one of the local television stations. And, as production and circulation costs mount, more and more papers are bought up by large chains like Hearst, Times-Mirror, or Newhouse. More than half of all the nation's dailies are now under chain ownership and frequently reflect the editorial viewpoints of the parent organizations.

Moreover, the media's interpretations of political occurrences are rarely unbiased. Newspapers, magazines, and television stations— whether considered liberal or conservative—interpret events in terms of their own political perceptions, rarely offering totally dispassionate or nonideological coverage. Even when political reports aim toward objectivity, selective perception and interpretation remain as inescapable for those in the media as for anyone else. In deciding which stories to emphasize, for example, and which ones to downplay, those in the media, in effect, set the political "agenda." They not only tell people what to think, but what to think about. They define what are the important issues and what aspect of those issues should be deliberated. Thus, although most people may realize that the evening news consists largely of selective views of the "important" events of the day, they may still mistake the news as a total portrait of reality. They may still confuse the compelling and highly selective fragments pieced together by reporters and media executives with the whole of politics for that day.

There is also a tendency to view the interaction between the news media and government principally in terms of an adversary relationship. Reporters are often romantically seen as neutral and tireless conveyers of information, seeking the facts about politicians completely independent of government in their search for the truth. Yet, while much of this romantic image may hold true, it tends to obscure the enormous amount of cooperation that takes place between the press and government. Governmental officials depend greatly on the publicity that the press can provide, while reporters depend on official briefings, "leaks," and handouts for the news they receive.

Even the social climate of Washington politics tends to foster this "cooperation." There is some question whether reporters can remain objective when they socialize with the political figures they are supposed to cover. It is not uncommon for Washington journalists to mingle with politicians on the dinner-party circuit or on the tennis courts. Although such social functions are perceived by journalists as a way of gaining access, the danger is that they may pull their punches on those they drink beer or have dinner with. Some observers wondered, for example, whether Henry Kissinger may have escaped much of the criticism he deserved for his role in the Vietnam War because he played the dinner circuit and charmed plenty of journalists. As columnist Mary McGrory reflected, it should not "matter that Henry Kissinger rolls his eyes and sighs a lot over the Christmas bombing of Hanoi. The important thing is the record—that's what he did."[10]

However, despite these limitations, television and other media have not neglected to provide essential political information. The media, contrary to the ruling-elite view, have furnished citizens with information on the activities of public officials and have helped expose deception in government. In fact, the news media frequently have collided with governmental officials who have tried to bring reporters around to an uncritical view of governmental policies—often without success.

This conflict flared frequently during the Nixon administration, which suffered repeated embarrassment from a number of sensational revelations in the press and on television: the Watergate break-in, the illegal campaign contributions, the White House tapes and transcripts, and evidence of Nixon's own culpability in the Watergate cover-up. In fact, the Nixon administration had been hostile to the news media from its inception, unleashing biting criticisms of the media through Vice-President Spiro Agnew's alliterative speeches, refusing to divulge details to the press about administration policies, threatening local radio and television stations with withdrawal of their licenses, and employing the Justice Department to intimidate news reporters into handing over confidential information to grand juries. As NBC correspondent John Chancellor remarked, "Other administrations have had a love-hate relationship with the press. The Nixon administration has had a hate-hate relationship."

The role of the press in uncovering the Watergate scandal particularly illuminated the bitter conflict that can erupt between the news media and government. At the initial outbreak of the story in the summer of 1972, administration officials complained sarcastically about the willingness of the press to play fast and loose with information derived from "hearsay" and "unofficial sources." Shortly after the break-in at the Watergate office and apartment complex, White House Press Secretary Ronald Zeigler chastised the *Washington Post* for blowing a "third-rate burglary" out of proportion. He chided reporters for printing "stories based on hearsay, character assassination, innuendo or guilt by association." The press, however, justified its stories on the principle of the public's "right to know." In fact, as the Watergate story unfolded, the press contended that the multitude of leaks on Watergate were warranted by the growing evidence that members of the administration were engaged in a wide-ranging cover-up of criminal activities. When official statements turned out to be false, the press felt it could not be blamed for turning to unofficial sources to get at the truth.

There were clearly dangers in this approach, as there would be in any effort to separate fact from rumor. As reporters Bob Woodward and Carl Bernstein acknowledged, there were times when they resorted to unorthodox methods to get the low-down on the Watergate story.[11] But it is certain that without persistent investigation and reporting by the press, the full dimensions of the scandal would have remained hidden. Despite the powers of the presidency used to try to cover up the scandal, the press—together with the courts and independent prosecutors—succeeded in unraveling many of the threads. As *New York Times* columnist James Reston wondered, "Would this scandal have reached the present point of disclosure if the press had not reported the secret testimony of witnesses in this case? Is a government which had knowledge of this kind of political espionage and sabotage, and then tried to conceal the facts, entitled to bar reporters from getting beyond the screen of

Bob Woodward and Carl Bernstein

secrecy?"[12] Even the administration and the Pulitzer Prize Committee eventually acknowledged the press's responsibilities in the case. By May 1973, the *Washington Post* received not only a public apology from Ronald Zeigler for his earlier comments but the coveted Pulitzer Prize for its coverage of the Watergate story.

Political Interest and Awareness

In addition to considering whether the media have provided useful and accurate information, we might consider whether television programs in particular have had much impact on political awareness, interest, and participation. When television first burst upon the political scene in the 1950 and 1952 elections, many observers believed it to be the greatest innovation in politics since radio. They marveled at television's ability to bring the outside world into American homes, at its capacity to make millions of viewers direct witnesses to the pageantry of politics. Indeed, for the first time in history, most Americans could observe, in the quiet leisure of their living rooms, the sweaty hoopla of a party convention, the tensions of a presidential address, even the machinations of a committee hearing in Congress.

Yet, has the advent of television raised the level of public involvement and interest in politics? Has it broadened public understanding of major issues and events? According to several studies, television does not appear to have stimulated greater interest and participation in politics.[13] In fact, as we will see shortly, there is even a possibility that television has discouraged such interest and participation.

One popular signpost of public attention to politics is the turnout in elections. Supposedly, if television has heightened political interest, one would find a larger percentage of Americans marching to the polls. Yet, as we may recall from Chapter 5, voter turnout in presidential elections since 1960 has been declining almost steadily. In the 1976 elections, the number of voters fell to only 54 percent, a percentage lower than in either 1936 or 1940, well before the advent of television. And, in the 1978 congressional elections, voter turnout plunged to only 36 percent. Although a number of factors—including increased mobility, a breakdown in party loyalties, and a deepening cynicism toward politics—also may be depressing voting levels, the expanding role of television in political affairs has not been accompanied by a surge in voter turnout.

Nor does there appear to have been any dramatic rise in the public's awareness of governmental and political affairs. As we also saw in Chapter 5, only 46 percent of those polled in 1973 could correctly identify their representative in Congress, a proportion only slightly higher than in the late 1940s. In 1977, a Gallup poll found that only 56 percent of Americans said they had "heard something about" Sen. Robert Dole of Kansas, the Republican party's vice-presidential nominee in the 1976 presidential election.[14] In other words, despite television, there is little evidence of the kind of accelerated public interest in, and awareness of, politics that many had anticipated.

Several explanations for this exist, including the charge that television has failed to educate the public. As stated earlier, American television has been criticized for saturating the airwaves with commercial entertainment that "disturbs no gray cells." Although most Americans report television as their main source of news, the amount of television time devoted to provocative political questions has been miniscule. Except for coverage of unusual political happenings, such as Watergate, there have been few broad and sophisticated presentations of current social and political events.

Indeed, some critics charge persuasively that the very presence of television has dulled sensibilities. Despite its capacity for exciting visual drama, most television fare has been low-keyed, commercial, and dull. It has encouraged passivity, demanding—unlike books and radio—almost no imagination or involvement from the viewer. Anthropologist Margaret Mead made an observation years ago that perhaps still remains applicable today. Television, she warned, "threatens to be a negative social influence, a way of accustoming people to dreary half-attention, just satisfying enough to dampen anyone's desire to read a book, or go out, or start a conversation; a way of keeping husbands home with their shoes off, of entertaining in-laws without effort. . . . Without a very large admixture of real events, real plays, real political excitement, real music, TV threatens the country with apathy at a time when we grievously need a stimulant."[15]

But the total responsibility does not rest with television alone. The same selective processes discussed earlier probably keep many people from watching even the few educational programs about politics that do surface on television. Those who remain disinterested in politics simply will not sit through programs of a political nature, regardless of their content or frequency. When the Senate Watergate hearings were televised during the summer of 1973, the networks were flooded by thousands of letters from irate viewers who complained angrily about the hearings' preemption of their favorite afternoon soap operas and game shows. Even though television can bring dramatic historical events into American homes, it cannot ensure that people will pay attention; it cannot guarantee that the ideas and images it projects will stimulate people to reflect on their significance.

Perceptions of Politics and Government

There may be an added consequence of television, however, that affects people's perceptions of politics and desire to participate. As we have seen, most Americans today regard politics as a "dirty business" and cast a cynical eye on the activities of government. Perhaps, as Kurt and Gladys Lang suggest, this cynicism has been nurtured by the tendency of television news programs to highlight the unusual and negative aspects of politics—the battles, the scandals, and the crises—and thus to present a distorted view of the political process. "Television's style in chronicling political events," they argue, "can effect the fundamental orientations of the voter toward his government. It can undermine or bolster public confidence in the viability of political institutions and in the ability of political leaders to discharge their responsibilities."[16] During the 1970s, for example, the highlights of television coverage of Washington politics included the Watergate hearings, the White House tapes controversy, the indictment and conviction of high governmental officials, the impeachment deliberations, and the resignations of President Nixon and Vice-President Agnew. Although these events did not mark all of the accomplishments of national government during the decade, the extensive coverage of these events on television undoubtedly reinforced many people's distrust of politicians. Whereas before, people may have suspected that politics was riddled with corruption and dishonesty, now they had proof.

Obviously, television does not create such events; crises and scandals in government were inflicted on citizens long before the introduction of television. But the ability of the medium to dramatize these events and bring them visually into the living room may reinforce defensive reactions to politics and serve to justify lack of interest and participation—a condition one study refers to as "television malaise."[17]

Also television coverage may create an added sense of remoteness in that political and social events often gain a distant and unreal aura. The disgust with politics, Kurt and Gladys Lang reflect, may be "nothing but a defensive reaction against . . . reality that is overbearing, against the unfamiliar and the frightening, where 'remote' events and invisible powers seem to determine the destiny of the individual who can do nothing about it."[18] Indeed, we cannot expect information to motivate people to participate if they feel they do not have access to power. If television is indeed a window on the political world, it is also a partition. It keeps viewers at arm's length, showing them crises and suffering thousands of miles away that they feel they cannot prevent. In this society, a wide chasm separates the enormous flow of information and the opportunities to act. Television exposes people to problems of society, yet does not offer them a corresponding channel for effective action. Thus, it can be argued that television and other media can breed frustration. In the absence of a meaningful relationship between information and the ability to act, viewers receive no alleviation of the tensions produced by knowing that a problem exists and yet feeling too impotent to solve it. (For more on this point, see Chapter 15.)

DOONESBURY   **by Garry Trudeau**

Television and Political Personality

A final, and somewhat different, question about television is what long-term effect it may have on our choice of political leaders. Because of television, do politicians with the best "images"—the most careful packaging—stand the best chance of winning public office?

According to some observers, the introduction of the "television personality" into political campaigns has been one of the most significant developments in the age of television. Although campaigns revolved around personalities long before television arrived, the medium, they charge, has placed a greater premium on superficial characteristics—the attractive face, the broad smile, the commanding presence—than on intelligence and ability. It has given tremendous impetus to politicians like Ronald Reagan and Edward Kennedy, who conform to the expectations of a commercial entertainment medium in which a physically attractive appearance is a definite plus. Some observers have even argued that several former presidents, if they were alive today, might have had a more difficult time winning national office. Although Abraham Lincoln, for example, was a striking man in several respects, his high-pitched voice, angular features, and trimmed beard might not endear him to a contemporary television audience.

Sociologist Marshall McLuhan even suggests that television favors not only attractive politicians but those with certain kinds of personalities.[19] For office seekers to be embraced by viewers today, he contends, their projected images must be attractive and soft, an image he defines in part as "cool." They must not appear too loud or abrasive, invading the intimacy of the living room with an overbearing presence—a tendency of Hubert Humphrey's that some observers believed ensured his presidential election defeats. Thus, according to McLuhan, during the Great Debates in the 1960 presidential campaigns, the "blurry, shaggy texture" of John Kennedy triumphed over the "sharp, intense image" of Richard Nixon. To many voters who watched the debates, Nixon did not appear as appealing as Kennedy, regardless of what the two men were actually saying. As Theodore White recounted, "Probably no picture in American politics tells a better story . . . than that famous shot of the camera on the Vice-President as he half slouched, his 'Lazy Shave' powder faintly streaked with sweat, his eyes exaggerated hollows of blackness, his jaw, jowls, and face drooping with strain."[20] Even Nixon himself admitted, "I spent too much time . . . on substance and too little on appearance. I paid too much attention to what I was going to say and too little to how I would look"[21]

We must not, of course, carry this point too far; certain appearances do not always ensure victory or defeat. Many people are elected to

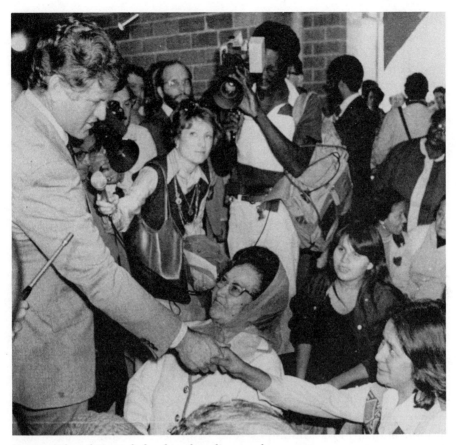
Senator Edward Kennedy has broad media appeal.

public office who do not fit the stereotypes established by McLuhan or anyone else. Nevertheless, media specialists and campaign managers do take account of appearance and personality in the broadest sense, deliberately placing candidates in staged settings—whether in the Oval Office or on a Georgia peanut farm—that offer selected views of their most pleasing qualities.

This then raises the question we began with: Does television give advertising agencies and campaign managers a chance to fool the American public—to corrupt their vote—with staged presentations and false images? Does television, in other words, permit a potential leader's qualifications (or lack of them) to become more perceptible to the public, or does it allow them to remain hidden and disguised?

Some believe that, because of the pervasiveness of media campaigns, office seekers are not required to stand exposed before the voters. Apart from such occasional media "events" as presidential debates (which we will examine shortly), candidates do not have to reveal their true personalities. Instead, most of their appearances are controlled and staged, and their media campaigns offer only one-sided, artificial images fabricated by their campaign managers.

Others believe, however, that television tends to reveal more than disguise the qualities of those seeking public office. In a typical national campaign, candidates are in the spotlight so many times, and seen in so many different circumstances, that most voters *can* get a good idea of what sorts of persons they really are. During the 1972 presidential primaries, for example, Sen. Edmund Muskie was mercilessly unmasked by television. In the most dramatic instance, network television caught him sobbing in front of the *Manchester Union Leader* offices as he tried to respond to charges contained in a phony letter published by that New Hampshire newspaper. "It changed people's minds about me, of what kind of guy I was," Muskie later lamented. "They were looking for a strong, steady man, and here I was weak."[22] Thus, in the opinion of some observers, despite the efforts of image makers to present only the most favorable aspects of their candidates, television will reveal many of the true qualities of those hoping to gain public office.

It should be pointed out, of course, that it is difficult for most people to know from television alone whether the images of candidates are accurate. Only those who know them personally can gauge the degree of distortion, if any, by television. In fact, television may both reveal and mask the qualifications of office seekers, depending on the style of their campaigns. Nevertheless, given the reliance on advertising and staged presentations, most campaigns tend to project the images campaign managers want voters to see. As one scholar has concluded, "Possibly a more reasonable approach would be to state that television can unmask a charlatan, if those responsible for use of camera and microphone want to do so. But given control over the television situation—makeup, lighting, camera angles, speechwriting, teleprompting, and the like—there is no reason in the world that the basic appearance of a candidate cannot be acceptable. (It may not be a crashing success, but there are specialists in the field of personal public relations and deportment who could get a man past either Emily Post or the casual voter.)"[23]

Evaluation: Televised Debates and the Press

In view of the controversy surrounding the media's role in political campaigns, it is not surprising that a number of media-related reforms

The Nixon/Kennedy debate, 1960

have come under consideration. Because of the manipulation and packaging involved in past television campaigning, a growing demand has been heard for campaigns in the 1980s to rely less on trying to "sell" candidates and to become more issue oriented. Instead of using traditional advertising techniques, campaigns should be structured around press conferences and debates, in which candidates must demonstrate an understanding of political problems and an ability to handle them. Televised debates especially have been advocated as a proper forum for presenting candidates to the viewers. They have the advantage of bringing together the major adversaries and thus overcoming the tendency of voters to become exposed to only one side. And they presumably give voters a better opportunity to assess the candidates' qualifications.

Many observers were heartened by the effort made in 1967 to deal with political issues through televised debates between Jimmy Carter and Gerald Ford. Not since the Kennedy-Nixon debates in 1960 had a similar televised confrontation been staged between the presidential candidates of the two major parties. Under the sponsorship of the League of Women Voters, Ford and Carter met face to face in three ninety-minute televised debates. (A fourth debate was also held between the two vice-presidential candidates, Walter Mondale and Robert Dole.)

The debates took place at a time when public confidence in government was extremely low. Both men were aware of this fact and pitched their presentations to it, trying to appear trustworthy and presidential. According to opinion polls, most of those surveyed thought Ford "won" the first debate on domestic issues, while Carter edged Ford in both the second debate on foreign affairs and the third covering a wide range of issues. And at least 57 percent of those polled considered the debates "helpful" in making a choice between the candidates.[24]

Under most circumstances, it is not to an incumbent's advantage to engage in a televised debate. A debate tends to give the lesser-known challenger needed exposure, provides him with a stature equal to the incumbent's in the eyes of voters, and puts the incumbent in a position of having to defend his policies. (It was largely for these reasons that Lyndon Johnson backed away from confronting Barry Goldwater in 1964 and that Richard Nixon refused to debate George McGovern in 1972.) Ford, however, was far behind in the polls and felt he had more to gain than lose from a televised showdown with Carter.

Still, there is some doubt whether televised debates truly provide a significantly more rational approach to campaigning, especially considering that what candidates say may not be as important as how they look. As stated earlier, many who witnessed the 1960 Kennedy-Nixon debates responded more favorably to Kennedy's overall style than to Nixon's, allowing details of appearance to overshadow what the two men were actually saying. "Some scanty evidence from the Kennedy-Nixon debates," Kurt and Gladys Lang point out, "suggests that the dramatic improvement of Kennedy's personal image that followed the first debate did not extend to radio listeners. The relatively few who listened (mainly to car radios) were apt to call the debate a 'draw,' while viewers, who were witnesses to Kennedy's drive and energy and Nixon's apparent discomfort, credited Kennedy with a clear 'win.'"[25]

What about press coverage of political campaigns? There is a common belief that television newscasts and press reports provide voters with more complete and accurate information on the candidates than does political advertising. Yet, in several respects, campaign news coverage also falls short in providing substantive information. This is particularly true of television journalism. TV reporters covering the campaign trail often fall captive to media "events," focusing on the campaign stories that make for the flashiest pictures: the crowds, motorcades, rallies, and other hoopla. What the voters tend to get is a great deal of information on the campaign skirmishes and activities of the participants, and little on the problems facing the country and the solutions proposed by the candidates. One study of the 1972 elections, for instance, found that most of the network coverage was devoted to "horse race" trivia—who was "ahead" in the race for delegates, who would receive the most endorsements, and so on. Less than 3 percent was devoted to reporting on the candidates' stands on the issues. "By contrast," the study concluded, "newspapers were far more effective than television in making voters better informed on the issues."[26]

In the 1976 elections, television and newspaper reporters alike seemed preoccupied with the candidates' blunders. A great deal of attention was focused on Ford's gaffe in the second presidential debate when he said that Poland was free of Soviet influence and on Carter's famous *Playboy* interview (November 1976) in which he admitted his "lust" for women. Carter himself complained in the same interview that "the traveling press has zero interest in any issue unless it's a matter of making a mistake." No reporter following his campaign, Carter said, "would ask an issue question unless he thought he could trick me into some crazy statement."

Reporters respond, with some justification, that such lapses in reporting are largely the result of the emptiness of the campaigns themselves. As they see it, the candidates encourage poor press coverage by avoiding discussions of controversial issues. Reporters do confess, however, that they sometimes fall prey to another problem in campaign coverage: "pack journalism." After sitting in the same buses and planes week after

The Carter/Ford debate, 1976

week following the candidates, they come to share certain perceptions, going after the same stories and covering them in the same way. They not only share their drinks and cigarettes, but their notes and story leads as well. According to journalist Timothy Crouse, this pack syndrome stems inevitably from the reporter's determination to cover every aspect of the campaign and to publish the pap each day because every other reporter is doing the same thing.[27]

But whatever the merits or weaknesses of debates and press reporting, many people clearly would welcome an alternative to paid political advertising. As it stands now, instead of using the media to illuminate the issues and present their qualifications, politicians allow themselves to be "packaged" with all the razzle-dazzle of commercial advertising. As former television correspondent Eric Sevaried once concluded, "This is the age of appearances, when the wrapping seems more important than the contents."[28]

Key Terms

    mass media

    spot commercial

    selective exposure/perception

Notes

1. Snell Putney and Gail J. Putney, *The Adjusted American* (New York: Harper & Row, 1966), p. 188.

2. Quoted in Robert MacNeil, *The People Machine: The Influence of Television on American Politics* (New York: Harper & Row, 1968), p. 210.

3. Joe McGinniss, *The Selling of the President 1968* (New York: Trident Press, 1969).

4. MacNeil, *The People Machine*, pp. 193–194.

5. See, for example, Joseph T. Klapper, *The Effects of Mass Communication* (New York: Free Press, 1960); David O. Sears and Jonathan Freedman, "Selective Exposure to Information: A Critical Review," *Public Opinion Quarterly*, Summer 1967, pp. 194–213.

6. See, for example, W. H. Ittleson and F. P. Kilpatrick, "Experiments in Perception," *Scientific American*, August 1951, pp. 50–55.

7. William H. Flanigan, *Political Behavior of the American Electorate*, 2nd ed. (Boston: Allyn and Bacon, 1972), p. 108.

8. Dan Nimmo, *The Political Persuaders: The Techniques of Modern Election Campaings* (Englewood Cliffs, N.J.: Prentice-Hall, 1970), p. 138

9. George Gerbner and Larry Gross, "The Scary World of TV's Heavy Viewer," *Psychology Today*, April 1976.

10. Mary McGrory, quoted in *Newsweek*, 1 December 1975, p. 90.

11. Bob Woodward and Carl Bernstein, *All the President's Men* (New York: Simon and Schuster, 1974).

12. James Reston, *New York Times*, 9 May 1973.

13. See, for example, Angus Campbell, "Has Television Reshaped Politics?" pp. 318–323 in *Political Opinion and Electoral Behavior*, (Belmont, Calif.: Wadsworth, 1966).

14. *Gallup Opinion Index*, November, 1977.

15. Margaret Mead, "A Force That Can Change the Nature of Society." *TV Guide*, 10 March 1962, pp. 9–11.

16. Kurt Lang and Gladys E. Lang, *Politics and Television* (New York: Quadrangle/The New York Times Co., 1968), p. 306.

17. Michael J. Robinson, "Public Affairs Television and the Growth of Political Malaise: The Case of the 'The Selling of the Pentagon,'" *American Political Science Review*, June 1976, pp. 409–432.

18. Lang and Lang, *Politics and Television*, p. 307.

19. Marshall McLuhan, *Understanding Media* (New York: McGraw-Hill, 1964).

20. Theodore H. White, *The Making of the President 1960* (New York: Atheneum, 1961), p. 289.

21 Richard M. Nixon, *Six Crises* (Garden City, N.J.: Doubleday, 1962), p. 341.

22. Quoted in Theodore H. White, *The Making of the President 1972* (New York: Atheneum, 1973), p. 82.

23. Charles A. H. Thomson, *Television and Presidential Politics* (Washington, D.C.: Brookings Institution, 1956), p. 139.

24. *Newsweek*, 8 November 1976, p. 20.

25. Lang and Lang, *Politics and Television*, p. 296.

26. Thomas E. Patterson and Robert D. McClure, "Political Campaigns: TV Power is a Myth," *Psychology Today*, July 1976. See also Doris A. Graber, "Press and TV as Opinion Resources in Presidential Campaigns," *Public Opinion Quarterly*, Fall 1976, pp. 285–303.

27. Timothy Crouse, *The Boys on the Bus* (New York: Random House, 1973).

28. Quoted in Bernard Rubin, *Political Television* (Belmont, Calif.: Wadsworth, 1967), p. 33.

Recommended Reading

CROUSE, TIMOTHY. *The Boys on the Bus.* New York: Random House, 1973.

EPSTEIN, EDWARD J. *News From Nowhere.* New York: Random House, 1973.

LANG, KURT, and GLADYS E. LANG. *Politics and Television.* New York: Quadrangle/The New York Times Co., 1968.

McGinniss, Joe. *The Selling of the President 1968*. New York: Trident Press, 1969.

McLuhan, Marshall. *Understanding Media*. New York: McGraw-Hill, 1964.

MacNeil, Robert. *The People Machine: The Influence of Television on American Politics*. New York: Harper & Row, 1968.

Mickelson, Sig. *The Electric Mirror*, New York: Dodd, Mead, 1972.

Nimmo, Dan, and Robert Savage. *Candidates and Their Images*. Santa Monica, Calif.: Goodyear, 1976.

Patterson, Thomas E., and Robert D. McClure. *The Unseeing Eye: The Myth of Television Power in National Elections*. New York: Putnam, 1976.

Rivers, William L., and Michael J. Nyhan, eds. *Aspen Notebook on Government and the Media*. New York: Praeger, 1973.

Rubin, Bernard. *Media, Politics, and Democracy*. New York: Oxford University Press, 1977.

Woodward, Bob, and Carl Bernstein. *All the President's Men*. New York: Simon and Schuster, 1974.

PART THREE

The Policy Makers: Participation at the Higher Levels

9

The President: High Rolling in Politics

Those of us who have ever dreamed of wielding great political power probably have tried to envision what it would be like to be president of the United States. For many of us, the presidency traditionally evokes images of great pomp and ceremony, of subordinates jumping to obey authoritative commands, and of economic and social crises being effectively challenged by the force of executive decision. The president appears to be an individual who has achieved the ultimate success in gaining access to and influence over the machinery of government.

Similar visions of success undoubtedly propel those candidates who campaign for the presidency. Seduced by the glamor and power of the office, they will sacrifice almost anything to gain command of the White House. They will endure the hardships and humiliations of a national campaign, expose themselves and their families to endless probings and personal criticisms, and pump friends and enemies alike for the funds needed to "sell" their candidacy to the voters. Rather than accept James Bryce's warning that "great men are not elected President," they will view their campaign for the office as a testament to their own call to political eminence.

Part of the great lure of the presidency is, of course, that it is an extremely adaptive office, responsive to the personality of each individual who sits in the White House. The vague duties of the office stated in the opening line of Article II—"The executive power shall be vested in a President of the United States of America"—ultimately allow for a great deal of flexibility. Each president has room to interpret his responsibilities to suit not only the needs of the times but also his own personal philosophy. Although some presidents have been reluctant to exercise great authority (Calvin Coolidge, for example, believed there already were too many laws and pledged not to recommend many new ones), other, more forceful chief executives (like Lincoln, Wilson, and the two Roosevelts) have interpreted the vague constitutional language to mean an absence of specific prohibitions and have acted accordingly to broaden their powers, setting precedents for future White House occupants. The nature of the office, John Kennedy reflected, demands that "the President place himself in the very thick of the fight" and that he "be prepared to exercise the fullest powers of his office—all that are specified and some that are not."[1]

Yet, the presidency is not without its political hazards. As Jimmy Carter discovered, those who eventually attain the office may experience frustration and defeat on a par with the glory and fame. As is true of any gamble involving high stakes, the pursuit of presidential power may either elevate an individual to greatness or plunge him into public disrepute. In fact, as shown by experiences with Vietnam and Watergate, errors of judgment and misconduct on the part of a president can result in blunders of tragic proportions, tragic not only for the person occupying the office but for those affected by his decisions. Instead of winning a reputation for goodwill, a president may become a historic anomaly, a public mistake shared by all who supported him.

Consider the case of Richard Nixon. With his resignation in August 1974, he left behind a legacy of public distrust and cynicism that damaged more than his own reputation. By abusing the powers of his office, he helped intensify public suspicion of politicians and governmental institutions alike. His complicity in the Watergate cover-up, compounded by his and Lyndon Johnson's calamitous Vietnam policies, took the presidency through a period of deep public distrust that may be unrivaled in U.S. history.[2] The very legitimacy of the presidency was tested, with enormous pressures put upon his immediate successors, Ford and Carter, to restore public confidence in the office—a task, incidentally, which still awaits history's final report card. And, as for Nixon himself, columnist George Will summarized it this way: "The disgrace is permanent. There are not going to be any Richard M. Nixon high schools, parks, highways, stadiums."[3]

August 9, 1974

Dear Mr. Secretary:

I hereby resign the Office of President of the
United States.

Sincerely,

[signature: Richard Nixon]

11.35 AM

HK

The Honorable Henry A. Kissinger
The Secretary of State
Washington, D.C. 20520

National Archives

Personality and Presidential Performance

The possibility of failing or succeeding in the presidency should remind
us that a president's personality can affect both his performance and his
responsiveness to the citizenry. His sensitivity to citizen concerns and
his capacity and willingness to confront social problems is inextricably
bound up, not only with his possible ties to certain elite interests (see
Chapter 2), but with his character, motivations, and view of his office.
Indeed, those hoping to sway executive decision making—through letters, interest-group activity, or demonstrations—must confront the
question of presidential personality. Some observers insist, for instance,
that the reluctance of both Lyndon Johnson and Richard Nixon to face
up to the mounting protests against the Vietnam War revealed not only
a stubborn commitment to military policy but also a hypersensitivity to
criticism and alternate views.

The realization, in fact, that personality ties in with conduct has led to some highly controversial "psychobiographical" studies of presidential behavior. Political scientist James David Barber, for instance, has drawn biographical sketches of thirteen recent chief executives in an effort to understand more clearly the influence of personality on the exercise of presidential power.[4] Because a president's personality—his character, style, and world view—may have a profound impact on national affairs, Barber suggests we analyze each future chief executive to predict his likely performance under stress, insisting that we can make such a prediction if we study his "psychological makeup." By examining his earliest childhood and adult experiences, we can anticipate what he will do while in the White House. Show us a child with an overbearing, cantankerous father and a domineering mother, and we may find a president beset by hostility and unpredictable impulses.

Taking this thesis even further, Barber contends that early experiences usually result in one of four different presidential types: "active-positives," "active-negatives," "passive-positives," and "passive-negatives." Barber uses the "active/passive" dichotomy to describe the amount of energy a president invests in the office and the "positive/negative" dichotomy to indicate how a president feels about what he does. Thus, "active-positive" presidents want most to achieve results and enjoy exercising power. They tend to possess relatively high self-esteem, as well as an ability to adapt to changing circumstances (Franklin Roosevelt, Truman, Kennedy, Ford, and Carter). "Active-negatives" also seek results, but seldom get as much pleasure from the task. Their actions seem more compulsive, and they tend to view life as a hard struggle to gain and maintain political power (Wilson, Hoover, Johnson, and Nixon). "Passive-positive" presidents search for affection as a reward for being agreeable. They do not accomplish much, but enjoy the adulation that comes with the office (Taft and Harding). The "passive-negatives" not only accomplish little but retreat from the demands and conflicts of the job by stressing vague civic virtues. For them, the burdens of politics tend to outweigh the enjoyments (Coolidge and Eisenhower).

Barber issues a special warning about the second type of presidential character: the "active-negative." This type of individual, Barber believes, tends to be motivated by anxieties and guilts, and has difficulty controlling his aggressions. Because such a person sometimes confuses national policy with his own ambitions and becomes fixated on a policy regardless of the consequences—as Johnson did with Vietnam and as Nixon did with the Watergate cover-up—the "active-negative" president can be an especially dangerous individual who may bring on disaster.

Some critics, of course, have questioned Barber's categories, pointing out that even "active-positive" presidents can act aggressively and irresponsibly. President Kennedy, for example, may have had a more healthy view of life, but he was still capable of approving a debacle like the invasion of Cuba at the Bay of Pigs in 1961.

Indeed, there are problems in making psychological interpretations from a distance. While it may be possible to augment our understanding of presidential behavior by examining early childhood and adult experiences, there are dangers in merely picking out certain incidents in the past to account for later actions. Such incidents may only seem to tie in with later actions and may not be typical of the individual's past or future behavior. When it comes to predicting presidential behavior, it may be difficult to know which experiences are truly relevant and which are not.

The Burdens and the Glories

In any event, we should not become so involved in examining the personality differences between individuals who occupy the White House that we ignore the special requirements of the office. The relationship between personality and performance works both ways, in that the office influences the incumbent's behavior just as his behavior affects the office. Persons seeking the presidency and those struggling to influence it must take into account the scope and complexity of the president's many competing responsibilities. As adaptive as the presidency may be, the job still carries with it certain expectations.

The Constitution and tradition have assigned to the office a number of duties that every president is expected to perform. He is supposed to direct the federal bureaucracy, propose new federal programs, serve as ceremonial head of state, lead his party, and assume major responsibility for foreign and military affairs. Although the discretionary nature of the office permits him to choose which of these duties to emphasize, he cannot ignore any of them. At various times during his term of office, he will find himself immersed in a problem that, as party leader or commander in chief, he is expected to solve. And he will find himself judged not only by the policies he personally initiates as president, but by how well he handles the other responsibilities thrust upon him.

The Weight of Bureaucracy

When a president takes office, he assumes command of one of the largest government bureaucracies in the world, an administrative enterprise with close to three million civilian employees. This is because the framers of the Constitution expected the president to take charge of the federal agencies that administer the nation's social and legal services. They stipulated in Article II that "the executive power shall be vested in a President of the United States" who shall "take care that the laws be faithfully executed."

Indeed, it is a safe bet that no other executive in government or industry has as many administrative responsibilities as the president. No other executive has as many buttons to push, as much money to spend, as many employees to supervise. As a result of the provisions in Article II and congressional statutes, the president is expected to oversee the entire federal bureaucracy and to appoint (or discharge) thousands of top officials outside the civil service system, including department and agency heads and U.S. ambassadors. On top of that, Congress since 1921 has expected the president each year to submit a budget covering the operating expenses of all federal agencies and programs, a budget that by 1980 exceeded $530 billion.

Of course, the president is not expected to administer the bureaucracy single-handedly. Most of the day-to-day responsibilities are delegated to subordinates who in turn place most of the burden on their underlings. Over the years, a number of agencies have been created to help the president make administrative decisions. In addition to his cabinet and personal White House Office staff (which we will discuss later), the president is served by a number of agencies in the *Executive Office of the President* (see Figure 9-1). One of the most important of these agencies is the Office of Management and Budget (OMB), which helps prepare the federal budget the president submits each year to Congress. The OMB reviews the financial requests of other federal agencies, makes sure the requests conform with the president's overall program, and suggests ways the agencies may improve their performance. Another is the Council of Economic Advisers, whose three economists (hired by the president) help him interpret and attempt to manage national economic developments.

Despite the president's numerous assistants, however, his command of the federal bureaucracy is not absolute. It would be a mistake to assume that the president simply takes charge and issues orders instantly obeyed by subordinates. Several features of the bureaucracy encourage its independence from presidential direction. For one thing, while the agencies of the Executive Office of the President (such as the OMB) operate in close contact with the president, most of the regulatory agencies (such as the Federal Communications Commission and Federal Reserve Board) are exempt from presidential domination because of their legislative and judicial functions (see Chapter 12). Even though the

Figure 9-1. Organization of the U.S. Government

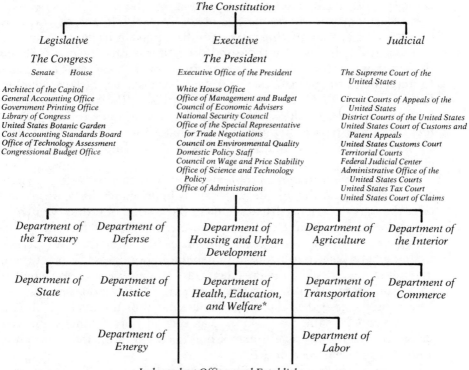

The Constitution

Legislative — **Executive** — **Judicial**

The Congress

Senate   House

Architect of the Capitol
General Accounting Office
Government Printing Office
Library of Congress
United States Botanic Garden
Cost Accounting Standards Board
Office of Technology Assessment
Congressional Budget Office

The President

Executive Office of the President

White House Office
Office of Management and Budget
Council of Economic Advisers
National Security Council
Office of the Special Representative
   for Trade Negotiations
Council on Environmental Quality
Domestic Policy Staff
Council on Wage and Price Stability
Office of Science and Technology
   Policy
Office of Administration

The Supreme Court of the
*   United States*

Circuit Courts of Appeals of the
   United States
District Courts of the United States
United States Court of Customs and
   Patent Appeals
United States Customs Court
Territorial Courts
Federal Judicial Center
Administrative Office of the
   United States Courts
United States Tax Court
United States Court of Claims

Department of the Treasury — **Department of Defense** — **Department of Housing and Urban Development** — **Department of Agriculture** — **Department of the Interior**

Department of State — **Department of Justice** — **Department of Health, Education, and Welfare*** — **Department of Transportation** — **Department of Commerce**

Department of Energy — **Department of Labor**

Independent Offices and Establishments

Action
Administrative Conference of the U.S.
American Battle Monuments
   Commission
Appalachian Regional Commission
Board for International Broadcasting
Canal Zone Government
Civil Aeronautics Board
Commission on Civil Rights
Commission of Fine Arts
Commodity Futures Trading
   Commission
Community Services Administration
Consumer Product Safety Commission
Environmental Protection Agency
Equal Employment Opportunity
   Commission
Export-Import Bank of the U.S.
Farm Credit Administration
Federal Communications Commission
Federal Deposit Insurance Corporation
Federal Election Commission
Federal Home Loan Bank Board

Federal Maritime Commission
Federal Mediation and Conciliation
   Service
Federal Reserve System, Board of
   Governors of the
Federal Trade Commission
Foreign Claims Settlement Commission
   of the U.S.
General Services Administration
Indian Claims Commission
Inter-American Foundation
International Communication Agency
Interstate Commerce Commission
National Aeronautics and Space
   Administration
National Credit Union Administration
National Foundation on the Arts and
   the Humanities
National Labor Relations Board
National Mediation Board
National Science Foundation
National Transportation Safety Board

Nuclear Regulatory Commission
Occupational Safety and Health Review
   Commission
Overseas Private Investment
   Corporation
Panama Canal Company
Pennsylvania Avenue Development
   Corporation
Pension Benefit Guaranty Corporation
Postal Rate Commission
Railroad Retirement Board
Renegotiation Board
Securities and Exchange Commission
Selective Service System
Small Business Administration
Tennessee Valley Authority
U.S. Arms Control and Disarmament
   Agency
U.S. Civil Service Commission
U.S. International Trade Commission
U.S. Postal Service
Veterans Administration

* In 1979 the Department of Health, Education, and Welfare was changed to The Department
of Health and Human Services. A new cabinet department, Education, was added.

Source: U.S. Government Organization Manual, 1978–79.

members of these agencies are appointed by the president, they are not subject to removal by him. Most serve long, overlapping terms so that no one president can make all of the appointments.

Furthermore, the enormous size of the federal bureaucracy and the president's many competing responsibilities make it impossible for him to keep in touch with the thousands of administrative workers. Even though the president establishes guidelines for the programs he wishes to implement, the bureaucracy is so vast he can never be sure whether his programs will be carried out as he intends. The sheer size of the federal bureaucracy, one scholar notes, "makes it impossible for a President to know or see or influence personally more than a handful of those men whose day-to-day activities will determine whether some cherished policy is to succeed or fail."[5]

Adding to the president's problems is the bureaucracy's sluggishness and evasiveness. Although the president is in principle the "chief executive," he may experience frustration similar to that of ordinary citizens who have become entangled in bureaucratic red tape. In fact, the president may encounter even greater difficulties in getting the bureaucracy to implement his programs than in persuading Congress to enact them in the first place. "Were the Presidents of the last fifty years to be polled on this question," Clinton Rossiter has written, "all but one or two, I am sure, would agree that the 'natural obstinacy' of the average bureau chief or commissioner or colonel was second only to the 'ingrained suspicions' of the average Congressman as a check on the President's ability to do either good or evil."[6]

In many respects, the federal bureaucracy has a will of its own separate from that of the White House or any other branch of government. Civil servants (who are not elected by the people) frequently make independent decisions that drastically affect other people's lives: where roads will be built, who will be eligible for welfare assistance, how safe drugs and automobiles must be. Many of these civil servants have toiled at their jobs for years, serving presidents of both major parties. As Richard Nixon once remarked, "Presidents come and go, but the bureaucracy goes on forever." Often these civil servants are allied with influential members of Congress or special interest groups who may not approve of a president's policies. In such instances, they may take policy matters into their own hands, purposely stalling the implementation of a president's program or even failing to carry it out at all. In Harry Truman's words, many of these "career men in government look upon the occupant of the White House as only a temporary nuisance who will soon be succeeded by another temporary occupant who won't find out what it's all about for a long time and then it will be too late to do anything about it."[7]

Sometimes, a president may even be reluctant to pursue implementation of a program vigorously, especially if doing so might sour his relations with key members of Congress or special interest groups whose support he desperately needs. As long as he has satisfied certain people by getting a program through Congress, he may not wish to risk further antagonizing those who opposed the program by forcing the bureaucracy to carry it out as intended.

An Architect of Policy

The president is deeply involved also in policy making and is, in fact, judged by the kinds of programs he proposes to Congress. Although the Constitution does not specifically refer to him as an architect of policy, it does outline a number of major legislative responsibilities—responsibilities that many presidents regard as their principal reasons for assuming the office in the first place.

One of these responsibilities is expressed in the annual State of the Union message to Congress, in which the president spells out what needs to be done to settle the nation's woes. The constitutional basis for this message is found in the statement that he "shall from time to time give to the Congress information of the State of the Union, and recommend to their consideration such measures as he shall judge necessary and expedient."

Usually, the president addresses both houses of Congress after the opening of each session in January, taking full advantage of television coverage. Because he cannot personally introduce a bill into the House or Senate, he can use this annual address—as well as more detailed messages later on—to convince members of his party to enact certain policies. Most members of Congress, in fact, look to the president for policy leadership. Because the president heads the federal bureaucracy and enjoys a national constituency, he is regarded by them as a focal point of legislation.

This is not to say, however, that a president can usually count on success. It is easier for members of Congress to thwart White House plans than to initiate constructive policies of their own. Jimmy Carter, for example, ran for the presidency as an outsider against the Washington establishment. But once in the White House, he discovered how difficult it was to win support for his proposals in an independent-minded Congress. His lack of long-term congressional relationships and experience with Washington's political ways got him into immediate trouble on several of his major energy and economic-stimulus programs. He had to learn the same tricks as his predecessors: how to soothe congressional egos, do a little mutual back-scratching, and otherwise acquire allies for his legislative battles.

Indeed, ruling-elite theorists and pluralists alike contend that the powers of the presidency over legislation vary with the personalities of those who occupy the office and that a president's real power depends on his ability to persuade. To win support for his programs, he must be able to bargain aggressively, employ publicity, or do whatever else is required to convince skeptical legislators that, as one scholar noted, "what the White House wants of them is what they ought to do for their sake and on their authority."[8] In Harry Truman's words, "There are a lot of other powers written in the Constitution and given to the President, but it's that power to persuade people to do what they ought to do anyway that's the biggest. And if the man who is President doesn't understand that, if he thinks he's too big to do the necessary persuading, then he's in for big trouble, and so is the country."[9]

Proposing legislation is, of course, only the beginning. Another important legislative responsibility is to provide an occasional check on Congress by wielding the potent constitutional weapon of the *veto*—a weapon, incidentally, that plays no minor role in his ability to persuade. Because all new bills must be signed by the president, he has a virtual life-or-death power over policy. The mere threat of a veto may force a bill's sponsors in Congress to scurry to shape it to the president's desires.

The reason the veto is such a potent weapon is that a two-thirds majority of both the House and Senate is required to override it. In fact, any bill the president receives within ten days before Congress adjourns that he does not sign (called a *pocket veto*) automatically dies and cannot be overridden. As we can see in Table 9-1, between 1933 and late 1978, Congress was able to override only about 3 percent of all presidential vetoes.

One major limitation of the veto is that the president must turn thumbs down on an entire bill, even though he might object to only a small part of it. Most state governors command even greater power over some kinds of legislation than does the president, for they can employ an *item veto*. This device allows them to strike out or "bluepencil" any part of an appropriations bill they disapprove of, while leaving the remainder intact. Because the president cannot use an item veto, members of Congress sometimes can push through favored policies by attaching amendments (*riders*) to bills the president is known to want. They know the president must either accept or reject the entire package; he cannot veto just the amendment. This was the very strategy that enabled Congress in 1973 to end the bombing in Cambodia and Laos. By attaching the measure to an emergency $3.4 billion supplementary ap-

Table 9-1. Presidential Vetoes, 1933–1978

President	Total Number of Vetoes	Vetoes Overridden
Roosevelt (1933–1945)	635	9
Truman (1945–1953)	250	12
Eisenhower (1953–1961)	181	2
Kennedy (1961–1963)	21	0
Johnson (1963–1969)	30	0
Nixon (1969–1974)	43	5
Ford (1974–1977)	66	12
Carter (1977–Nov. 1978)	19	0

Source: Congressional Quarterly Weekly Report, 18 November 1978, p. 3326.

propriations bill, members of Congress averted a veto of the antiwar amendment by President Nixon.

The Ceremonial Side

In addition to his political chores as head of government, the president can find his calendar clogged with endless ceremonial functions as the nation's symbolic head of state. In countries like England and Norway, the two jobs are performed by different persons; the figurehead queen or king discharges most of the ceremonial duties as titular head of state— such as knighting prominent public figures or welcoming new foreign ambassadors—while the prime minister wields the real political power as head of government. But because the president by tradition holds both jobs at once, he may spend his time not only proposing and vetoing legislation but decorating astronauts, rolling out the first egg for the Easter Bunny, or hosting delegations of Campfire Girls and World War II veterans. When he enters a hall on state occasions, he is usually welcomed with the presidential anthem, "Hail to the Chief" (only Carter so far has discouraged the practice), and is inaugurated—or buried—with all the ceremony and pomp reserved in other countries for royalty.

Although these ceremonial duties and trappings may seem unimportant, they are not. Often a president's personal magnetism and appeal can be augmented by his activities as the symbolic representative of the American people. Indeed, a good performance as chief of state can greatly enhance a president's public prestige, and thus become a potent weapon in his political arsenal.

Naturally, the President's featured role in the spotlight can also attract attention to his character and style in ways not entirely flattering. Certainly most presidents have been subject to typecasting: Nixon as the used-car salesman; Johnson as the southern wheeler-dealer; Kennedy as the youthful sophisticate; and Carter as the humble, down-home peanut farmer. Ford suffered an image of being less than brilliant—an image fostered largely by Lyndon Johnson's famous wisecracks that Ford "could not walk and chew gum at the same time" and that he "played football too long without his helmet." Satirist Mort Sahl remarked dryly that Ford reminded him of the clerk who okays a customer's check at the supermarket.

But whatever relationship exists between a president's popular image and his role as ceremonial leader, his image can have a decided effect both on his popularity and on public confidence in the presidency. Even though Ford, for example, was belittled for his presumed lack of intelligence, he seemed to offer to many Americans a welcome contrast in style to that of his predecessor. Where Nixon's presidency had been widely viewed as insular and devious, Ford's was immediately regarded as open and relaxed. Apparently, the public mood had been so depressed by Watergate as to be at least temporarily bolstered by seeing the presidency pass from the used-car salesman to the supermarket clerk.

The President and His Party

An interesting paradox each president must face is that he not only must serve as the ceremonial representative of the entire nation but must provide partisan leadership for his party as well. Because of his powerful position, he is expected to lead his party from the moment he is nominated at the national convention—to select the party national chairman, campaign for local and state party candidates, use his prestige to attract needed campaign contributions, and help set policy goals. "He is at once," Clinton Rossiter observed, "the least political and the most political of all heads of government."[10]

However, the president's leadership of the party can never extend too far. Because of the decentralized nature of the Democratic and Republican parties, the president has little direct control over state and local party organizations; for instance, he can impose only marginal discipline over most congressional members of his party. Although some presidents have exercised more leadership than others, a president's relations with other members of his party tend to rest on mutual benefits: he requires their support for his legislative proposals, and they depend on his prestige, policy direction, and such special favors as appointments.

There are also times when a president, due to loss of credibility and public support, is unable to provide his party with any effective leadership. This has happened to a number of presidents, including Andrew Johnson, Warren Harding, and Harry Truman. Perhaps the most extreme example of a recent president who fell from party favor was Richard Nixon. His rapid decline in popularity during the Watergate investigations prompted a majority of Republicans to disavow ties to his policies. During the special off-year elections in the spring of 1974, Republican candidates, instead of seeking his appearance in their districts, pleaded for his absence. Even so, the party lost four normally strong GOP congressional districts that spring, including the one in Michigan previously represented by Gerald Ford. Given such a record of defeats—and the placing of the blame directly on Nixon's ties with Watergate—it came as no surprise that many Republicans, up for reelection in November, welcomed with relief the news of Nixon's resignation from office.

Director of Diplomacy

Some presidents have regarded their role as chief diplomat to be the inspiration for their most ambitious and important policies. Certainly some have had great expectations of influencing world affairs, as we are reminded by Woodrow Wilson's determination to "make the world safe for democracy," Richard Nixon's goal to create a "lasting structure of peace in the world," and Jimmy Carter's global push for human rights. Even those presidents who have seen the office primarily in domestic terms often have found their attentions diverted to foreign policy matters. In Lyndon Johnson's case, foreign affairs proved to be the critical factor in undermining an otherwise promising presidency.

Generally, the president's command over foreign-policy making exceeds his command over domestic legislation and the bureaucracy. Although the president must share his diplomatic responsibilities with the Senate, which can either approve or reject his treaties and appointments of ambassadors, his position remains paramount. For example, only the president or his agents can legally represent the United States in its relations with foreign governments. In 1936, the Supreme Court ruled that the president has "exclusive power . . . as the sole organ of the Federal Government in the field of international relations."[11] Neither members of Congress nor private citizens may negotiate independently with other governments on behalf of the United States. It is argued that diplomatic negotiations with other countries require a "single voice" and an occasional element of secrecy that Congress, with its 535 diverse and conflicting personalities, cannot provide.

As a result, the president has the sole responsibility to decide if and when the United States shall officially recognize or break off relations with foreign governments. It was Dwight Eisenhower, for example, not Congress, who decided to sever diplomatic relations with Cuba in the late 1950s. It was Jimmy Carter, not Congress, who moved to resume full diplomatic relations with China and sever relations with Taiwan in 1979.

The president also has the sole constitutional authority to negotiate *treaties* with other countries. Although the Senate must approve all treaties by a two-thirds vote, it seldom has failed to do so; historically, it has approved more than 90 percent of the treaties submitted. In the late 1970s, however, President Carter faced two strong challenges to his treaty-making powers. In 1978, he barely mustered sufficient Senate support for the two Panama Canal treaties (one guaranteeing the Canal's neutrality; the other transferring the Canal to Panama in the year 2000). And in 1979, he faced a tough battle trying to win Senate approval of SALT II, the second phase of the Strategic Arms Limitations Talks with the Soviet Union (see Chapter 12).

Actually, the president does not even have to depend on Senate consent for most negotiations with other countries. He may bypass it through the use of *executive agreements*, which, unlike treaties, do not require formal Senate approval (although they may be thwarted by Congress if appropriations are required to carry them out). Executive agreements have been used for a variety of purposes, such as establishing foreign military bases, freezing the development of nuclear weapons, and negotiating tariff agreements.

Although the Constitution does not specifically authorize executive agreements, the Supreme Court declared in 1937 that the president may independently negotiate with foreign governments and establish international compacts.[12] Thus, each year a president may sign about 200 executive agreements, while resorting to treaties only in matters of great international significance or when Senate approval is assured. From 1789 until the end of 1976, for example, the United States concluded 8,475 executive agreements and only 1,280 treaties, according to State Department figures.

Naturally, the frequent use of this device has sparked considerable criticism. Some critics fear that the president's resort to executive agreements places too great a responsibility in one person's hands. In 1953, Sen. John Bricker proposed a constitutional amendment to prohibit the practice entirely, but it failed to win Senate approval by one

Carter and Brezhnev signing the SALT II treaty, 1979

vote. Later, in 1972, after it had been revealed that some of President Nixon's agreements with foreign governments had been kept secret from Congress, the House and Senate passed a new law requiring the president to submit to Congress within sixty days the text of any international agreement. But, while the new law curtails the president's independence to some degree, it does not limit his authority to make such agreements in the first place.

Command over the Military

The president can also back up his diplomatic responsibilities with his command over the military. The Constitution empowers the President to "be Commander in Chief of the Army and Navy . . . and of the militia of the several states, when called into the actual service of the United States." This means that the president can draw his sword and personally lead troops into battle—an action, however, to which only George Washington resorted during the Whiskey Rebellion in 1794. It is generally forgotten that almost one-fourth of our presidents have been army generals, including: George Washington, Andrew Jackson, Zachary Taylor, Franklin Pierce, Ulysses S. Grant, Rutherford B. Hayes, James Garfield, Benjamin Harrison, and Dwight Eisenhower.

Although the Constitution grants Congress the sole authority to "declare" war and appropriate military funds, presidents have had virtually a free hand to conduct military operations. Over the years, the United States has been engaged in more foreign military adventures under presidential direction than in wars formally declared by Congress. One estimate is that presidents have ordered troops into battle without a congressional declaration of war at least 150 times. In fact, even the five wars declared by Congress—the War of 1812, the War with Mexico, the Spanish-American War, and the two World Wars—were sanctioned only at the insistence of the president. Since the close of World War II alone, presidents have taken a number of dramatic military steps without formal congressional approval: the "intervention" in Korea in 1950; the invasion of Cuba at the Bay of Pigs in 1961; the landing of more than twenty thousand troops in the Dominican Republic in 1965; and the invasion of Cambodia in 1970.

Many scholars contend that the framers of the Constitution never intended the president to command such sweeping military power. Abraham Lincoln, long before assuming office, wrote that the Founding Fathers understood the power of kings to involve their citizens in war to be "the most oppressive of all Kingly oppressions; and they resolved to so frame the Constitution that no one man should hold the power of bringing this oppression upon us."[13] The major reasons the framers gave the president command of the military were to ensure civilian control over the armed forces and to allow quick response to a sudden attack on the United States. Any protracted or offensive conflict, however, would be conducted only after a congressional declaration of war. But, because the framers did not define the difference between "war" and any action short of it, presidents have felt relatively free to initiate military actions.

As a result, many citizens have been frustrated in their attempts to influence the president in military matters. Despite the framers' avowed intentions to ensure civilian control over the armed forces, many Americans have complained that the White House has too frequently assumed a fortress stance—a "Pentagon mentality"—in the face of citizen pressures. Protesters against the Vietnam War, for example, continually met firm resistance from Presidents Johnson and Nixon on the issue of American withdrawal from Southeast Asia. In fact, ruling-elite theorists make a persuasive argument that the ties between the White House and the Pentagon have too often resulted in a rigidity of thought, an unwillingness on the part of presidents and their advisers to accept criticism of military policies.

This is not to deny that attempts have been made to limit presidential control over military policy. In 1973, in a vote overturning President Nixon's veto, Congress passed the War Powers Resolution, forbidding the President to send combat troops abroad for more than sixty days without congressional approval. The president would still be free to take "emergency" military actions, but he would be required to report the reasons for his actions to Congress within forty-eight hours. Congress could then reverse his decision by passing a concurrent resolution of both houses, which would not be subject to his veto. Furthermore, unless Congress gave specific authorization to continue the military action, the president would be required to halt the operation after sixty days. In other words, the operation would have to cease if Congress simply did nothing. The president could extend this sixty-day period for an additional thirty days, but only to permit the safe withdrawal of troops.

President Nixon, in his veto message, insisted the War Powers Resolution was unconstitutional because it "would purport to take away, by a mere legislative act, authorities which the President has properly exercised under the Constitution for almost 200 years." He, as well as other critics of the resolution, feared the president could no longer respond effectively to a foreign crisis that called for strong military action. However, supporters of the resolution replied that many previous crises—such as the Cuban missile threat in 1962—ended well under ninety days. And, in an age of possible nuclear attack, too much decisiveness by a president can occur within ninety minutes, let alone ninety days. For these reasons, ironically, several members of Congress who were critical of presidential military power also opposed the resolution, fearing it would give the president a free hand to undertake military adventures for ninety days without congressional approval—a fear borne out when Cambodian gunboats seized the American freighter *Mayaguez* in 1975. Not until Ford had already ordered marines to rescue the ship's crew did he notify Congress of his action; and for this he encountered little criticism from Congress. More will be said about the president's foreign and military powers in Chapter 14.

The Judicial Side

Finally, although the Constitution assigns "the judicial power of the United States" to the courts, the president (as a check on the judicial branch) also undertakes certain judicial tasks. For one thing, he may overturn a court ruling by pardoning a person convicted of a federal (but not a state) crime, as Carter did for Patty Hearst in early 1979. He may also reduce a sentence by granting a commutation, or temporarily delay a punishment by granting a reprieve. In rare instances, he may even pardon an entire group, as both Ford and Carter did in limited form for Vietnam War resisters.

A pardon may, of course, stir considerable public controversy, as when President Ford stunned the nation in August 1974 by granting a

Patricia Hearst on her release from prison

"full, free and absolute" pardon to Richard Nixon. In an unprecedented display of presidential judicial prerogative, Ford pardoned his White House predecessor before any formal charges could be levied. The pardon covered not only Watergate-related activities but all other federal crimes Nixon might have committed as president. Although Ford claimed his pardon was an act of mercy in view of Nixon's deteriorated health at the time, and that a trial would only "cause prolonged and divisive debate" in the country, most critics felt it was premature and violated the principle of equal justice.

In addition to the pardoning power, a president has the authority to fill all vacancies on the federal courts, including the Supreme Court. The power to appoint Supreme Court justices—which, as we will see in Chapter 11, has tended to be based on partisan considerations—remains one of the president's most sweeping powers. Because justices are appointed for life, their selection can influence national policy long after a president has left office. William O. Douglas, for example, the most outspoken liberal force on the Court up until the mid-1970s, was appointed by Franklin Roosevelt in 1939.

This important power is restricted by the fact that only a few vacancies on the Court may occur during a president's term. On the average, each president has been able to select only two Supreme Court justices, although Nixon during his five-and-one-half-year term appointed four. Moreover, the president's power to appoint Supreme Court justices is limited constitutionally by the fact that a majority of the Senate must confirm his choices. Although the Senate has approved most appointments to the Court, it nevertheless has turned down 28 of the 140 Supreme Court nominations made in history. In recent years, the Senate not only failed to act on Lyndon Johnson's nominations of Abe Fortas as Chief Justice and Homer Thornberry as associate justice in 1968, but also tossed out Richard Nixon's nominations of Clement Haynesworth in 1969 and G. Harold Carswell in 1970—a spectacular four rebuffs in a three-year period.

In Payment For Services

Confirming the special place of the presidency in American politics, a number of special compensations and benefits have been bestowed on the incumbent. In addition to being serviced by a large personal staff, the president enjoys a salary of $200,000 a year (taxable), plus an annual expense allowance of $50,000. For his personal comfort and convenience, he has at his disposal a fleet of jets ("Air Force One"), helicopters, a staff of gourmet cooks and chefs, and even a White House projection room for private showings of first-run films. It has been estimated that an ordinary citizen would require an annual income of more than $50 million to live in the style of an American president.

When a president leaves office, he receives a lifetime annual pension of $60,000, free office space, up to $96,000 a year for staff assistance, and continued protection by the Secret Service. He receives these compensations, incidentally, even if he resigns. Even though Richard Nixon resigned following accusations of illegal activities, he was still granted a pension and allowances for his years of White House service. He would not have received these benefits, however, if he had been removed from office through impeachment.

We might wonder whether all the perquisites of the office—especially the doting assistants and "yes men" who inevitably come with the job—do not eventually take their toll, sheltering a president from "the real universe of living." As George Reedy, former special assistant to Lyndon Johnson, observed after serving in the White House, "A President moves through his day surrounded by literally hundreds of people whose relationship to him is that of a doting mother to a spoiled child. Whatever he wants is brought to him immediately—food, drink, helicopters, airplanes, people, everything but relief from the political problems." In fact, Reedy hypothesized, perhaps "the burdens would be lighter, the urban poor would be better served . . . if Presidents had to face the same minor penalties that the rest of us do. An occasional 'go soak your head' or 'that's stupid' would clear the murky, turgid atmosphere of the White House and let in some health-giving fresh air."[14]

Naturally, the degree to which a president allows the trappings of the office to go to his head depends a great deal on the individual. As we have noted, each president responds differently to the office, depending on his character and style. Some find comfort in the fact that Jimmy Carter, on entering the White House, quickly disposed of the large black limousines, sold the presidental yacht *Sequoia*, and was seen lounging around the office in levis and cardigan sweaters. Carter seemed more aware than his predecessors of the dangers of presidential insulation, taking pains to "keep in touch" with ordinary Americans. Early in his term, he took phone calls from citizens on a nation-wide radio show, stayed overnight with several American families, and appeared at mock town meetings answering questions from the audience. Whether Carter's new style was only a superficial guise or just a temporary pause in a long line of successive presidential "monarchs," however, is uncertain. Ironically, some Americans take the presidential role of ceremonial leader seriously, and would prefer to keep an atmosphere of royalty in the White House. For them, the sooner all the levis in the White House are replaced by grey business suits, the better.

Recruitment to the Presidency

Most Americans, it is true, will never discover what sort of president they would become. Most do not have enough money for an extensive campaign, cannot claim the required past service in a high political office like senator or governor, and cannot muster the ambition or make the personal sacrifices to be a full-time politician.

The legal qualifications for the job are actually not very restrictive. One only has to be at least thirty-five years old, native-born, and a resident of the United States for at least fourteen years. However, as a result of tradition and social prejudices, the presidency has been occupied almost exclusively by white, well-to-do men. So far, of the thirty-eight presidents in history, none has been a woman or a member of a prominent minority group.

Jimmy Carter

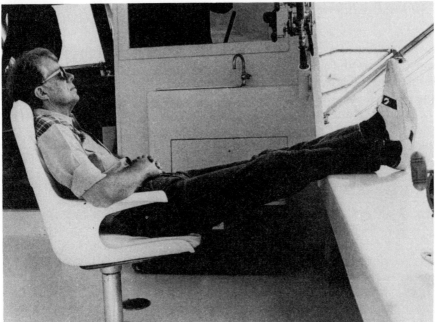

There are at least some signs that this situation may eventually change. As Table 9-2 shows, the number of Americans saying they would vote for a woman for president has climbed noticeably during the past several decades, a period that has witnessed intensified efforts by women to gain equal rights. In a 1978 Gallup poll, 76 percent of those interviewed said they would support a woman for president, up from 31 percent in 1937.

Public-support for a nonwhite candidate for president also appears to be climbing. For example, as Table 9-3 indicates, 77 percent of Americans in 1978 said they would vote for a black candidate for President, up from 38 percent in 1958.

It should be noted, however, that about one-fifth of those surveyed still refused to support qualified candidates solely on the basis of their sex or race. Moreover, even the positive responses among the majority may have reflected largely what the respondents considered to be socially acceptable views. Still, if we take the responses at face value, the fact that support for women and black candidates has increased over the years may signal an eventual change in presidential politics. We may expect at the very least that someday the pronoun "he" will no longer be the exclusive referent to the president.

"All the President's Men"

In any review of presidential powers and duties, it is hardly sufficient to consider only the activities of the president. Roaming around the White House and the Executive Office Building next door are hundreds of men and women who help the president perform his duties. In addition to the aides serving in the Executive Office agencies mentioned earlier

Table 9-2. Vote for a Woman for President?

	Yes	No	No Opinion
1978	76%	19%	5%
1971	66	29	5
1969	54	39	7
1967	57	39	4
1955	52	44	4
1948	48	48	4
1937	31	65	4

Source: Gallup Opinion Index, August 1971, and November 1978.

Table 9-3. Vote for a Black Candidate for President?

	Yes	No	No Opinion
1978	77%	18%	5%
1971	70	23	7
1969	67	23	10
1967	54	40	6
1965	59	34	7
1963	47	45	8
1958	38	53	9

Source: Gallup Opinion Index, November 1978.

(such as the Office of Management and Budget), two basic groups stand out in recognition and importance: the *cabinet* and the "inner circle" of the White House Office staff. Let us consider each in turn.

The Cabinet

Many people do not realize that the presidential cabinet stems, not from the Constitution, but from a politically expedient tradition honored by successive presidents. Although the Constitution calls for the appointment of a "principal officer in each of the Executive Departments," it says nothing about these department heads coming together as a group. Instead, each president has tended to form a cabinet to help him administer the executive branch. In addition to the vice-president and a few other top officials, the cabinet usually consists of the heads (or secretaries) of the thirteen executive departments, who are appointed by the president with the consent of the Senate. Their ostensible duties are to supervise the work of their departments and to serve as advisers to the president.

However, unlike the British cabinet, in which elected members of Parliament share responsibility with the prime minister for policy direction, members of the American cabinet often remain on the fringes of presidential decision making. The cabinet in this country rarely has had the influence commanded by its counterparts in Britain and most other parliamentary systems. In fact, each president tends to use his cabinet and individual secretaries as he sees fit. Whereas one president may meet frequently with his cabinet for its collective advice, another may make little use of it as an advisory body, preferring instead to see his secretaries one at a time or to ignore their advice almost completely.

For the most part, each president selects cabinet members who share his political views or who may help accommodate some interest group

Table 9-4. The President's Cabinet

Department	Date Formed
State	1789
Treasury	1789
Interior	1849
Agriculture	1862
Justice	1870
Commerce	1903
Labor	1913
Defense (replaced the War and Navy departments)	1947
Health and Human Services (formerly H.E.W.)	1953
Housing and Urban Development	1965
Transportation	1966
Energy	1977
Education	1979

or faction of the party. As ruling-elite theorists point out, cabinet officers frequently are brought in from private industry and finance, resulting in some overlapping of interests between the White House and economic elites. A president, for varying reasons, may even snatch someone from the opposition party, as when Richard Nixon picked southern Democrat (and later Republican) John Connally in 1971 to head the Treasury Department. And, although most cabinet members are chosen for their expertise, some are selected who have little or no experience in the subject areas of their departments, as was true when President Kennedy selected Robert McNamara (former head of Ford Motor Company) to be secretary of defense and when President Carter appointed Charles Duncan (former head of Coca-Cola) to be secretary of energy.

It should be understood that, even though cabinet secretaries are ultimately dependent on the president, they must also be responsive to Congress. Because their departments are funded by Congress, they may find themselves caught in the middle between congressional and presidential demands, an often tight and uncomfortable position. (For more on the executive departments, see Chapter 12.)

The White House Staff

While most presidents do not rely heavily on their cabinet for daily advice and policy direction, they do lean on a cadre of special assistants in the White House Office. Members of this "inner circle" are not subject to Senate confirmation and are selected primarily for their technical expertise, political savvy, and/or personal loyalties.

Each president molds this White House staff according to his own style, assigning titles and duties to suit his needs. Some assistants may serve as his links with Congress or the executive agencies. Others may smooth his relations with the press and handle his appointments. Still others may advise him on foreign policy, provide legal counsel, or help draft his speeches. A president may assign the same individual a variety of tasks, switching him from assignment to assignment, and then dumping him when he no longer proves useful.

Occasionally, a struggle may erupt between a president's policy advisers and his political advisers, the first prodding him to fight for what he thinks is right, and the second urging him to be careful and work for a second term. It is up to each president to decide how much to compromise between the two, how much to ignore the "political realities" and fight the legislative battles of the moment.

Because of their proximity to the president, White House aides can command considerable power. Ordinary citizens and governmental officials alike who have tried to gain access to a president have at times found themselves unable to vault over a wall of White House aides insensitive to their desires. This was especially true during the Nixon administration when chief of staff H. R. Haldeman and presidential counsel John Ehrlichman virtually dominated the executive branch. "By Nixon's time," Arthur Schlesinger reflected, "White House aides were no longer channels of communication. They were powerful figures in themselves, making decisions and issuing instructions in their own right, more powerful than members of the cabinet. . . . But they were not, like members of the cabinet, subject to confirmation by the Senate or (pre-Watergate) to interrogation by committees of Congress."[15] Until the Watergate scandal removed him from office, White House chief of staff H. R. Haldeman was especially influential, deciding who would have access to President Nixon and who would not. Whenever a Senator or member of the cabinet tried to phone the president, his call usually went first to Haldeman. Or, whenever an official wished to see the president personally, it was Haldeman who decided whether he would be admitted. "Rather than the President telling someone to do something," Haldeman boasted, "I'll tell the guy. If he wants to find out something from somebody, I'll do it."[16]

At least two clear dangers may arise from presidential use of staff. One is that a president may become too insulated in the White House, shielded by overzealous aides from outside citizen influence and alternative information sources. Obviously, the way a president makes policy decisions is of great importance to us all. Generally, the first thing a president must do is demand up-to-date information. This information is then collected and analyzed by White House aides, in order to present meaningful options for the chief executive to consider. Only too late a president may discover that he received one-sided information or was shielded from the advice of people he should have seen. Of course, most presidents, by selecting assistants who share their policy views, encourage this one-sidedness. They set the tone of the White House by choosing aides who are most like themselves.

Moreover, the personal ambitions of the aides themselves contribute to this one-sidedness of information. As assistants to a president, they exercise a degree of influence few other Americans can experience and are under great pressure to remain in the chief executive's good graces. As one scholar has observed, "The Presidency is the supreme prize offered in American political life, but very few men can become President. For those to whom the White House is the symbol of the ultimate goal, the next best thing to the Presidency itself is the role of presidential adviser. Those playing the role must suffer from the omnipresent, albeit subconscious knowledge that the fall from grace will be a very long and humiliating one. Under the circumstances, one can hardly expect the majority of advisers to escape the trap of yes-men."[17]

The other danger is that a president may delegate too much responsibility to his aides. Assistants anxious to please their boss may take, on his behalf, independent actions that go well beyond the confines of the law. Although Nixon promised in 1968 to select "men who will command the public's respect," and who "will not have to check their conscience at the door," the actions of his staff heaped further disaster on his presidency. The Senate Watergate hearings in the summer of 1973 revealed that top Nixon aides had employed the White House Office—apparently with Nixon's encouragement—as a private instrument to intimidate political opponents and carry out assorted forms of espionage. While presidential counsel John Ehrlichman promoted the investigation of opponents' drinking and sexual habits, counsel Charles Colson helped draft an "enemies list" of presumed White House "adversaries," ranging from Sen. Edward Kennedy to actor Paul Newman.

We will probably never know the extent to which other administrations were tainted by similar illegal activities of presidential aides. And, although both Gerald Ford and Jimmy Carter made efforts to keep a "palace guard" mentality out of the White House, the possibility exists that future administrations could become tainted by similar excesses. Such a possibility has inspired several proposals for keeping White House aides in line, such as expanding congressional oversight and making aides subject to Senate confirmation. We might wonder, however, whether these or other reforms would do much good. After all,

White House aides ultimately reflect the character and style of the president they serve and will behave the way he wants them to behave. "They stand as both a symbol and reflection of the President," one observer has noted. "They act in his image. They revel in his glory."[18]

The Vice-Presidency: "The Hollow Shell"

While the presidency has evolved into one of the most powerful offices in the world, the vice-presidency has remained merely a "hollow shell of an office."[19] Some of the Founding Fathers even doubted the need for a vice-president. In fact, several vice-presidents have felt that the office has been only a source of humiliation. John Adams, the first person to hold the job, lamented that "my country has in its wisdom contrived for me the most insignificant office that ever the invention of man contrived or his imagination conceived." John Nance Garner, vice-president under Franklin Roosevelt, went even further, contending that "the vice-presidency isn't worth a pitcher of warm spit." Indeed, although most of us probably can name all previous presidents, how many are familiar with former vice-presidents? Consider some of the vice-presidents who have been lost to history:

George Clinton (1805–1812)
Elbridge Gerry (1813–1814)
Daniel D. Tompkins (1817–1825)
Richard M. Johnson (1837–1841)
George M. Dallas (1845–1849)
William R. King (1853)
John C. Breckinridge (1857–1861)
Hannibal Hamlin (1861–1865)
Schuyler Colfax (1869–1873)

Henry Wilson (1873–1875)
William A. Wheeler (1877–1881)
Thomas A. Hendricks (1885)
Levi P. Morton (1889–1893)
Garret A. Hobart (1897–1899)
Charles W. Fairbanks (1905–1909)
James S. Sherman (1909–1912)
Thomas R. Marshall (1913–1921)
Charles G. Dawes (1925–1929)

The vice-president actually draws only three clear duties from the Constitution: (1) to serve as the constitutional heir to the president; (2) to preside over the Senate; and (3) to exercise a vote in case of a Senate tie. As a measure of the insignificance of the last two tasks, former vice-president Spiro Agnew, during the first half of the 1973 session in the Senate, presided for only 2½ hours of the 667 hours the Senate had been sitting.[20] During the rest of the time, either the Senate pro tempore or a junior senator wielded the Senate gavel. And, during his entire term as vice-president, Spiro Agnew cast a deciding vote in the Senate only once: to break a tie in favor of the Alaskan pipeline amendment in July 1973.

Most contemporary vice-presidents are, of course, assigned other duties by the president. They serve on the National Security Council, attend cabinet meetings, travel abroad as the president's personal ambassador, and make public speeches that the president may not wish to make. Jimmy Carter even used Vice-President Walter Mondale as a close personal adviser, breaking precedent by installing Mondale in an office in the White House. But because these duties are at the president's request, they do not provide an independent power base for a vice-president. In other words, a vice-president's powers generally are what the president chooses to make them.

If the vice-presidency seems to be such an insignificant office, why then would any prominent politician want the job? One reason perhaps, apart from the high salary and fringe benefits, is that it may offer a convenient springboard to the presidency. Although few vice-presidents have advanced to the White House by their own efforts, John Adams, Thomas Jefferson, Martin Van Buren, and Richard Nixon did succeed to the office in this manner. Moreover, eight vice-presidents have been thrust into the presidency as a result of the death of the incumbent, and one (Gerald Ford) succeeded as a result of his predecessor's resignation. In all, thirteen of the forty-two vice-presidents in history—almost one-third—eventually became president.

In view of these statistics, we might expect the selection of a vice-president to be a careful process, aimed at choosing a person with great leadership capabilities. Yet the choice of vice-presidents, Theodore White observes, "is the most perfunctory and generally the most thoughtless in the entire American political system."[21] Traditionally, the vice-president is chosen by the presidential nominee in the closing hours of the national convention, with an eye to "balancing the ticket," adding regional and ideological strength to the campaign.

To many critics, this method of hurriedly picking a vice-president, and for political expediency, is a mistake—a mistake made clear by the disastrous impact of Thomas Eagleton's selection on George McGovern's candidacy in 1972 and by Spiro Agnew's indictment and resignation in 1973. Indeed, Agnew will probably be saved from the obscurity of most vice-presidents. In October 1973, he became the second vice-president to resign, and the only one to do so after pleading "no contest" to a charge of federal income tax evasion. (John C. Calhoun also resigned the office, in 1832, to become a U.S. senator.)

Although no way exists to prevent any vice-presidential choice from turning into a disaster, pressure has been mounting for a change in the selection process. In addition to the suggestion that the vice-presidency simply be abolished,[22] at least two major reform proposals have been discussed. One is to force presidential and vice-presidential candidates to pair up for the primary races. The other is to have a separate primary for all those campaigning solely for the vice-presidency. In each case, vice-presidential candidates would be exposed to the voters during the long ordeal of the primaries, offering the voters a chance to decide for themselves who would be best suited for the job.

One significant aftereffect of Agnew's resignation, of course, was to permit Richard Nixon to become the first president to select a new vice-president (Gerald Ford) during his administration. Before the ratification of the Twenty-Fifth Amendment in 1967, there was no provision for filling the vice-presidency between elections if the office became vacant. Even though few people may have noticed, the United States prior to Agnew's resignation had to limp along without a vice-president sixteen times, for a total of more than forty years (see Table 9-5).

The Relativity of Presidential Power

Having begun this chapter with a discussion of presidential personality and the possibility of failing or succeeding in the White House, it seems fitting to conclude with a brief analysis of presidential power. Clearly, the desire of a president to command power at the highest political level must be sufficiently restrained to protect the freedom and well-being of other citizens. The Watergate scandal and Vietnam War have forced many observers to worry seriously about the misuse of presidential power and to wonder how to resolve the conflict between the need for a strong chief executive and the potential for abuse of the executive office. Although Carter and other presidents have encountered great difficulties in translating many of their policy goals into reality, there remains the concern that the presidency has been entrusted with too much power and that, in the hands of the wrong individual, the power will be misused.

This concern is, of course, hardly new. The framers of the Constitution in the late eighteenth century not only expressed similarly divided feelings about executive power but were deeply worried about its potential misuse. In fact, part of the reason the Constitution is so vague about the duties of the president is that the framers disagreed over how much responsibility to assign the office. On the one hand, they were convinced of the shortcomings of purely "legislative government" and believed the United States required a reasonably strong, independent executive. As Thomas Jefferson warned, "The tyranny of the legislature is really the danger most to be feared, and will continue to be so for many years to come." As a result, they provided for a president who was chosen sepa-

---

Table 9-5. Vacancies in the Vice-Presidency

Vice-President	Term Elected	Date of Vacancy	Reason	President
George Clinton (R)	1809–1813	4/20/1812	Death	James Madison
Elbridge Gerry (R)	1813–1817	11/23/1814	Death	James Madison
John C. Calhoun (D)	1829–1833	12/28/1832	Resignation	Andrew Jackson
John Tyler (Whig)	1841–1845	4/6/1841	Succeeded to presidency on death of President Harrison	William Henry Harrison
Millard Fillmore (Whig)	1841–1853	7/10/1850	Succeeded to presidency on death of President Taylor	Zachary Taylor
William King (D)	1853–1857	4/18/1853	Death	Franklin Pierce
Andrew Johnson (R)	1865–1869	4/15/1865	Succeeded to presidency following assassination of President Lincoln	Abraham Lincoln
Henry Wilson (R)	1873–1877	11/22/1875	Death	Ulysses S. Grant
Chester A. Arthur (R)	1881–1885	9/20/1881	Succeeded to presidency following assassination of President Garfield	James A. Garfield
Thomas Hendricks (D)	1885–1889	11/25/1885	Death	Grover Cleveland
Garrett A. Hobart (R)	1897–1901	11/21/1899	Death	William McKinley
Theodore Roosevelt (R)	1901–1905	9/14/1901	Succeeded to presidency following assassination of President McKinley	William McKinley
James S. Sherman (R)	1909–1913	10/30/1912	Death	William Howard Taft
Calvin Coolidge (R)	1921–1925	9/3/1923	Succeeded to presidency on death of President Harding	Warren G. Harding
Harry S. Truman (D)	1945–1949	4/12/1945	Succeeded to presidency on death of President Roosevelt	Franklin D. Roosevelt
Lyndon B. Johnson (D)	1961–1965	11/22/1963	Succeeded to presidency following assassination of President Kennedy	John F. Kennedy

---

Source: Congressional Quarterly Weekly Report, 22 September 1973.

rately from Congress, who originally could be elected for any number of terms, and who could veto all bills passed by Congress.

Yet, at the same time, the framers were afraid of the potential danger posed by too strong an executive. Following their experiences with the British king, George III, they were careful to restrict the president's powers through a complex system of checks and balances: his appointments and treaties had to be approved by the Senate, his vetoes could be overridden by a two-thirds vote in Congress, and he could be impeached by the House and removed by the Senate.

But even though the framers expressed divided feelings about executive power, the historical tendency has been for the powers of the presidency to expand. Despite the framers' expectation, for example, that Congress would be responsible for initiating new laws, all modern presidents have introduced major legislative proposals. Despite the framers' intention to give Congress the constitutional authority to declare war, more military actions—such as in Korea and Vietnam—have been initiated by presidential decree than by congressional declaration of war.

This expansion of presidential power has stemmed largely from the actions of forceful and ambitious presidents, such as Lincoln, Wilson, and Franklin Roosevelt, who refused to accept limited roles for their presidencies. Faced with new crises and challenging social demands, they extended the duties of their office and used its resources to accomplish goals they believed in. And they succeeded in getting away with it because a change in the times—a civil war, an industrial revolution, a world war, or a depression—called for strong actions.

Other factors also have been important. For example, members of Congress have contributed to an increase in presidential power by abdicating some of their responsibilities. As a result of a decentralized party system and Congress's own cumbersome procedures, senators and representatives alike have been either unable or unwilling to respond to new social and economic problems. Until recently, instead of setting their own agenda, they have been satisfied to let most of the major initiatives come from the White House.

In fact, the evolution of American society itself has augmented presidential responsibility in decision making. As the United States has grown in population (from 3 million people to more than 220 million) and has become plagued with all of the social ills of a large urban, industrial society, the president's responsibilities as chief executive have mushroomed. Although Congress has continued to exercise its constitutional obligation to pass the laws and approve the federal budget, the president has been expected to carry the major responsibility for implementing large-scale social programs.

Even the advent of radio and television probably has helped magnify the president's role. In contrast to the 535 members of Congress, the president is a single individual whose activities are under the constant watch of the news media and the subject of public gossip. And, although most presidents have criticized the media, each has used the media to his own advantage, relying on free air time—such as that provided for press conferences and televised addresses—to reach the public over the heads of critics.

But, whatever may have contributed to the expansion of presidential power during the past two centuries, the debate over its consequences is unlikely to subside. Indeed, no issue in American politics is less likely to fade away than whether presidential power is too extensive and potentially dangerous. On the one hand, some political observers—notably the advocates of the ruling-elite theory—point out that presidential power has at times exceeded constitutional limits and been used to subvert the basic principles of American government. This criticism has been echoed by scholars and members of Congress who insist that both Lyndon Johnson and Richard Nixon pushed the nation too close to a one-branch government. The House Judiciary Committee's impeachment inquiry, for example, pointed out that Nixon not only impounded funds appropriated by Congress, but also withheld important information from the courts pertaining to criminal activities, directed the secret surveillance of private citizens, and ordered an invasion of Cambodia without consulting Congress.

Ironically, some of the most vocal critics of presidential power used to foster an almost uncritical cult of a strong chief executive. Such well-known scholars as Arthur Schlesinger, Jr., George Kennan, and Richard Neustadt championed strong-willed presidents like John Kennedy and Lyndon Johnson (in his early years) who tried to use their office to solve such domestic problems as racial discrimination and poverty. They were critical of the fact that both presidents were hampered in their efforts by a coalition of conservative Congress members loyal to the status quo.

Yet, following Vietnam and Watergate, many of these scholars joined the chorus denouncing the burgeoning of executive power—the "runaway presidency," as Arthur Schlesinger dubbed it. While still believing in the need for strong executive leadership in domestic affairs, they began to lament the ever-expanding powers of the president in foreign and military affairs. Despite the long tradition of presidential control over military policy, they insisted that Johnson and Nixon went far beyond the limits of their predecessors in exercising military authority. Indeed, they felt, the structure of presidential power had become a true paradox in the last half of the twentieth century. "We have given power to the President," James MacGregor Burns commented, "precisely in the area where his rash action might be uncheckable and irreversible—

that is, in foreign and military policy—and we carefully fence him in, in those areas where presidential errors could be limited and reversed—notably in domestic fiscal policy."[23]

Other political observers, however, have insisted that the powers of the presidency are not too extensive, and that recent congressional actions, such as the impeachment hearings and passage of the 1973 War Powers Resolution, show the resilient strength of the legislative branch. In fact, they argue, presidential power is difficult to measure; how one views it depends on the policy area with which a president deals. Although most presidents have been more than a match for Congress in foreign affairs, they have been greatly constrained in domestic affairs, as Jimmy Carter discovered when Congress rewrote his energy and tax reform proposals (see Chapter 13).

Moreover, whether or not the president's powers are too great often depends on whether one agrees with his policies. If one's interests are not being served by a president, there may be a greater temptation to believe he enjoys too much power. Thus, Carter's decision in early 1979 to switch U.S. recognition from Taiwan to China (and his giving notice of plans to terminate a twenty-four-year-old defense treaty with Taiwan) focused new attention on the president's foreign policy powers. While supporters applauded the decision as a bold diplomatic move, critics lambasted it as an "illegal" exercise of presidential license.

In any event, the argument continues, if presidential power should be limited further, who could then take the initiative in policy making? Could Congress, with its 535 diverse personalities and cumbersome structure of rules and committees, possibly fill the vacuum? Certainly any decision to alter the balance of power between the White House and Congress would require major changes in Congress to make it more responsive to the times, to make it capable of exerting policy leadership. How far such changes would have to go is the subject of the next chapter.

Key Terms

Executive Office of the President	*rider*
veto	*treaty*
pocket veto	*executive agreement*
item veto	*cabinet*

Notes

1. Quoted in Arthur M. Schlesinger, Jr., *A Thousand Days* (Boston: Houghton Mifflin, 1965), p. 120.

2. U.S. Senate, Committee on Government Operations, "Confidence and Concern: Citizens View American Government, A Survey of Public Attitudes," pt. 1 (Washington, D.C.: U.S. Government Printing Office, 1973).

3. George Will, *Washington Post*, December 1974.

4. James David Barber, *The Presidential Character: Predicting Performance in the White House*, 2nd ed. (Englewood Cliffs, N.J.: Prentice-Hall, 1977).

5. Clinton Rossiter, *The American Presidency*, rev. ed. (New York: Harcourt Brace Jovanovich, 1960), p. 57.

6. Ibid., p. 55.

7. Quoted in Barber, *The Presidential Character*, 1972, p. 276.

8. Richard E. Neustadt, *Presidential Power* (New York: Wiley, 1960), p. 34.

9. Quoted in Merle Miller, *Plain Speaking: An Oral Biography of Harry S. Truman* (New York: Berkley Publishing Co., 1974), p. 10.

10. Rossiter, *The American Presidency*, p. 128.

11. *United States* v. *Curtiss-Wright Corp.* (1936).

12. *United States* v. *Belmont* (1937).

13. Quoted in Arthur M. Schlesinger, Jr., *The Imperial Presidency* (Boston: Houghton Mifflin, 1973), p. 43.

14. George E. Reedy, *The Twilight of the Presidency* (New York: New American Library, 1970), pp. 33–34.

15. Schlesinger, *The Imperial Presidency*, pp. 221–22.

16. Ibid., p. 222.

17. Philippa Strum, *Presidential Power and American Democracy*, 2nd ed. (Santa Monica, Calif.: Goodyear, 1978), p. 99.

18. Dom Bonafede, "White House Staffing: The Nixon-Ford Era," in Thomas E. Cronin and Rexford G. Tugwell, *The Presidency Reappraised*, 2nd ed. (New York: Praeger, 1977), p. 151.

19. Rossiter, *The American Presidency*, p. 129.

20. *Newsweek*, 27 August 1973, p. 11.

21. Theodore H. White, *The Making of the President 1972* (New York: Atheneum, 1973), p. 193.

22. See, for example, Arthur M. Schlesinger, Jr., "Is the Vice Presidency Necessary?" *The Atlantic*, May 1974, pp. 37–44.

23. James MacGregor Burns, "The Presidency at the Crossroads," in Hans J. Morgenthau, ed., *The Crossroads Papers: A Look into the American Future* (New York: W. W. Norton, 1965), p. 197.

BARBER, JAMES DAVID. *The Presidential Character: Predicting Performance in the White House.* 2nd ed. Englewood Cliffs, N.J.: Prentice-Hall, 1977.

CRONIN, THOMAS E. *The State of the Presidency.* Boston: Little, Brown, 1975.

CRONIN, THOMAS E., and REXFORD G. TUGWELL, *The Presidency Reappraised.* 2nd ed. New York: Praeger, 1977.

CRONIN, THOMAS E., and SANFORD D. GREENBERG, eds. *The Presidential Advisory System.* New York: Harper & Row, 1969.

KOENING, LOUIS W. *The Chief Executive.* 3rd ed. New York: Harcourt Brace Jovanovich, 1975.

NEUSTADT, RICHARD E. *Presidential Power.* New York: Wiley, 1960.

REEDY, GEORGE E. *The Twilight of the Presidency.* New York: New American Library, 1970.

ROSSITER, CLINTON. *The American Presidency.* Rev. ed. New York: Harcourt Brace Jovanovich, 1960.

SCHLESINGER, ARTHUR M., JR. *The Imperial Presidency.* Boston: Houghton Mifflin, 1973.

ALLAN P. SINDLER. *Unchosen Presidents: The Vice President and Other Frustrations of Presidential Succession.* Berkeley: University of California Press, 1976.

STRUM, PHILIPPA. *Presidential Power and American Democracy,* 2nd ed. Santa Monica, Calif.: Goodyear, 1978.

10

Congress:
The Legislative Labyrinth

When it comes to influencing policy, senators and representatives would seem to be in enviable positions. As members of Congress, they share a unique responsibility for enacting, or blocking, legislation affecting the health and well-being of millions of Americans. Indeed, to many who seek political power, Congress has the allure of an exciting arena in which new legislation is constantly being created. The men and women in Congress are seen as participants in a dynamic process in which they share a great opportunity to translate their dreams into political reality. Undoubtedly, it is this vision that compels many citizens to try to influence their senator or representative, to sway his or her vote on pending legislation.

A Sense of Impotency

Yet, in some ways, such a vision of creative potential is deceptive, obscuring both the difficulties Congress has experienced in serving as a productive law-making body and the obstacles many members have faced in trying to achieve even modest political goals. One finds, in fact, that how one views power in Congress depends greatly on which senators and representatives one chooses to examine. If one looks at those committee chairmen who serve as the spokesmen for wealthy and powerful interests—the oil companies, the banking lobby, or the military—then the opportunities for influence may seem boundless. But if one examines instead those members who come to Washington ostensibly to work on behalf of people without strong representation and leadership, such as the poor and the elderly, then the chances of achieving meaningful goals in Congress may appear more remote. As newly elected members soon discover, Congress does not provide immediate gratification of the thirst for power or the desire for reform that may have been the driving force behind their campaigns. "A new Congressman," Rep. Shirley Chisholm has written, "faces a lot of disappointments. One most freshman House members share is the discovery that, while getting elected made him a big man back home, Washington has seen green representatives arrive by the thousands and is not very impressed. Then, unless he has had legislative experience, he will be frustrated to learn that his plans for laws that will solve the problems of the country, whatever he deems them to be, are doomed because he is a very junior member of a rather large group."[1]

Nor are such frustrations confined to freshman members. Even seasoned congressional veterans can find their efforts blocked. With its committees that decentralize decision making, its complex procedures, and the inordinate influence of special interests, Congress can be a source of irritation even to those familiar with its ways. Members seeking solutions to social problems complain time and again that Congress is a difficult place in which to assume a constructive role. Explaining why he chose to retire from the House after serving fourteen years, one representative snapped, "It's the system. I can't do anything unless I'm chairman of an important committee—and I could wait forever for that."[2]

Even senators occasionally feel drowned. While they have the advantage over House members of enjoying greater prestige, having a six-year rather than two-year term, and serving in a smaller body with less rigid rules and procedures, each remains only one voice among many. Even if a senator wins the support on a bill of a majority of his own chamber, he still must contend with a majority of members of the House.

Also, members of Congress cannot count on basking in the warmth of public adulation once they have reached this lofty position. Based on past congressional failures, the attitude of citizens is often skeptical and cynical toward their claims of noble intentions. Indeed, senators and representatives would have to go to considerable lengths to restore public confidence in their law-making abilities. According to a June 1977 Gallup poll, only 34 percent of Americans interviewed said they approved of the job performed by Congress, as compared with 42 percent who said they disapproved, and 24 percent who were undecided.

In fact, for years, Congress has been chided for lacking the will to confront social problems and for serving as an obstacle to reform. Generations of commentators, satirists, and cartoonists have decried what the nineteenth-century French writer Alexis de Tocqueville once described as its "vulgarity and its poverty of talent." Even the venerable satirist Mark Twain had scathing things to say about Congress:

It could probably be shown by facts and figures that there is no distinctly native American criminal class except Congress.

I . . . was a reporter in a legislature two sessions and the same in Congress one session—and thus learned to know personally three sample-bodies of the smallest minds and the selfishest souls and the cowardliest hearts that God makes.

. . . those burglars that broke into my house recently . . . are in jail, and if they keep on they will go to Congress. When a person starts downhill you can never tell when he's going to stop.

While most Americans today may be amused by Twain's iconoclastic views of Congress, many also harbor similar negative feelings. They hear tales of senators and representatives traveling abroad on "pleasure junkets" at taxpayers' expense, attending cocktail parties when they should be legislating, or accepting bribes for political favors. Indeed, how can a favorable view of Congress be expected when scandals involving legislators continue to splash on the front pages of newspapers? Since 1971, more than a dozen members of Congress have been indicted for crimes ranging from perjury and tax evasion to bribery and extortion. But perhaps the most widespread feeling is that Congress remains unresponsive to people's needs. Crime still rages in the streets, prices continue to skyrocket, and millions of elderly citizens go on living in run-down tenements while members of Congress seem to coast along making promises that are rarely fulfilled.

Yet, there is irony in all of this. Although people seem to have a low opinion of Congress, they are generally content with the performance of their own representative. The same 1977 Gallup poll cited above found that only 17 percent of those interviewed said they disapproved of the job performed by their representative, while 55 percent said they approved. (The rest still had no opinion on the matter.) This perhaps suggests one reason most members of Congress continue to be reelected year after year.

Some reform-minded members have been heartened, of course, by efforts in recent years to reform its legislative machinery. As we will see, Congress during the 1970s approved a variety of changes in the way it does business, including placing new curbs on the seniority system and the powers of committee chairmen. It also made significant strides, following Vietnam and Watergate, to regain some of the powers lost to the White House, such as placing new limits on the president's war powers and assuming greater control over the federal budget. With these changes has come the hope that Congress can now respond more decisively to the nation's social and economic ills, and that each member can play a more assertive role in policy making. However, whether members of Congress are prepared to assume such an assertive role on a permanent basis, without allowing the balance to swing back to the White House again, remains to be seen.

To better understand the action potential of serving on Capitol Hill, we will examine some of the powers and duties of senators and representatives. We will also look at the evolving power structure in Congress, especially at how that structure may or may not be suitable to the goals of individual members. Obviously, those of us who desire to feed our own ideas into the legislative labyrinth also need to know what our senators and representatives can, or cannot, do for us—what sort of obstacles we as citizens can expect to face.

The Tools of Congressional Power

An incredible diversity of powers and duties remains the most striking feature of a congressional career. Apart from such rarely exercised powers as declaring war, proposing amendments to the Constitution, and removing federal officials through impeachment (see Chapter 3), members of Congress have four major responsibilities: forging new laws, overseeing the executive branch through investigations and "advice and consent," raising and spending money, and helping *constituents* back home. On any given day, a senator or representative may cast the crucial vote on a foreign aid bill, chair an important committee hearing on bureaucratic waste, help trim or fatten the federal budget, or even help a constituent retrieve a lost social security check. Let us take a look at how each of these powers and duties may be exercised.

Forging New Laws

As we would expect, the greatest potential for political power enjoyed by members of Congress is the opportunity to forge new laws. Because the Constitution declares that "all legislative powers herein granted shall be vested in a Congress of the United States," each senator and representative may introduce and help pass legislation designed to promote the general welfare of the country (or at least some special group).

However, it is important to remember that the actual amount of influence on policy making varies with each member. Some senators and representatives are clearly more or less ambitious than others and expect, or refuse, to wield the maximum power they can draw from their positions. Moreover, the hurdles of Congress can at times seem insurmountable. Because most policy making takes place in committees, for example, a member may find it difficult to push through legislation unless the proper committee shares his concerns. Not only may the committee not share his concerns, but many other bills may be competing for its attention. After all, Congress receives legislative proposals from a grab bag of sources: lobbyists pushing pet causes, leftover bills not passed earlier, as well as policy brainstorms of powerful committee chairmen and budding presidential hopefuls. And, because the president has been handed the responsibility to set Congress's legislative agenda, a senator or representative may find his or her own pet project placed on the back burner while the president's policy recommendations receive priority.

Thus, while constituents back home dash off letters urgently pleading for legislation to cure society's ills, the policy maker in Congress struggles with the legislative machinery. Despite pressures from home, few members of Congress actually succeed each year in getting important new legislation passed. Although some members remain indebted to special interests and could not care less about serving constituents, others find their dreams of legislative knighthood vaporized. As one representative lamented, "I came here thinking I would immediately share in the drafting of legislation. As all of us soon discover, the likelihood of first or second termers, and particularly minority members, doing any major drafting of legislation that passes is slim if not completely unknown."[3]

Nor does the average member of Congress wield tremendous influence with his or her vote on the floor. Although voting is one of a member's most important legislative responsibilities—after all, it is through voting that a senator or representative theoretically expresses the will of constituents—few members perceive their votes as decisive on most pieces of legislation. This is particularly true in the House of Representatives with its 435 members. "Since I've been here," one Representative has proclaimed, "only one major bill has been decided by a single vote. If you try to evaluate your incremental impact, you have to decide that, unless you're Speaker, chairman of an important committee, or part of the House leadership, you just can't have much impact on normal Congressional operations."[4]

However, as we will see, a member can wield significant influence in his or her own committee, where a single vote can be decisive in determining the life or death of a bill. The question then becomes how to decide whether to support or reject a bill. One standard view is that members of Congress ultimately are "delegates" of their constituents and should honor constituents' wishes. As one representative has stated, "You cannot buck district sentiment on certain issues. In my area, oil, coal, and mining are extremely important, and if you're 'right' on these things you have a much easier time of it. But you are opening yourself up to criticism if you vote against them often."[5]

Supporters of the ruling-elite theory insist, of course, that most members of Congress are the delegates of powerful local elites. They point out that senators and representatives tend to communicate more with active special interests in their home states and districts than with the majority of their constituents, who are ignorant of congressional activities. This means that in a district where the main industry is coal mining, the key and relevant constituency will be those who dominate that industry. However, whether the interests of the local elite necessarily conflict with the interests of a majority of the legislator's constituents is another question. Conceivably, a majority of those back home may feel that congressional policy benefiting local industry also benefits them in terms of jobs and other economic services.

In any event, how can legislators know what the majority of their constituents want on most issues? Although tools are available to sample opinions—including polls and mailed questionnaires—they are impractical on an issue-by-issue basis. As John Kennedy discovered when he served in Congress, "In Washington I frequently find myself believing that forty or fifty letters, six visits from professional politicians and lobbyists, and three editorials in Massachusetts newspapers constitute public opinion on a given issue. Yet in truth I rarely know how the great majority of the voters feel, or even how much they know of the issues that seem so burning in Washington."[6] Such doubts have convinced many legislators that they are ultimately "trustees" of the people, and must make their own decisions as to what is to their district's best advantage. "The voters selected us," Kennedy concluded, "because they had confidence in our judgment and our ability to exercise that judgment from a position where we could determine what were their own best interests, as a part of the nation's interests."[7]

In practice, the views of most members of Congress toward law making vary from policy to policy. On issues not specifically pertaining to their districts, such as foreign aid, lawmakers often will act in response to their own sentiments, or to the wishes of colleagues or the party leadership; but on matters closer to home, such as economic issues, they often will try to vote more in keeping with local interests. As one survey of Congress members discovered, 28 percent tended to regard themselves primarily as "delegates" of their districts, 23 percent as "trustees," and 46 percent as a combination of both.[8]

Serving Constituents

Although senators and representatives face interesting challenges in legislating for the nation, they are not solely lawmakers. As the federal bureaucracy expands its influence over people's lives, members of Congress must spend an increasing amount of time helping constituents cut red tape or correct bureaucratic injustices. Perhaps an elderly constituent has not received his monthly social security check, or perhaps a teacher wants help obtaining a visa to visit China or the Soviet Union. As one Representative discovered, "Much of the work that comes across a Congressman's desk has absolutely no relationship to legislation. All of these casework problems probably could not easily be sent elsewhere. Certainly the people don't know where else to take them."[9]

The only complaint is that having to deal with constituent requests takes time away from purely legislative matters. Even though most of the mail pouring into the office is handled by a hired staff, the average representative, according to one estimate, spends almost 30 percent of his or her time receiving visitors, answering letters, and handling constituent problems.[10] Although members of Congress prefer to remain cordial and diplomatic when dealing with constituents, diplomacy sometimes evaporates. In one famous incident, former Rep. John Steven McGroarty of California wrote back to a constituent: "One of the countless drawbacks of being in Congress is that I am compelled to receive impertinent letters from a jackass like you in which you say I promised to have the Sierra Madre mountains reforested and I have been in Congress two months and haven't done it. Will you please take two running jumps and go to hell."[11]

Still, most senators and representatives place great importance on their constituent-service function. They believe their continuation in office depends in large part on satisfying those who request personal assistance. Even though most voters may not be familiar with the work of their legislators, few Congress members are willing to alienate those who do contact them with a problem. In the opinion of one representa-

Senator Edward Kennedy meeting with some of his constituents

tive, "Unless you can keep constantly in contact with your people, serving them and letting them know what you are doing, you are in a bad way. My experience is that people don't care how I vote on foreign aid, federal aid to education, and all those big issues, but they are very much interested in whether I answer their letters."[12]

In the final chapter, we will consider this point further, taking a look at the constituent-service function of Congress members from the point of view of citizens who write the letters.

Investigating

Over the years, members of Congress have been able to broaden their influence by using an "implied power" not spelled out in the Constitution. The right to hold committee hearings and conduct investigations has evolved over time as part of their law-making and *legislative oversight* responsibilities. In fact, senators and representatives have come to rely on hearings and investigations to serve several crucial functions: (1) to gather information on proposed bills; (2) to haul up existing policies for review; (3) to oversee the executive branch; and (4) to inform the public on current issues and problems. When bills of an important or controversial nature are being considered, hearings and investigations can last for weeks, during which testimony may be obtained from dozens of experts, lobbyists, and other citizens.

Two of the most sensational investigations in recent years were those conducted by the Senate Watergate Committee in 1973 and by the House Judiciary Committee in 1974. The Senate Watergate Committee first riveted national attention on the scandals that eventually led to President Nixon's fall from office. Chaired by Sen. Sam Ervin, a seventy-six-year-old constitutional law expert from North Carolina, the committee (known officially as the Senate Select Committee on Presidential Campaign Activities) set out to investigate the break-in at the Democratic party headquarters in the Watergate complex during the 1972 presidential campaign. Its ostensible purpose was to uncover the part played in the burglary by the Committee for the Reelection of the President (CREEP) and to recommend legislation preventing future campaign abuses. In the process, the committee heard weeks of televised testimony by key Nixon aides, most notably by John Dean, who implicated Nixon in the subsequent cover-up of the affair. As its final official action, the committee in July 1974 released a ponderous three-volume report spelling out some recommendations for reform. Among them was the suggestion (later carried out) that an independent Federal Election Commission be created to supervise and enforce the campaign finance laws.

Equally sensational were the deliberations of the House Judiciary Committee a year later. The thirty-eight-member committee, headed by raspy-voiced Peter Rodino, was delegated the historic responsibility, in Rodino's words, "to investigate fully and completely whether sufficient grounds exist for the House of Representatives to exercise its constitutional power to impeach Richard Milhous Nixon, President of the United States of America." After months of research, hearings, and heated debate, the committee in July 1974 played out its final five days of deliberations over network television. As cameras panned along the long mahogany bench to capture the "aye" or "no" vote of each member, the committee handed down the first recommendation for the impeachment of a president since 1868. It charged Nixon with "obstruction of justice" in the Watergate cover-up, "abuse of power" in his dealings with governmental agencies, and "contempt of Congress" through his defiance of congressional subpoenas. (For more on impeachment, see Chapter 3.)

One significant aspect of these two committee investigations is that they were watched on television and discussed by more people than perhaps any other investigations in history. Indeed, the televised coverage of the committees may have done more to elevate public interest in congressional activities—normally overshadowed by those of the president—than anything else undertaken by Congress during the past several decades.

Senate Watergate Committee hearing

Congressional investigations are not always highly praised, of course. A common complaint is that committee hearings and investigations are often used as a "political cop-out," as a smoke screen for inaction. Some representatives and senators, eager to appear concerned about a problem—such as Indian rights or housing conditions in urban slums—hold public hearings, even though the information already is abundant and the problem cries for immediate solution. In the opinion of Rep. Shirley Chisholm, "Most congressional hearings are ridiculous. They are held to impress the public, to get someone's name in the papers and on television. . . . Witnesses come in and earnestly testify about something they know and care about, hoping that the committee will be moved. They think if they give Congress the truth, they will get justice in return. Then their testimony is printed in book after book of hearing records, which are piled on shelves to gather dust."[13]

Another complaint is that investigations are often carried out in an incompetent and unproductive manner. Although one of the most common uses of investigations is to see whether the federal bureaucracy is properly administering the laws passed by Congress, investigations often prove inadequate. Administrative errors and fraud, cost overruns, and general bureaucratic incompetence frequently slip by unnoticed or are tacitly accepted with a mutual shrugging of shoulders by administrators and members of Congress. Some members complain, of course, that they are at a disadvantage when it comes to checking the activities of the executive branch. They are unable to compete with the thousands of experts and enormous technical resources of the federal bureaucracy, and thus are unable to catch or prevent every irresponsible policy decision. However, while this excuse may be justified in part, the lack of resources could be resolved through added staff or new legislation stiffening penalties for bureaucratic mismanagement if the will existed to do a vigorous job of legislative oversight. Unfortunately, as some critics note, the will to do so often seems to be lacking.

Raising and Spending Money

Many members of Congress feel that a great deal of their power rests with their constitutional authority to regulate the flow of money. Although the president draws up elaborate budget recommendations each fiscal year, members of Congress ultimately determine where the money will come from (such as taxes and government bonds) and how much will be spent. In other words, without their approval, no money can be doled out for foreign aid, salaries for army generals, or paper clips for bureaucrats.

Members of the House of Representatives have traditionally exercised most financial control. If the president requests more money for defense or some other purpose, bills must be introduced in the House authorizing and *appropriating* such funds. By custom, the House Appropriations Committee, which has the primary authority for spending, is the first to review the president's budget requests. It then sends its recommendations to the Senate Appropriations Committee, which may add amendments. Members of the House also have the constitutional authority to initiate revenue bills (see Article I, section 7). This means that all new tax bills must go first to the House Ways and Means Committee, whose members consider the ways and means of raising money. Only after a tax bill winds its way through this committee and the House will it reach its Senate counterpart, the Finance Committee, for review.

For many years, controversy has raged over how Congress's power of the purse affects its relations with the White House. Some observers believe Congress's control over raising and spending money has tended to suffer a decline similar to that over military policy. Ever since the Bureau of the Budget (now the Office of Management and Budget) was created in 1921, members of Congress have had to play largely by the president's rules, making only slight alterations in a budget sent over from the White House. Yet, it is also true that control over the purse strings provides representatives and senators with their greatest influence over the executive branch. Because few of the president's programs can succeed without funds, a decision to increase or reduce his budget requests can drastically affect his administration's performance.

In fact, during the past decade, Congress has taken steps to expand its influence over the budget. In 1974, it passed the Budget and Impoundment Control Act, establishing new House and Senate Budget Committees and a joint Congressional Budget Office of fiscal experts. The act was designed to improve Congress's ability to determine what the total of government spending should be each year. That is, instead of just looking piecemeal at the budget proposals offered by the president, Congress can now set its own overall spending targets for each broad area of governmental activity, targets that the revenue and appropriations committees (and the president) must keep in mind when considering new tax laws and spending bills.

The act also contained a provision to limit presidential *impoundments*. This provision coincided with a series of lower federal court cases curtailing the president's power to hold back funds. Ever since Thomas Jefferson's term, presidents have occasionally balked at spending money appropriated by Congress. When the House and Senate in 1972, for example, authorized $25 billion to clean up the nation's polluted rivers, President Nixon vetoed the bill in an effort, he said, to hold down federal spending. Then, after Congress overrode his veto, Nixon simply impounded $6 billion by ordering that it not be spent. He argued that, as chief executive, he had the authority to impound any funds alloted by Congress. Many members of Congress objected, however, that under the Constitution the president may veto a bill only in its entirety; he may not "item veto" specific appropriations. As a result, the 1974 Budget Act was passed, limiting the president's power to hold back funds approved by Congress.

Providing "Advice and Consent"

Although members of the House may have an edge over senators in revenue matters, senators have the sole constitutional authority to oversee the White House by reviewing the president's appointments and treaties. Just as the president can veto bills passed by Congress, so can senators "veto" his appointments and treaties.

The Constitution stipulates that the president's appointments of federal officers—such as department heads, ambassadors, and federal court judges—are subject to the *advice and consent* of a simple majority of senators present and voting. Members of the House do not share this duty with the Senate, except when a president (under the Twenty-Fifth Amendment) must pick a new vice-president. When President Nixon in 1973 selected Gerald Ford to replace Spiro Agnew and when President Ford, a year later, selected Nelson Rockefeller, both houses of Congress were called upon to give formal approval by a majority vote.

Although most appointees are confirmed without difficulty, senators on occasion do turn thumbs down on a nominee. Several of Ford's appointees, for example, were turned down by the Senate, and Carter's nominee for director of the CIA, Ted Sorenson, withdrew in the face of certain Senate rejection. Presidents must bear in mind that, even though senators will give them considerable freedom to appoint federal officers (only eight Cabinet nominees since 1789, for example, have been rejected), it is still wise to clear prospective nominees with key senators—especially those from a state in which an appointee like a federal judge is to serve—before making an appointment.

The same need for Senate consultation is true for treaties, which, unlike appointments, require the approval of *two-thirds* of the senators present and voting. The possibility that the Senate may reject a treaty compels the president to seek the support of key senators in advance, especially those on the powerful Foreign Relations Committee who are the first to review new treaties. Although the Senate historically has approved more than 90 percent of the treaties submitted, senators occasionally have demanded last-minute changes as their price for support (as they did before approving the two Panama Canal treaties in 1978). In 1919, Woodrow Wilson made the disastrous mistake of not compromising with the Senate Republican leadership on the Treaty of Versailles, and thereby helped doom the League of Nations. Of course, as noted in the preceding chapter, one response of presidents to the risk of treaty rejection has been to rely on executive agreements, which do not require formal Senate approval.

Recruitment to Congress

If one concludes that a congressional career is desirable from the standpoint of political action, the immediate concern becomes: Who is most likely to attain the post? The Constitution stipulates only a few legal qualifications for election to Congress: that Representatives (who serve two-year terms) must be at least twenty-five years old, and Senators (who serve six-year terms) must be at least thirty; that the former must have been American citizens for at least seven years and the latter for at least nine; and that they must reside in the states in which they are elected.

However, although most Americans may legally qualify to serve in Congress, neither the House nor Senate truly reflects a cross-section of our society. As ruling-elite theorists are quick to point out, the vast majority of those serving on Capitol Hill are white males, whose professions are either in law, business, banking, or education. As Table 10-1 shows, women are remarkably underrepresented in Congress: although they comprise more than half of the nation's population, they account for only 3 percent of the 96th Congress (1979–1981), with a total of seventeen members. A similar underrepresentation of minority groups also prevails: although 12 percent of the population is black, for example, the 96th Congress includes only sixteen black members, also less than 3 percent. Most other minority groups, such as Hispanics and Native Americans, have few or no members in either the House or the Senate.

Congress probably will never reflect a true cross-section of the population in every respect (obviously, it is not surprising that lawyers predominate in a law-making body). Yet, it is difficult to justify such underrepresentation of women and other large groups in our society. Such underrepresentation may lead not only to disillusionment with the governing process but also to a neglect of social problems that many

Table 10-1. Characteristics of the 96th Congress, 1979–1981

	House	Senate	Total
Sex and Race			
Men	419	99	518
Women	16	1	17
White	417	97	514
Black	16	0	16
Oriental	2	3	5
Prior Occupations			
Agriculture	19	6	25
Business or Banking	127	29	156
Education	57	7	64
Engineering	2	0	2
Journalism	11	2	13
Labor leaders	4	0	4
Law	205	65	270
Law enforcement	5	0	5
Medicine	6	1	7
Clergy	6	1	7
Scientists	2	2	4
Religion			
Baptist	43	11	54
Episcopal	51	17	68
Jewish	23	7	30
Methodist	58	19	77
Presbyterian	52	12	64
Catholic	116	13	129
Other	92	21	113

Source: Congressional Quarterly Weekly Report, 20 January 1979.

senators and representatives simply do not identify with or understand. While it may be true that Congress members do not need to resemble their constituents to represent their interests, we might wonder how a group of predominately white, college-educated male senators can possibly feel the despair of an elderly black woman trying to survive in an urban slum. (Could this be part of the reason urban slums are permitted to exist?)

How broader representation can be achieved, however, remains a perplexing question. Certainly the prejudices of many voters, the inequalities of campaign financing, and other roadblocks need to be overcome to erase the inequalities of representation.

The Structure of Power: Implications for Action

Although the ability of senators and representatives to gain significant political influence has much to do with their talents and ambitions, ultimately it depends on the positions they attain in the congressional power structure. Like most organizations, Congress is not a body of equals. Some senators and representatives, by virtue of their committee assignments and leadership roles, can attain positions of power that elude other members.

Indeed, as already stated, many newly elected members are shocked to find how little influence they can exert outside the limited policy areas of their committees and how often Congress can tear apart meaningful legislation. They discover not only that the procedures and power structure in Congress can be quite foreboding but that a handful of legislators can impede or permanently block bills favored by a majority of members and the public. While the seniority tradition, Senate filibuster, and other hallowed procedures have been the targets of reform, disturbing questions about the responsiveness of Congress remain.

Many historians point out, of course, that the framers of the Constitution never intended Congress to be a particularly responsive institution. The fact that they created a bicameral (two-house) legislature composed of an often competitive and mutually hostile House and Senate (the latter originally not even directly elected by the voters) suggested a willingness to allow delay and deadlock in its law making. As we saw in Chapter 3, many of the Founding Fathers were fearful about creating a national legislature that might respond too speedily to the changing moods of future majorities.

In this section, therefore, let us consider some of the main features of the congressional power structure, features that can often frustrate those hoping to see constructive policies emerge from the legislative labyrinth.

The Committees

With rare exceptions, all legislative craftsmanship in the House and Senate takes place in committees. Each bill introduced on Capitol Hill is referred to a committee for consideration; and it is in the committee, not on the floor, that its fate usually is determined. After being ushered into the House and Senate galleries, tourists often are amazed to see perhaps only a dozen or so members on the floor, speaking to rows of empty seats. Unless an important vote is about to take place, most members probably will remain in their offices or attend to the business of their committees.

Congress relies on committees to divide the workload and to enable each member to specialize in a few fields. (It is common today for most representatives to serve on one or two standing committees, and for senators to serve on two or three.) With more than twenty thousand bills introduced each session on Capitol Hill, few members can become familiar with the details of each bill. As a result, each committee in the House and Senate has jurisdiction over a certain broad area, such as foreign relations, education, or agriculture (see Table 10-2).

At present, there are fifteen permanent or *standing committees* in the Senate and twenty-two in the House. Because each standing committee is supposed to mirror the party composition of the entire body, each is bipartisan, with its seats distributed according to the relative strength of the two major parties. This means that, for most of the past fifty years, a majority on each committee—as well as *all* committee chairmen—have been Democrats because that has been the majority party.

To most of the men and women in Congress, their committee assignments are of crucial importance: it is in their committees, not on the

---

Table 10-2. The Standing Committees of Congress

Senate Committees	*House Committees*
Agriculture, Nutrition, and Forestry	Agriculture
Appropriations	Appropriations
Armed Services	Armed Services
Banking, Housing, and Urban Affairs	Banking, Finance, and Urban Affairs
Budget	Budget
Commerce, Science, and Transportation	District of Columbia
Energy and Natural Resources	Education and Labor
Environment and Public Works	Government Operations
Finance	House Administration
Foreign Relations	Interior and Insular Affairs
Governmental Affairs	International Relations
Human Resources	Interstate and Foreign Commerce
Judiciary	Judiciary
Rules and Administration	Merchant Marine and Fisheries
Veterans' Affairs	Post Office and Civil Service
	Public Works and Transportation
	Rules
	Science and Technology
	Small Business
	Standards of Official Conduct
	Veterans' Affairs
	Ways and Means

Shirley Chisholm

floor, that they will have the best chance to guide legislation and establish their reputations. Obviously, some committees, such as the Foreign Relations Committee in the Senate and the Appropriations Committee in the House, have greater prestige and more important responsibilities than others, and thus positions on them are highly prized.

Basically, the decision as to who gets assigned to which committee is made by special committees dominated by the party leadership in each house. An effort usually is made to help members politically by assigning them to committees that reflect their interests or the concerns of voters back home. However, it is not unknown for new members (particularly in the House) to be placed on committees having little to do with their concerns. Rep. Shirley Chisholm, for example, was shocked to find herself at one time assigned to the House Agriculture Committee. She objected vehemently to the appointment, insisting that service on that committee was an absurd way for her to represent her urban and mostly black district in Brooklyn. "Apparently, all they know here in Washington about Brooklyn," she commented sarcastically, "is that a tree grew there."[14] Her committee assignment was eventually changed to Education and Labor.

The standing committees are themselves broken down into more than 260 smaller subcommittees to handle specialized subjects. The House

Judiciary Committee, for instance, has subcommittees on Civil and Constitutional Rights, Crime and Monopolies, and Commercial Laws. Over the years, subcommittees have become increasingly powerful forces in Congress. Because the members of subcommittees tend to become specialists in their own narrow policy areas, other Senate and House members, including the members of their parent standing committees, usually defer to their decisions. This means that, on issues ranging from atomic energy to tax legislation, a few subcommittee members often rule the day. In fact, the House Democrats in 1973 passed a "subcommittee bill of rights" granting the Democrats on each standing committee (rather than the chairman) the authority to select subcommittee chairmen and stipulating that no member could chair more than one subcommittee. This ruling in effect reduced the powers of committee chairmen and fragmented power in the House to an even greater degree than before. Subcommittee chairmanships were dispersed widely among the Democrats, giving more members a chance to play a major role in at least one narrow policy area.

Congress also relies on *conference committees* to iron out differences in bills passed by both houses, as well as *select committees* to conduct special investigations. An example of the latter was the Senate Watergate Committee, chaired by the former senator with the dancing eyebrows, Sam Ervin.

Needless to say, a great deal of criticism has been levied against the committee system. One major complaint is that much of what Congress *does not do* is determined by the committees. Because committees have the power to change drastically or refuse consideration of bills, only a small fraction of the bills introduced (about 5 or 10 percent) ever show up on the floor for a vote (see Table 10-3). When a bill is referred to a committee, Woodrow Wilson once remarked, it "crosses a parliamentary bridge . . . to dim dungeons of silence whence it will never return."[15]

Although many bills undoubtedly deserve this fate, important bills having wide public and congressional support sometimes are killed in committee by a small number of lawmakers. Indeed, few representatives and senators (not to mention concerned citizens) have escaped the disappointment of seeing a desired bill destroyed by a handful of hostile committee members. In 1972, for instance, the House Judiciary Committee, under pressure from the gun lobby, quashed a bill by Sen. Birch Bayh to ban cheap handguns called "Saturday night specials," the type of weapons used to kill Sen. Robert Kennedy and cripple Alabama Governor George Wallace. The bill already had passed the Senate and, according to opinion polls, had the support of a majority of Americans. But because the House as a whole was not sufficiently committed to the

Table 10-3. Passing a Law (bills may be introduced first in either chamber or simultaneously in both).

Senate

Bill Introduced: A bill is introduced by a senator, perhaps as suggested by the president. It is given an identification number and then referred to the proper standing committee.

Committee Considers: If the committee does not kill the bill outright, it may refer the bill to a subcommittee and hold hearings. After the bill wins a majority vote in the committee (possibly with amendments), it is scheduled for debate on the floor.

Floor Action: The bill goes before the entire Senate, where it is debated and voted on. Once the bill is passed (possibly with amendments), it is sent to the House of Representatives where it must clear similar hurdles.

House

Bill Introduced: The bill is sent to the Speaker, who refers it to the proper standing committee.

Committee Considers: Again, if this committee does not kill the bill outright, it also may add amendments. After the bill wins a majority vote in the committee, it is sent to the Rules Committee (only appropriations and revenue bills usually bypass the Rules Committee).

Rules Committee: If the Rules Committee decides not to kill the bill, it determines *when* the bill will be heard on the floor, *how long* debate on it may last, and *whether* it can be amended on the floor.

Floor Action: The bill goes before the entire House, where it is debated and voted on.

Final Action: Once the bill wins House approval, it may be sent either (1) directly to the president for his signature or veto, (2) back to the Senate for approval of amendments added in the House, or (3) to a conference committee of Senate and House members, where the differences may be hammered out (in which case another vote on the bill must take place in both chambers).

issue, it allowed a handful of committee members to determine the fate of Senator Bayh's bill.

In fact, even if a senator or representative succeeds in propelling a bill through both houses, the bill may still become useless because of an appropriations committee's actions. This is because any bill approved by Congress, especially one setting up a new federal program, is only an "authorization" for the program: money still has to be raised to put it into effect. To get that money, the Appropriations Committees in the House and Senate must support a new bill alloting the funds. Historically, many programs have never been given full funding simply because an appropriations committee, or one of its subcommittees, did not support them.

However, it is not only members of Congress who may find their will obstructed by a committee's actions. Ordinary citizens may be similarly affected. Because the destiny of most bills is decided in committee, special interest groups—oil companies, labor unions, the gun lobby, or banking interests—can concentrate their pressures on a handful of committee members known to support their concerns. If they wish to bury a bill favored by a majority of the public, such as the one banning cheap handguns, the support of a simple majority of members on the right committee can do the trick. The diffusion of power among committees, each virtually monopolizing policy decisions in a given area, makes Congress particularly susceptible to the pressures of well-organized interests. Such interests can have considerably greater impact on legislation than if they had to deal with the entire membership of Congress, often to the detriment of an unalerted public.

Moreover, the presence of committees encourages unequal representation. Those of us fortunate enough to live in a district served by a member who sits on, or possibly even heads, a powerful House committee like Appropriations or Ways and Means can sometimes count on more immediate return for our votes than those living in a district served by a junior representative with little experience or position. Although a working relationship (if any) between citizens and their representative depends on many conditions, a representative who has been assigned to a minor committee and who commands little influence imposes a handicap on those seeking an effective political voice.

In fact, it has been said that how much constituents benefit from legislation depends greatly on how long their representative has served in Congress and on what position he or she holds. Chairmen of committees can be especially effective in catering to the economic interests of constituents and local industry alike, helping to channel funds into their districts for such projects as military installations and veterans' hospitals. Congress-watchers noted that, while Mendel Rivers served as chairman of the House Armed Services Committee from 1965 to 1970, more military funds were pumped into his South Carolina district than it knew what to do with. Meanwhile, other districts went hungry.

The Rules Committee

One of the most striking examples of committee influence on legislation is found in the House Rules Committee. Because the House of Representatives has more than four times as many members as the Senate (435 as compared with 100), more bills are introduced in that body each year. To save the members from drowning in endless pieces of legislation, most bills approved by the standing committees must pass through the Rules Committee on their way to the House floor. The committee determines (1) the sequence in which bills will be taken up by the entire House (they do not have to be reported out in the order they come in from other committees), (2) how much time will be allotted for debate, and (3) whether amendments can be offered on the floor.

Although these functions appear necessary, the Rules Committee occasionally has been lambasted for lacking objectivity and for wielding life-or-death power over legislation. Members of the committee have been known to insist that a bill be amended as the price for permitting it on the floor and even to substitute an entirely new bill for the one originally proposed. In fact, whenever a majority of the committee has decided to delay or table a bill, it has usually died, even when it was favored by most House members and the public at large. In 1974, for instance, the committee killed an important mass transit bill aimed at helping traffic-clogged cities. Although a majority of members can petition to "discharge" a bill from the committee, such action has been rare. One reason is that few members have been willing to antagonize the committee that could decide the fate of their own bills.

Only in recent years has the power of the Rules Committee been curtailed. As a result of reforms passed during the mid-1970s, the committee has tended to behave less dictatorially than in the past. The Speaker now has the power to name its Democratic members and thus to keep them more in line with the party leadership.

The Filibuster

Although the Senate operates without a Rules Committee, it has its own procedures that can obstruct the flow of legislation—most notably the *filibuster*. Because the Senate, unlike the larger and more unwieldy House, permits almost unlimited discussion on a bill, any senator can try to stop a bill by talking continuously or otherwise procrastinating (such as by asking for endless roll-call votes and points of order). To filibuster, all he must do is remain standing and keep talking; the subject does not even have to be relevant to the bill at hand. A senator may entertain colleagues with Mother Goose nursery rhymes or recipes from a cookbook. Passage of the 1957 Civil Rights Act, for example, was delayed by Strom Thurmond, who bored the Senate for more than twenty-four hours by reading editorials in southern newspapers and the opinions of former Chief Justice Taft on jury trials in contempt cases.

However, because individual Senators cannot rely on iron vocal cords to carry them through, the most effective filibuster strategy is for a group of senators to speak in succession. When one senator tires, he can simply yield the floor to a colleague who continues the "debate." Such a group filibuster may drag on for days or even weeks. The longest group filibuster in the Senate's history was staged by a coalition of southern senators who tried unsuccessfully to block passage of the 1964 Civil Rights Act. Their filibuster lasted more than eighty-three weary days.

In 1975, the Senate made a historic change in the filibuster by revising the time-honored *cloture rule* for cutting off debate. Under the old rule, if two-thirds of the senators on the floor supported a petition to restrict debate, all further discussion on a bill would be limited to one hour per member. The revised cloture rule reduces the number needed to stop a filibuster from two-thirds of those present to three-fifths of the total Senate membership. This means that, with no vacancies in the Senate, sixty votes would be required at all times to end debate.

The new rule came after a long, twenty-year campaign to soften the two-thirds requirement. Senate reformers had complained that the old two-thirds rule made it extremely hard to cut off a filibuster. Indeed, prior to the 1975 revision, the cloture rule had been used successfully only a few times, although success had become more frequent during the early 1970s. Of the 101 cloture votes taken between 1917 and early 1975, only 22 succeeded. Since 1975, a majority of cloture votes have been successful.

But why should a filibuster pose a threat at all? Why should senators be afraid of seeing a few of their colleagues taking control of the floor for an extended period of time? The major reason is that as long as a filibuster continues, they will be unable to enact other important legislation. Even when most senators support a bill, they may have a difficult time trying to muster the necessary sixty votes to stop a minority talkathon. A filibuster can be especially effective toward the end of the year when time is running short and members have pet legislation they wish to pass. A handful of senators can threaten to bury dozens of bills, simply by gaining the floor and refusing to yield until their demands are met.

Yet, despite the filibuster's apparent threat to majority rule, many senators continue to champion its use. One reason is that it allows added influence over legislation by a senator who, although greatly affected by a bill, had not been part of the crucial legislative machinery. By filibustering, he can try to stop a bill that he views as disastrous for his state. In addition, the filibuster may sometimes be used by a majority against a minority. It may be employed as a "holding action" by one or two senators to prevent a minority of their colleagues from passing legislation while the rest of the members are not present. Whether these justifications, however, surmount the criticisms of the filibuster remains a matter of dispute.

The Committee Chairmen

We should also consider the special powers of committee chairmen. Although their style and influence may vary from committee to committee, most chairmen exercise considerable influence over policy making. For one thing, because hundreds of bills may be brought before a committee, they have the authority to determine the order in which bills will be inspected and can occasionally even refuse to consider bills they oppose. When hearings on a bill are held, the chairmen often decide who will testify and how much time each member has to cross-examine. And, in rare instances, they can even kill a bill outright simply by refusing to schedule any hearings at all. When Emanuel Celler, the former chairman of the House Judiciary Committee, was asked how he stood on a bill, he replied defiantly: "I don't stand on it. I am sitting on it. It rests four-square under my fanny and will never see the light of day."[16]

Until recently, committee members had done little to change matters. Only during the past decade has the autocracy of committee chairmen been challenged through an assault on the seniority tradition and through the growing powers of subcommittees (and their chairmen). For most of Congress's history, the decisions of committee chairmen have tended to prevail. They have been able to veto policy, preventing or stalling majority action, and to push through their own pet projects irrespective of majority sentiment. As one former representative noted scornfully, "There are all sorts of ways to get things done in Congress. The best way is to live long enough to get to be a committee chairman."[17]

The Tradition of Seniority

This brings us then to the *seniority system*, a controversial, long-standing tradition that only in recent years has come under heavy assault. For most of this century, power and position have been determined not by expertise, intelligence, or party loyalty but primarily on the basis of time spent on the same committee. This has meant that whenever a member dies, resigns, or is defeated at the polls, everyone remaining moves up a step on the seniority ladder. And the member of the majority party who has served longest on the committee almost automatically becomes its chairman.

One might ask why this custom has been followed. What could justify the selection of chairmen on the basis of their longevity? One popular argument in favor of seniority has been that it promotes internal harmony in Congress by providing a peaceful route to power. If the heads of committees were selected by other means, such as by election, more conflict and bitterness might result. Another is that it encourages the selection of experienced and able chairmen. It rewards those who know first-hand the technicalities of legislation and who have had long exposure to the subject matters of their committees.

The drawback, however, has been that seniority does not reward experience gained outside Congress by younger members. Nor does it seem consistent with the fact that other important positions in Congress, such as the Speaker of the House and the floor leaders, have been filled through elections. Indeed, although many members of Congress have been inclined to support the seniority tradition in one form or another, others have been strongly critical of the practice. In the words of one group, "Even the 'law of the jungle' operates on a higher level than the 'law' of seniority; the first works to assure the survival of the fittest: the latter operates only to assure the survival of the oldest."[18]

Because of the seniority tradition, Congress has been reproached for being dominated by a "council of elders," by chairmen who are on the average older than the majority of Congress. Of course, it is not age by itself that has been the great issue. "If the ancient fools of Congress were weeded out," journalist Robert Sherrill has exclaimed, "there is no assurance that they would be replaced by young whizbangs, nor any assurance that some of the wise old men wouldn't be replaced by young asses."[19] Rather, the concern has been that long tenure in Congress breeds chairmen who are insulated from the contemporary problems of society. Just as a president may become insulated in the White House, senators and representatives serving long terms in Congress may become insensitive to changing social conditions.

Of equal concern has been the tendency of the seniority tradition to favor members from certain states and districts. To gain enough seniority to head a committee, members usually have had to be continually reelected from "safe" districts where there is little stiff opposition from the other major party. Until the mid-1970s, southern Democrats used to get the lion's share of the chairmanships because two-party competition tended to be weakest in the Democrat-dominated South. In 1975, for instance, eleven of the twenty-two standing committees in the House were headed by southerners (with Texas alone accounting for four of the chairmen). However, as Republicans have made more inroads into the South, and as older southern Democrats have left Congress, the picture has been changing. In fact, some of the safest seats are now held by black members of Congress, who represent mostly black urban districts in the North.

But perhaps the strongest criticism against seniority has been that it splinters party responsibility and makes Congress less internally democratic. If chairmen are not selected on the basis of party loyalty and service, they cannot be held accountable to other committee members or to the elected party leadership. As long as their power derives from just staying alive and getting reelected, they can continue to wield power in autocratic fashion with little fear of being removed.

Thus, it is not surprising that critics of the seniority tradition applauded the actions of the House Democrats in 1975. In a major break with the seniority tradition, the House Democratic caucus (comprising all the Democratic members) voted to strip the committee chairmanships from three crusty old Democrats, all from the South. The three were removed in a wave of resentment among young and liberal members, many of whom were swept into the House in the 1974 Democratic landslide.

This assault was made possible by a number of changes in House rules. In 1971, the House Democrats (following a similar move by the Republicans) voted to allow any ten members of a committee to demand a vote before the party caucus on the status of their chairman. Realizing later that an open challenge to a chairman might intimidate some members, the Democrats decided in 1973 to make any chairman subject to a *secret ballot* vote if 20 percent of the party members asked for it. This ruling was then strengthened in 1975 when secret ballot elections were required for *all* House committee chairmen every two years. Senate Democrats also caught the fever of reform and voted to select their committee chairmen by secret ballot whenever 20 percent of their colleagues demanded it.

It should be pointed out, of course, that seniority has not been entirely abandoned as a result of these reforms. Most of the current chairmen are members with many years of congressional service, and seniority is still being used as a principal guide for deciding who will head a committee. Still, in early 1979, three junior Democrats did succeed in defeating more senior members in elections for subcommittee chairmanships, potentially setting a new antiseniority precedent. Instead of just displacing chairmen who were considered autocratic (as was largely true in 1975), in the 1979 action, as one Representative put it, "members were voting on whether one's candidate's views were closer to theirs than the others." Thus, selection on the basis of ideology and merit could conceivably displace seniority altogether.

The Parties and the Party Leadership

When tourists visit the Senate and House chambers, they notice that the Democrats sit on one side of the aisle and the Republicans on the other, and that the members of each party enter and leave through separate swinging doors. Although the two major parties, as we saw in Chapter 6, are fragmented and undisciplined bodies, they provide some important cues to senators and representatives on how to vote and help bring some order to the chaos existing on Capitol Hill.

One of the major contributions of the parties is in providing some organization to manage the flow of legislation. In fact, some of the most powerful and prestigious positions in Congress are held by a handful of senators and representatives chosen by their party to keep other members in line and provide policy leadership. In many respects, the job of these party leaders remains one of the most challenging in Congress. Despite the assaults on the seniority tradition and the powers of committee chairmen, the party leaders have experienced considerable difficulty in achieving party unity. Members of Congress continue to be responsive to local pressures independent of the congressional party leadership and frequently vote in special interest blocs that cross party lines. The "conservative" coalition of Republicans and southern Democrats, for example, and the rise of informal groups (such as the Congressional Black Caucus and Northeast-Midwest Economic Advancement Coalition) provide potent challenges to the authority of the elected party leaders.

Who are these elected party leaders? And what do they do? Let us begin with those in the House.

The House

The most powerful elected leader in the House is the *Speaker*, who not only commands the rostrum as presiding officer but also serves as the majority party leader of the House. He is elected by the entire body every two years and, because of a straight party-line vote, is always a member of the majority party (presently the Democrats).

In presiding over the House, the Speaker has the power to recognize members on the floor and to interpret parliamentary rules. He also refers bills to committees and appoints members to select and conference committees. In fact, as a result of several reforms passed in the 1970s, he also chairs the powerful Democratic Steering and Policy Committee and selects most members of the Rules Committee. And, although the crisis has never occurred, the Speaker may even assume the presidency if both the president and vice-president die or become disabled.

In the final analysis, the extent of the Speaker's power depends on his style and character. While some Speakers (like Sam Rayburn, who ruled during the 1940s and 1950s) have used their position to great advantage—serving effectively as their party's "contact" with the president, deciding who gets the best committee seats, and so on—other Speakers (like Carl Albert, who served from 1971 to 1977) have used their position to far less political advantage.

The Speaker is assisted by a *majority floor leader*, who is chosen by the party caucus. He helps the Speaker plan party strategy, bargain with committee chairmen, and reconcile disputes between party members. The job usually serves as a stepping stone to the Speaker's post, as when Thomas "Tip" O'Neill rose from House majority leader to Speaker in 1977. Helping the floor leader is a *majority whip*, who communicates the wishes of the leadership to the party rank and file, and rounds up members for important votes on the floor. (The title "whip," incidentally, comes from the term "whipper-in," used in Britain to describe the person assigned during fox hunts to keep the dogs from straying.)

The minority party (presently the Republicans) also elects a floor leader and whip to help manage the legislative programs of their party, direct party strategy, and work occasionally with the majority leader and the president to iron out differences on bills.

The members of each party in the House also occasionally come together in *caucus* (called a *conference* by the Republicans). The caucus votes on committee assignments, elects party leaders, and discusses party policy. Since the mid-1970s, the party caucuses have been asserting considerable influence over party matters. In 1975, for example, the House Democratic caucus stripped the Ways and Means Committee of its right to make Democratic committee assignments and gave it to the caucus's Steering and Policy Committee, composed of the elected party

---

Table 10-4. The Elected Party Leaders, 96th Congress, 1979–1981

House

Speaker: Thomas "Tip" O'Neill (Mass.)
Majority Leader: Jim Wright (Tex.)
Majority Whip: John Brademas (Ind.)
Minority Leader: John Rhodes (Ariz.)
Minority Whip: Robert Michel (Ill.)

Senate

President Pro Tempore: Warren G. Magnuson (Wash.)
Majority Leader: Robert Byrd (W. Va.)
Majority Whip: Alan Cranston (Calif.)
Minority Leader: Howard Baker (Tenn.)
Minority Whip: Ted Stevens (Alaska)

---

leadership and other members appointed by the Speaker. The caucus also sacked three powerful committee chairmen and imposed new restraints on the seniority system. Whether this trend toward greater assertiveness will continue during the 1980s, however, remains to be seen.

The Senate

In the Senate, there is no powerful presiding officer similar to the Speaker of the House. The vice-president holds the constitutional office of "President of the Senate," and the *president pro tempore* occasionally presides in the vice-president's absence, but neither official wields much clout. In fact, the job of presiding usually falls to junior senators who take turns wielding the Senate gavel.

The *majority leader* of the Senate is actually the most influential party leader of that body. Like the Speaker of the House, he is the chief strategist of the majority party in his chamber, mobilizing the members behind bills the leadership decides are in the party's best interests. Naturally, in view of the decentralized, undisciplined character of American parties, this is quite an ambitious task. Generally, he strives to achieve as much party unity as possible. To this end, he helps parcel out committee assignments to other Democrats, works with the minority leader to determine the sequence of bills on the floor, and serves with the Speaker of the House as his party's liaison with the president. As with other party posts, however, the majority leader's success ultimately depends on his persuasiveness—his ability to coax, bargain with, even flatter other senators in the party. A leader who is weak and unpersuasive will have little success in keeping other party members, especially committee chairmen, in line.

As in the House, the Senate majority leader is assisted by a whip, who performs many of the same duties as his House counterpart. There are also a minority leader and whip for the Republicans, as well as party caucuses for both parties.

Legislative Staffs: Our Nonelected Lawmakers

Senators and representatives are not the only policy makers in Congress. Scurrying in and out of their offices and through the halls are a group of "shadow lawmakers" who write the speeches, handle the constituent mail, do the research, and occasionally even help draft new pieces of legislation. These are the more than 18,000 men and women who staff the committees and offices of members of Congress. Most of them are under forty years of age, have college degrees, and earn anywhere from $20,000 to $40,000 a year.

As the role of government has increased, this growing army of anonymous congressional aides has played an ever-expanding role in policy making. In order to oversee the vast federal bureaucracy and to keep up with the growing complexity of legislation, members of Congress have become increasingly dependent on their staffs to gather, process, and evaluate information, much as the president has come to rely on his personal White House assistants. Although many aides have little say on policy, sitting in cramped offices all day answering constituent letters or tracking down lost social security checks, other aides are actively involved in legislative decision making. This is especially true for committee staff aides, who arrange the hearings, select the witnesses, prepare the questions, brief the members, and draft the bills.

Many aides develop more technical expertise than the senator or representative they serve and provide the advice that may determine how a busy legislator will vote on a bill. During a vote on the controversial

Congressman Harrington meeting with his aides.

Federal Election Commission (FEC) in 1976, for example, a top staff aide was on the Senate floor telling his boss to vote against an amendment crippling the commission. "I did what I thought was the responsible thing," the aide recalled. "As it turned out, the amendment was defeated by a single vote. . . . If I had told him to vote the other way, the FEC would be out of existence now. . . . I had the power—me, an appointed staff member, elected by nobody and responsible to nobody—to overturn a major law in this country. It's scary."[20]

The power may indeed be scary, but it is also a source of excitement to many aides who as ordinary citizens would have little political clout. By attaching themselves to a senator or representative, they can help think up new laws, tell pushy bureaucrats where to place their pencil sharpeners, and write impassioned speeches on current issues without once having to endure the hardships of a political campaign. In fact, aides with long tenure who serve in key positions are often as likely to initiate bills as the senator or representative they serve.

The danger comes when aides begin to think of themselves as senators or representatives, manipulating the process to satisfy their own policy goals. Aides have been known to influence legislative decisions by giving only select information to their boss, cutting out that which conflicts with their own political views. A few aides have even used their position for private gain, resulting in front-page scandals similar to that surrounding Lyndon Johnson's senate aide, Bobby Baker.

But perhaps the most important consequence of an ever-expanding professional staff is that Congress has been creating its own bureaucracy, with all the features (good and bad) of the executive bureaucracy it is supposed to oversee. Instead of just 435 Representatives and 100 Senators, Congress now comprises thousands of hopeful policy makers stumbling over one another in their striving for legislative impact.

Congress and Social Action

The feelings of impotency and frustration that overcome some of the men and women in Congress largely reflect the difficulty in getting Congress as a whole to move. As the country's primary law-making body, Congress has not been adept at setting policy priorities and responding to many of the major social and economic problems facing the country. Crime and inflation continue on the rampage, poverty and environmental pollution still ravage the nation, while people in large numbers cast a weary and cynical eye on government.

Advocates of congressional reform used to argue (and perhaps still do) that the rules and customs of Congress frustrating many members, such as the emphasis on seniority and the wide dispersion of power among committees, also interfere with Congress's ability to fulfill many of its law-making responsibilities. Even when a major social problem has reared its ugly head, Congress has been too splintered by internal bickering, too indebted to special interests, too encumbered by an antiquated, slipshod organization to do much about it. "Clumsy, unresponsive, controlled in large part by its most ordinary members," one observer has argued, "the national legislature blunders on, facing nuclear problems with colonial procedures, insisting all the while that nothing is wrong."[21]

In many respects, of course, Congress has become a different institution in recent years. Although the dispersion of power among committees and a lack of party discipline continue to frustrate passage of important legislation, many of the old procedures and rules have been reformed. The seniority system has been weakened, the filibuster has been modified, autocratic committee chairmen have been deposed, and Congress as a whole has become a more open institution by exposing most committee sessions to the public and the press. As we noted at the beginning of the chapter, many members of Congress and others have been heartened by these reforms, insisting that Congress is now in a better position than ever before to respond to the nation's social and economic ills.

Yet, there is another perspective on Congress worth considering. Many ruling-elite theorists insist that the ability of Congress to respond to social problems depends on more than the reform of its procedures. They argue that the very goals of Congress are shaped and limited by the power structure of the society in which it thrives. Congress simply mirrors the prevailing inequities of the political and economic system, serving mainly as an instrument of elite interests. "As long as Congress reflects the distribution of economic power in the wider society," one writer argues, "it is not likely to change much even if liberals in both houses manage to gain control of the major committees, and even if the cloture rule is changed to enable the Senate to rid itself of the filibuster, and even if the Rules Committee is deprived of its arbitrary powers, and even if seniority is done away with. For what remains is the entire system of organized corporate power with its elitist institutions, business-controlled media and mass propaganda, organized pressure groups, high-paid lobbyists and influence-peddling lawyers, campaign contributions and bribes—all of which operate with such telling effect on legislators, including most of the professedly liberal ones."[22]

These are harsh criticisms. Undoubtedly, Congress does serve elite interests and has been slow in responding to the needs of a large part of our society. But if we have to wait until the capitalist system is replaced before meaningful improvements in the responsiveness of Congress are realized, we are probably in for a long wait. In the meantime, we can continue to debate the role of Congress and find new ways to make it responsive to those who, up to now, have been slighted in the struggle for political favors.

Key Terms

constituents

legislative oversight

appropriation

impoundment

advice and consent

standing committee

conference committee

select committee

filibuster

cloture rule

seniority system

caucus (conference)

Notes

1. Shirley Chisholm, *Unbought and Unbossed* (Boston: Houghton Mifflin, 1970), p. 100.
2. "Dropout's Lament," in *U.S. News & World Report*, 25 March 1974, p. 96.
3. Quoted in Charles L. Clapp, *The Congressman: His Work As He Sees It* (Washington, D.C.: Brookings Institution, 1963), p. 426.
4. Donald Riegle, *O Congress* (New York: Doubleday, 1972), p. 65.
5. Quoted in Clapp, *The Congressman*, p. 377.
6. John F. Kennedy, *Profiles in Courage* (New York: Harper & Row, 1955), p. 18.
7. Ibid., p. 16.
8. Roger H. Davidson, *The Role of the Congressman* (Indianapolis: Pegasus, 1969), pp. 117–119.
9. Quoted in Clapp, *The Congressman*, p. 54.
10. Donald G. Tacheron and Morris K. Udall, *The Job of the Congressman*, 2nd ed. (New York: Bobbs-Merrill, 1970), pp. 303–304.
11. Quoted in Kennedy, *Profiles in Courage*, p. 10.
12. Quoted in Clapp, *The Congressman*, p. 52.
13. Chisholm, *Unbought and Unbossed*, p. 104.

14. Quoted in Mark J. Green, et al., *Who Runs Congress?* (New York: Bantam Books, 1972), p. 56.

15. Woodrow Wilson, *Congressional Government* (New York: Meridian Books, 1956), p. 63. Originally published in 1885.

16. Quoted in Jim Wright, *You and Your Congressman* (New York: Coward-McCann, 1965), p. 134.

17. Clem Miller, *Member of the House: Letters of a Congressman* (New York: Charles Scribner's Sons, 1962), p. 39.

18. House Republican Task Force on Congressional Reform, *We Propose: A Modern Congress* (New York: McGraw-Hill, 1966), p. 26.

19. Robert Sherrill, *Why They Call It Politics,* 2nd ed. (New York: Harcourt Brace Jovanovich, 1974), p. 117.

20. *Newsweek,* 17 January 1977, p. 20.

21. Warren Weaver, Jr., *Both Your Houses: The Truth About Congress* (New York: Praeger, 1972), p. 4.

22. Michael Parenti, *Democracy for the Few* (New York: St. Martin's Press, 1974), pp. 205–206.

Recommended Reading

CLAPP, CHARLES L. *The Congressman: His Work As He Sees It.* Washington, D.C.: Brookings Institution, 1963.

DAVIDSON, ROGER H. *The Role of the Congressman.* Indianapolis: Pegasus, 1969.

FENNO, RICHARD F., JR. *Congressmen in Committees.* Boston: Little, Brown, 1973.

GREEN, MARK J., et al. *Who Runs Congress?* New York: Bantam, 1972.

KINGDON, JOHN W. *Congressmen's Voting Decisions.* New York: Harper & Row, 1973.

MAYHEW, DAVID R. *Congress: The Electoral Connection.* New Haven: Yale University Press, 1974.

ORFIELD, GARY. *Congressional Power: Congress and Social Change.* New York: Harcourt Brace Jovanovich, 1975.

REDMAN, ERIC. *The Dance of Legislation.* New York: Simon and Schuster, 1973.

RIEGLE, DONALD. *O Congress.* New York: Doubleday, 1972.

WEAVER, WARREN, JR. *Both Your Houses: The Truth About Congress.* New York: Praeger, 1972.

11

"Politicians in Black Robes:" The Judicial Branch

There are many Americans who, essentially disgusted with politicians and bureaucrats, retain a certain reverence for the judicial process, as exemplified by the Supreme Court. In contrast to members of Congress, presidents, and lobbyists, who appear to be locked forever in partisan battle, the robed judges who sit on the high bench—while certainly not immune to controversy—seem to tower above the usual pettiness and strife of political ambition. If public opinion polls are to be believed, the justices of the Supreme Court have enjoyed greater prestige than any other officials in government.[1]

Yet, while the popular image of Supreme Court justices may suggest an aloofness from partisan politics, the justices are as much practitioners of political art as any other elected or appointed officials. Indeed, they must be viewed in a similar light as presidents and members of Congress: as individuals who have achieved high positions of power and who exercise that power in terms of their own personal views and perceptions. Once appointed to the Supreme Court, justices do not relinquish their claims to personal opinion, nor forego prejudice and political ambition. As former Justice James McReynolds once stated, a Supreme Court justice does not become an "amorphous dummy, unspotted by human emotions."

One writer many years ago poked fun at the popular image of justices as impartial and dispassionate beings in an irreverent little piece entitled the "Song of the Supreme Court."

Song of the Supreme Court

We're nine judicial gentlemen who shun the common herd,
Nine official mental men who speak the final word.
We do not issue postage stamps or face the microphones,
Or osculate with infants, or preside at corner-stones.
But we're the court of last resort in litigation legal.
(See: Case of Brooklyn Chicken *versus* Washington Blue Eagle.)
We never heed the demagogues, their millions and their minions,
But use *this* handy yardstick when in doubt about opinions:

   Chorus

   If it's In The Constitution, it's the law,
   For The Constitution hasn't got a flaw.
   If it's In The Constitution, it's okay,
   Whether yesterday, tomorrow, or today—
   Hooray!

If it's In The Constitution, it must stay!
Like oysters in our cloisters, we avoid the storm and strife.
Some President appoints us, and we're put away for life.
When Congress passes laws that lack historical foundation,
We hasten from a huddle and reverse the legislation,
The sainted Constitution, that great document for students,
Provides an airtight alibi for all our jurisprudence.
So don't blame us if now and then we seem to act like bounders;
Blame Hamilton and Franklin and the patriotic founders.

   Chorus

   If it's In The Constitution, it's the law, *etc.*

Source: Arthur L. Lippman, *Life* magazine, August 1935; reprinted in Glendon Schubert, *Constitutional Politics* (New York: Holt, Rinehart and Winston, 1960), pp. 11–12. Used with permission of Henry T. Rockwell.

Some have cynically suggested that the justices enjoy high prestige because of the public's overall ignorance of their activities. If people knew more about how justices are appointed and understood the motivations for their rulings, public respect for them would be no greater than for other governmental officials.

Whatever the merits of this observation, social scientists have discovered that an overwhelming majority of Americans scarcely know what the Court is doing. Few can name more than a handful of the Court's nine justices, describe its procedures, or recount the nature and history of its role in the political system. And, apart from a few highly controversial cases—such as those concerning busing and prayer in the public schools—most Court decisions stir little public interest. One study revealed that more than 55 percent of Americans could not describe any recent Supreme Court rulings.[2]

The Court's press coverage, of course, has not been as extensive as that of the president and Congress, and many of the Court's decisions have abounded in legal technicalities that defy most people's understanding. Moreover, most Americans have neither the opportunity nor the desire to become intimately acquainted with the Court's activities. They do not write letters to the justices, are unable to penetrate the secrecy in which much of the Court's work is accomplished, and have few of the required resources to bring an injustice to the Court's attention. Some scholars, such as the ruling-elite theorists, aptly conclude that among the various governmental institutions in this country, the Supreme Court remains one of the least open to citizen scrutiny and influence—a conclusion that, if shared by most Americans, may indeed inhibit understanding and awareness.

The Power to Nullify "Laws"

The widespread ignorance of Supreme Court activities should not obscure the enormous power the nine justices command in the political system. Nor should it obscure the occasional storms of controversy accompanying their decisions. During the past few decades alone, the justices have handed down opinions of far-reaching significance affecting the very fabric of American society.

From the standpoint of political action, for example, the role of the justices has been profound. Their decisions have ranged over a wide area of political expression, touching on voting rights, freedom of speech, freedom of the press, and freedom of association. Their rulings in the 1960s on the issue of what constitutes permissible acts of public protest carried broad implications for those seeking constitutional protection for political expression. In response to widespread civil rights and anti-Vietnam War protests, the justices confronted federal, state, and local laws restraining public speech and assembly. In 1963, for example, the Court upheld the right of almost two hundred students to demonstrate on the South Carolina state capitol grounds, ruling that the students were exercising "basic constitutional rights in their most pristine and classic form."[3] Similarly, in 1966, the Court upheld a sit-in by five black adults protesting the segregationist policies of a regional library.[4] However, in a number of cases, the Court also came down hard against political protest. In 1967, it sustained the convictions of two hundred college students demonstrating against a segregated county jail on the grounds that the jail was not on public property.[5] And in 1968, it upheld the convictions of four persons who had burned their draft cards in violation of federal law.[6]

The basis for these and other rulings is the justices' sweeping power to exercise "judicial review." By law and tradition, the nine Court justices can overturn decisions of Congress, the president, and state legislatures that in their opinion conflict with the Constitution. Although the president and members of Congress also continually interpret the Constitution through their actions, Supreme Court justices usually have the final word in interpreting the document's meaning. As former Chief Justice Charles Evans Hughes stated bluntly in 1907, "We are under a Constitution, but the Constitution is what the judges say it is."

Take one recent and dramatic example. In July 1974, the Supreme Court justices held an extraordinary midsummer hearing on whether President Nixon had to surrender sixty-four White House tape recordings sought by Special Prosecutor Leon Jaworski. Titled *The United States of America* v. *Richard M. Nixon*, the case marked the first appearance of the Watergate scandal in the highest court. In their historic decision, the justices ruled against President Nixon, upholding a previous order by District Court Judge John Sirica requiring the president to hand over the tapes as evidence in the Watergate cover-up trial of six former Nixon aides.

Simply stated, the justices rejected Nixon's sweeping assertion that only a president can decide what White House materials can be used as evidence in criminal proceedings. The doctrine of separation of powers and the need for confidential communication within the executive branch, the justices ruled, does not give the president absolute privilege to withhold material from the courts. In a criminal case such as the cover-up trial, where the claim of confidentiality is not based on grounds of military or diplomatic secrecy, the president's assertion of *executive privilege* must yield to the need for evidence.

Clearly, the case represented one of the most significant disputes over governmental powers in American history and strongly bolstered the Court's position relative to that of the president in the area of law. Nixon's compliance with the ruling reaffirmed the Court's preeminence among the three branches of government in interpreting the Constitution.

Interpreting the Constitution is not all that the Court does, of course. Much of its time is also spent interpreting the meaning of acts of Congress and rules of federal regulatory agencies. Because federal laws and regulations are often ambiguously worded, the Court frequently is asked to resolve conflicts of statutory interpretation. And in interpreting law, the Court is also *making* law. Thus, in matters ranging from federal trade practices and corporate mergers to taxation and welfare, the Court's rulings are often as important in policy making as its rulings on constitutional issues.

How Judicial Review Began

Considering that *judicial review*, however, remains the Court's most awesome power, it is interesting to realize that the Constitution does not specifically authorize the Court to exercise it. Although Article III stipulates that the justices may consider "all cases, in law and equity, arising under the Constitution," this provision does not clearly empower them to strike down acts they consider to be unconstitutional.

However, many historians point out that the use of judicial review had been anticipated before the Constitution was drafted and that many state courts already had invalidated acts that conflicted with state constitutions. Furthermore, many members of the Constitutional Convention in 1787 had championed judicial review as one of the vital functions of the Court.[7] An early study by historian Charles Beard revealed that at least seventeen of the twenty-five most influential members of the convention were "on record in favor of the proposition that the Judiciary would in the natural course of things pass upon the constitutionality of acts of Congress." And of the less prominent members, Beard found, six were on record who "understood and approved" the doctrine.[8]

Moreover, in *The Federalist*, a series of essays promoting ratification of the Constitution by the states, Alexander Hamilton pleaded for the right of the judicial branch to decide whether legislative acts were constitutional. "The complete independence of the courts of justice is peculiarly essential in a limited constitution," he argued, and such a limited constitution "can be preserved in practice no other way than through the courts of justice, whose duty it must be to declare all acts contrary to the manifest tenor of the Constitution void. Without this, all the reservations of particular rights or privileges would amount to nothing."[9] In fact, in the Judiciary Act of 1789 (which established the federal court system), Congress handed Supreme Court justices limited power over state court decisions. By doing so, many historians contend, Congress implied that the justices could overturn laws contradicting the federal Constitution.

But because the Constitution was silent on the Court's right to review congressional or presidential acts (for reasons still being debated), the justices gradually acquired this power through their own interpretations of the document. The celebrated case of *Marbury* v. *Madison* (1803) was especially important in this regard, since it set the precedent for reviewing acts of Congress. The case developed in 1801 when John Adams, just before stepping down from the presidency, hurriedly appointed a number of Federalist party judges, among them William Marbury as justice of the peace in the District of Columbia. When Thomas Jefferson, Adams's Republican successor, learned that Marbury's commission had not been delivered in time, he decided to appoint someone else. Marbury, evidently disappointed and angered by Jefferson's refusal to honor his appointment, appealed directly to the Supreme Court. He insisted that the justices should force Jefferson's secretary of state, James Madison, to deliver the commission. He based his appeal on the fact that Congress, in the Judiciary Act of 1789, had stated that requests for a *writ of mandamus* (an order demanding a public official to do his duty) could be taken directly to the Supreme Court; that is, such requests were part of the Court's *original jurisdiction.*

Clearly, the justices were placed in an uncomfortable position. On the one hand, if they tried to order Madison to deliver the commission, Madison would probably just ignore the order and thereby humiliate the Court. But, on the other hand, if they refused to support Marbury, they would be admitting the Court's weakness.

Chief Justice John Marshall's majority opinion was a masterpiece of strategy. He admitted that Marbury should be given his commission, but stated that the justices did not have the power to help him get it. This was because the section of the Judiciary Act authorizing them to honor direct requests for writs of mandamus in the first place was unconstitutional. Congress had no authority, Marshall said, to enlarge the Court's original jurisdiction by handing the justices the added authority to issue such writs. The Court's original jurisdiction is limited by the Constitution to disputes involving diplomats or one of the states and cannot be enhanced by Congress. And because Marbury was neither a diplomat nor a state, the justices had no authority to issue a writ of mandamus on his behalf. Thus, even though Marbury did not benefit by this decision, the justices and the Court clearly did. By ruling that a section of the Judiciary Act was unconstitutional, they avoided a fight with the Jefferson administration and simultaneously established the Court's authority to interpret the constitutionality of congressional acts.

Ironically, in the years since the Marbury decision, Supreme Court justices have not overturned many other acts of Congress: only about one hundred such acts have been declared totally or partly unconstitutional. Most of the Court's judicial review power has been directed instead against the states. One estimate is that more than one thousand state and local acts have been thrown out by the Court. In the opinion of some observers, in fact, the power to review state acts has been more important than the power to review legislation of Congress. Without the power to interpret state acts, there would be little to prevent the states from going their independent legal ways to the detriment of the federal Constitution. As former Justice Oliver Wendell Holmes concluded, "I do not think the United States would come to an end if we lost our power to declare an act of Congress void. I do think the Union would be imperiled if we could not make that declaration as to the laws of the several states."[10]

Justifications for Judicial Review

What possible justifications can we find for allowing Supreme Court justices to wield judicial review? Why should nine robed judges who never face the voters command the awesome power to overturn the decisions of elected officials? Such power, according to ruling-elite theorists, would appear to conflict with the "democratic" ideal that no group, particularly an elite appointed for life, should determine policy for a majority of society.

One justification, as we saw in Chapter 3, is that our political system is based on more than majority rule, that it ultimately rests on a foundation of constitutional law. As Alexander Hamilton wrote in *Federalist* No. 78 and as Chief Justice John Marshall ruled in *Marbury* v. *Madison* (1803), the Constitution must be regarded as the supreme law of the land, superior to any acts of Congress, the president, lower courts, or state legislatures. And, because the responsibility of the courts is to interpret the law, Supreme Court justices must be the ultimate interpreters of the Constitution. They must determine whether any legislation passed by Congress or other legislative bodies is in accord with it. If the justices should find a conflict between such legislation and the Constitution, it is their duty to declare that legislation invalid.

Related to this legalistic justification is the more obvious fact that many of the Founding Fathers were never willing to put full trust in the majority or their elected representatives. They feared that the majority might trample on the rights of those individuals or minorities who happen to offend the prevailing prejudices of the times. And, because every citizen is likely to be a member of some minority at one time or another, no individual might be spared persecution by the many. "It is of great importance in a republic," James Madison warned in *Federalist No. 51*, "not only to guard the society against the oppression of its rulers, but to guard one part of the society against the injustice of the other. . . . If a majority be united by a common interest, the rights of the minority will be insecure." Thus, in the opinion of many of the Founding Fathers, it would be unrealistic to entrust members of Congress or state legislatures with the sole responsibility to define the boundaries of their authority or the rights of minorities. These bodies are elected by temporary majorities whose prejudices and passions at any moment might be unleashed against unpopular groups. In contrast, Supreme Court justices, who are not elected by the voters and who serve for life, are in a more independent position to protect individual rights guaranteed by the Constitution.

Naturally, this does not mean that Supreme Court justices have always provided such protection. As we will see, constraints have been imposed on the Court to prevent the justices from challenging the majority will for long periods of time. In fact, Supreme Court justices even have aided the repression of individual rights at various times in history. In *Dred Scott* v. *Sanford* (1857), they ruled that descendants of slaves were not United States citizens and that Congress could not halt

the expansion of slavery into the territories. In *Plessy* v. *Ferguson* (1896), a majority of the justices supported the concept of "separate but equal" facilities for different races. And in *Korematsu* v. *United States* (1944), a similar majority upheld President Roosevelt's order placing thousands of loyal Japanese-Americans in makeshift detention camps during World War II. While these rulings may be regarded as exceptional in the Court's history, they offer little reassurance to those expecting judicial "knights in shining armor" always to wield their swords of judicial review to defend the rights of individuals in distress.

History of the Supreme Court

The exercise of judicial review by Supreme Court justices has had an interesting and somewhat mixed history. The rulings of the Court during the past 190 years reveal that the orientations of the justices have tended to shift quite remarkably, reflecting changes in both social concerns and legal perspectives. It is possible, in fact, to distinguish several periods in the Court's history during which certain issues dominated the justices' attention.

1789–1865

During the initial period of the Court's history, from 1789 until the Civil War, the justices were primarily involved in power disputes between the federal government and the states. Under Chief Justice John Marshall (1801–1835), they labored not only to establish the Court as the supreme interpreter of the Constitution[11] but to strengthen the authority of the federal government. They ruled in *McCulloch* v. *Maryland* (1819), for instance, that the states could not interfere with the authority of Congress to create a national bank by the use of their taxing power. They also declared in *Gibbons* v. *Ogden* (1824) that Congress, not the states, had the ultimate authority to regulate interstate commerce. Because the federal government, Marshall stated, is "emphatically, and truly, a government of all the people," its decisions in certain matters must prevail.

Even after Marshall's death in 1835, the justices continued to be preoccupied with the nation-state issue. However, under Chief Justice Roger B. Taney (1836–1864), they retreated from the strong support previously given to the claims of the federal government and gave greater (although not exclusive) support to the claims of the states. They asserted that the two levels of government were basically coequal and that powers delegated to the federal government were clearly limited by the powers reserved to the states in the Tenth Amendment. The reputation of the Taney Court was badly tarnished, however, by the notorious *Dred Scott* v. *Sanford* decision in 1857 stating that Congress had no right to exclude slavery from the new territories. This decision greatly undermined the Court's prestige in the North for more than a generation and may even have helped bring on the Civil War.

1865–1941

From the Civil War until the New Deal in the 1930s, the Court turned its attention from the nation-state issue toward guarding capitalist industrial development from governmental regulation. Although previous justices under Marshall and Taney had been concerned with business and property rights as well, most of the justices during this second period reflected the general spirit of the times and sided with business interests in their efforts to ward off governmental regulations of free enterprise. Under a succession of chief justices, the Court held that a provision of the Fourteenth Amendment (ratified in 1868) prohibiting the taking of a person's property without "due process" also protected business enterprises from governmental interference. It ruled that corporations were "persons," and that employers and employees had a right to bargain in any way they wished. In due course, it struck down the federal income tax in 1895,[12], overturned legislation curbing child labor in 1918,[13] and repealed minimum wage laws for women in 1923.[14] These and similar rulings were condemned by Progressives, who viewed the justices as merely defenders of industrial "robber barons."

Interestingly, the Great Depression in the 1930s brought the Court's probusiness orientation into direct conflict with Franklin Roosevelt's New Deal. Maintaining a laissez-faire philosophy, the Court declared more than eleven major New Deal policies unconstitutional. President Roosevelt sharply attacked their destruction of his policies and vowed revenge. In a message to Congress in 1937, he asked for legislation to increase the Court's size from nine to fifteen justices and thereby ensure a majority sympathetic to the New Deal. Although this "Court-packing" plan failed to win congressional support, the president's determination eventually sparked some changes. Several of the justices switched their positions ("the switch in time that saved nine"), and vacancies on the bench finally allowed Roosevelt to appoint new justices who favored his policies. As a result, the Court upheld both the Social Security Act and the National Labor Relations Act as valid federal legislation.

Following the United States' entry into World War II, the major concern
(and controversy) facing the Court began to involve, not business-
government disputes, but the issues of equal rights and due process.
And, at different times during this twenty-eight year period, a majority
of justices were found on both sides of these issues. During the reigns of
Chief Justice Harlan F. Stone (1941–1946) and Chief Justice Fred M.
Vinson (1946–1953), the Court generally refused to challenge the federal
government's repressions of individual rights. Not only did the justices,
in *Korematsu* v. *United States* (1944), uphold the infamous order incar-
cerating thousands of Japanese-Americans in detention camps during
World War II, but they also, in *Dennis* v. *United States* (1951), upheld the
Smith Act prohibiting freedom of speech for certain political groups.

Not until Earl Warren was appointed chief justice in 1953 did the
Court actively employ judicial review to extend the protections of the
Bill of Rights. The Warren Court ruled in numerous cases that the pro-

William O. Douglas and Chief Justice Earl Warren.

visions of the Bill of Rights (applying mainly to Congress) also applied to the states via the "due process" and "equal protection" clauses of the Fourteenth Amendment. This meant, as we saw in Chapter 4, that the states had to recognize and uphold the same rights as did Congress and that state laws violating these rights were unconstitutional. (The Supreme Court, in *Gitlow* v. *New York*, 1925, had already ruled that freedom of speech and of the press—protected by the First Amendment from abridgement by Congress—were also protected by the due process clause of the Fourteenth Amendment from abridgement by the states.) Thus, among its other rulings, the Warren Court struck down state laws supporting segregation in the public schools,[15], required the states to furnish an attorney for any defendant who could not afford one,[16] and prohibited state prosecution of criminal suspects not notified of their rights or provided with counsel during interrogations.[17] These and other rulings won favorable notice from many Americans who felt the justices had performed a valuable service for individual rights too long ignored or resisted by other governmental agencies. But they also won a surprising amount of criticism from those who thought the justices' decisions had gone too far in the direction of social reform.

1969–Present

Many observers expected that Richard Nixon's appointments of four so-called judicial conservatives, beginning in 1969, would initiate a new period for the Supreme Court. Under Chief Justice Warren Burger, the Court appeared to retreat somewhat from the strong activist philosophy touted by its immediate predecessor. Burger frequently asserted, for instance, that Americans had come to rely too heavily on the Court to solve pressing social problems. Instead of seeking the Court's intervention, he declared, they should lobby Congress and state legislatures to enact laws requiring policy changes. And in keeping with this view, the Burger Court began imposing added procedural roadblocks (such as restrictions on the use of class action suits) limiting access to the Court by civil rights and other plaintiffs.[18]

In stating this position, Burger echoed the views of those who had criticized the Warren Court for making policy decisions they felt belonged to the elected branches of government. They had argued that Supreme Court justices should keep their hands off social problems and not substitute their own social values for statutes passed by elected officials. Taking a similar view, President Nixon had promised to appoint only *strict constructionists* who would interpret the Constitution according to the precise meaning of its words. "It is my belief," he

Chief Justice Warren E. Burger

declared, "that it is the duty of a judge to interpret the Constitution and not to place himself above the Constitution or outside the Constitution. He should not twist or bend the Constitution in order to perpetuate his personal political and social values."[19] Thus, he expected his appointments of Burger, Harry A. Blackmun, Lewis F. Powell, Jr., and William H. Rehnquist would force the Court to conform with his standards of judicial conservatism and not make sweeping changes in existing law.

Of course, as many scholars have pointed out, such labels as "strict constructionist" and "judicial conservative" are oversimplifications. Certainly many of the Burger Court's decisions—notably its 1973 rulings striking down state laws against abortions[20]—reflect as broad an interpretation of the Constitution as any decision handed down by the Warren Court. Few justices are likely to pass up the chance to apply their own values to legal interpretations or to ignore completely their unique opportunity to influence American life. In fact, the vagueness of key phrases in the Constitution—such as "due process of law" and "probable cause" for arrest, search, or seizure—compels the justices to apply their own criteria, to choose among alternative and competing values.

Table 11-1. The Supreme Court 1980

	Age	Appointed by	Date
Chief Justice			
Warren E. Burger	70	Nixon	1969
Associate Justices			
William J. Brennan, Jr.	73	Eisenhower	1956
Potter Stewart	64	Eisenhower	1958
Byron R. White	62	Kennedy	1962
Thurgood Marshall	71	Johnson	1967
Harry A. Blackmun	71	Nixon	1970
Lewis F. Powell, Jr.	72	Nixon	1971
William H. Rehnquist	55	Nixon	1971
John Paul Stevens	59	Ford	1975

In several respects, the Burger Court's patchwork of rulings since 1969 has defied most efforts to determine its judicial character and direction. While it has upheld many previous rulings of the Warren Court, it has also weakened others. It has been especially unpredictable in the area of individual rights. While it has continued to rule against sex and race discrimination, has extended the rights of prisoners, and refused to stop publication of the *Pentagon Papers*, it has also weakened the rights of criminal suspects,[21] sustained the death penalty,[22] made it easier for local officials to define and crack down on "obscenity,"[23] and upheld the Bank Secrecy Act allowing governmental officials broad access to citizens' banking records.[24] It has also been criticized for being inconsistent in its judgments. For example, the Court's 1973 rulings upholding the right of women to have abortions were partly undermined four years later by rulings upholding the denial of public funds for abortions by women who could not afford them.[25]

The interesting thing about both the Warren and Burger Courts, however, has been their enormous impact on governmental policy. Despite the avowed intentions of Burger and Nixon to restrain the Court's activist role, the Burger Court has followed in the Warren Court's footsteps in telling elected officials what they must do. As one scholar has noted, the tendency of courts in the past was "to *restrict* the executive and legislature in what they could do. The distinctive characteristic of more recent activist courts has been to *extend* the role of what the government could do, even when the government did not want to do it. The *Swann* and *Keyes* decisions[26] meant that government *must* move children around to distant schools against the will of their parents. The *Griggs* decision[27] meant that government *must* monitor the race and ethnicity of job applicants and test-takers."[28] In these and other decisions, the Burger Court continued rather than discarded the activist policy-making role exemplified by the Warren Court.

A point to remember is that the Court's policy-making role has been criticized by different sides at different times in history. While many self-proclaimed conservatives, for example, lambasted the frequent use of judicial review by the Warren Court in the 1950s and 1960s, they applauded its use in the 1930s when an earlier Court overturned many of Franklin Roosevelt's New Deal policies. Similarly, while many self-professed liberals were gratified to see the Warren Court flex its judicial review muscles, they were strongly critical of such displays by more conservative, probusiness Courts in the past. In view of such changes of opinion, it is apparent that the major issue has not been the Supreme Court's activism or restraint, but rather the substantive nature of its decisions. To put it more bluntly, support or rejection of the Court's activist role has often depended merely on whose ox is being gored by its rulings.

Constraints on Judicial Action

Although ruling-elite theorists and others may consider the Supreme Court one of the nation's most elitist institutions, the justices remain under considerable constraint. The president, Congress, even ordinary citizens can employ weapons against the justices to circumvent their rulings. Let us first consider Congress.

Congress

If members of Congress become sufficiently upset over the decisions of the justices, they have several alternative weapons to employ. For one, they may impeach a justice in an attempt to intimidate or remove him for actions they consider offensive. When Gerald Ford was House minority leader in 1970, he introduced a resolution to impeach Justice William O. Douglas. Ford apparently disliked the "radical" political views expressed in Douglas's book *Points of Rebellion*, excerpts of which surfaced in an issue of *Evergreen* magazine featuring photographs of nudes. Ford's threat to impeach the reputable justice was based on the elusive constitutional provision that judges "shall hold their offices during good behavior," as well as Ford's own remarkable view that "an impeachable offense is whatever a majority of the House of Representatives considers it to be at a given moment in history" (see Chapter 3). However, Ford's efforts to impeach Douglas fizzled when the House Judiciary committee concluded that sufficient grounds for impeachment did not exist.

Actually, impeachment has not been a potent weapon against Supreme Court justices. Although four lower federal court judges have been removed by Congress, not a single member of the Supreme Court has been deposed. The only Supreme Court justice who has been impeached—that is, formally accused of an offense by the House—was Samuel Chase, who was accused in 1805 of making seditious public statements against the Jefferson administration; but the Senate did not find Chase guilty.

Members of Congress also have the constitutional power to take away the justices' appellate jurisdiction in certain kinds of cases. Article III states that, except for original jurisdiction in a few areas, the Court's right to hear appeals on federal questions is subject to "such exceptions, and under such regulations as the Congress shall make." Although Congress has not exercised it in more than one hundred years, this power remains a potentially significant threat to the Court's independence.

If members of Congress are reluctant to impeach Court justices or strip them of their appellate jurisdiction, they can always try to pass constitutional amendments reversing their decisions. As we saw in Chapter 3, the Constitution empowers Congress to amend the Constitution if it can muster the support of three-fourths of the state legislatures. In 1909, for example, Congress proposed the Sixteenth Amendment (ratified by the states in 1913) establishing the federal income tax. This amendment overturned an earlier Court ruling that such a tax would be unconstitutional.[29] Although this and other procedures have not been resorted to often, the possibility of congressional retaliation always exists.

The President

Supreme Court Justices must be concerned about the challenges of the president, as well as of Congress. While the president's weapons may not be as dramatic as those of Congress, his influence tends to be more immediate and direct. For one thing, he can alter the philosophy of the Court by appointing new justices. Although some presidents have had little opportunity to place new justices on the bench (Calvin Coolidge, for example, appointed only one), others have appointed sufficient numbers to affect the Court's judicial orientation. Richard Nixon, for example, by filling four vacancies on the Court, considerably altered the

Court's philosophical character during his five and one-half years in office.

Equally significant is the president's command of the federal bureaucracy that enforces the law. Because Supreme Court justices can boast no police or army of their own—that is, no independent enforcement machinery—they must rely on the president and Justice Department to carry out their decisions. If they were to make a decision offensive to the president (as well as to Congress and most other Americans), they might find themselves in a helpless position. When President Lincoln suspended the *writ of habeas corpus* during the Civil War, the Court could not even muster the courage to scold him for his actions until after Lincoln had died. And, when the Court ruled in 1954 that segregation in the public schools was unconstitutional, many schools throughout the country remained—and still remain—segregated. Little or no effort was made by President Eisenhower or by state officials to enforce the Court's ruling. As the governor of Texas stated flatly in 1956, "The Supreme Court passed the law, so let the Supreme Court enforce it."

The Lower Courts

The Supreme Court also must depend on lower courts to carry out its rulings. Although we may believe that lower courts jump to attention whenever the Supreme Court sneezes, the fact is that they sometimes delay or alter the Court's broad interpretations of federal law to fit local and specific situations. The lower courts often have a great deal of discretion in interpreting the Court's rulings, especially when the Court provides less than a clear mandate in its opinions. They may even openly defy its rulings in response to local pressures or out of a basic difference in philosophy. Efforts to undermine the Court by distorting the meaning of its interpretations have been seen in such highly emotional and controversial areas as school integration, school prayers, and reapportionment of legislative districts.[30]

The People

Indeed, the justices' reliance on public support can significantly constrain their power. In the opinion of many scholars, Supreme Court justices must remain sensitive to the changing climates of opinion or run the risk of sacrificing the Court's legitimacy. Because the justices ultimately depend on the president and the cooperation of the public to enforce their rulings, they cannot afford to make too many decisions running counter to the political temper of the times. In the words of the late Justice Felix Frankfurter, "The Court's authority—possessed neither of the purse nor the sword—ultimately rests on sustained public confidence in its moral sanction." This means that even the justices' support of individual rights can never extend too far beyond the tolerance of majority opinion. If it did, the public could ignore their decisions or encourage Congress to supersede the justices' authority through a constitutional amendment.

In recent years attempts have been made to measure the impact of Supreme Court decisions and to determine the extent of public compliance with its rulings.[31] One conclusion is that although most Court decisions are obeyed—especially those requiring the compliance of only a few officials, such as a ruling on the death penalty—other decisions directed toward major social reform have been more difficult to enforce. On matters of racial discrimination, for example, justices have found their decisions on desegregating public schools, busing school children, and open housing ignored for long periods of time by large segments of the population. These decisions have aggravated deeply ingrained prejudices and depend for their effectiveness on the cooperation of millions of people.

The Justices Themselves

Finally, Supreme Court justices observe their own restrictions on judicial review. Because their jurisdiction is primarily appellate, they cannot take the initiative. They must wait for a case to be appealed to the Court before they can pass judgment. And even when such an appeal surfaces, at least four of the justices must agree on the importance of the case before it can be considered.

Furthermore, justices tend to fashion their own doctrine of "judicial restraint." Although they are not likely to pass up every temptation to exercise the powers of their office, they know such temptations must be restrained by political realities. They must at least retreat from cases that might jeopardize the Court's independence. Most justices have been reluctant, for example, to interfere with presidential decisions in foreign and military affairs, even when those decisions have raised serious constitutional questions. In 1970, the Massachusetts state legislature filed a suit challenging the constitutionality of United States involvement in Vietnam. The suit requested the justices to declare American participation "unconstitutional in that it was not initially authorized or subsequently ratified by Congressional declaration." But a majority of the justices refused to review the suit, just as they refused to entertain suits challenging the legality of the draft in an undeclared war and the right of President Nixon to send troops into Cambodia without formal congressional authorization. Given the long-standing concern about "national security"—as well as the fear that the president would ignore the Court's ruling anyway—little serious thought was given to challenging executive authority in military matters.

One effect of this reluctance has been to frustrate many citizens who have looked to the Court for help in defeating foreign policy and other decisions with which they disagree. Their attempts to gain access to the Court have been shadowed by the political considerations that may influence the justices' decision whether to hear a case, regardless of the case's constitutional implications. Because the justices either may refuse to consider the constitutionality of certain governmental policies or may be unable to enforce their decisions, citizens have faced innumerable obstacles trying to confront existing laws and practices through the Court. (For more on litigation as a political tactic, see Chapter 15.)

Approaching the Bench: Access to the Court

Since judicial review can be exercised only after a case is brought before the Court, we should consider some of the ways a case may reach the Court and be decided. Occasionally we hear people proclaim defiantly that they will fight an issue "all the way to the Supreme Court." What these people may not realize is that, even if they could afford to spend thousands of dollars to appeal a case to the highest court, there is no assurance the case would be heard. Apart from political considerations weighed by the justices, a case will not be heard unless it raises constitutional questions having greater significance than the outcome of a single dispute. The kinds of cases typically reaching the Court involve issues affecting a large segment of society.

In fact, the justices severely limit the number of cases they review each year, despite the enormous quantity of petitions pouring in. Unlike members of Congress, Supreme Court justices have no committee system to divide the workload; they must all help decide each case. In a typical year, they may receive petitions to hear more than 4,500 cases. If they had to rule on all of the petitions they receive, they would have to decide more than 15 cases a day! Instead, they usually rule on only about 200 cases, which means that more than 95 percent of the appeals to the Court are dismissed.

This does not mean that citizens face impossible odds in winning a Supreme Court hearing. In exceptional cases, even individuals with little money and legal support have successfully brought civil rights and criminal justice cases before the Court. In the early 1960s, a prisoner in Florida named Clarence Gideon submitted a handwritten petition asking the Court to review his conviction. According to federal statutes, persons too poor to pay the usual costs of a court appeal may proceed "in forma pauperis" ("in the manner of a pauper"). Thus, although Gideon had little money and had drafted his petition in pencil on lined paper, the justices accepted his case. They eventually ruled in his favor, finding that, because he did not have the benefit of an attorney in his original trial, his conviction was invalid, thus establishing the landmark decision *Gideon* v. *Wainwright* (1963).[32]

Jurisdiction of the Court

Essentially, two principal ways exist to gain access to the Supreme Court. The first is to rely on the Court's *original jurisdiction* which, as described in the Constitution, permits a case to be brought directly before the Court. Because the Supreme Court is the final arbiter or

Clarence Gideon

umpire of the federal system, it has the original jurisdiction to settle major disputes between different levels and branches of government. However, the Court normally will hear such disputes only when they involve "Ambassadors, other public Ministers and Consuls, or those in which a state shall be Party." In fact, such original cases have been quite rare, having been settled by the Court only about 150 times. A frequently cited example is the 1963 dispute between Arizona and California over Colorado River water rights.

A more common path to the Court is through its *appellate jurisdiction* as established by Congress. The Supreme Court will entertain a request for a hearing from any citizen whose case raises a substantial federal question (such as a potential violation of the Bill of Rights). A formal request usually is made by the losing party in a state or lower federal court case who claims the judge wrongly interpreted the Constitution. Although the Supreme Court has a basic obligation to hear certain kinds of cases on *appeal*—for example, when a state court overturns an act of Congress, or when a federal court strikes down a state law—most of the cases reaching the Court do so through a petition for a discretionary *writ of certiorari* (Latin for "to be made more certain"). Essentially, such a petition is a request by the losing party that the Supreme Court order a lower court to send up the records of the case for review. Normally, the justices will agree to issue a writ (to hear the case) only when at least four of them feel the issue at stake involves a serious constitutional question or falls within the Court's jurisdiction. In fact, the decision whether to hear a case may even be based on the unique policy interests of the justices who happen to be sitting on the Court at the time. And as we have seen, those policy interests may differ considerably from one historical period to another.[33] This means that even though the Court may be flooded by thousands of petitions for a writ of certiorari each year, the justices will grant only a few hundred; the decision as to which cases to accept is entirely up to them.

Deciding the Cases

How then do the nine justices process the cases they agree to hear? Usually, they hear cases in open court two weeks each month during the October–June term, scheduling the other two weeks for research and opinion writing. On the Mondays through Thursdays when open court sessions are held, the justices march into the marble-columned courtroom at precisely 10:00 A.M. dressed in flowing black robes. (No wigs are worn, however, since United States justices do not mimic this aspect of the British judicial costume.)

After the justices have read their decisions on previously heard cases, the chief justice calls for the first case of the day, to be presented by opposing attorneys seated at the counsel tables in front of the bench. Although the justices already will have reviewed the written briefs of all sides of the case, they will allow the lawyers to present brief oral arguments. They usually allow only thirty minutes for each side, although in some important cases they will allot more time. To the chagrin of the lawyers, the justices may interrupt their speeches to ask questions or contradict their arguments. At times, the justices may even talk among themselves, scribble notes, or, as in the exceptional case of Oliver Wendell Holmes, who frequently had already made up his mind, take a nap.

But, as imposing as these public sessions may be, the real work of the justices takes place behind the scenes. Each justice spends most of his time researching and studying cases alone or with law clerks. Then, every Friday, the justices assemble in an ornate conference room to decide which new petitions for review to accept and to vote on the cases already presented in chamber. These conferences may last all day and are totally confidential—not even law clerks or secretaries are allowed to attend. The junior justice (the last member appointed to the Court) usually acts as the "guardian of the door," dashing from the conference table to accept or deliver messages.

Although it is difficult to learn what goes on in these meetings, we do know that the chief justice presides and usually begins by summarizing the cases and how he feels they should be decided. He then yields to the other justices, who take turns voicing their opinions. When they are ready to vote—sometimes after heated debate—the junior justice votes first and the chief justice, last. After a case has been decided, a majority opinion must be drafted explaining the Court's decision. If the chief justice sides with the majority, he will assign the job either to himself or to another justice who supported the same view; otherwise, the senior associate justice in the majority will make the assignment.

Usually, the drafting of an opinion is an intricate process taking weeks or even months to complete. An initial draft will likely circulate among the justices for many rewritings until it is approved by everyone in the majority. Those justices who disagree with the majority may, of course, write a dissenting opinion. Sometimes, justices writing a dissenting opinion can persuade their colleagues to change their minds before the final decision is read in open court.

Ironically, some observers see this practice of dissenting as weakening the Court's prestige by revealing its internal divisions. The fact that many important Court decisions have been split five to four or six to three convinces some critics that the Court often cannot provide a definitive solution to a legal controversy. Yet, many powerful legal ex-

"My dissenting opinion will be brief: You're all full of crap!"

pressions have been voiced in dissenting opinions, such as in those by Oliver Wendell Holmes, Louis Brandeis, and Hugo Black. In fact, many dissenting opinions eventually become the Court's majority opinion, reflecting changes in the times and new perspectives on legal issues. (Indeed, since 1789, the Supreme Court has reversed itself at least 140 times!)

The Chief Justice

It should be understood that judicial influence is not shared equally by all nine justices. Just as some members of Congress exert a disproportionate influence on policy making, some justices, by virtue of their superior legal skills, exert considerably greater influence on judicial decisions.

The role of the chief justice is important in this regard, for if he is an especially forceful individual, he can stamp his own character on the

Court. The chief justice gains special authority by presiding over open court sessions and by directing the secret Friday conferences. Although, like other justices, he has but one vote, he sets the time limits on debate, establishes the ground rules for discussion, and assigns the writing of Court opinions. In addition, he is the Court's symbolic head and holds in some respects the highest governmental office next to that of the president. By virtue of his position, he may guide the Court toward making a profound and lasting imprint on national policy.

Recruitment to the High Court

As we would expect, a major influence on judicial decision making is the background of each person appointed to the Court. Yet, while the Constitution outlines legal requirements for other political offices, like the presidency and Congress, it is silent about the qualifications of a Supreme Court justice. As far as the Constitution is concerned, a justice could be foreign born (and not even a United States citizen), too young to vote, and totally without legal training.

In fact, the Constitution does not even specify how many justices there should be. This responsibility was handed to Congress. In the beginning, the Court was composed of only six members; but this number was changed half a dozen times until Congress finally settled on nine justices in 1869.

Although the Constitution does not specify any formal legal qualifications to be a Supreme Court justice, other, informal qualifications have tended to prevail. The backgrounds of justices have been similar to those of presidents and members of Congress in that they have not been representative of the general population. Most have been Protestant, financially independent, and about fifty-five years of age at the time of their appointment. Only about 10 percent have been Catholic or Jewish; only one has been black; and so far, none has been a woman.

Interestingly enough, although every Supreme Court justice has been a lawyer, few have had much prior experience as a judge. Almost half of the 105 justices in the Court's history have had no prior judicial training at all. This includes some of the Court's most eminent members, such as John Marshall, Louis Brandeis, Felix Frankfurter, and Earl Warren. Generally speaking, justices do not reach the Supreme Court by advancing up through the lower federal or state courts. Instead, they are more likely to come from positions in government, as former members of Congress, cabinet officials, governors, or even (as was true of William Howard Taft) president of the United States.

The Role of the President

Although a seat on the high bench is a top prize for those seeking political influence, it cannot be campaigned for like a seat in Congress or won through a public popularity contest. Like other federal judgeships, a Supreme Court seat must be filled by presidential appointment, subject to Senate approval.

Historically, presidents have tended to select justices who reflect their own political and judicial philosophies, using the appointive process to augment their political influence. Because Supreme Court rulings can greatly affect national policy, the appointment of justices has been a prime way for presidents to implant their own ideas on American law. As Richard Nixon once stated, "There is probably no more important legacy that a President of the United States can leave in these times than his appointments to the Supreme Court. . . . You will recall, I am sure, that during my campaign for the Presidency I pledged to nominate to the Supreme Court individuals who shared my judicial philosophy."[34] Given this perspective, it should not be surprising that about 90 percent of all Supreme Court justices appointed since 1789 have belonged to the same party as the appointing president.

Although President Carter pledged to appoint federal judges strictly on the basis of merit, the selective process has tended to be a political one. Federal district judgeships have tended to be filled on the recommendations of state party officials or senators from each state, while vacancies on the Supreme Court have been filled after the president has received recommendations from a variety of sources, including members of Congress, judges, interest groups, and bar associations. There has usually been an effort to maintain some religious, ethnic, and geographic balance on the Court to help legitimize its decisions and gain political support from influential groups; however, as we have seen, such considerations have not applied to most minority groups or to women, who generally have been excluded from the appointive process.

Naturally, the ability of presidents to shape the Court to their own philosophies has been limited by the necessity of winning Senate approval. For example, Richard Nixon saw both of his southern nominees, Clement Haynesworth and G. Harold Carswell, rejected by the Senate in 1969 and 1970. The record for rejections, however, is held by John Tyler (1841–1844), who saw four of his nominees turned down. Although the Senate does not customarily resist presidential nominations in such fashion, at least one of every five has been either withdrawn, rejected, or not acted on at all.[35]

Presidents sometimes also make mistakes and discover that their appointees take positions contrary to what they expected. Supreme Court

Justices tend to become quite independent once they reach the bench, especially since they are appointed for life. President Eisenhower, for example, was less than happy to find Earl Warren—a California Republican governor whom he appointed chief justice in 1953—leading one of the most activist Courts in American history. The appointment of Warren, Eisenhower reportedly lamented, was "the biggest damnfool mistake I ever made." As we will see, some critics suggest that Supreme Court justices, rather than being appointed by the president, should be elected by the voters.

Other Courts, Other Judges

Although Supreme Court justices stand at the pinnacle of the federal judicial system, the rulings of lower federal and state court judges also can have tremendous political and legal significance. Without the diligence of District Court Judge John Sirica (*Time* magazine's "Man of the Year" for 1973), the Watergate scandal might have attracted consid-

Judge John Sirica

erably less attention. It was Judge Sirica, a Republican who headed the federal district court in the nation's capital, who presided at the trial of the seven Watergate burglars and who broke open the case by agreeing to review their penalties if they talked—as James McCord eventually did. Not only did the disclosures in Judge Sirica's courtroom help elevate the original burglary into a national scandal, but it was there that the White House, the Senate Watergate Committee, and the special prosecutor battled over possession of the elusive White House tapes. It was Judge Sirica, not the justices of the Supreme Court, who first pitted the judicial branch against the president of the United States by ordering Richard Nixon to turn over the tapes for court inspection.

Given the latent political importance and legal power of judges like Sirica in the American judicial system, we should consider the structures and duties of their courts. Article III of the Constitution specifies that "the judicial power of the United States shall be vested in one supreme Court, and in such inferior Courts as the Congress may from time to time ordain and establish." This means that although the Constitution specifically provides for the Supreme Court, it gives Congress the sole authority to determine the number and jurisdiction of other federal courts. Beginning with the Judiciary Act of 1789, which established the first federal district and circuit courts, Congress has been creating an increasing number of federal courts to meet the country's growing size and judicial workload.

Federal District Courts

The largest number of federal courts are those at the base of the federal judicial system, the district courts. At present, there are ninety-four federal district courts in the United States, with at least one in each state and territory. Containing anywhere from one to twenty-seven judges each, these district trial courts settle civil disputes between citizens of different states, resolve federal questions arising under the Constitution (such as the constitutional controversy surrounding the White House tapes), and conduct trials for violations of federal law (such as counterfeiting, illegal immigration, and mail fraud). These district courts have original jurisdiction only, and do not hear cases on appeal.

The work of these district courts has received a great deal of attention in recent years, not only as a result of the original Watergate revelations in Judge Sirica's courtroom but also as a result of the trials of several former Nixon associates, including Attorney General John Mitchell, White House chief of staff H. R. Haldeman, and presidential assistant John Ehrlichman. These trials, as much as anything, underscored the Watergate issues and helped bring down the Nixon administration.

Courts of Appeals

Because the rulings of district court judges are occasionally controversial or imprecise, the federal judicial system also provides eleven courts of appeals to review their decisions. Each of these courts of appeals serves one of the eleven judicial circuits into which the country has been divided and contains anywhere from three to fifteen judgeships. They have the responsibility not only to hear appeals from the lower district courts but occasionally to review decisions of the federal regulatory agencies. Because these courts hear cases only on appeal, they do not use juries; instead, three judges normally sit as a panel to hear each case.

It may be recalled that the federal courts of appeals also received publicity from the Watergate scandal, especially in 1973 when the court of appeals in Washington, D.C., upheld Judge Sirica's order directing President Nixon to hand over the White House tapes. Although Nixon later appealed a similar case to the Supreme Court, he obeyed the court of appeals' rulings in the first confrontation, setting a precedent future presidents may find difficult to ignore. This same court of appeals also attracted national publicity by overturning the government's prosecutions of 12,000 demonstrators arrested during the Washington, D.C., May Day protests in 1971.

Special Federal Courts

In addition to the district and appeals courts, a number of other federal courts have been created by Congress to deal with special kinds of cases. Briefly stated, these courts include the United States Court of Claims, Customs Court, Court of Customs and Patent Appeals, Tax Court, Court of Military Appeals, and the Territorial Courts. The judges of these courts, like the judges of the district and appeals courts, are appointed by the president with the consent of the Senate. And the decisions of these courts also may be appealed to the Supreme Court.

State Courts

Finally, we should remember that there are two different sets of courts in this United States: federal and state. Each of the fifty states has its own court system to handle cases not within the judicial power granted to the federal courts by the Constitution and Congress. Theoretically, neither set of courts is inferior to the other, but the state courts must obey the rulings of the United States Supreme Court in cases involving national constitutional issues.

State courts not only possess the judicial review power to interpret acts of state legislatures and other state officials, but they, not federal court judges, try most of the nation's civil and criminal cases. This is because the bulk of criminal and civil laws—such as those covering divorce, burglary, and homicide—are enacted by the states and not by the federal government. Thus, although most Americans probably will never be a party in a federal court case, there are few who have not at least paid for a traffic ticket in a state municipal court.

It might be added that, even though the nature of state courts varies throughout the country, most state courts are organized along a similar hierarchy: municipal and justice courts; superior (or county) courts; district courts of appeals; and a state supreme court. And, in contrast to all federal judges, who are appointed by the president with the approval of the Senate, in most states the judges are elected at the polls.[36]

The Court and Its Critics

In its long history, the Supreme Court has faced a large number of reform proposals. Some of these proposals have been made by those who strongly support an activist role for the Court but who feel it urgently needs reorganizing and streamlining. Still other proposals have been made by those who are critical of the justices' exercise of power and who wish to see such power curtailed. Although the two types of reform proposals overlap in some ways, let us consider an example of each.

Reducing the Workload

The practice of hearing cases for only two weeks each month might seem to give Supreme Court justices a great deal of time to research and study cases. Yet there have been complaints that their workload has become increasingly hard to bear. As the Court's annual number of appeals and petitions for certiorari has climbed from about 1,000 cases in the early 1950s to more than 4,500 cases today, concern has been expressed that the justices have become entangled in too much legal paperwork. With so many cases to consider each year, the justices have not had enough time properly to oversee the judicial process. And with so many cases competing for the justices' attention, citizens with legitimate grievances find the opportunities for judicial redress restricted.

One proposal to meet this problem was made in 1972 by a study group headed by Harvard Law Professor Paul Freund. This study group, appointed by Chief Justice Burger, recommended the creation of a national court of appeals composed of judges chosen on a rotating basis from the federal courts of appeals. This new court would screen all cases now referred to the Supreme Court and would decide which cases were important enough for the highest court to see. Supreme Court justices would retain the right to hear any case they wanted, but would be relieved of handling the large volume of mostly trivial and insubstantial petitions.

However, a number of people denounced the study group's proposal on the grounds that Supreme Court justices would only lose much of their independent authority to decide which new petitions to consider. Former Chief Justice Earl Warren, for instance, felt the creation of a new national court of appeals would do "irreparable harm to the prestige, the power and the function of the Supreme Court." It would simply add to the bureaucracy of justice and impose goals and values conflicting with those expressed by the high Court. Moreover, it would serve as another means of restricting access to the Supreme Court by ordinary citizens, adding another procedural roadblock to those already imposed by the Burger Court. Thus, in view of these objections, the proposal to establish an intermediary court of appeals was not put into effect.

Curbing the Court's Powers

Far more dramatic suggestions for reforming the Court have been offered as a result of repeated criticisms of its decisions. As we have seen, Supreme Court justices have had their share of critics who accuse them of wielding too much power. While some attacked the justices in the 1930s for obstructing the policies of the New Deal, others criticized the justices in the 1950s and 1960s for their rulings on school desegregation, police procedures, and prayers in public schools. Such criticisms have given rise to a number of proposals to curb the justices' powers, such as requiring more than a simple five-to-four majority to render any law or action unconstitutional and narrowing the justices' appellate jurisdiction.

Perhaps the most dramatic suggestion has been to elect justices for limited and fixed terms. Critics argue that because the Court plays a major role in policy making, justices should be elected at the polls instead of appointed by the president for life terms. They contend there is adequate precedent for such a change, since most states currently elect their highest court judges for terms ranging anywhere from six to twelve years. Even though these state court judges also exercise judicial review, the voters still have an opportunity to express their disapproval without having to resort to impeachment.

Such a proposal has not been vigorously championed, however, partly because the constraints on the justices already mentioned have been considered adequate. The public, through the president and Congress as well as through their own actions, ultimately can circumvent unpopular Court decisions. In addition, there has been a reluctance to extend majority control over the Court for reasons discussed earlier. If the justices of the nation's highest court were required to run periodically for reelection, they might be subject to greater pressures from special interests and would lose much of their independent authority to protect individual and minority rights from majority prejudices. "The very purpose of having a written Constitution," Chief Justice Burger has stated, "is to provide safeguards for certain rights that cannot yield to public opinion. . . . The Justices' duty is to stand firm in defense of basic constitutional values, as they see them, even against momentary tides of public opinion."[37] In any event, as two scholars have concluded in their review of California's judicial system, "There are problems with both methods: executive appointment may result in numerous political hacks on the bench, while election assumes that the people are knowledgeable in the area of judicial qualifications and care enough to become informed."[38]

Key Terms

executive privilege

mandamus, writ of

strict construction

appeal

judicial review

original jurisdiction

appelate jurisdiction

certiorari, writ of

Notes

1. See, for example, Rober Hodge, Paul Siegel, and Peter Rossi, "Occupational Prestige in the United States, 1925–1963," *American Journal of Sociology*, November 1964, pp. 286–302.

2. Walter F. Murphy and Joseph Tanenhaus, "Public Opinion and the United States Supreme Court," in Joel B. Grossman and Joseph Tanenhaus, eds., *Frontiers of Judicial Research* (New York: Wiley, 1969).

3. *Edwards* v. *South Carolina* (1963).

4. *Brown* v. *Louisiana* (1966).

5. *Adderly* v. *Florida* (1967).

6. *United States* v. *O'Brien* (1968).

7. See Edward S. Corwin, ed., *The Constitution of the United States of America: Analysis and Interpretation* (Washington, D.C.: U.S. Government Printing Office, 1953).

8. Charles Beard, "The Supreme Court—Usurper or Grantee?" *Political Science Quarterly*, March 1912, pp. 1–35.

9. *The Federalist*, No. 78.

10. "Law and the Court," *Speeches* (Boston: Little, Brown, 1934), p. 102.

11. *Marbury* v. *Madison* (1803).

12. *Pollock* v. *Farmer's Loan and Trust Company* (1895).

13. *Hammer* v. *Dagenhart* (1918).

14. *Adkins* v. *Children's Hospital* (1923).

15. *Brown* v. *Board of Education* (1954).

16. *Gideon* v. *Wainwright* (1963).

17. *Miranda* v. *Arizona* (1966).

18. See Stephen L. Wasby, *Continuity and Change: From the Warren Court to the Burger Court* (Pacific Palisades, Calif.: Goodyear, 1976), Chap. 2.

19. Richard M. Nixon, speech of 21 October 1971.

20. *Roe* v. *Wade* (1973); *Doe* v. *Bolton* (1973).

21. *Harris* v. *New York* (1971).

22. *Gregg* v. *Georgia* (1976).

23. *Miller* v. *California* (1973).

24. *California Bankers Association* v. *Schultz* (1974).

25. *Beal* v. *Doe* (1977); *Maher* v. *Roe* (1977).

26. *Swann* v. *Charlotte-Mecklenburg Board of Education* (1971); *Keyes* v. *School District #1*, Denver, Colorado (1973).

27. *Griggs* v. *Duke Power Co.* (1971).

28. Nathan Glazer, "Towards an Imperial Judiciary?" *The Public Interest*, Fall 1975, p. 109.

29. *Pollock* v. *Farmer's Loan and Trust Company* (1895).

30. See, for example, Theodore L. Becker and Malcolm M. Feeley, eds., *The Impact of Supreme Court Decisions*, 2nd ed. (New York: Oxford University Press, 1973); Neil Romans, "The Role of State Supreme Courts in Judicial Policy Making," *Western Political Quarterly*, March 1974, pp. 38–59.

31. Becker and Feely, *The Impact of Supreme Court Decisions*.

32. For more on the case, see Anthony Lewis, *Gideon's Trumpet* (New York: Random House, 1964).

33. See Lawrence Baum, "Policy Goals in Judicial Gatekeeping: A Proximity Model of Discretionary Jurisdiction," *American Journal of Political Science*, February 1977, pp. 13–36.

34. Richard M. Nixon, speech of 21 October 1971.

35. Congressional Quarterly's *Guide to Congress*, 2nd ed., 1976, p. 647.

36. For more information, see Henry J. Abraham, *The Judicial Process*, 3rd ed. (New York: Oxford University Press, 1975).

37. "Thie Chief Justice Talks About the Court," *Reader's Digest*, February 1973.
38. Ruth A. Ross and Barbara S. Stone, *California's Political Process* (New York: Random House, 1973), p. 140.

Recommended Reading

ABRAHAM, HENRY J. *The Judiciary: The Supreme Court in the Governmental Process.* 4th ed. Boston: Allyn and Bacon, 1977.

BECKER, THEODORE L., and MALCOLM M. FEELEY, eds. *The Impact of Supreme Court Decisions.* 2nd ed. New York: Oxford University Press, 1973.

COX, ARCHIBALD. *The Role of the Supreme Court in American Government.* New York: Oxford University Press, 1976.

McCLOSKEY, ROBERT G. *The American Supreme Court.* Chicago: University of Chicago Press, 1960.

DEAN, HOWARD E. *Judicial Review and Democracy.* New York: Random House, 1966.

FORTE, DAVID F., ed. *The Supreme Court in American Politics: Judicial Activism vs. Judicial Restraint.* Lexington, Mass: D. C. Heath, 1972.

LEWIS, ANTHONY. *Gideon's Trumpet.* New York: Random House, 1964.

MITAU, G. THEODORE. *Decade of Decision: The Supreme Court and the Constitutional Revolution 1954–1964.* New York: Charles Scribner's Sons, 1967.

ROHDE, DAVID, and HAROLD SPAETH. *Supreme Court Decision Making.* San Francisco: W. H. Freeman and Co., 1976.

WASBY, STEPHEN L. *Continuity and Change: From the Warren Court to the Burger Court.* Pacific Palisades, Calif.: Goodyear, 1976.

12

The Bureaucracy: "Alphabet Agencies Spell Power"

As we saw in Chapter 2, the debate between the ruling-elite theorists and the pluralists over who governs in America has been joined by a third group of theorists who contend that ultimately *no one* is in charge. They argue that our political system has become so enveloped in the tentacles of bureaucracy, so beset by a growing complexity of problems and solutions, that control over policy making by any group has become virtually impossible.

Although this theory embraces a variety of concepts and concerns, it is ultimately a response to the seemingly pervasive "bureaucratization" of American society. In the federal government, especially, the bureaucracy seems to be everywhere, comprising a potent and independent "fourth branch" elected by, and seemingly accountable to, no one. With its labyrinth of departments, agencies, and bureaus, the federal bureaucracy has become so vast that neither the president nor Congress nor even those working within it can fully comprehend its scope. According to a report issued by the Library of Congress, for example, "The Federal Government now spends nearly four billion dollars annually on research and development in its laboratories, but it does not know exactly how many laboratories it now has, where they are, what kind of people work in them, or what they are doing." Some critics suggest that the bureaucracy merely feeds upon itself, swelling under its own internal pressure, as a perfect illustration of Parkinson's Law: "Work expands so as to fill the time available for its completion."[1]

In this chapter, we will examine some of the features of the federal bureaucracy and the impact it has on our lives. We will address a number of questions, including: What exactly is this bureaucracy we hear so much about? How did we end up with it? And what opportunities (if any) exist for citizens to make the bureaucracy work for them?

The Nature and Growth of Bureaucracy

The word *bureaucracy*, according to one scholar, was first coined in eighteenth-century France.[2] It was formed from a combination of the term *bureau* (which originally referred to a cloth covering the desks of government officials) and the term *cracy* (signifying rule of government). As used today, the word bureaucracy signifies certain arrangements and conditions. In the broadest sense, it implies an organization having a hierarchy of command, with a specialization of roles and a division of labor, and governed by formal rules and regulations. To some observers, it also signifies certain ideals: an emphasis on rationality and expertise, and a political neutrality. If a group of people suddenly found themselves stranded on a deserted island (pardon the familiar analogy), they would not constitute a bureaucracy—that is, not unless they formed a pyramidal chain of command, with each person assigned responsibilities based on his or her expertise. (If they began to sit behind desks piled with paper, gave themselves pompous titles, and erected massive wooden huts to house alphabet-soup agencies, they would certainly be on the bureaucratic track.)

Bureaucracies can be found almost everywhere, from large corporations and universities to church organizations and hospitals. In the federal government, the bureaucracy refers principally to the executive agencies and departments under the president's command which carry out the laws passed by Congress.

During the early part of American history, few people thought much about the bureaucracy. As late as the 1880s, fewer than 150,000 people were employed by the federal government. Only a handful of executive departments and agencies existed, performing such tasks as collecting taxes, printing money, and delivering the mail.

Today, close to three million people work for Uncle Sam, with another two million employed in the armed forces (see Table 12-1). The Veterans Administration alone has more employees than the total number of federal bureaucrats on hand at the turn of the century. Only during the past few decades, in fact, has the number of federal employees leveled off. Since the 1950s, the size of the bureaucracy has remained generally below three million people. (Of course, federal agencies now "contract out" many of their activities to private firms, thus indirectly employing many additional people. And where the federal bureaucracy has remained constant, state and local bureaucracies have been taking up the slack. About four times as many people today are employed by state and local governments as by the federal government.) In terms of money spent, the federal budget in 1980 exceeded $540 billion a year, up more than 300 percent since 1960. And during the past twenty years, close to 250 new agencies and bureaus have been added, while only a few dozen have been scrapped.

It seems likely that the Founding Fathers did not anticipate the enormous growth of the federal bureaucracy. As noted in Chapter 3, the Constitution is silent about how the bureaucracy should be structured and what duties it should perform. The document makes only a few casual references to the bureaucracy, such as that the president "may

Table 12-1. Federal Civilian Bureaucracy

Department or Agency	Employees
Defense	982,198
U.S. Postal Service	648-419
Veterans Administration	227,903
Health and Human Services	140,000*
Treasury	132,393
Agriculture	114,099
Interior	75,937
Transportation	74,445
Justice	52,962
Tennessee Valley Authority	40,121
Commerce	38,645
General Services Administration	37,624
State	30,092
National Aeronautics and Space Administration	24,191
Energy	19,743
Education	18,000*
Housing and Urban Development	17,575
Labor	17,271

Source: U.S. Bureau of the Census, *Statistical Abstract of the United States*, 1978, pp. 280–281.
* 1979 estimates

require the Opinion, in writing, of the principal Officer in each of the executive Departments." Although the Founding Fathers realized that some apparatus would be needed to carry out the laws passed by Congress, they did not foresee how the government would expand. They did not foresee that as Congress faced growing demands for legislation to cure society's ills, there would also be a need for more agencies and administrators to carry out that legislation.

Indeed, the federal bureaucracy did not spring into being overnight. It evolved gradually in response to new economic forces, technological developments, and a changing population. It grew in response to demands for government to solve such problems as unemployment, housing, education, and transportation. The emergence of giant industrial corporations in the late 1880s, for example, spurred demands for regulatory legislation to protect workers and to preserve a competitive market system. Similarly, the Great Depression of the 1930s stimulated the need for new federal programs and agencies (such as the Social Security Administration) to provide greater financial security for citizens and to help maintain the economic order. These pressures continued to mount over the years, reaching a peak in the 1960s during the Johnson administration when massive new programs in the name of the "Great Society" were offered as solutions to virtually every major social problem.

The growth of the bureaucracy, of course, has also stimulated considerable apprehension and criticism. Few issues in American politics have been as hotly debated in recent years as how to put a brake on its expansion. The growing "taxpayers' revolt," for example, is only one expression of a general public reaction against the broadening reach and soaring costs of government. To many Americans, the bureaucracy has become the major symbol of governmental waste and inefficiency, a symbol perhaps few of the Founding Fathers could have fully imagined.

Staffing the Bureaucracy

As the bureaucracy has grown, so has the concern over how it should be staffed. Where should all of the bureaucrats come from, and how should they be selected and governed?

Prior to the Civil War, presidents commonly appointed to the bureaucracy people who had demonstrated their partisan loyalties. Providing a job on the federal payroll was a handy way for a newly elected chief executive to reward someone for his support during the campaign. This practice, known widely as the *spoils system* (from the expression, "To the victor go the spoils"), was used not only to fill cabinet and other high governmental posts, but also such lesser positions as postal clerk and justice of the peace. And with each turnover in administrations, a large number of civil servants would be sacked and replaced by opposition-party supporters. To put it mildly, job security was hardly a major feature of a federal appointment, especially around election time.

Following the Civil War, this patronage system came under increased attack. Many saw the bureaucracy riddled by political corruption and staffed with incompetents. Then, in 1881, a Chicago lawyer named Charles Guiteau assassinated President James Garfield. Guiteau was apparently disappointed that he did not get the spoils job he expected, and thus he shot Garfield in the back. (Guiteau was later hanged.) The push for reform soon reached fever pitch and, in 1883, Congress passed the Pendleton Act, setting up a bipartisan Civil Service Commission to recruit and regulate federal employees.

Today, about 90 percent of all federal jobs are filled under the rules and regulations of the *civil service* system. Most federal employees are hired through competitive examinations, are promoted on the basis of evaluations by their superiors, and are largely protected from dismissal for partisan reasons. Only about 6,500 top policy-making positions, such as the heads of the cabinet departments and independent agencies, are still filled directly by the president.

This is not to say that political considerations and personal favoritism have been entirely removed from the civil service system. Despite examinations and other controls, a person with pull can still manage to land a federal job. Many bureaus and agencies occasionally use special referral procedures to bypass normal channels and make room for those with political connections or special skills.

Nor has the present system guaranteed equal opportunities in job advancement. Although minority groups and women are well represented in most agencies, they tend to be concentrated at the lower grades. Women, for example, hold about 35 percent of all white-collar positions in the federal bureaucracy, but only about 9 percent of the high-salaried positions ($21,000+).[3]

In fact, since its creation the civil service system has frequently been rapped by critics who demand changes in its procedures. However, instead of attacking the way federal employees are hired, they have been more critical of the way incompetent and inefficient employees are retained and even promoted. In 1978, President Carter finally persuaded Congress to pass a Civil Service Reform Act. The act provided for the reorganization of the Civil Service Commission by splitting it into two new entities: (1) a Merit System Protection Board to handle employee complaints and protect employee rights, and (2) an Office of Personnel Management to conduct civil service examinations, regulate employee salaries and benefits, and stimulate productivity. The act was designed to eliminate the "schizophrenic" nature of the Civil Service Commission, where responsibilities for overseeing employee rights and encouraging productivity were lodged in the same agency.

Carter agreed with critics who contended that it was easier to promote or transfer an incompetent employee than it was to fire one. He cited the statistic offered by Civil Service Commission Chairman Alan Campbell that only 226 of 2.8 million federal workers were discharged for incompetence in 1977. That was no way, Carter said, to run a farm, a factory, or a government. He also observed that "there is not enough merit in the merit system; there is inadequate motivation because we have too few rewards for excellence and too few penalties for unsatisfactory work." As a result, the Civil Service Reform Act also set up a merit-pay system for middle-level management, modified provisions for firing incompetent workers, and even established a special board to protect "whistle blowers," employees who emerge from the bureaucratic shadows to expose governmental waste or corruption. How well the new act will satisfy critics, however, remains to be seen.

The Bureaucratic Network

Since the Constitution does not spell out how the federal bureaucracy should be organized, it has been left to the president and Congress to decide which bureaucrats will perform which duties and in which building. They determine when new agencies will be established, what their responsibilities will be, and how much officials will be paid. As a result, we have inherited an administrative enterprise formed in sporadic and piecemeal fashion. Like a small village that has taken centuries to grow into a metropolis, with its streets and boulevards laid out in a haphazard pattern formed by years of circumstance and changing needs, the federal bureaucracy has gradually evolved into its present desultory form. For a federal bureaucracy we have inherited not the planned symmetry of a Paris, but the unplanned sprawl of a Los Angeles.

For the sake of description, we can lump most of the agencies of the federal bureaucracy into four basic groups: the cabinet-level departments, the independent agencies, the government corporations, and the regulatory commissions. Let us first look at the cabinet departments.

The Cabinet Departments

The largest and most important agencies of the federal bureaucracy are the thirteen cabinet level *executive departments* (or "line agencies," as

Table 12-2. The Cabinet Departments

Department	Founded	Major Duties
State	1789	Advises president on foreign policy; negotiates treaties; oversees foreign aid programs.
Treasury	1789	Enforces federal revenue laws; coins money; collects taxes.
Interior	1849	Oversees nation's parks, natural resources, and Indian reservations.
Agriculture	1862	Supports farm productivity research; administers crop surplus subsidies.
Justice	1870	Enforces federal laws; represents federal government in legal matters.
Commerce	1903	Promotes U.S. exports; administers Census Bureau and Patent Office.
Labor	1913	Enforces minimum wage laws and labor safety regulations; oversees pension programs services; decides wage disputes.
Defense (replaced the War and Navy Departments)	1947	Maintains and directs U.S. military forces; awards defense contracts.
Health and Human Services (formerly Health, Education, and Welfare)	1953	Administers food and drug laws, public health research, and social security programs.
Housing and Urban Development	1965	Coordinates urban renewal, and public housing assistance
Transportation	1966	Oversees federal highway and mass transit programs; enforces auto and air safety standards.
Energy	1977	Coordinates U.S. energy research and development programs.
Education	1979	Administers federal education programs.

they are sometimes called). They provide most of the social services and carry out most of the laws passed by Congress (see Table 12-2). They vary in size from the specialized Labor Department with roughly 17,000 employees to the mammoth Defense Department with nearly 1 million employees. While some of the departments—such as State and Treasury—have been around since colonial times, others—such as Health and Human Services, and Housing and Urban Development (HUD)—are relative newcomers whose staffs and responsibilities have mushroomed in response to the nation's growth.

Each department is headed by a secretary (an attorney general in the case of the Justice Department) appointed by the president with the consent of the Senate. The secretaries enjoy considerable public prestige as members of the president's cabinet, and are assisted by at least one undersecretary and several assistant secretaries, also appointed by the president. Each department is splintered into many smaller bureaus and divisions that handle special functions or serve particular geographical areas. (Figure 12-1 shows the configuration of one typical department.)

The structures of the departments, however, vary considerably. While some are neatly centralized with authority flowing in clear vertical lines, others are little more than collections of relatively independent bureaus with their own concerns and clientele. The Federal Bureau of Investigation (FBI) in the Justice Department, for example, and the Corps of Engineers in the Defense Department have considerable autonomy in carrying out their functions.

Furthermore, although the official duties of the departments are to provide essential governmental services and apply the laws, some of the departments also have a third mission: to represent the interests of client groups. The Department of Agriculture, for instance, was set up in 1862 primarily to assist and regulate the farming industry. Similarly, the Department of Labor came into being in 1913 largely in response to demands for cabinet representation of labor interests. Presidents usually face considerable political pressure to appoint department secretaries who are sympathetic to their departments' client groups.

The Independent Agencies

In addition to the cabinet departments, there are dozens of *independent agencies* that also answer to the president. They are "independent" only because they exist outside the cabinet departments, not because they are free of presidential oversight. The directors of these agencies are appointed by the president with the consent of the Senate and may be removed from their posts by the president.

These independent agencies vary considerably in size, organization, and power. While some are headed by a single administrator, others are

Figure 12-1. Department of Housing and Urban Development

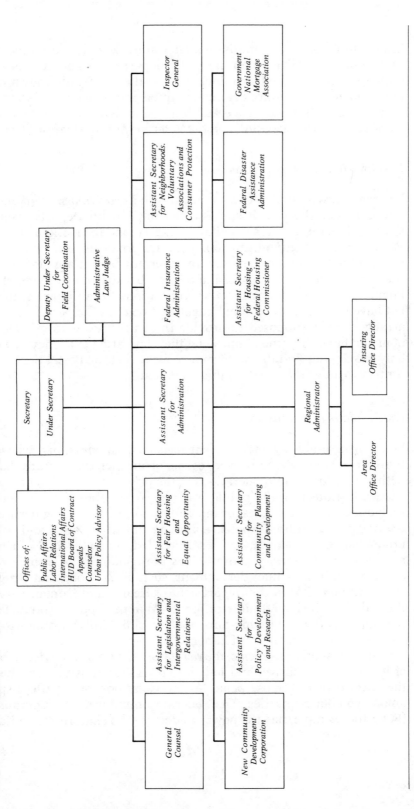

Offices of:

Public Affairs
Labor Relations
International Affairs
HUD Board of Contract
Appeals
Counselor
Urban Policy Advisor

Secretary
Under Secretary

Deputy Under Secretary for Field Coordination

Administrative Law Judge

General Counsel

Assistant Secretary for Legislation and Intergovernmental Relations

Assistant Secretary for Fair Housing and Equal Opportunity

Assistant Secretary for Administration

Federal Insurance Administration

Assistant Secretary for Neighborhoods, Voluntary Associations and Consumer Protection

Inspector General

New Community Development Corporation

Assistant Secretary for Policy Development and Research

Assistant Secretary for Community Planning and Development

Assistant Secretary for Housing– Federal Housing Commissioner

Federal Disaster Assistance Administration

Government National Mortgage Association

Regional Administrator

Area Office Director

Insuring Office Director

Source: U.S. Government Organization Manual, 1978–1979.

headed by a board or commission. They are alike only in that they tend to be more specialized than the major departments and are not represented in the president's cabinet. Among the most well known of the independent agencies are the Central Intelligence Agency (CIA), the National Aeronautics and Space Administration (NASA), the General Services Administration (GSA), and the Veterans Administration (VA).

The Government Corporations

There are also a number of agencies known as *government corporations.* These include the U.S. Postal Service, the Federal Deposit Insurance Corporation, the Tennessee Valley Authority, and the National Railroad Passenger Corporation (Amtrak). They are organized and run like private profit-making companies, with governing boards appointed by the president with the consent of the Senate. Because they are either self-financing or receive long-term appropriations from Congress, they do not have to present operating budgets to Congress each fiscal year. This arrangement is supposed to provide these agencies with greater freedom and flexibility, thus improving their operating efficiency. (One has only to keep in mind the performance records of the Postal Service and Amtrak to judge the merits of this argument.)

The Regulatory Commissions

Finally, there are the independent *regulatory commissions,* whose activities reach into virtually every corner of our society. They are charged with regulating certain operations in the private sector of the economy and with protecting the public from corporate abuses. They perform such duties as setting rates for interstate commerce, issuing licenses for television and radio stations, enforcing antitrust laws, and setting product safety standards. (For a selected list, see Table 12-3.) Included among these regulatory commissions are a number of agencies that operate within a cabinet department, such as the Food and Drug Administration (FDA) in the Department of Health and Human Services, the Federal Aviation Administration (FAA) in the Department of Transportation, and the Occupational Safety and Health Administration (OSHA) in the Department of Labor.

Unlike most other agencies, the regulatory commissions wield a blend of legislative, executive, and judicial powers. They issue rules having the effect of law, impose penalties for violations, and settle disputes among conflicting parties. The Federal Communications Commission (FCC), for example, has the power to decide who shall receive a license to operate a television or radio station, and can revoke a license if a station fails to satisfy certain operating conditions. Barring federal court action, the FCC's judgment is final.

Because the regulatory commissions wield such a blend of legislative, executive, and judicial powers, they are supposed to remain relatively independent of both the president and Congress. They are headed by boards of several members instead of by single individuals, for example, and must be bipartisan. And even though commissioners are appointed by the president, they do not report directly to him and cannot easily be removed. Most serve long, overlapping terms so that no one president can make all of the appointments.

However, the "independence" of the regulatory commissions is only partial. The president designates the chairman of each commission—thus exercising some measure of control over policy direction—while Congress controls the flow of money to keep the commissions operating.

Table 12-3. Some Regulatory Commissions

Commissions	Founded	Major Duties
Interstate Commerce Commission	1887	Eleven commissioners regulate rates and routes of interstate railroads, trucking and bus companies, and pipelines.
Federal Reserve Board	1913	Seven-member board regulates banking industry and sets monetary and credit policy.
Federal Trade Commission	1914	Five commissioners enforce antitrust laws, prohibit unfair competition, and enforce truth-in-labeling laws.
Federal Communications Commission	1934	Seven commissioners license television and radio stations and regulate interstate telephone services.
Securities and Exchange Commission	1934	Five commissioners regulate stock exchanges and investment companies.
Equal Employment Opportunity Commission	1964	Five commissioners enforce rules prohibiting job discrimination.
Consumer Product Safety Commission	1972	Five commissioners set product safety standards and initiate recall notices for defective products.

In addition, the regulatory commissions are often criticized for yielding to pressures from the industries they are supposed to regulate. Because commission rulings can affect the profits of industries in a direct way, such as by banning a company's product or denying an operating license, regulatory commissions face intense lobbying efforts urging them to support rather than challenge industry concerns. These efforts are often successful, especially since commission members are frequently selected from the same industries they oversee. As critics have noted, some of the commissions seem more concerned with promoting the interests of industry groups than with protecting the public from corporate abuses. More on this point later.

How the Bureaucracy Affects Our Lives

Probably to most people the agencies and departments just described are little more than vaguely familiar names. The officials who run them are largely unknown, tucked away in massive buildings along the mall in Washington, D.C., and in other cities across the country. Yet, in several respects, the decisions of these anonymous men and women affect us more directly than those of any other governmental officials—more than those of the members of Congress, state legislators, city council members, or presidents we elect to office. Each day they issue regulations governing virtually all aspects of our lives, ranging from the softness of our mattresses to the shape of our toilet seats. They tell us whether we can use saccharin in our coffee, whether our hair sprays and shave creams can come in aerosol cans, and whether our children's pajamas are to be treated with flame-retardant chemicals.

If the past is any guide, the influence of these civil servants will increase rather than diminish. The growth in the number of federal regulations over the years has been striking. According to one report, federal agencies in 1975 had under consideration over 10,000 regulations, up more than 14 percent over the previous year alone.[4]

Theoretically, bureaucrats are supposed to do what elected officials tell them to do, which is to administer the laws. In practice, however, they have great discretionary authority. Although agencies like the Food and Drug Administration (FDA) and the Internal Revenue Service (IRS) administer policies made by Congress and the White House, policies rarely are so specific that these agencies cannot use discretion in carrying them out. For instance, when Congress stipulated that new drugs on the market had to be safe and effective, the Food and Drug Administration was handed the power to establish the actual standards of safety and effectiveness. It was given the authority to make policy decisions concerning the kinds of products that reach consumers—in effect, determining both the health and well-being of millions of Americans and the economic fate of entire industries.

Several reasons have been given to explain why such discretionary policy-making power has been handed to nonelected bureaucrats. One is that such power is an unavoidable consequence of a growing technological society. Many social and economic problems have become so highly complex that people with technical expertise are required to handle them. Elected officials, including members of Congress, usually do not have such expertise and must delegate considerable policy-making authority to bureaucrats.

Another reason is that the defects of our economic system—unemployment, price fixing, monopolies, unsafe working conditions, and consumer fraud—have placed increased responsibilities on bureaucratic officials charged with solving social and economic problems. The FDA, for example, has been handed its enormous policy-making authority in recognition of the fact that consumers require some protection against the occasional abuses of the drug industry. Without the scientific expertise and governmental authority commanded by fed-

eral agencies like the FDA, it is extremely doubtful whether safety standards for many of the products we use would have been achieved.

However, although the need for administrative expertise and oversight has long been accepted as a necessary part of government, the rash of new regulations in recent years—for consumer product quality, industrial safety, and environmental protection—has sparked new debates about the highly visible regulatory aspect of the bureaucracy. Have bureaucratic officials, as some critics contend, been handed too much power in regulating American society? Have they been properly serving the interests of American citizens, or have they instead been serving the interests of the industries they are supposed to regulate?

Because the outcome of this debate could have a profound impact on our lives, we should examine some of the criticisms of, and justifications for, the bureaucracy's regulatory activities. Exploring the debate over this prominent function of the breaucracy should shed some light on the principles and problems of the bureaucracy as a whole.

The Uses of Regulation

Several years ago, it was revealed that the Ford Motor Company knowingly produced Pintos with gas tanks that could explode if hit from the rear. The National Highway Traffic Safety Administration (NHTSA), prodded by consumer groups into investigating the safety of the Pinto fuel systems, reported in May 1978 that it knew of thirty-eight Pinto rear-end collisions resulting in twenty-seven deaths that involved fuel tank explosions. In September of the same year, the Ford Motor Company was indicted by an Indiana grand jury on three counts of reckless homicide and one count of criminal recklessness in connection with the deaths of three teen-age girls whose 1973 Pinto burst into flames after being hit from the rear. (No individuals employed by Ford were indicted, however, and the maximum amount Ford could be fined was $35,000.)

This startling news was accompanied by reports of other corporate insensitivities, such as the revelation that the Firestone Tire and Rubber Company was continuing to market defective 500 steel-belted radial tires suspected in auto accidents killing forty-one people. Despite alarming data on the tires compiled by the NHTSA, and despite protests from consumer action groups like the Center for Auto Safety, Firestone persisted in dumping its inventories of 500s in Florida and Alabama. Finally, in October 1978, Firestone yielded to government pressures and agreed to recall more than ten million tires, one of the largest recalls in the nation's history.

Although not all corporations show the same disregard for human life demonstrated by Ford and Firestone in these instances, the sad fact is that citizens cannot rely exclusively on the good intentions of profit-oriented enterprises. Some additional mechanisms are needed to protect against fraud and against products that could endanger public health. Experience has shown that governmental programs in such areas as drug regulation, food inspection, and industrial and product safety have served legitimate public needs and should be continued.

Consider one dramatic example. In the early 1960s, Dr. Frances Kelsey of the FDA received national publicity for keeping a sedative called Thalidomide off the shelves. She resisted a drug company's efforts to introduce the sedative into the American market, even though it already had been widely prescribed in Europe. As it turned out, the drug was found to have caused thousands of European children to be born deformed because their mothers had taken it during pregnancy.

This does not mean that regulatory officials should be viewed as a band of fearless knights protecting us against hordes of vicious corporate scoundrels. As we will see, federal regulators have been criticized on numerous counts, including for being "captured" by the industries

Dr. Frances Kelsey of the FDA

they are supposed to oversee. Rather, federal regulators like Dr. Kelsey can provide additional checks on the abuses of private industry which we, as consumers, may be unable to detect or prevent. As stated earlier, without the scientific expertise and governmental authority commanded by federal regulators, it is extremely doubtful whether many of the safety standards we take for granted today would have been implemented.

The Negative Side of Regulation

A number of criticisms, however, have also been lodged against federal regulators. One criticism has been the sheer cost of all the regulations they issue. Officials in President Ford's administration once estimated that the average American family ends up paying an additional $2,000 a year above its income taxes to help foot the bill.[5] Equipment alone mandated by the federal government, for example, adds over $660 to the average price of a new car and as much as $2,500 to the price of a new house. And this cost does not include the enormous amount of paperwork generated. One governmental commission established to study the problem reported that the federal bureaucracy issues enough regulations and documents each year to fill fifty-one major league baseball stadiums.[6]

To make matters worse, federal regulators occasionally have been shown to be inconsistent and inept. In 1972, for example, the Consumer Product Safety Commission (CPSC) demanded that children's sleepwear be treated with flame-retardant chemicals such as Tris. The requirement immediately resulted in a 20 percent price hike in children's pajamas, imposed by manufacturers to cover the added expense of treatment. Then, several years later, the same commission, concerned about reports that Tris was a suspected cancer-causing agent, banned the use of the chemical in children's sleepwear. It was unable to explain to parents why they had been required during the previous years to pay higher prices to expose their children to a potential carcinogen.

An even more serious criticism of the regulatory bureaucracy is that it fails to do enough for the consumer. Despite examples of regulatory heroism displayed by Dr. Frances Kelsey of the FDA, federal agencies have not responded quickly and effectively enough to many of the harmful products that show up in the market place. The Consumer Product Safety Commission, for example, from 1973 to 1978, issued mandatory safety standards for only three kinds of products: swimming pool slides, architectural glass, and matchbook covers.[7] Considering that an estimated 20 million Americans are injured or killed annually by defective products, the commission's limited actions during those five years hardly demonstrated a high commitment to consumer safety.

Perhaps no event in recent years has dramatized the absence of adequate regulatory controls more than the Three Mile Island nuclear reactor accident near Middletown, Pennsylvania, in April 1979. Over a period of days, radioactive steam periodically escaped from the nuclear plant into the surrounding atmosphere, prompting thousands of local residents to flee the area. As nuclear power foes had argued for years, the fail-safe systems of the nuclear industry proved to be as fallible as the humans who designed and operated them. The reactor accident, the worst in American history, cast a shadow not only over the future of the nuclear industry, but also over the performance of the Nuclear Regulatory Commission (NRC), which is charged with licensing and inspecting all commercial power reactors. Critics argued that the NRC was aware of design flaws at Three Mile Island and had been lax about safety standards at nuclear plants around the country. They charged that NRC inspectors tended to rely too heavily on test results provided by those who built the nuclear plants and not enough on independent on-site

Three Mile Island

investigations. Even the General Accounting Office (GAO), a "watch-dog" agency responsible to Congress, joined the chorus of criticism, chastising the NRC for not requiring detailed emergency and evacuation plans.

One common explanation for such bureaucratic inaction and failure is that regulatory agencies are often too close to the industries they regulate. The NRC, FDA, and other regulatory commissions have been staffed at the highest levels with former industry members who compromise the independence of regulatory decision making. (A 1975 study by Common Cause, for example, revealed that 65 percent of NRC staffers had been employed by companies licensed by, or holding contracts with, the commission.) These regulatory officials often enjoy the support of key members of congressional committees who are "sympathetic" to the same industries, forming what has been frequently described as a "cozy triangle" of bureaucrats, members of Congress, and industry lobbyists.[8] Although a major function of regulatory agencies is to provide private industry with central services, such as maintaining a healthy climate of competition and arbitrating disputes, the interests of ordinary citizens have often been slighted or overlooked. Instead of championing the rights of consumers, regulatory agencies have served as defenders of the industries they are supposed to oversee, protecting the interests of their client groups.

Some regulators insist, however, that they are not given enough support from the White House and Congress to meet their responsibilities. While the public clamors for more consumer protection, bureaucrats claim they are unable to obtain sufficient funds and staffs to carry the added load. The FDA, for example, may take several years to complete the testing of a new drug. Since hundreds of new drugs are submitted for approval each year and thousands of other drugs are already on the market, the pressure to satisfy all parties is simply too great to bear under present conditions.

Moreover, regulators argue, they are constantly dealing with highly charged issues of individual rights. The growing demand for consumer protection has brought with it the contradictory criticism that regulatory agencies are intruding too much into people's lives. For each person who demands greater passenger protection in the event of an auto accident, there is another who resents seatbelts that must be buckled before his car can start. It may be recalled that the FDA's disapproval of the cancer drug Laetrile prompted enormous controversy during the late 1970s. While the FDA claimed that the drug (derived from apricot pits and bitter almonds) had little medical value and refused to certify it, Laetrile supporters insisted that cancer patients should have the freedom of choice to use it if their doctor approved. The controversy was sufficiently intense to inspire nearly a dozen states to try to bypass the FDA by legalizing the drug within their boundaries.

In the final analysis, of course, many people's attitudes toward governmental regulation—and the bureaucracy in general—reflect their political views or personal experiences. Those who deplore in principle any large-scale regulation of free enterprise, for example, will continue to object to the government's butting into business activities, regardless of how many instances of corporate insensitivity are cited. Similarly, those who have been hassled or mistreated by the Postal Service, the IRS, or any other bureaucratic agency will not likely be enthusiastic about expanding governmental influence over their lives. Some even see the activities of governmental regulators as an insufficient response to the basic defects of a capitalist economy. Merely banning an occasional product or slapping a few industrialists' wrists will not dramatically alter the deficiencies of the present economic system.

Who Controls the Bureaucracy?

As we have seen, there is the view that the bureaucracy is an omnipotent force in its own right, a powerful and independent "fourth branch" of government elected by, and seemingly accountable to, no one. With its army of obedient officials, it reaches into every corner of our society, creating and enforcing rules that often bear little relation to reason or justice. How valid is this view? Does it represent an accurate portrait of the federal bureaucracy?

It can be argued that such a view exaggerates the power and independence of the bureaucracy by ignoring the important interplay of political forces in our society. In view of the checks and balances in the American political system, bureaucratic agencies can hardly remain immune to the influences of other governmental and political interests. As participants in the policy-making process, bureaucratic agencies must share power with other governmental institutions and be subject to a number of important legal and political restraints.

Congress, for example, not only has the constitutional authority to set up the agencies in the first place, it also holds the power of the purse. Congress regulates the flow of money to pay for bureaucrats' salaries and paper clips, and thus can doom agencies and programs by cutting off their funds. Moreover, through appropriations hearings and special investigations, members of Congress can review the activities of bureaucratic agencies and amend the laws under which they operate.

These congressional restraints are supplemented by those imposed by the White House. Despite the president's inability to keep a close watch on thousands of administrators, he does screen all agency requests for funds through the Office of Management and Budget (OMB). He can appoint and remove many key officials, and, together with Congress, can reorganize or eliminate federal agencies.

Even the courts have an impact, albeit a more limited one, on bureaucratic behavior. The courts can overturn a regulatory action if it is not in accord with the law the agency is supposed to enforce. Just as the courts can exercise the power of judicial review over the actions of the president and Congress, they also impose their will on administrators. Indeed, citizens who believe they have been wronged by an administrative act have successfully used the courts to challenge agency rules and procedures.

There are other checks as well, including the influence of powerful interest groups, the press and public opinion, and even—as some observers have noted—the professional norms and conduct of the bureaucrats themselves.[9]

In fact, it can be argued that if the bureaucracy has not been adequately restrained, it is because the president and Congress have been lax in exercising their powers of control. As noted in Chapter 10, Congress frequently has been accused of incompetence in carrying out its legislative oversight responsibilities. Bureaucratic irregularities and mismanagement often slip by unnoticed or are tacitly accepted by members of Congress, who are too involved in legislative and other pursuits. As one scholar has noted, even in cases "where the public interest and a committee-defined constitutional mandate govern committee roles, there is still little, if any, systematic concern for comprehensive oversight."[10]

A balance, of course, must also be struck between responsiveness and responsibility. A bureaucracy that surrenders all of its autonomy to elected officials can pose almost as much danger as one that shows its independence. As the Watergate investigations revealed, there is always a danger that a president may abuse his influence over agencies like the Internal Revenue Service (IRS) and Federal Bureau of Investigation (FBI) by setting them against his political opponents. Without proper limits on the compliance of the bureaucracy with the directives of elected officials, citizens could face the double threat of an "imperial" presidency aligned with an omnipotent bureaucracy.

The main point is that the bureaucracy, for all its growth and influence, cannot prevail on its own. It can grow and multiply only with the consent of the White House and Congress. If the president and Congress should decide to trim the bureaucracy, to scrap certain agencies or reform their procedures, the constitutional authority exists for them to do so. As the elected representatives of the people, they must carry the major responsibility for the character and performance of the federal bureaucracy.

Taking on the Bureaucracy: Citizen Access to Federal Agencies

During the past decade, there has been an intensified effort by citizens and public interest groups to influence bureaucratic decision making. Citizens have descended on governmental agencies in growing numbers to demand fuller participation in administrative proceedings.

Because bureaucrats are not elected at the polls, broadened citizen participation has long been advocated as a way to improve bureaucratic responsiveness and accountability. Direct citizen involvement— through advisory boards, public hearings, and local councils—is thought to contribute to better decision making by exposing administrators to a broader range of views. Although there is always a danger that labels like "public interest," "consumer," and "environmental" may be abused by individuals and groups pursuing their own selfish aims, positive benefits are seen in admitting those who speak for a variety of public concerns into agency proceedings.[11]

Until a few years ago, participation in bureaucratic decision making was limited primarily to well-heeled corporate interests. Legal and financial obstacles tended to prevent other groups from gaining access to federal agencies where they could voice their concerns. But in the mid-1960s, a series of court rulings defined new rights of citizen participation. Federal agencies were ordered to admit citizen groups into more of their proceedings. These court rulings were supplemented by congressional legislation authorizing financial support for citizen groups wanting to participate in certain regulatory areas, such as those partly covered by the Federal Trade Commission, the Environmental Protection Agency, and the Consumer Product Safety Commission. The Community Action Programs started in the 1960s also provided federal grants to encourage the "maximum feasible participation" of the poor in local antipoverty programs, while a few agencies set up special "in-house" advocacy units to represent consumer and other interests.

More recently, there have been efforts to improve citizen access to all federal agencies and to provide additional financial support for those wanting to participate in bureaucratic decision making. Despite past court rulings and congressional legislation, many citizens still cannot afford the attorney's fees and other expenses that are sometimes necessary to penetrate the bureaucracy and compete effectively against well-financed corporate interests. In 1978, President Carter pushed for congressional legislation to help citizens cover the costs of participating in federal agency proceedings. The money would go to citizens and groups, such as the elderly, consumers, and small business interests, who represent important segments of the community but who do not have sufficient funds to promote their cause on an ongoing basis. Not surprisingly, Carter's proposal was endorsed by such groups as Common Cause, the Consumers' Union, and the National Council of Senior Citizens. Opposing it were the National Association of Manufacturers, the Grocery Manufacturers of America, and several utility and nuclear power firms. But the proposal gained little support in either the House or the Senate and died a quiet death in committee.

Many people, of course, express doubts about their ability to influence the federal bureaucracy, with or without financial assistance. Apart from the high costs, there is the time and expertise needed to become effectively involved. The rule-making process of a federal agency is often lengthy and complicated, requiring great patience and the ability to master the procedural maze. Considering the usual pressures of working at a full-time job and supporting a family, the average citizen, if he or she is to become involved at all, may find it difficult to do more than testify at a local hearing or dash off an occasional letter to an administrator.

Even those who have participated have sometimes come away disillusioned. Citizens who have testified at agency hearings or have even gained representation on advisory and policy-making boards have

---

Access and the Freedom of Information Act

Government agencies, like the FBI, Internal Revenue Service, and Census Bureau, traditionally have been able to decide what information they would release to the public and the press. In 1966, however, Congress passed the Freedom of Information Act. This act requires federal agencies to make documents and records available to citizens who request them, unless the material falls under one of nine exempted categories. Exempted from disclosure, for example, are personnel and medical files, sensitive national security information, and criminal investigation records.

In 1974, Congress amended the act (over President Ford's veto) to make it even stronger. Agencies are now required to reply to requests within ten working days and to charge reasonable fees for the information they provide. This was designed to discourage agencies from dragging their feet in responding to requests and from charging expensive "search fees" to hinder the release of documents. Citizens are permitted to appeal to the courts if an agency refuses to comply; and it is up to the agency to prove that information should be withheld for national security or other reasons.

Congress also passed the Privacy Act of 1974 to protect citizens from invasions of privacy by federal agencies. It permits individuals to inspect personal records about them compiled by government agencies and to challenge or correct any inaccurate information. It also prohibits an agency from making an individual's file available to other agencies without that individual's consent.

Although these two acts have not been entirely successful in encouraging disclosure of information to the public, they have given reporters, public interest groups, and ordinary citizens greater access to government agencies.

---

complained of not being taken seriously. Their feeling has been that administrators do not value citizen input as much as the information obtained from special interests or community leaders. In fact, some observers (notably ruling-elite theorists) believe that agencies often use citizen participation as a means of gaining public support for their policies and to "co-opt" or "pacify" potential forces of opposition.

Indeed, effective citizen participation in bureaucratic decision making is still largely an unrealized goal. Citizen groups wishing to sway the minds and hearts of bureaucrats will have to continue to press for greater access and for more support from government. And there is every indication they will do so. As long as bureaucratic agencies affect the quality of life for so many Americans, there will be demands for more citizen participation in agency deliberations.

Bureaucratic Reform

The growing concern over the inefficiencies, unresponsiveness, and excesses of bureaucracy has inspired a number of proposals for reform. Some of these proposals have been offered by those who see the "capture" of federal agencies by private industry as the primary obstacle to effective regulation. They have suggested that Congress adopt more rigorous conflict-of-interest laws and that more consumer-oriented officials be recruited from outside private industry.

Other suggestions have been offered by those wanting more controls on government spending. One proposal has been to expand the use of *zero-base budgeting*, which requires agencies to defend every dollar they plan to spend each fiscal year, not just requests for increases over last year's appropriations. Another has been to adopt the kind of *sunset laws* used in several states, which require agencies to justify their existence every few years or face abolition.

There have even been moves toward whittling down the number of regulations and rewriting them in plainer English. In 1977, for example, the Federal Trade Commission, traditionally one of the worst enemies of the English language, hired Rudolph Flesch, the author of *Why Johnny Can't Read*, as a consultant to work on its regulations. His job was to eliminate the linguistic gobbledegook that infests so many documents and letters to citizens. In an agency where phrases like "ongoing collaborative discussion revision process" are thrown around, his assigned task could hardly be less than monumental.

But the most dramatic calls for reform have come from critics who wish to see the structure of the federal bureaucracy overhauled. Included among these critics was Jimmy Carter, who pledged as president to do something about "the horrible Washington bureaucracy." At a news conference in 1978, he proclaimed: "I came to Washington with the promise to rebuild the faith of the American people in our government. We want a government that can be trusted, not feared; [one] that will be efficient, not mired in its own red tape; a government that will respond to the needs of the American people, and not be preoccupied with needs of its own."

After taking office, Carter persuaded Congress to extend the Reorganization Act of 1949, which had expired in 1973. The act, originally proposed by President Truman, authorized the president to submit plans for reshaping the federal bureaucracy, subject to congressional veto. Presidents from Truman to Nixon had used the act to create new federal agencies, such as the Office of Management and Budget (OMB) and the Environmental Protection Agency (EPA), and to try to extend presidential control over the bureaucracy by reshuffling the lines of authority. But, while most of their plans were approved by Congress, they did not greatly simplify the operations of government. Carter hoped that by reinstating presidential authority to reorganize the executive branch, he would succeed where others had failed: to streamline the bureaucracy by making deep cuts in the number of agencies and to improve governmental efficiency.

Certainly few critics of the bureaucracy dispute the need for reorganization. As Harold Seidman has observed, "Reorganization has become almost a religion in Washington." Demands for revamping the bureauc-

"This could be trouble — get those desks into a circle..!"

racy have ranged from calls for decentralizing decision making to consolidating administrative functions into fewer agencies. Perhaps the greatest impetus for reform has been the overlapping and duplicating efforts of various agencies and departments. "Examples of mission redundancy," notes one observer, "abound within national administration. ... The Federal Trade Commission and the Justice Department have jurisdiction in the antitrust field. The Justice Department shares civil rights enforcement authority with the Civil Rights Commission. Jurisdiction over the airwaves is divided between the Federal Aviation Agency and the Civil Aeronautics Board."[12] Sometimes, the competition and overlap reaches absurd levels. In one recent case, the Occupational Safety and Health Administration (OSHA) ordered the use of back-up beepers by all vehicles on worksites. The order, however, was then challenged by the Environmental Protection Agency (EPA) because the beepers made too much noise.[13]

Yet, resistance to change has also been marked. Many groups in and out of government have established firm ties to existing agencies and regard proposals for reorganization as a potential threat to their influence. In the early 1970s, for instance, President Nixon proposed combining seven cabinet departments (Agriculture; Commerce; Health, Education and Welfare; Housing and Urban Development; Interior; Labor; and Transportation) into four new "superdepartments" organized in such broad categories as Community Development, Economic Affairs,

Human Resources, and Natural Resources. However, his plan ran into strong opposition from interest groups and Congress, and was scrapped.

President Carter, during his first years in office, tried to soften the opposition to his own reorganization plans by courting key legislators and interest groups in advance of his proposed reforms. In his eagerness to trim bureaucratic waste, he eliminated close to five hundred advisory committees. He terminated such groups as the Advisory Committee on Salmonella, the Board of Tea Exports, the Condor Advisory Committee, and even the National Peanut Advisory Committee. He also reduced the number of units within the executive office, dropping such offices as the Economic Policy Board and the Federal Property Council, and as we saw earlier, reorganized the Civil Service Commission. In late 1978, he also signed a bill gradually phasing out the Civil Aeronautics Board (CAB), which regulates the routes and fares of interstate airlines. The bill was passed to reduce governmental restraints on free-market competition among passenger airlines, allowing them to drop (or raise) fares and scrap unprofitable routes.

In early 1979, Carter considered a major reorganization of governmental agencies concerned with economic assistance, education, and natural resources. He persuaded Congress in September of 1979 to create a separate Department of Education, removing it from the Department of Health, Education, and Welfare (renamed the Department of Health and Human Services). He also proposed centralizing most development functions of the Department of Housing and Urban Development (HUD) by creating a new Department of Development Assistance (DDA). And he proposed a new Department of Natural Resources to replace the Department of Interior and take over land, water, and oceanic programs from the departments of Commerce and Agriculture.

Carter's most publicized achievement, however, was the creation of a new Department of Energy in 1977. The new department absorbed dozens of energy-related functions spread throughout the federal government. It consolidated the Energy Research and Development Administration (ERDA), the Federal Power Commission (FPC), and the Federal Energy Administration (FEA). It also absorbed the energy-related functions of several cabinet departments, including those of Defense, Interior, and Commerce.

Yet, as a sign of the continuing controversy surrounding reorganization, the new Energy Department quickly drew fire. Before the department could even obtain office space for its new employees, doubts were expressed over whether the consolidation of separate energy functions was a good idea after all. As a spokesman for the environmental group Friends of the Earth commented, "We don't believe the creation of this superagency will provide anything except a monolithic structure that is much bigger, more rigid, and more inaccessible to the public than the existing energy agencies."[14]

The problems of reorganization are complex and perhaps are unlikely to be resolved. Those who desire multiple routes of access to bureaucratic decision making will continue to suspect plans to combine separate agencies into monolithic blocs. Likewise, those who attack the overlapping and competitive efforts of separate agencies will continue to criticize any presidential failure to pursue a consolidating course. Although the needs of both groups may not be mutually exclusive, differing perceptions of what reorganization means in terms of efficiency and responsiveness will probably continue to stall sweeping reform of the bureaucracy.

Key Terms

bureaucracy

spoils system

civil service

executive department

independent agency

government corporation

regulatory commission

zero-base budgeting

sunset laws

Notes

1. C. Northcote Parkinson, *Parkinson's Law* (Boston: Houghton Mifflin, 1957), p. 2.

2. Reinhard Bendix, *International Encyclopedia of the Social Sciences*, 2nd ed., vol. 2, p. 206.

3. U.S. Bureau of the Census, *Statistical Abstract of the United States*, 1977, p. 272.

4. William Lilly and James Miller, "The New 'Social Regulation,'" *The Public Interest*, Spring 1977, pp. 49–61.

5. *U.S. News & World Report*, 30 June 1975, p. 24.

6. *Time*, 2 January 1978, p. 48.

7. *Congressional Quarterly Weekly Report*, 18 February 1978, p. 391.

8. See, for example, Douglass Cater, *Power in Washington* (New York: Pegasus, 1969).

9. See, for example, W. Lloyd Warner et al., *The American Federal Executive*, Yale University Press, 1963.

10. William L. Morrow, *Public Administration* (New York: Random House, 1975), p. 114.

11. See, for example, "Symposium on Neighborhoods and Citizen Involvement," *Public Administration Review*, May/June 1972.

12. Morrow, *Public Administration*, p. 84.

13. *Newsweek*, 15 December 1975, p. 35.

14. Quoted in *Newsweek*, 11 July 1977, p. 59.

Recommended Reading

ALTSHULER, ALAN A. and NORMAN C. THOMAS. *The Politics of the Federal Bureaucracy.* 2nd ed. New York: Harper & Row, 1977.

BENVENISTE, GUY. *Bureaucracy.* San Francisco: Boyd & Fraser, 1977.

DOWNS, ANTHONY. *Inside Bureaucracy.* Boston: Little, Brown, 1967.

FRIED, ROBERT C. *Performance in American Bureaucracy.* Boston: Little, Brown, 1976.

MICHAEL, JAMES R., ed. *Working on the System: A Comprehensive Manual for Citizen Access to Federal Agencies.* New York: Basic Books, 1974.

MORROW, WILLIAM L. *Public Administration.* New York: Random House, 1975.

ROURKE, FRANCIS E. *Bureaucracy, Politics, and Public Policy.* 3rd ed. Boston: Little, Brown, 1976.

SEIDMAN, HAROLD. *Politics, Position, and Power: The Dynamics of Federal Organization.* 2nd ed. New York: Oxford University Press, 1975.

SHARKANSKY, IRA. *Public Administration: Policy Making in Government Agencies.* 3rd ed. Chicago: Rand McNally, 1975.

SIMON, HERBERT A. *Administrative Behavior: A Study of Decision-Making Processes in Administrative Organizations.* 3rd ed. New York: Free Press, 1976.

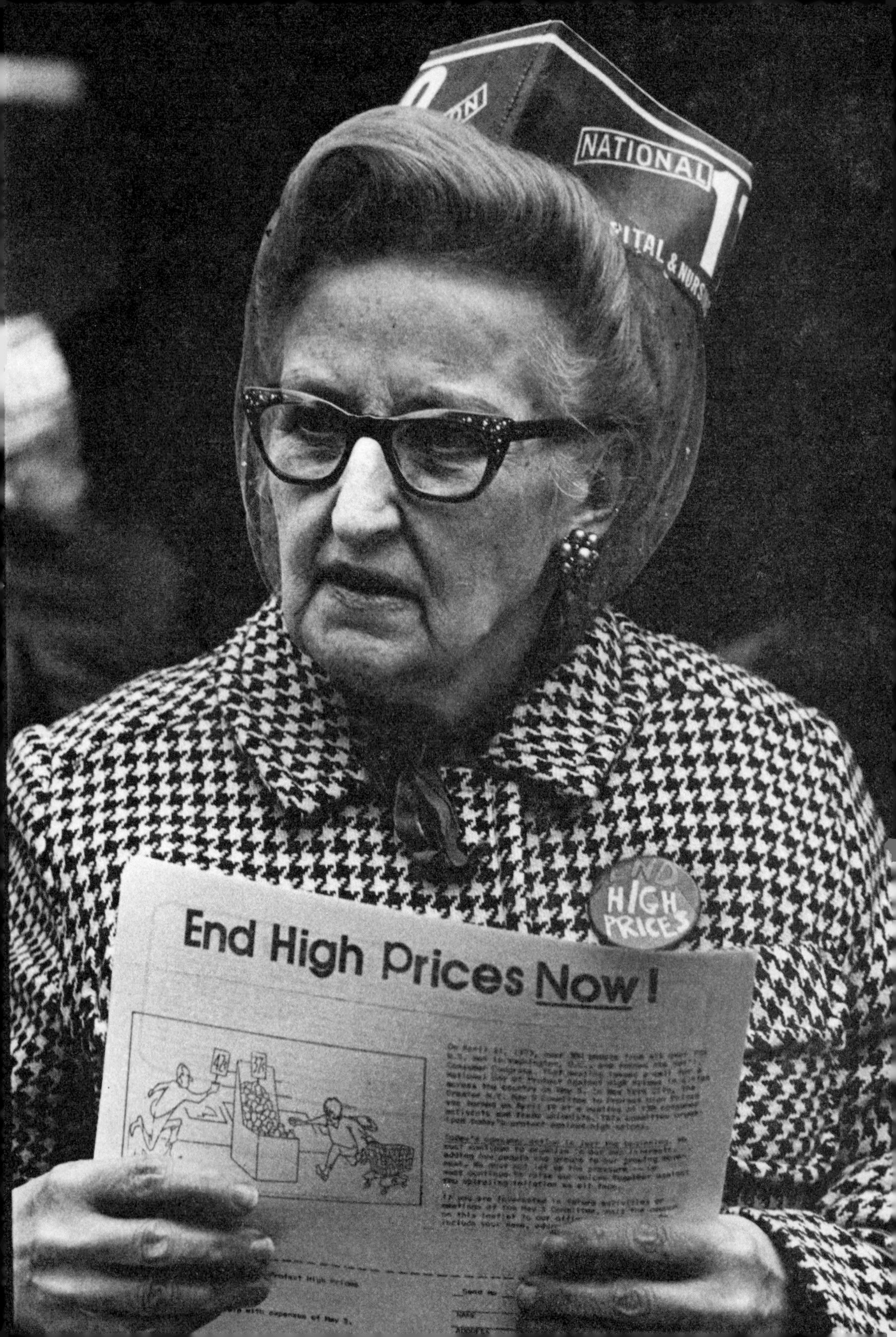

NATIONAL
ITAL & NURS
HIGH PRICES
End High Prices Now!

PART FOUR

Government in Action: Policies for the Eighties

13

Public Policy:
Turning Issues into Answers

One might suspect that if the Founding Fathers were somehow transferred from the rather simple era of the Revolution to the bustle and confusion of the 1980s, they would be hard pressed to cope with the evolution of American society, let alone its government. The average citizen today is left in a similar state of bewilderment. Government has become massive in scope and extensive in responsibilities.

Most of us know when we are upset about a given issue, although few of us ever view the same issue in an identical light. When enough individuals or groups express a common concern about an issue, that issue becomes a public issue, and their views are transmitted to the respective offices of government. The tough part is in transforming often conflicting ideas about the same issue into acceptable answers. When this transformation takes place—that is, when a commitment is made—government leaders are making public policy. Simply stated, public policy represents the combination of decisions and policy commitments made by those who hold governmental positions of authority.

The concern about public policy is relatively new to the study of American politics. Until recently, most political scientists were content to examine the relationship between the needs of citizens and the capacities of institutions. These considerations, while worthy, do not tell us what *causes* government to make policies or *how* these policies are made. The study of public policy takes us a step further by focusing on the kinds of decisions government leaders choose to make as a result of their perceptions of public needs and demands. Moreover, these decisions may change over time as the values of society change.

This chapter begins with a focus on the concept of public policy. We will identify those who participate in the decision-making process and the factors that turn social and economic issues into public policies. Agencies and branches of government are designed in part to receive demands and needs expressed by individuals, groups, and society as a whole. The task here is to understand how these feelings are interpreted and refined by policy makers and translated into new directives or laws.

Who Makes Public Policy?

At first glance, public policy seems to result from various government commitments. Indeed, as the holder of public power, government has the ability to perform a wide range of tasks and functions. In the words of one scholar, "Public policy is whatever governments choose to do or not to do. . . . [It is] the description and explanation of the causes and consequences of government activity."[1] Yet, it is important to realize that public policy means government response to the demands voiced by individual citizens, groups, and other members of government. As the authors of a recent book on the subject suggested, "Public policy is the accomplishment of some goal."[2]

However, to refer to government as the source of public policy is not enough. We know that the term "government" is rather vague. At best, government is a diffuse combination of officeholders and institutions involved in making public policy. For example, when the president signs an executive order limiting federal employment opportunities in the name of reduced government, he is exercising his powers to make policy. Likewise, when the president commits the nation to the Strategic Arms Limitations Treaty (SALT) negotiations, he is directing public policy in the arena of foreign affairs. Although some may question his judgment, the fact remains that a large portion of a president's leadership comes in the form of establishing priorities and commitments.

There are other sources of public policy in addition to the presidency. As the nation's chief legislative body, Congress each year passes hundreds of new statutes or laws. In 1977, for example, President Carter handed Congress a comprehensive program for national energy policy. The program was controversial because it increased the nation's energy costs in the hope of limiting dependence on oil imports. Congress grappled with the Carter proposal for nineteen months. Hundreds of committee hearings and thousands of testimonies later, Congress passed its own version of an energy program. After the president signed the various pieces of legislation in the complicated energy package, he praised Congress for moving the country in a new policy direction.

The courts also play an important role in policy making. Although they are not as active in the legislative process as Congress, they do make policy through their interpretations of the law. In deciding the merits of the *Bakke* case, for example (see Chapter 4), the Supreme Court responded to the policy issue of "reverse discrimination." On the basis of the Court's decision, civil rights policy was tilted in a direction protecting majority as well as minority rights.

While the three branches of government mentioned above receive most public attention in the policy-making process, policies also stem from a number of other less obvious sources. The bureaucracy, for example, has become so vital in modern industrial society that one author refers to it as a "fourth branch" of government.[3] On paper, most bureaucratic agencies administer policies created by Congress and the White House. Yet, it is often difficult to determine where the administration of policy ends and the making of policy begins. To this extent, even the lowest-level bureaucrat may have the power to make decisions and, hence, establish policy.

Moreover, many of the same powers exercised at the national level are also wielded by state and local governments. Our system of federalism enables these other levels of government to pursue more limited policy areas. Thus, a variety of decisions on the same question may be made by several jurisdictions.

Finally, there are many opportunities for citizens to initiate policy from outside formal governmental structures. As we will see in Chapter 15, referenda and initiatives are permitted in more than half of the states. While the referendum allows voters to accept or reject policies suggested by the legislature, the initiative permits voters "to propose changes in the constitution, charter, laws, or ordinances which are then accepted or rejected by the voters at the polls."[4]

In light of the many complicated questions and overlapping decision-making institutions, it is easy to understand why citizens are confused about the origins of public policy. More often than not, they are apt to throw up their hands in disgust and to blame "the government" for the wrongdoings perpetrated on society.

The Birth of Issues: Building the Public Agenda

Not all disputes in our society evolve into policy questions for the public agenda. If two individuals disagree on clothing styles and chide each other for bad taste, their disagreement does not constitute a public policy issue. In such an instance, there would be no need for government intervention because the issue at stake involves little more than a private disagreement. However, if a government agency decided that the material used in clothing was highly flammable, the agency could spark a public policy issue by ordering the material off the market.

Stated another way, public policy issues develop when a conflict arises over how government should distribute authority or resources.[5] If government assumes responsibility for resolving the conflict, its activity makes the issue a question of public policy.

In many instances, government response mirrors the intensity of the conflict. Thus, citizen participation is fundamental to placing provocative questions on the public agenda. A vocal public can help direct government's attention to an area of mounting public concern.

The biggest questions regarding policy issues center on costs and benefits. Costs are important to citizens because policies may extract charges (such as new taxes) that citizens are unwilling to bear. Benefits are equally important because citizens expect their "money's worth" from government. To complicate matters, the "cost" for one segment of society may be the "benefit" for another.

Most of us read daily newspaper accounts of new policy areas with sizable price tags. When President Carter's energy program was carefully scrutinized in 1978, the bulk of the debate focused on the cost of the energy bill to consumers. Opinion polls showed that most Americans were aghast at the steep rise in energy prices between 1973 and 1978. Nevertheless, the Carter administration pushed for higher energy costs in the name of reduced energy consumption and, hence, independence from foreign energy sources. As the president hammered away at the virtues of a comprehensive (and expensive) energy policy, a public policy issue developed.

Another example of the concern for cost can be seen in the national health insurance issue. Virtually all experts acknowledge the astronomical leap in health care costs. Critics have clamored for relief in the health care area through a government-financed program. Yet, the latest estimates are that a modest governmental response to the problem of catastrophic illness alone would cost between $60 billion and $110 billion annually. Moreover, many economists argue that such expenditures would spark an inflationary spiral that could harm the U.S. economy. Given these pressures, President Carter decided to reverse himself and refrain from proposing a national health insurance plan. In other words, Carter reasoned, the best policy in this instance was no public policy.

If costs give reason to dismiss policy proposals from the public agenda, benefits provide motivation to adopt new policy ideas. Recent propositions regarding airline deregulation and reduced numbers of public works projects exemplify both successful and unsuccessful efforts to tie policy and public benefits together. In the former instance, it was widely believed by representatives of the airline industry and public alike that deregulation would yield substantial savings in the price of air travel and, hence, provide direct public benefits. In response to this contention, Congress passed legislation paving the way for deregulation.

In the matter of public works projects (referred to by some critics as *pork barrel legislation*), President Carter consistently urged Congress to cut back its appropriations for new dams and water projects on the grounds that the costs outweighed the benefits. He argued that any gains from such projects would be restricted to a narrow group of citizens, while the costs would be absorbed by the general public. However, despite his appeals to hold the line, Carter was largely unsuccessful in convincing Congress of the merits of his proposal. Because many members of Congress felt that their popularity (and reelection chances) were tied to water issues, they continued to fund the vast majority of public works projects.

Thus, costs and benefits are important elements in the development of the public policy agenda. Both reflect the struggle by interested parties over the government's authority and distribution of resources. If enough government leaders think the costs are necessary, then the policy may be in a good position to win approval. However, the pressures on policy makers are enormous. There are few clear-cut examples of policies benefiting all, costing little, and harming no one.

Costs and benefits are not the only considerations, however. After an issue has been placed on the public agenda, policy makers must turn to the difficult task of predicting the public's reactions. If the consequences of a policy can be anticipated, then the officials can adjust their goals to cope with objections.

Predicting the consequences of proposed policies is a risky business. While it is fairly easy to foresee the short-term consequences of a new policy, it is another matter to comprehend the long-term consequences. Too many mistakes of this nature can cost a policy maker his job, as was true of President Lyndon Johnson and his military policy in Vietnam. Johnson may have misjudged the mood of the electorate to the extent that it cost him the presidency in 1968.

Indeed, unintended consequences may emerge from even the most carefully developed policies. One example was observed when the United States government changed its agricultural policy toward the Soviet Union in 1972. As George Edwards and Ira Sharkansky noted, "the large, unprecedented, government-approved sale of wheat to the Soviet Union that year depleted surplus stocks and tied up transportation facilities. Governmental policy therefore produced significant rises in the prices of domestic wheat, flour-based products, beef, pork, poultry, eggs, dairy products, and transportation."[6] Had these consequences been anticipated prior to the sale, the terms of the transaction could have been adjusted and the policy changed.

Given such unintended consequences—not to mention the almost daily bombardments of new pressures and social needs—it is not surprising that few policies are cast in concrete. Government leaders often will settle on the best possible solutions for problems even though they know their decisions may be temporary. If one solution does not work, government officials will usually find out through negative comments from those affected.

If a newly implemented policy does not satisfy the needs as anticipated, policy makers must face the task of developing a more acceptable solution. Aside from basic questions like defense, education, or social security, the majority of policy commitments may be altered if enough pressure develops. Policy makers are valuable not only for their ability to develop programs and commitments, but also for their ability to modify policies if negative reactions warrant reconsideration. On most occasions the policy changes will be *incremental*, or marginal in nature. In other instances, a policy may be completely overhauled. To determine the extent of change, policy makers often look to citizens and the feelings they express in letters, marches, and votes.

The drive for an Equal Rights Amendment points to one example of changing social values. The Constitution does not guarantee equal rights for men and women. Rather, the Preamble states that "all *men* are created equal." Despite the implication of male dominance, women began clamoring for change in the early nineteenth century. In 1920, the Nineteenth Amendment granting women's suffrage was incorporated into the Constitution. Nevertheless, as the twentieth century wore on, a number of leaders and groups insisted that voting rights were not synonymous with full equality. Congress seriously considered proposals for an Equal Rights Amendment on at least four separate occasions (1946, 1950, 1953 and 1970), but each time to no avail.[7]

By 1970, women comprised 38 percent of the labor force, yet studies showed that their salaries lagged considerably behind those of their male counterparts. Women activists and others close to the feminist cause blamed the differences on the lack of constitutional guarantees for women. In 1972, Congress finally agreed to submit the Equal Rights Amendment (ERA) to the fifty states for ratification.

The ERA exemplified the ability of policy makers to respond to new values. As the petitioners for ERA increased both in numbers and intensity, Congress and a number of the states responded accordingly and reversed previous policies.

Although the Equal Rights Amendment illustrated a policy reversal that was the culmination of more than a century of pressure and changing values, other public policy reversals have taken place in less time. The controversial decision of the Supreme Court in the *Bakke* case represented a public policy change occurring relatively soon after the original policy's development and implementation.

During the 1960s, a combination of executive orders, congressional legislation, and Supreme Court decisions in the area of civil rights policy signaled a new direction in the treatment of blacks and other minorities. The government embarked on a policy of nondiscrimination to "prevent indefinite perpetuation of inequalities caused by past discrimination."[8] In response to the flurry of government activity, public institutions adopted "affirmative action" programs, which offered special opportunities to members of minority groups who had suffered long periods of discrimination.

As part of an effort to guarantee admission for minorities who might not otherwise compete with whites, the medical school at the University of California, Davis, reserved sixteen of its one hundred slots for disadvantaged minority persons. When Allan Bakke, a white male, was denied admission to the medical school in 1973 and again in 1974, his test scores were above the majority who had been admitted under Davis's special admissions program.

After a series of unsuccessful appeals, Bakke filed suit on the grounds that he was denied "equal protection of the laws" as guaranteed in the Fourteenth Amendment. The case ultimately landed in the Supreme Court. In 1978 the Court decided that while race was a legitimate issue in the admissions process, the special admissions program at Davis was unconstitutional because of the predetermined number (sixteen) of minority entrance slots. The Court then ordered the Davis medical school to admit Bakke into its program. In the process, the Court redefined national policy toward affirmative action, modifying the direction of the previous decade.

The ERA and the *Bakke* case exemplify changes in the direction of public policies. When policy commitments go beyond the level of general acceptance, policy makers must redirect their efforts at acceptable alternatives. Thus, most public policies are vulnerable to modification even after they have been adopted.

Limits on the Policy Process

Political scientists have pointed to three factors that may limit public policy making. These are political feasibility, institutional relationships, and historical perspective. Moreover, the existence of these elements helps explain the potential detours that can prevent a proposal from becoming policy.

Political feasibility refers to the "practical realities" policy makers must face in their proposed changes of the status quo. Regardless of its merit, a suggested alteration will not be acceptable if the proposal does not mesh with the political values of those affected. Thus, a state whose economy relies heavily on strip-mining is not likely to pursue strong environmental controls on strip-mining operations. In such a climate, policy makers will be quick to realize that clean water does not keep people employed if the industry responsible for polluting the water is severely curtailed or put out of business. State and community values can be significant deterrents to national public policy.

Institutional relationships can also impede the policy process if the leaders in different branches of government cannot agree on major issues. When the framers provided for a "separation of powers," for instance, they assured themselves and successive generations that no individual or institution could change the law without the cooperation of others. Edwards and Sharkansky noted that "the venerable age of our government impresses the sanctity of tradition on current debates about policy. . . . Each branch of government remains viable, especially in its ability to block proposals for changing policy that come from another branch."[9] If the president wants to reduce expenditures significantly, for example, he can do so only with the blessing of Congress. Thus, while the separation of powers provides built-in checks and balances, the concept also frustrates the ambitions of policy makers in some branches of government, who lack the necessary support of other branches. Occasionally, a policy may become stalled indefinitely between proposal and adoption because more than one government office or branch assumes responsibility for it. In the area of water policy, the Bureau of Reclamation and Army Corps of Engineers regularly battle each other for Congress's ear. In the process, Congress may be reluctant to support either agency and, hence, be unable to make water policy.

In addition to feasibility and institutional problems, policy efforts may be stymied because of past behavior. The weight of history can be great in preventing a policy from being accepted. Let us consider social security as an example. From the early days of our nation's history, Americans had little sympathy for government involvement in social welfare regardless of economic conditions. Those who were genuinely needy were attended by charitable organizations, while others who appeared to be healthy were forced to take care of themselves. This belief was reinforced as the country endured serious recessions and economic depressions. Only with the Great Depression in the 1930s did many Americans reconsider the questions of poverty and income security. The constant refrain was, "Government has *never* provided for income security, so why should it do so now?" Unlike previous economic downturns, the Great Depression did not abate. Finally, in 1935, President Roosevelt persuaded Congress to pass the Social Security Act. While few Americans question the value of social security today, many cited lack of a precedent as the reason for their refusal to support it in the 1930s. History can be a strong obstacle to the adoption of new policy proposals.

These factors represent important constraints on the ability of public officials to make policy commitments. Establishment of an issue alone is not sufficient to make public policy. To do so requires the ability to overcome a series of political impediments and sources of opposition.

Carter's Tax Reform and Jarvis's Tax Revolt: Two Cases in Public Policy

In the first part of this chapter, we learned that issues become questions of public policy when a sizable sector (or sectors) of the public captures the eyes and ears of government leaders. Depending on the seriousness of the issue and the number of persons affected, government may respond to a new problem in a variety of ways. Sometimes a problem may be addressed through the action of a single officeholder or institution. More often than not, however, public policies are cautiously developed through the cooperative efforts of several branches of government.

In 1978, the question of taxation reached a point of negative public reaction unparalleled in recent years. Caught between the ravages of inflation, higher energy costs, and Social Security tax increases, taxpayers at all levels began to demand changes in tax structures. Because 1978 was an election year, incumbents throughout the country were particularly sensitive to the growing public outcry.

President Carter's tax reform proposal and the tax revolt in California led by Howard Jarvis represent two different approaches to public policy concerning taxation. The Carter package was a carefully drafted proposal designed to go through the traditional channels of the public policy process. Because the president and Congress had to work closely together for legislative purposes, the final tax package was considerably different from the original bill. In contrast, the tax revolt in California reached its climax as a frustrated coalition of voters made statewide legislation through an initiative. The voters assumed the policy-making responsibility because the state's elected political machinery—the governor, legislature, and local governments—had repeatedly failed to respond to the public mood on taxation. Despite these different approaches to public policy, both showed the relationship between the public and its policy makers trying to solve the problem of excessive tax burdens.

The Carter Tax Reform Proposal

En route to his presidential victory in 1976, Jimmy Carter described the American taxation system as a "national disgrace." He criticized the complicated tax structure for its inequities and loopholes, almost all of which tended to benefit the rich at the expense of the poor and middle classes. Referring to his policy agenda in his 1977 inaugural address, Carter asked Congress for a restructured tax system during the course of his four-year administration. By the end of his first year in office, however, Carter realized that opposition to tax reform was so great that any changes would be incremental.

On January 21, 1978, President Carter sent a special message to Congress on tax reform. In this message, he suggested a series of proposals designed to reform the methods of taxation and relieve the burden on the bulk of the taxpaying community. He also proposed some relief for the corporate community. Specifically, his recommendations included:

- $17 billion in net income tax cuts for individuals, through across-the-board rate reductions and a new personal credit, focused on low- and middle-income taxpayers.
- $6 billion in net income tax cuts for small and large corporations, through reductions in the corporate tax rates and extensions of the investment tax credit.
- $2 billion for elimination of the excise tax on telephone calls and a reduction in the payroll tax for unemployment insurance.[10] Carter concluded that "this program will eliminate a number of the inequities that undermine the integrity of the tax system."

In reality, Carter's proposal represented a *shift* in the tax burden as well as a tax cut. While the program called for net reductions of $25 billion, the entire package consisted of $34 billion in cuts and $9 billion in new taxes. It was in the area of additional revenues that the bill generated the most controversy. Almost all of the proposed new taxes were aimed at eliminating loopholes for the wealthy and corporate sectors. These ranged from restrictions on deductions for business meals (the "three-martini lunch") to various tax shelters and deferred annuity programs.

No one made the case for tax reform better than Carter himself when he stated: "Low and middle-income workers, struggling to make ends meet, are discouraged by tax laws that permit a few individuals to live extravagantly at the expense of government tax revenues. The privileged few are being subsidized by the rest of the taxpaying public when they routinely deduct the cost of country club dues, hunting lodges, elegant meals, theatre and sports tickets and nightclub shows."[11] Under his plan, Carter claimed that 96 percent of American taxpayers would see reductions in their income taxes, with the average family saving more than $250 per year.

Despite widespread support for tax reductions, opposition quickly developed to some of the details surrounding the Carter proposal. Congress had the responsibility for passing the president's proposal into law. Inasmuch as many senators and representatives reflected the needs

of special groups affected by the tax package in a negative way, a number of influential members sought to tone down some of the bill's more controversial portions.

What followed during the next few months was a process common in policy making. Various leaders inside and outside government jockeyed for position and influence in the struggle over the Carter tax proposal. Afraid that the pressures for too much tax reduction might foster increased inflation, Carter pressed for his legislative package through public statements and press conferences. He also threatened to veto the measure if the final bill produced in Congress strayed too far from his plan, stating that he was open to "reasonable" compromises. As part of the Carter offensive, the administration's two biggest economic guns, Treasury Secretary W. Michael Blumenthal and the chairman of the Council of Economic Advisors, Charles Schultze, fired away at opposition from both Congress and the private sector.

Meanwhile, the administration's tax package was squeezed from all sides. Congressional Republicans launched their own effort to reduce federal taxation and spending. Known as the Kemp-Roth bill, the counterproposal called for an across-the-board tax cut of 30 percent during the next three years amounting to $113 billion. The plan, co-sponsored by 25 senators and 151 representatives, was endorsed by the conservative National Taxpayers Union and became official policy of the national Republican party.

In addition to Republican opposition, the Carter tax proposal received criticism from fellow Democrats as well. Among the first to respond was Al Ullman, chairman of the House Ways and Means Committee. While the House leader favored tax relief, he balked at Carter's proposals to tighten corporate loopholes, saying that some of them were too controversial and likely to throw people out of work. And although the House of Representatives ultimately agreed to a modest tax cut with no loophole closures, efforts in the Senate were made toward expanding the size of the tax cut. In March 1978, the Senate Finance Committee, chaired by Russell Long, proposed cutting taxes by an additional $10 billion. The combination of fewer closed loopholes and greater tax cuts left the Carter administration extremely upset. It was clear that, to salvage the bill, the administration would have to bargain extensively with key congressional leaders.

As the year progressed, it became clear that the tax reform objectives of the Carter administration and those of congressional leaders were guided by distinctly different principles. Whereas Carter modified his proposals in response to a fast-changing economic climate, many members of Congress based their decisions on the political demands of their states. The combination left the two branches of government far apart, with the president threatening to veto a proposal that began with his blessing and encouragement.

Inside the White House, Carter and his economic advisors began to fear that an extensive tax cut was no longer necessary. During the first half of 1978, unemployment steadily declined; at the same time, inflation increased without any sign of relief. In light of these developments, Carter decided that a sizable tax cut along his original lines would make inflation worse. Thus, the administration revised the tax cut proposal downward, first to $19.4 billion and ultimately to $15 billion.

In Congress, the trend was in the opposite direction. Instead of closing loopholes, congressional leaders seemed disposed to open them. One example of congressional attitude was the battle over capital gains, long believed by many to be a loophole for those making profits from the sales of stocks and bonds. The original Carter proposal tightened treatment of capital gains, yet the spirit in Congress was to the contrary. When an amendment was suggested to cut the taxes on capital gains, President Carter condemned the proposal as providing "huge tax windfalls for millionaires and two bits for the average American." Ultimately, the House version lowered the tax from 50 percent to 35 percent. In other words, rather than shift the tax burden to the wealthy, the House offered more benefits to the affluent sector. House Ways and Means Chairman Ullman summed up the differences in approach this way: "I told the President we needed an economic tax cut, not a tax reform package. . . . You can only pass tax reform every dozen years or so."[12] Ullman's reluctance to shift the tax burden was echoed by another committee member who said, "It's no sin to make a profit anymore, or to be rich."

Responding to the mood of the House, the president complained that 80 percent of the proposed benefits would go to less than one percent of the taxpayers who earn more than $100,000 a year. These revelations represented a huge difference between the Carter objectives and those of Congress.

When the House of Representatives enacted its tax reform legislation in August, the bill only faintly resembled the Carter package. While the cut amounted to $16.3 billion, the bulk of the benefits went to corporations and wealthy individuals. Although the House ignored virtually all of the Carter proposals to tighten loopholes, the legislative body voted corporate tax cuts of $4.0 billion and capital gains tax reductions amounting to $1.9 billion. Unlike the Carter plan, which would increase individual taxes for the wealthy and decrease taxes for the poor and middle classes, the House proposal offered an across-the-board cut of 6 percent.

And so ended another stage of the bargaining process in the making of public policy. Even though the president and the House agreed on the general objective of tax reform, their differing interpretations of that objective led to considerable conflict.

As the Carter tax reform proposal traveled through the Senate, the impetus for tax reform waned while the movement for tax breaks gathered steam. Senate Finance Committee Chairman Russell Long recommended massive cuts across the board, with a reduction in the capital gains tax that made 30 percent rather than 50 percent of the profits subject to taxation. Moreover, the size of the cuts seemed to grow as the November elections neared.

The Senate version was much more generous to the corporate and wealthy communities than the House version in the areas of capital gains taxes, minimum income taxes, and corporate tax rates. Whereas the House package provided total tax reductions amounting to $16.3 billion, the Senate recommended cuts of $29.1 billion, almost twice the amount voted in the House and considerably larger than the reductions advocated by the president.

Ultimately, the Senate and the House versions collided in conference committee, where compromises yielded a version of the bill that bore little resemblance to the tax program proposed by President Carter. Although reductions totaled $18.7 billion, the figures alone did not tell the entire story. The battle over capital gains taxes ended with the tax now applied to 28 percent of the profits, benefiting mostly those who earned more than $50,000 annually. In the words of one summary, "Almost all of his [Carter's] proposed 'reforms', except a few tokens, had been scrapped, and the cuts were skewed much more towards the upper end of the income scale than he had recommended."[13]

Hoping the president might veto the bill, opponents launched a last-ditch effort to gain political support. Ralph Brandon, director of the Ralph Nader Tax Reform Research Group, asserted that the bill abandoned the public interest: "This bill reverses over ten years of tax reform efforts. The long effort to eliminate the special treatment of capital gains—the biggest loophole in the tax system for the wealthy—would be dealt a knockout blow unless the president rejects the bill."[14] Yet, reform was no longer the policy question.

In November 1978, President Carter signed into law the Revenue Act of 1978. As finally written, the measure contained a considerably different combination of tax changes than those he originally proposed. Although Carter began the year with a call for reform and tax shifts, Congress ended the year with a call for tax reductions and incentives for the corporate and affluent portions of society. The question of improved capital gains benefits, absent from public debate in January, became the burning tax issue as the year wore on. Even though tax reform was

Table 13-1. The Revenue Act of 1978

Category	Carter (Jan. 20, 1978)	House (Aug. 10, 1978)	Senate (Oct. 10, 1978)	Conference (Oct. 15, 1978)
Personal Income	$ 17.0 billion	$10.4 billion	$21.1 billion	$12.2 billion
Business[a]	$ 8.0 billion	$ 4.0 billion	$ 5.0 billion	$ 4.3 billion
Capital Gains	$ 0 billion	$ 1.9 billion	$ 3.0 billion	$ 2.2 billion
Total	$25.0 billion	$16.3 billion	$29.1 billion	$18.7 billion

[a]includes cuts in excise taxes and reduction in the payroll tax for unemployment insurance.

Sources: New York Times, 21 January 1978; U.S. code Congressional and Administrative News (Revenue Act of 1978), p. 289; Congressional Quarterly Weekly Reports, pp. 2933 and 3028.

placed on the public agenda by the president, Congress adopted a different view of the agenda. Such things happen when controversial matters are placed before policy makers who must base their own decisions on political feasibility. Clearly, the members of Congress were persuaded that the potential benefits of tax reductions were more appropriate than the potential costs stemming from tax reform. Even the threat of a presidential veto could not convince them otherwise.

Table 13-1 traces the activity of the Carter tax reform proposal. We can see that the conference committee version adopted by Congress represented a significant departure from the president's plan. Yet Carter signed the bill, knowing that in an election year, a tax relief bill was better than no tax reform bill.

As observed through the discussion above, the Revenue Act of 1978 emerged as a hybrid from several conflicting proposals. The president played a key role in placing the bill on the public agenda. Both houses of Congress were also prominent in designing parts of the tax package. Aside from the public institutions and officeholders, numerous interests sought to make imprints on the tax bill as it traveled the legislative road. Several reports suggested that while public interest lobbies like the Nader Research group were pulling the bill in one direction, the American Council on Capital Formation, the National Association of Manufacturers, and prestigious Wall Street stockbrokerage firms were pulling the bill in another direction.[15]

The battle over tax reform in 1978 is instructive for the lessons it offers about public policy. First, public policy is often little more than a compromise. It provides what is minimally acceptable to the greatest number of those concerned with the issue. Neither the president nor Congress achieved desired goals, yet both compromised to make some legislation possible. Second, it is difficult for public policy to be developed by any single institution. Even the president was limited in his ability to convince Congress to support his tax proposals; thus, the most powerful office in the nation was checked by another branch of government. Third, public policy can change as it develops. The public agenda on the question of tax reform shifted as the issue gained attention. As a result, the original goals of the president were replaced in part by the objectives of Congress.

Jarvis and the California Tax Revolt: Grass-Roots Public Policy

As the 1978 election year unfolded, two themes gained public attention across the country: government waste and taxation. For years citizens had become increasingly aware of welfare fraud, over-lucrative defense contracts, and growing numbers of expensive government-funded social programs. Wisconsin Senator William Proxmire openly chastised the national government with his monthly "Golden Fleece" awards. The smoldering public resentment toward these activities burst into political flames by the late 1970s. In 1958, a Gallup Poll found that 56 percent of those interviewed thought that "government was spending too much money." By 1978, a *New York Times* poll found that 78 percent agreed with the statement that "people in government waste a lot of money."[16] Public irritation had become public outrage.

If some citizens had problems in relating taxes to big government, their difficulty disappeared by 1978. Inflation had pushed the small income gains of many wage earners into considerably higher tax brackets, forcing them into the unenviable position of paying more taxes and enduring a lower standard of living. But nowhere was the tax revolt more explosive than in California, where particular ire had focused on the state's property tax methods.

Unlike many states, California employs the property tax as a crucial source of revenue. Collected as a major tax at the local government level, property taxes have been used to finance fire and police departments, school districts, local welfare assistance, and a variety of special programs ranging from cemetery care to sewage disposal. In 1978, local governments were scheduled to collect a total of $11.5 billion in property tax revenues. The tax amounted to 27 percent of all city revenues, 40 percent of all county revenues, 47 percent of all school district revenues, and 90 percent of the revenues collected by fire districts.[17]

As the combination of growth and inflation affected California, the property tax grew proportionately large and unpopular. One national study found that the tax amounted to $32 per $1,000 personal income in

1942, only 89 percent of the national average; but by 1976, it doubled to $63 per $1,000 personal income and 142 percent of the national average.[18] Moreover, while property values nearly tripled between 1968 and 1978, property taxes climbed almost as high. Local governments played the numbers game of lowering property tax rates slightly every year, although the actual taxes collected skyrocketed as a result of the higher assessed values of properties. The stage was set for a revolt in the Golden State.

California's lawmakers attempted to quell public anger before the tax issue became an election issue. In 1977, it became clear that the state would have a surplus for the foreseeable future. Although Governor Jerry Brown and the legislature attempted to devise tax relief legislation, they could not agree. Throughout 1977, the governor insisted on a plan designed to give maximum relief to renters (about half of the state's dwellers) and low-income families, while opponents in the state Senate wanted an approach giving more assistance to homeowners.

Meanwhile, as the state government fumbled about, political activist Howard Jarvis promoted a citizen-sponsored initiative providing much more extensive tax relief than any plan contemplated by the governor or legislature. In December 1977, Jarvis and his Sacramento-based ally, Paul Gann, collected 1,200,000 signatures (more than double the amount needed) to qualify their property tax relief initiative for the June 1978 election. Pressure mounted on state officials to counter Jarvis with some immediate relief. The voters now had a choice, and the officials knew it.

The state government remained paralyzed in the early months of 1978. Even though Governor Brown abandoned his low-income assistance "circuit-breaker" approach, the legislature remained split into several factions. Finally, in late March, the legislature placed a modest tax relief measure on the June ballot which reduced property taxes for homeowners by 32 percent. Despite the fanfare from organized business, labor, and government leaders alike, the legislature's counterproposal was soon seen as "too little, too late," as the ballot initiative paled beside the 57 percent relief (amounting to $7 billion) provided in the Jarvis initiative. Clearly, Howard Jarvis was now the man of the hour.

The California taxpayers' revolt and Howard Jarvis became inseparable themes in 1978. While Jarvis did not place the question of excessive taxation on the public agenda, he played a valuable role in convincing the voters of the issue's importance. As the June elections for state offices neared, more debate surrounded noncandidate Jarvis and his tax relief proposal than any of the candidates contesting California's elected positions. Praised by some as a messiah and chastised by others as a demagogue, Jarvis emerged as a leading citizen activist in 1978.

Who was Howard Jarvis? In California politics, he was long considered by many as a gadfly for conservative causes. After retiring as a wealthy newspaper publisher and manufacturer in 1962, Jarvis lost handily in his bid to win the Republican nomination to the United States Senate. He suffered the same fate in 1972 when seeking the Republican nomination to the state's elected tax agency, the Board of Equalization. In 1977, Jarvis ran for mayor of Los Angeles but finished far down the list.

Poor showings at the polls were of little concern to Jarvis. He used his candidacies as an ongoing forum to hammer away at excessive taxation and big government. Moreover, Jarvis contended, he was now resorting to the initiative process because "the people are fed up with politicians and their promises."[19] For fifteen years, Jarvis pursued his objectives with little public fanfare.

As public resentment toward government officials grew, many who previously ridiculed Jarvis for his unconventional behavior paid tribute to him in 1978. (One gubernatorial candidate actually promised a state appointment to Jarvis if elected, but the candidate failed to win his party's nomination.) Over and over, Jarvis canvassed the state to relate his own tax miseries to those of the general public. Describing himself

Howard Jarvis

as "a rugged bastard who's had his head kicked in a thousand times by the government,"[20] Howard Jarvis became a household word in California. Now serving as the paid director of the Apartment Association of Los Angeles, the 75-year-old activist offered a permanent tax relief plan which would give help to all and promised that California would be the starting point for a nationwide wave of taxpayer revolts. "I'm not interested in my own taxes," Jarvis said at one point. "I'm not gonna be here much longer to pay taxes. What I'm concerned about is the thousands of people—both elderly people in drastic situations and the young people who have no way to build anything for themselves. These people need help."[21] Apparently millions of Californians had similar concerns.

The battle over property tax relief began in earnest during the early months of 1978. Ultimately, the voters were presented with two radically different alternatives on the June ballot. In December 1977, Jarvis submitted his initiative petition to the secretary of state, who subsequently numbered the proposed law as Proposition 13. Under its provisions, the initiative limited all property taxes to one percent of the market value for the 1975–76 fiscal year. Homeowners, apartment building owners, and businesses of all sizes would qualify for local property tax reductions averaging 57 percent. In the future, county assessors would be permitted to raise property values for cost-of-living purposes by no more than 2 percent during any single year. (For example, a house worth $100,000 one year could be raised in value to $102,000 the next year, with the one percent tax adjusted accordingly.) Only when the property was resold could the tax assessor reappraise the house or business at current market value. If passed, Proposition 13 would slash property taxes by $7 billion.

In Sacramento, the legislature finally produced its own tax reduction proposal in March 1978. Known as Proposition 8, the legislature's measure would reduce property taxes on all owner-occupied homes by approximately 32 percent. Apartment building owners, businesses, and corporate interests would continue to pay property taxes at the current rates, thus providing for what became known as a "split assessment roll" (one assessment rate for businesses, a lower assessment rate for homeowners). Whereas Proposition 13 offered no direct relief to renters, Proposition 8 gave the state's renters a tax credit of $75 per taxpayer. If passed, Proposition 8 would cut residential property taxes by $1.4 billion.

As the voters contemplated the two alternatives, various organizations and political personalities voiced their own opinions on tax relief in California. A citizens group headed by Jarvis called the United Organization of Taxpayers actively promoted the initiative along with dozens of homeowners associations across the state. The California Farm Bureau, an organization consisting of the largest agricultural interests in the state, sided with Jarvis early in the Proposition 13 campaign. Most of the half-dozen candidates for the Republican gubernatorial nomination also expressed support for the proposition. Contrary to the concerns of crippled government, Jarvis pointed to the several billion dollar surplus in Sacramento and promised that the $7 billion in tax reductions represented only some of the "fat" in government. Thousands of bumper stickers expressed support for the Jarvis measure with the slogan: "Save the American dream. Vote for Proposition 13."

Despite considerable grass-roots support for Proposition 13, the list of well-known opponents to the measure (and proponents of Proposition 8) was much more substantial and diverse than that favoring the initiative. Governor Brown and a lopsided majority of the legislature criticized the Jarvis measure as an attempt to dismantle state and local governments. Virtually all city and county government units along with local boards of education and police and fire departments took issue with Proposition 13 for the extensive cuts the initiative would make in the local tax base. Outside the public sector, the *Los Angeles Times*, the state's most respected and widely read newspaper, charged in an editorial that "enactment of Proposition 13 would create fiscal havoc among cities and counties in California, and the new and higher state taxes necessary to restore their stability would fall heaviest on those whom the initiative purports to benefit."[22] Organized labor and a majority of leaders in the corporate sector also joined the fight against the Jarvis initiative. The state's major financial institutions, insurance companies, and utilities raised more than $1 million to oppose Proposition 13, even though the business sector would receive two-thirds of the total tax savings from the proposed change. Before the campaign was over, the "No on 13" committees had outspent the "Yes on 13" committees by a margin of two to one. Thus, on paper the opponents seemed to be in a position to defeat the Jarvis tax relief measure. Yet, they were not able to do so.

During the early course of the tax relief battle, public opinion remained indecisive on the Jarvis issue. In March 1978, for example, a *Los Angeles Times* survey found that 35 percent of those interviewed favored Proposition 13, 27 percent opposed it, and 38 percent remained undecided. By late May, however, public opinion had shifted decisively in the direction of the proposed change with 52 percent in favor, 35 percent against, and 13 percent undecided.

The breaking point on the tax relief question came three weeks before the June elections. In mid-May, the Los Angeles County tax assessor sent out the latest tax assessments to the 1.7 million property owners in the county. Because Los Angeles county contains 35 percent of the state's

population, voter sentiment there was particularly crucial to the up-coming election. Fuming over new property tax hikes of 100 percent and more, thousands of residents converged on the assessor's office in pro-test. For Howard Jarvis, the timing could not have been better. Publicly calling upon the state's voters to reject the smaller cuts suggested by the legislature, Jarvis reminded the voters of their opportunity to directly affect public policy: "We have the people's amendment [in Proposition 13]. . . . This is the first time since the Boston Tea Party that we have a chance to vote for ourselves . . ."[23] Jarvis's cry was heard around the state.

On June 6, 1978, California voters went to the polls in record numbers. The results were convincing. While Proposition 8 lost by 53 percent to 47 percent, Proposition 13 carried a near two-to-one majority, 65 percent to 35 percent. Moreover, the "Yes on 13" vote was equally distributed, with 55 of the state's 58 counties in support of the measure.

As for Howard Jarvis, the guiding force behind Proposition 13 emerged as a hero to millions. Basking in the success of his first political victory on election night, Jarvis summarized his triumph as the will of the people when he stated: "Tonight was a victory against money, the politicians, [and] the government."[24] For Howard Jarvis, it was also the night when his public image changed from conservative gadfly to political folk hero.

The property tax issue in California illustrates the power of citizen politics under the most difficult circumstances imaginable. The coalition behind Proposition 13 was ridiculed by leaders in the public and private sectors alike, condemned by the press, and outspent by a two-to-one margin. Yet, Proposition 13 became public policy in 1978. Why? First, a substantial portion of the California electorate lost confidence in the state's elected officials. Polls prior to the election indicated that voters felt taken for granted by the state and local governments. Many thought that Proposition 8 would never have been placed on the ballot had not Jarvis and his colleagues qualified Proposition 13. Thus, the voters wanted to teach government leaders a lesson on who *really* controls the public purse. Second, the voters saw the Jarvis initiative as a way to act fast. Jarvis presented them with a simple approach to a complicated problem, and the voters bought it. Third, the governor and legislature allowed the tax question to remain unsolved on the public agenda for too long; both underestimated the hostility of the public. Once an issue like excessive taxation is prominent on the public agenda, policy makers must respond to it.

Under normal conditions, officials who fail to respond might find themselves defeated in the next election. In California politics, however, the state has an initiative process that makes it possible for voters to qualify an issue for the ballot. Instead of just sending the state's policy makers a message, the voters assumed the policy-making role. At least in the field of property tax relief, Californians saw citizen politics become citizen government in 1978.

Proposition 13 in Perspective: A Mixed Bag of Tax Reform

On the surface, Proposition 13 brought substantial and immediate tax relief to California. In addition to property tax cuts of $7 billion, 100,000 jobs were eliminated from state and local governments. Far from the predicted aftershock of a statewide recession, the private sector boomed and incorporated most of those whose public jobs were terminated. To this extent, "doomsday" predictions were far off the mark. Nevertheless, many state officials continued to forecast that the huge state surplus of the late 1970's, now used to bail out depleted local governments, would be gone by the 1980–1981 fiscal year. Only then, they suggested, would Californians feel the wrath of the tax change.

If Proposition 13's passage failed to cause economic chaos in California, it also failed to bring much relief to homeowners. In July 1979, one study showed that of the $7 billion in reduced property taxes, only $1 billion was saved by California homeowners. The remaining $6 billion went to out-of-state property owners ($1 billion), apartment owners ($400 million), California corporations ($1.4 billion), increased state income taxes ($1 billion), and increased federal income taxes ($2.2 billion). Stated another way, the outcome of this public policy change was considerably different from the promises made by the proponents of Proposition 13. Such phenomena are known to occur in the public policy process.

Public Policy Assessed: Putting It Together

Few facets of any society remain unchanged for long. As our society and government have become more complex, the relationship between the two has become more intertwined. Public policy studies the connections between what society needs and what government produces. Clearly, the two components are intimately associated.

The study of public policy seems to reaffirm the pluralists' contention that government is not an institution totally removed from the citizens. Indeed, despite the ruling-elite view, our institutions are representative and accountable on many issues. On some occasions, policies may favor one sector of society; on other occasions, policies may benefit another sector. Inasmuch as domestic public conflicts are usually over scarce resources, such as money or land, the policies that emerge will usually be broad in nature and modest in change.

It is important to remember that while public policy is generally made by government officials, the public remains at both ends of the policy process. Through any of several methods (like personal contacts, demonstrations, public testimonies, electoral outcomes, and the like), individuals and groups place demands on government leaders for new policy directions. While ordinary citizens may be removed from the policy process most of the time, elected and appointed officials must stay attuned to changing public sentiment. As new areas of need arise, it is the task of government to filter and balance competing claims and transform them into public policies.

Should government leaders fail in their responsibility to make acceptable public policies, they may find themselves as election victims of alienated citizens. This happened in 1978, when a number of liberal domestic "spenders" were defeated by voters expressing the mood of "fiscal conservatives." In many instances, citizens have something to say on the acceptability of the policies adopted by government. Moreover, if government policies fail entirely to meet public demands, citizens may enact policies in their own behalf. The California experience discussed above shows how this possibility can become vivid reality.

Just as the public mood shifts in policy areas, government leaders often respond to the public pulse. The difficulty in reading that pulse does not always arise from a lack of concern or interest. The president and Congress, for example, are elected by different constituencies (or publics) and may not share identical perceptions of the same issue. The national struggle over tax reform (the president) versus tax relief (the Congress) shows the difficulty in securing agreement over public policy. Even when policy commitments are finally determined, the bureaucracy and other interests may delay implementation for years and sometimes decades.

Nevertheless, even if change is slow, change can be accomplished. And in the area of public policy, citizens may assume substantial responsibility for ordering priorities and directing the results of the policy process.

Key Terms

pork barrel legislation

Notes

1. Thomas Dye, *Understanding Public Policy*, 3d ed. (Englewood Cliffs, N.J.: Prentice-Hall, 1978), pp. 3–5.

2. James E. Anderson, David W. Brady, and Charles Bullock, III, *Public Policy and Politics in America* (North Scituate, Mass.: Duxbury Press, 1978), p. 4.

3. David A. Caputo, *Politics and Public Policy in America* (Philadelphia: Lippincott, 1974), p. 105.

4. Charles R. Adrian, *State and Local Governments*, 4th ed. (New York: McGraw-Hill, 1976), p. 134.

5. Theodore Lowi argues that there are three major types of public policy: distributive, regulatory, and redistributive. In all three areas, however, government is called upon to use its authority in ways that will affect society. See "American Business, Public Policy, Case-Studies, and Political Theory," *World Politics*, July 1964, pp. 677–715.

6. George Edwards and Ira Sharkansky, *The Policy Predicament* (San Francisco: Freeman, 1978), p. 183.

7. Marcia M. Lee, "The Equal Rights Amendment: Public Policy Making by Means of a Constitutional Amendment," in David A. Caputo, ed., *The Politics of Policy Making in America* (San Francisco: Freeman, 1977), p. 26.

8. Allan P. Sindler, *Bakke, Defunis, and Minority Admissions* (New York: Longman, 1978), p. 18.

9. Edwards and Sharkansky, *The Policy Predicament*, pp. 243–244.

10. "Special Message to Congress on Taxes," as quoted in the *New York Times*, 21 January 1978.

11. "President Submits Tax Cut Plan for 'Fairer and Simpler' System," *New York Times*, 22 January 1978.

12. "Political Demand Exceeds Supply of Economic Logic," *New York Times*, 23 July 1978.

13. "Congress Approves $18.7 billion Tax Cut," *Congressional Quarterly Weekly Reports*, 21 October 1978, p. 3027.

14. Ibid.

15. "Momentum for Tax Cut," *New York Times*, 17 July 1978.

16. "Poll Discloses Property Tax Cuts Are Widely Backed Around The Nation," *New York Times*, 28 June 1978.

17. "Ballot Proposition Analysis," *California Journal*, May 1978, p. 6.

18. "Sound and Fury over Taxes," *Time*, 19 June 1978, p. 19.

19. "Jarvis Initiative Poses Headache for Candidates," *Los Angeles Times*, 16 January 1978.

20. "Maniac or Messiah?" *Time*, 19 June 1978, p. 21.

21. "Jarvis Riding a Whirlwind and Loving It," *Los Angeles Times*, 23 January 1978.

22. Ibid., 6 February 1978.

23. Ibid., 17 May 1978.

24. "Sound and Fury over Taxes," *Time*, 19 June 1978, p. 13.

Recommended Reading

ANDERSON, JAMES E., DAVID W. BRADY, and CHARLES BULLOCK III, *Public Policy and Politics in America*. North Scituate, Mass.: Duxbury Press, 1978.

BRIGHAM, JOHN, ed. *Making Public Policy*. Lexington, Mass.: D. C. Heath, 1977.

Dye, Thomas. *Understanding Public Policy*. 3rd ed. Englewood Cliffs, N.J.: Prentice-Hall, 1978.

Edwards, George, and Ira Sharkansky. *The Policy Predicament*. San Francisco: Freeman, 1978.

Jones, Charles O. *An Introduction to the Study of Public Policy*. North Scituate, Mass.: Duxbury Press, 1977.

Lindblom, Charles E. *The Policy-Making Process*. Englewood Cliffs, N.J.: Prentice-Hall, 1968.

Lineberry, Robert. *American Public Policy*. New York: Harper and Row, 1977.

Lowi, Theodore. *The End of Liberalism*. New York: W. W. Norton, 1969.

Sharkansky, Ira, and Donald Van Meter. *Policy and Politics in American Governments*. New York: McGraw-Hill, 1975.

Starling, Grover. *The Politics and Economics of Public Policy*. Homewood, Ill.: The Dorsey Press, 1979.

14

American Foreign Policy: Constraints and Challenges

Although the affairs of foreign nations may seem remote to us, our lives are increasingly dependent on what these other nations do. Despite our preoccupation with domestic policies and how we can influence them, the quality and security of our lives is inexorably bound up with decisions and events that take place thousands of miles from our shores. The "energy crisis" of recent years, for example, reminds us of our growing dependence on imported oil and its effects on our economy. When American citizens protest the slaughter of baby seals or whales by other countries, or express alarm at the denial of human rights in South Africa and elsewhere, they are acknowledging the impact of foreign affairs on their lives.

At the same time, the growing interaction among peoples of different nations can expand our sense of personal impotency. Our occasional feelings of despair at the remoteness of government in Washington or in our state capitals pales beside our seeming incapacity to affect the course of world events. Through foreign travel and the influence of television, we are becoming increasingly aware of the hopes, problems, and conditions of people in other lands, and yet we seem to have few corresponding channels through which to translate our awareness into meaningful actions. We are becoming increasingly citizens of the world, facing both new challenges and new frustrations.

Like other countries, the United States has had to wrestle with the problem of deciding what its foreign policy goals should be and how they should be achieved. Although some Americans may believe that these goals are etched in granite, they have undergone numerous changes in response to developments in both international and domestic affairs.

Indeed, the foreign policy of the United States has reflected a variety of goals and activities. It has included not only policies aimed at preserving America's security, but also policies aimed at advancing the country's broad economic interests and its values and ideals. Foreign policy, after all, involves more than ensuring a nation's defense. It represents the sum total of the goals and decisions a country pursues in its relations with other nations of the world. At times, these goals and decisions may clash. The United States may support democratic principles, for example, and yet give aid to dictatorial regimes as part of its overall defense strategy. Defining what the goals of American foreign policy should be has concerned U.S. policy makers and sparked domestic disagreements ever since the nation was founded more than two centuries ago.

In this chapter, we will take a closer look at foreign affairs as an important aspect of American policy making. We will briefly consider how this country's international role has changed over the past two centuries and who has the major responsibility for determining what that role will be in the future. And because all of us are affected in one form or another by international developments, we will also briefly consider the relationship of public opinion to foreign policy.

The Evolution of American Foreign Policy

Like many of the new countries of Africa and Asia in this century, the United States during the first decades of its existence was concerned mainly with protecting its newfound independence and restricting its involvement in the power struggles of other nations. In his farewell address in 1796, George Washington insisted that the United States should "steer clear of permanent alliances" with European countries. "Europe," he proclaimed, "has a set of primary interests which to us have none or a very remote relation. Hence she must be engaged in frequent controversies, the causes of which are essentially foreign to our concerns."

Such advice, however, was not taken to imply that the United States would completely ignore the rest of the world. In the Western Hemisphere, for example, the United States gradually began to carve out a major role. The 1823 *Monroe Doctrine* proclaimed that countries in the Western Hemisphere were off limits to European powers and that any interference in the affairs of Latin American nations would be viewed by the United States as an unfriendly act, "dangerous to our peace and safety." In return, the United States promised not to meddle in the internal affairs of Europe.

As the country's military and industrial power grew, the Monroe Doctrine became the justification for active U.S. involvement throughout the Western Hemisphere. It was interpreted to mean that the United States alone had a right to intervene in the political and economic affairs of Central American and Caribbean countries. President Theodore Roosevelt largely summed up this view by concluding that the United States had a "sacred duty" to exercise an "international police power" in the Western Hemisphere. Thus, partly to quell local rebellions and partly to protect overseas investments, the United States during the late nineteenth and early twentieth centuries sent troops into Mexico, Cuba, the Dominican Republic, Nicaragua, and Haiti. In 1903, it connived with local revolutionaries to obtain the right to construct and fortify the Panama Canal, making the new state of Panama a virtual outpost of the United States. Needless to say, these actions did not sit well with many people in Latin America, who charged the United States with practicing "Yankee imperialism."

The most dramatic aspect of U.S. foreign policy during the nineteenth century, however, was the struggle to gain dominance over the North American continent and to expand the nation's influence and trade in the Pacific. In a sustained effort to extend its borders, the United States purchased the Louisiana Territory from France, fought battles with Indian tribes to acquire western lands, annexed Texas, and seized California and parts of the American Southwest in the war with Mexico (1846–48). It also purchased Alaska from Russia, annexed the Hawaiian Islands, and acquired the Philippines, Guam, and Puerto Rico in the Spanish-American War (1898). To gain a share of the growing China trade, the United States insisted on equal commercial opportunities with the European powers in the "open door" policy of 1899.

To many Americans at the time, this military and economic expansionism was viewed as the nation's *manifest destiny*, as a righteous cause linked to the will of God. It is "our manifest destiny," *New York Morning News* editor John L. O'Sullivan boasted in 1845, "to overspread and to possess the whole of the continent which providence has given us for the development of the great experiment in liberty and federative self-government entrusted to us." Annexing the Philippines, President William McKinley reflected later, was a decision reached through prayer "to educate the Filipinos, and uplift and civilize and Christianize them, and, by God's grace, do the very best we could by them, as our fellow men for whom Christ also died." While there were many Americans who found this righteous crusade hard to swallow, others saw it as a natural corollary to America's expanding power and wealth.

A Reluctant World Power

If Washington's earlier advice still carried any weight, it was seen in the United States' continued neutrality toward Europe. Although the Spanish-American War and the acquisition of the Philippines and other territories signified expanded American involvement overseas, the United States largely held itself aloof from Europe's internal affairs. Even when war broke out in Europe in 1914, President Woodrow Wilson resolved that the United States would remain isolated from the conflict. In a speech reminiscent of Washington's farewell address, Wilson stated that "The United States must be impartial in fact as well as in name. . . . We must be impartial in thought as well as in action, must put a curb upon our sentiments as well as upon every transaction that might be construed as a preference of one party to the struggle before another."

But as American sympathies toward Great Britain and its allies began to grow and as Germany persisted in sinking American ships crossing the Atlantic, the United States found it increasingly difficult to support a position of neutrality. In 1917, the United States entered the war. America's participation then became, as with its manifest destiny earlier, a moral cause. World War I, Wilson declared, was a "war to end all wars," a noble crusade "to make the world safe for democracy."

This crusading zeal toward Europe did not last for long, however. Following the war, the Senate rejected the Treaty of Versailles and American membership in the new League of Nations, and the country retreated into isolationism. The United States focused its attention on such domestic matters as prohibition and the Depression, and concerned itself on the international front with signing treaties outlawing war (the Kellogg-Briand Peace Pact of 1928) and passing Neutrality Acts (1935–1937) barring U.S. support of any "belligerent nation." As historians have noted, during the two decades after World War I, most Americans clearly had no desire to enter into another foreign conflict unless the United States' own security was at stake.

But the spread of Nazism in Europe and the Japanese attack on Pearl Harbor on December 7, 1941, once again forced America to abandon its neutral position. The United States found itself engaged in a major war in both Europe and the Pacific, with an overriding interest in international developments and concern over America's security.

The war also had a long-term effect on America's international role. By the end of the war in 1945, the United States had become a superpower among nations. Having ushered in the nuclear age by exploding the world's first atomic bomb and having escaped the widespread devastation that afflicted Europe and Asia, the United States faced global responsibilities previously unknown in its history. In addition to helping rebuild the war-ravaged economies of Europe and fashioning a new constitution for Japan, the United States became involved in a *cold war* with its wartime ally, the Soviet Union.

The Doctrine of Containment

In his now-famous "iron curtain" speech delivered in Fulton, Missouri, in 1946, Winston Churchill criticized the Soviet Union's territorial advances in Eastern Europe. "From Stettin in the Baltic to Trieste in the Adriatic," he thundered, "an iron curtain has descended across the continent. . . . Warsaw, Berlin, Prague, Vienna, Budapest, Belgrade, Bucharest, and Sofia, all the famous cities and the populations around them lie in the Soviet sphere and all are subject in one form or another . . . to a very high and increasing control from Moscow."

Many top American policy makers agreed with Churchill's remarks, fearing that the Soviet Union was bent on world domination. They believed that it was the duty of the United States to defend the world against further Soviet expansionism and adopted a policy of *containment* designed to prevent the emergence of new communist regimes. Perhaps the most influential spokesman of containment was George F. Kennan, a high-ranking U.S. diplomat who first elaborated the policy in a 1947 article in *Foreign Affairs* magazine. Kennan argued that "the main element in any United States policy toward the Soviet Union must be that of a long-term, patient but firm and vigilant containment of Russian expansive tendencies."[1]

This policy of containment was first given substance in the *Truman Doctrine* of 1947. To prevent a possible communist takeover in Greece and Turkey, Truman proposed that the United States provide direct economic and military assistance to these two nations. "I believe that it must be the policy of the United States," Truman stated, "to support free peoples who are resisting attempted subjugation by armed minorities or by outside pressures." Congress agreed and voted over $400 million in aid to the Greek and Turkish governments.

The Truman Doctrine was soon expanded into a massive economic recovery program for all Western Europe. Through the *Marshall Plan* (named after Secretary of State George Marshall), sixteen European nations were given over $17 billion in economic aid between 1948 and 1952. The plan was an apparent success, for by 1953 the industrial output of the participating nations had risen above prewar levels. Since then, the United States has forged a series of foreign aid programs, pouring close to $200 billion into more than one hundred countries around the world.[2] While many have criticized such aid as a massive "give-away," it has been justified both on humanitarian grounds and as a means of gaining support for U.S. policies from recipient nations.

Security Through Alliances

In the opinion of most policy makers, however, foreign aid programs were not enough. Containment also required collective defense arrangements between the United States and other noncommunist countries. Thus, in 1949, the United States entered into its first peacetime European military alliance, the North Atlantic Treaty Organization (NATO). The NATO allies, comprising the United States, Canada, and ten Western European nations (followed later by Greece and Turkey), pledged to "unite their efforts for collective defense." They agreed that "an armed attack against one or more of them in Europe or North America shall be considered an attack against them all."

This collective defense approach was extended to other regions of the world when the United States also formally aligned itself with countries

of Latin America (OAS, 1948), with Australia and New Zealand (ANZUS, 1951), and with the countries of Southeast Asia (SEATO, 1954). In addition, the United States concluded mutual defense pacts with South Korea, the Philippines, Taiwan, and Japan. The Soviet Union, meanwhile, formed the Warsaw Pact (1955) with the countries of Eastern Europe.

Thus, by the 1950s, the United States had come a long way from the isolationism of the late eighteenth and early nineteenth centuries. Despite George Washington's advice to "steer clear of permanent alliances with any portion of the foreign world," the United States found itself tied economically, politically, and militarily to more than forty nations around the globe. Its top policy-making officials had adopted a strong anticommunist ideology to give additional credence to its expanded role in the international arena.

International Conflicts: Korea and the Cuban Missile Crisis

America's containment policies at times involved the United States in open conflict. In June 1948, the Soviet Union stopped all rail and road traffic into Berlin, which lay deep within the Soviet zone of Germany. The United States responded quickly to the blockade by airlifting supplies into the city. Before the blockade finally ended in 1949, the cold war had come very close to getting hot.

In the same period, Chinese communist forces under Mao Tse-tung crushed the nationalist forces of Chiang Kai-shek and established a communist regime in China. In 1949, the Soviet Union exploded its first atomic bomb. Then, in June 1950, communist North Korea invaded South Korea. The United States, together with fifteen other nations fighting under the United Nations flag, intervened on the side of South Korea. After three years of war, at a cost of more than 54,000 American, 14,000 allied, and untold numbers of Korean and Chinese lives, a stalemated truce was signed, with the borders between North and South Korea virtually unchanged. Domestically, the war had sparked a great deal of bitter debate. Some critics argued that the United States should have gone all out to win the war and should not have stopped short of invading North Korea and using nuclear weapons against China (which had backed North Korea); others insisted that repelling the invasion of a country ruled by a repressive right-wing regime hardly justified the loss of so many lives. Amid this debate, the United States committed itself to stationing thousands of American soldiers in South Korea as part of that country's continued defense.

Nor was Korea the end of American military engagements. On several other occasions in the 1950s (including Guatemala in 1954 and Lebanon in 1958), the United States intervened to prevent communist regimes from coming to power.

In fact, it seemed only a matter of time before the world would be hurled into a nuclear crisis. The time came in 1962, when Soviet-made missiles were detected in Cuba only ninety miles from the United States mainland. After weighing various alternatives, President Kennedy ordered a naval blockade of Cuba and warned that a Cuban-based missile attack on the United States would result in an immediate counterattack on the Soviet Union. Faced with the prospect of nuclear war, the Soviet Union agreed to remove the missiles from Cuba, and the blockade was lifted.[3] According to some observers, the United States' success in confronting the Soviet Union in Cuba helped boost America's confidence in its military and foreign policy capabilities—a confidence that carried it further into the mire of Vietnam.

The War in Vietnam

Vietnam was, in some respects, the logical and tragic result of U.S. containment policies. The guerrilla insurgency in Vietnam was widely viewed, not merely as a nationalist, anticolonialist movement, but as an example of the larger threat of world communism. Many top U.S. officials subscribed to the *domino theory,* which held that a failure to thwart communist advances anywhere in the world would only inspire similar advances elsewhere. If Vietnam "fell" to communism, they argued, then other nations in Southeast Asia would collapse like a row of dominoes.

American involvement in Vietnam grew gradually over a ten-year period. In 1954, Vietnam had won its war of liberation against France and had signed what became known as the Geneva Accords. These agreements provided for a temporary division of the country into a North Vietnam and a South Vietnam, pending free elections in 1956 to unite Vietnam under one government. (Although the United States participated in the Geneva talks, it did not sign the accords.) However, South Vietnam, headed by Ngo Dinh Diem and backed by the United States, refused to hold the elections, concerned that the communists might come to power. In response to this refusal, and to the fact that Diem's regime was becoming increasingly corrupt and autocratic, guerilla warfare erupted. By 1957, communist guerillas (the Viet Cong) had expanded their attacks throughout the south, with support provided by North Vietnam.

Fearing that an insurrection would topple Diem's government and lead to a communist takeover, Presidents Eisenhower and Kennedy stepped up military and economic aid. By November 1963, the month Kennedy was assassinated, more than 16,000 U.S. military "advisers" were stationed in Vietnam. Following Diem's assassination in 1963, and with divisions growing within the government, the Saigon regime appeared on the verge of collapse. Determined to prevent the country from falling into communist hands, President Johnson decided to commit American combat forces and to bomb North Vietnam. By 1968, American troops in Vietnam numbered more than 540,000, and the extensive bombing of North Vietnam had discharged more tons of explosives than were dropped on all enemy territory during World War II.

During the next four years, under President Nixon, American troops were slowly but gradually withdrawn and replaced by South Vietnamese troops, a policy Nixon dubbed "Vietnamization." This policy was part of the larger *Nixon Doctrine*, which held that the United States would honor its commitments but that other nations would have to bear the military burden of their own defense. The war, however, did not wind down. American troops were dispatched into Cambodia (1970), while Nixon increased the deployment and use of American air and naval power. In 1972, the massive aerial bombardment of North Vietnam was resumed, and the harbors of Haiphong and other northern cities were mined—all in an apparent effort to drive the North Vietnamese to the peace table. Finally, in 1973, a cease-fire agreement was signed, and the last U.S. troops were withdrawn. Despite administration hopes, however, that the South Vietnamese regime could sustain itself, the Saigon government in 1975 collapsed under a North Vietnamese offensive. The two Vietnams were reunited as the Socialist Republic of Vietnam, while America's allies in Cambodia and Laos were overrun by communist guerrila forces.

Dissent over the war divided the American people more than had any other conflict since the Civil War. America's support for a series of corrupt and repressive regimes, the questionable right of the United States to become involved in what seemed a local political struggle, and the reports of napalm bombing and the massacre of civilians at My Lai and elsewhere fueled a mounting wave of angry protest against the war. Protestors staged demonstration marches, teach-ins, and peace rallies, and engaged in violent confrontations in an effort to bring the war to an end.

Indeed, the war had been extremely costly to both the American and the Vietnamese people. By the time the war ended in 1975, the United States had lost more than 56,000 lives, suffered more than 300,000 wounded, and spent more than $140 billion. The total number of Vietnamese casualties will probably never be known, although most reports

place the number of North and South Vietnamese dead at more than a million. In the process of trying to "save" the Vietnamese from communism, the United States almost succeeded in destroying them. Particularly disturbing were the revelations that Henry Kissinger and other top officials believed America needed to show the communist nations that we could be as brutal as anyone, that these nations would have to bear an unacceptably high price for instigating insurgencies.[4] (A similar kind of view, ironically, was expressed by Chinese leaders following China's sudden invasion of Vietnam in early 1979. The invasion, they said, was necessary to "punish" Vietnam for its military action in Cambodia several months earlier.)

The final irony was that the Vietnam War (the longest in American history) was never officially declared by Congress. The legal basis for the buildup of American forces was provided by the so-called Tonkin Gulf Resolution. After American naval ships patrolling off the coast of Vietnam had been reportedly fired on by North Vietnamese PT boats in 1964 (later evidence indicated that reports of the attack had been greatly exaggerated), President Johnson asked for congressional support in taking retaliatory action. By an overwhelming vote, Congress passed the Tonkin Gulf Resolution, giving Johnson authority "to take all necessary measures" to prevent further aggression in Southeast Asia. Although the resolution was repealed in 1970, it served as the chief legal basis for U.S. involvement in its most disastrous war.

Détente and Arms Control

Following the debacle in Vietnam, many top U.S. policy makers concluded that America's containment crusade had to be modified. Despite this country's enormous military and economic power, it could no longer expect to impose its ideology on the world or maintain its we-will-go-anywhere policies of the previous decades. The Nixon Doctrine, which stated that the United States could not respond with troops to every communist advance, represented a major reassessment of America's twenty-year policy of containment. Instead of simply trying to contain communism as a matter of ideology, U.S. foreign policy would be based on "realism," on pursuit of America's own long-term economic and defense interests.

Thus, while continuing to stress a powerful defense posture, the United States in the 1970s began to place increased emphasis on improving its relations with the major communist powers. In 1972, President Nixon flew to China, ending several decades of official "nonrecognition" of the most populous nation on earth. Many Americans were startled to see Nixon, the old "cold war warrior," engaged in amiable conversations with Chairman Mao and other Chinese leaders. The visit paved the way for more extended contacts and led eventually to the establishment of formal diplomatic ties in 1979.

Similarly, in its relations with the Soviet Union, the United States began actively to pursue a policy of *détente*, of trying to thaw the cold war tensions between the two nations. Following his trip to Peking, President Nixon journeyed to Moscow for a summit meeting with Soviet party chief Leonid Brezhnev. While in Moscow, Nixon signed the Strategic Arms Limitations Talks (SALT) agreement, setting limits on nuclear weapons.

To many observers, the 1972 SALT agreement represented a major step forward in United States–Soviet relations. For many years, the two superpowers have accepted a policy of *strategic deterrence*. This policy assumes that peace can be maintained so long as each side possesses enough nuclear capability to deter the other side from attacking. So long as each adversary deploys enough weapons to kill everyone on the planet several times over—so long as there is a sufficient "balance of terror"—an all-out attack by either side would be self-defeating. This strategy, however, not only guarantees a spiraling arms race (to prevent either side from gaining an overwhelming superiority), but perpetuates mutual fear and suspicion. It also leaves open the possibility of an accidental nuclear war, stemming from a faulty radar signal, a misguided missile, or even a mentally unstable bomber pilot. And as more nations achieve a nuclear capability, the dangers of such an accidental war are multiplied.

Since the late 1940s, the United States has participated in a number of arms-control conferences in an effort to avoid a nuclear catastrophe. The first major breakthrough came in 1963, when the United States, the Soviet Union, and more than one hundred other nations signed the Limited Nuclear Test Ban Treaty, prohibiting above-ground testing of nuclear weapons (China and France did not sign). This was followed by the 1967 International Treaty on the Peaceful Uses of Outer Space, which banned the use of satellites to launch nuclear weapons, and the 1968 Nuclear Nonproliferation Treaty, which limited the transfer of nuclear weapons to nations that were not already members of the "atomic club." None of these treaties, however, confronted the central problem of reducing the growing arsenal of nuclear weapons held by the United States and the Soviet Union.

Thus, in 1969, the Strategic Arms Limitations Talks (SALT) were begun in Helsinki, Finland. As signed by President Nixon and Soviet leader Brezhnev in Moscow in 1972, the SALT treaty limited the de-

ployment of defensive antiballistic missile systems and placed a five-year freeze on the number of strategic offensive weapons each side could possess.

Further SALT negotiations continued during both the Ford and Carter administrations. The United States and the Soviet Union worked toward a new treaty that would further limit their nuclear stockpiles. Finally, after seven years of ardous bargaining, a second agreement (SALT II) was signed by President Carter and Soviet leader Brezhnev in Vienna in June 1979. The SALT II treaty limited each side to 2,250 long-range missiles and bombers by the end of 1985. It also placed restrictions on missile sizes, limited the introduction of new strategic weapons, and set guidelines for continuing the process toward an even more comprehensive SALT III agreement.

The treaty, however, faced a tough fight for approval in the U.S. Senate. The Senate threatened to add several "killer amendments" to the treaty that would be unacceptable to the Soviets, thereby sinking both the treaty and the entire SALT process. Some senators, for example, criticized the treaty on the grounds that it failed to halt the arms race. They pointed out that the treaty still permitted both countries to expand their nuclear arsenals (see Table 14-1). Other senators lambasted the treaty on the grounds that the United States was making too many concessions to the Soviet Union, allowing it to maintain or even gain superiority in nuclear warheads. In addition, with the fall of the American-backed Shah of Iran in 1978 and the loss of American monitoring stations, some Senate critics worried about how the United States could verify Soviet compliance with the treaty. President Carter, however, responded in his address to Congress that the treaty would impose "equal ceilings" on both countries' nuclear arsenals, "slow

Table 14-1. SALT II and the Arms Race

	Current U.S. Arsenal	Current Soviet Arsenal	What SALT II Allows
All strategic nuclear delivery vehicles (missiles and bombers)	2,060	2,570	2,250
Total missiles with multiple, independently targeted reentry vehicles (MIRVs)	1,046	795	1,320
Land-based and submarine-based missiles with MIRVs	1,046	725	1,200
Land-based missiles with MIRVs	550	600	820

Source: Adapted from *Time*, 21 May 1979, p. 24.

down—even reverse—the momentum of the Soviet arms buildup," and make future weapons competition "safer and more predictable."

Indeed, despite the continued arms race, Carter's efforts to win Senate approval of SALT II triggered one of the toughest ratification fights since Woodrow Wilson's losing battle to win Senate approval of the Treaty of Versailles more than half a century earlier. Not only was the SALT struggle in the Senate a major test of Carter's political leadership, but it also signified Congress' growing assertiveness in foreign-policy making, a point to which we will return in a moment.

A Changing World: New Actors in International Politics

The 1970s also brought a growing realization that the world situation could no longer be viewed merely as a "bipolar" conflict between the opposing ideologies of the United States and the communist world. The growing split between the Soviet Union and China, the expanding economic powers of Western Europe, Japan, and the oil-rich Arab states, and the rise of many new Asian and African countries had introduced a "multipolarity" to the world. Many of these countries showed an increased willingness to further their own political and economic goals independent of the superpowers.

Indeed, as the cold war tensions between the United States and the major communist nations appeared to thaw, other areas of the world emerged as major arenas of international conflict. Many of the *Third World* countries of Asia, Africa, Latin America, and the Middle East were being torn by border clashes and political upheavals that threatened to engulf entire regions and undermine the strategic and economic interests of the United States. Problems that had afflicted these countries for centuries—war, poverty, disease, and repression—were increasingly becoming matters of global concern. Many displayed open hostility toward the United States and other western industrialized nations, blaming them for advancing economic policies that victimized the Third World.

Many of these Third World countries were also rapidly arming themselves, spending billions of dollars on sophisticated weapons produced by the United States and other industrialized nations. (For years, the United States has been the world's leading arms merchant. In 1976, for example, U.S. corporations sold close to $13 billion worth of weapons to other nations—more than half of the world total.[5]) Moreover, with the birth of nearly one hundred new nations during the past several decades, the Third World was gaining numerical strength, dominating such organizations as the United Nations. And as their demands grew for a greater share of the world's political and economic resources, U.S. policy makers were forced to reassess this country's foreign policy goals.

To many observers, in fact, the United States' global influence was on the decline. The nation's ability to respond to external pressures had been sapped by the shattering experience of Vietnam and by changes in the international political and economic order. The surprise ouster in 1978 of the American-backed Shah of Iran by the Ayatollah Khomeini and his followers seemed only to highlight the growing impotence of the United States and its fragile relations with the Third World.

OPEC and the Energy Crisis

Perhaps the most dramatic sign of America's changing world position was its growing dependence on imported oil and its seeming vulnerability to events halfway around the world. In 1973, the Arab oil countries, displeased with the pro-Israeli policy of the United States and other countries during the October Middle East War, imposed an embargo halting shipments of oil. Americans suddenly found themselves sitting in long lines at service stations waiting to fill their tanks with ever more expensive gasoline. The quadrupling of the price of oil in a six-month period (from an average of $3 a barrel to more than $11.64) plunged the United States and other countries into a recession marked by a fall in industrial production, rising unemployment, and skyrocketing inflation. Airlines cut flights, gas stations closed, and a national 55-mile-per-hour speed limit was imposed to conserve fuel.

Despite the embargo, however, many Americans believed the "energy crisis" was contrived, that it was used as an excuse by the major oil companies to boost the price of gasoline, quell environmentalists' criticisms, and increase profits. (Indeed, Exxon reported a 39-percent profit rise for the first quarter of 1974; Texaco reported a whopping 123-percent rise.) Following more price hikes in early 1979, Americans found themselves again waiting in long lines at gas stations and again suspecting the oil companies of gouging the American consumer.

Yet, the long gasoline lines and skyrocketing gas prices also dramatized the United States' growing dependence on imported oil. Although the United States is the world's third leading oil producer (behind the Soviet Union and Saudi Arabia), by the late 1970s it was importing close to half of all the petroleum required to meet its needs.

In a sense, the giant American and European oil companies were partly the cause of the "crisis." In the late 1950s, they unilaterally announced they were going to pay less for Middle East oil. The oil-producing nations responded to the announcement by banding together in 1960 as the Organization of Petroleum Exporting Countries (OPEC).[6] They wanted not only more control over prices, but also more control over production. Thus, they moved to nationalize the oil fields by expropriating the refineries and pipelines previously held by the oil companies. Within a decade, the oil-consuming nations were at the mercy of the cartel. OPEC no longer negotiated directly with the oil companies, but set prices at meetings in Geneva and then flatly announced them to the world.

One major aspect of the "energy crisis" was the failure of the United States to anticipate the growing assertiveness of OPEC. When the oil embargo was imposed in 1973, the United States was caught without any long-term energy plan. Even when President Carter in 1977 presented Congress with a national energy policy emphasizing conservation of fuel, it was criticized and virtually torn apart in committee. Congress gutted his energy program, approving only the new Energy Department and a few other proposals.

Yet, as the price of imported oil continued to soar and as the lines grew longer at gas stations, it was Carter who was criticized for a lack of leadership in the energy area. Polls reflected this criticism, showing that public support for his presidency had slipped in 1979 to the same low levels reached by President Nixon as a result of the Watergate scandal and coverup.

Thus, in the summer of 1979, Carter tried again. He conferred with the leaders of the other major oil-consuming nations at a summit meeting in Tokyo and outlined a new domestic energy program in a nationally televised address. To reduce the nation's dependence on imported oil, Carter proposed the creation of a new Energy Security Corporation charged with developing 2.5 million barrels per day of synthetic fuels by 1990. He also called upon Congress to enact a windfall profits tax on the large oil companies to finance the development of new domestic energy sources. In addition, he froze U.S. oil imports at 1977 levels, asked for increased subsidies for mass transit, and sought funds to help the needy cope with rising fuel costs. He even announced a shakeup of his Cabinet, which included the firing of Energy Department Secretary James Schlesinger. And he urged Americans "to take no unnecessary trips, to use car pools or public transportation whenever you can, to park your car one extra day per week, to obey the speed limit and to set your thermostats to save fuel."

Whether all of Carter's energy proposals would be supported by Congress or by the American people, however, seemed doubtful. There was doubt, for example, whether Congress would resist the lobbying efforts of the oil companies and impose a strong windfall profits tax, or whether America's love for the automobile would yield to the call for fuel conservation. Many people were also unhappy with Carter's decision to rely more on nuclear energy and with the fact that making synthetic oil from coal and oil shale would harm the environment. Although most Americans by 1979 said they believed the energy situation was serious,[7] the commitment to reducing the nation's dependence on what Carter called "a thin line of oil tankers" stretching from the Middle East to America was by no means assured.

The Middle East: The Egyptian-Israeli Peace Treaty

America's growing dependence on Arab oil, however, was not the only basis for increased attention on the Middle East. The U.S. commitment to Israel—as arms supplier, business partner, and overseer—also firmly entrenched the United States in the affairs of that region.

The principal issues in the area had long been Israel's security and the fate of the Palestinian people. When the United Nations in 1948 partitioned Palestine into Arab and Israeli states, close to one million Arabs fled Israel, seeking refuge in neighboring Arab countries. Most of the Arab countries, however, refused to accept the Palestinians into their societies, while Israel was unwilling to allow them to return. As a result, by the late 1970s, an entire generation of Palestinian refugees had grown up hoping to return to their former homeland. Some insisted on the destruction of the Israeli state, giving support to international terrorism as a means to achieve that end.

Following the 1967 and 1973 Arab-Israeli wars, the United States began to play a more active role in the Middle East. Desiring to achieve regional stability and to protect its economic and strategic interests in the area, the United States sought to bring the opposing parties to the negotiating table. This effort began in earnest with Secretary of State Henry Kissinger's "shuttle diplomacy" between Israel and the major Arab states, and later continued during both the Ford and Carter administrations.

In 1978, President Carter took a personal political gamble by inviting Israeli Prime Minister Menachem Begin and Egyptian President Anwar Sadat to the presidential retreat at Camp David, Maryland. In two weeks of intense negotiations, Carter persuaded Sadat and Begin to resolve certain long-standing differences between the two nations and

to establish a framework for a Middle-East peace treaty. Following further negotiations over a year-long period, including a dramatic trip by President Carter to Egypt and Israel, an agreement between the two nations was reached. In April 1979, a peace treaty was signed on the lawn of the White House, ending the thirty-year state of war between Israel and its largest Arab neighbor. Although many problems were left unresolved—including the fate of the Palestinians—the treaty broke the solid Arab front against Israel, which for more than three decades had threatened to destroy the predominantly Jewish state. It also left Egypt estranged from its former Arab allies, many of whom called for an economic and diplomatic boycott of Egypt.

Implicit in the negotiations leading to the treaty was the assumption that the United States would provide massive military and economic aid to both Egypt and Israel. Estimates placed the total aid package at more than $4.8 billion. Thus, during the 1980s, the United States would serve as the benefactor and military overseer of both nations and would be drawn even further into the politics and conflicts of the Middle East.

Making Foreign Policy: The Major Participants

Like other areas of policy making, foreign policy decisions reflect the institutions and individuals who make them. The responsibility for foreign policy making rests mainly with the president and his personal staff, certain cabinet departments in the executive bureaucracy, Congress, and a number of other organizations both in and out of government. To better appreciate the complex maze of foreign policy making, let us briefly consider some of the main participants, beginning with the president.

The President

As we saw in Chapter 9, the president's powers in foreign relations have tended to be greater than in other areas of decision making. As commander in chief of the armed forces and as the nation's principal spokesman on the world stage, the president has tended to establish the general tone of American foreign policy. Jimmy Carter, for example, injected a moralistic tone into U.S. foreign policy by calling on all nations to advance human rights. While some criticized Carter's human rights stance, accusing him of meddling in the internal affairs of other nations and endangering U.S. relations with foreign governments, others saw it as a welcome goal of American foreign policy.

The Constitution grants the president the power "to make Treaties, provided two-thirds of the Senators present concur," to "appoint Ambassadors, other public Ministers and Consuls," to "receive Ambassadors and other public Ministers," and to serve as "Commander in Chief of the Army and Navy of the United States." From these provisions other presidential powers flow: he may choose to recognize or sever relations with governments of other nations; he may conclude executive agreements with foreign nations that do not require formal Senate approval; and he may send armed forces abroad in times of peace as well as war.

In fact, many Americans have come to accept the idea that the president should dominate military and foreign policy. With the coming of the nuclear age, many feel that only the president can respond to emergencies with appropriate speed and decisiveness, as John Kennedy did during the 1962 Cuban Missile Crisis. Only the president is supplied with daily intelligence reports compiled by the Central Intelligence Agency and the State and Defense departments, and thus has the information and expertise needed to act decisively. It is partly for these reasons, in fact, that Congress has been reluctant to curb the president in military and foreign policy matters—although, as we will see, that reluctance has been waning. During the Vietnam War, many of the same senators and representatives who complained bitterly about the war continued to appropriate the money to keep it going.

With rare exceptions, not even Supreme Court justices have mustered a serious challenge to the president's military and foreign policy authority. With the country's security possibly at stake, the justices have tended to turn down efforts to restrict presidential powers. They refused during World War II, for example, to interfere with Franklin Roosevelt's executive order placing thousands of Japanese-Americans in makeshift detention camps. They also refused during the Vietnam War to question the constitutional authority of Lyndon Johnson and Richard Nixon to carry out a prolonged war in Southeast Asia, or to decide whether the draft was legal without a congressional declaration of war (see Chapter 11).

At the same time, however, it has become increasingly apparent that the president must act within bounds set by events outside his control. Not only is he tied to many of the policies of his predecessors—foreign aid programs, mutual defense pacts, treaties, and so on—but his plans are constantly subject to changes in the affairs of other nations. A new foreign leader may come to power, a friendly government may be overthrown, or a war between two strategically important nations may erupt. In 1979, for instance, President Carter found himself confronted by a new and hostile government in Iran, an invasion of Vietnam by

China (and the frightening prospect of wider world conflict), and an international energy crisis fueled by enormous price hikes by the major oil-producing nations. These and other events restrict the options open to the president and have a direct impact on his foreign policy decisions.

Congress

As we have seen, the war in Vietnam raised new questions about the respective responsibilities of the president and Congress in foreign policy making. The Constitution officially requires the president to share his foreign policy duties with Congress. It grants Congress the power to declare war, regulate commerce with foreign nations, provide for the common defense, "raise and support Armies," "provide and maintain a Navy," "make Rules concerning Captures on Land and Water," and "define and punish Piracies and Felonies committed on the high seas, and Offenses against the Law of Nations." In addition, it grants the Senate the power to approve treaties and diplomatic appointments.

While some of these powers may have little significance today—such as defining and punishing piracies on the high seas—others are of great consequence. Perhaps the most potent of Congress's powers is its control over the purse strings. In the final analysis, Congress is responsible for appropriating the money used to maintain our embassies abroad, buy weapons, supply and pay the troops, and distribute U.S. foreign aid. By withholding the funds, Congress can reduce the size of America's armed forces, limit the president's diplomatic leverage with foreign nations, and even force the president to halt a military action.

Yet, as noted in earlier chapters, Congress's influence on foreign policy has, for years, been almost totally eclipsed by that of the president. During most of the post-World War II period, Congress tended to rubber stamp presidential initiatives and programs, bowing to the judgments of senior executive officials and the Pentagon.

In the early 1970s, however, Congress began to reassert its powers and to challenge executive authority in various areas of foreign policy making. Many senators and representatives felt they had been misled by President Johnson over Vietnam, that their support of the Tonkin Gulf Resolution had been deceitfully used to escalate the war throughout Indochina. With congressional opposition to the war slowly building, Congress in 1970 repealed the Tonkin Gulf Resolution and in 1973 cut off funds for American combat activities in Cambodia and Laos. In addition, Congress in 1973 passed the War Powers Resolution limiting the president's powers to commit U.S. forces abroad without congressional approval (see Chapter 9). It also required the president to submit to Congress the texts of executive agreements (1972); cut off arms shipments to Turkey following its invasion of Cyprus (1974); and barred the Ford administration from giving military and economic aid to anticommunist forces engaged in a civil war in Angola (1976).

This resurgence of congressional influence gained momentum during the Carter administration. Carter had to make concessions to several key Senators to muster sufficient Senate support for the Panama Canal treaties in 1978, and faced the prospect of seeing the SALT II treaty with the Soviet Union torn apart by Senate foes in 1979.

Some observers, of course, question whether the resurgence of congressional influence is desirable. While they agree that the president's decisions will not always be correct or wise, they are skeptical whether Congress can match the speed and decisiveness of the White House or become a truly coequal branch. They fear that the White House has already become so crippled by congressional constraints that the United States has lost effective leadership. In their view, any additional limits on executive power and flexibility would only reduce the country's capacity to tackle the growing complexity of international problems in the 1980s.

However, while such concerns may be valid, the era of congressional assertiveness may be only temporary. In an age of nuclear weapons, new power blocs, and a growing energy crisis, demands for presidential action could escalate, forcing the pendulum of power to swing back again to the White House. The "imperial presidency" may appear to be only an historical aberration of the Johnson and Nixon years, but its reappearance (whether welcome or not) cannot be discounted.

The National Security Council

Within the executive branch are a number of departments and agencies that help the president carry out American foreign policy. One of the most important of these agencies is the National Security Council (NSC), formed by Congress in 1947. The NSC's task is to "advise the President with respect to the integration of domestic, foreign, and military policies relating to the national security." Its members include the president, the vice-president, the secretaries of state and defense, and other high-ranking officials invited by the president (such as the director of the CIA and the chairman of the Joint Chiefs of Staff). Presiding over the NSC is the president's special assistant for national security affairs.

Until the Nixon administration, the NSC served primarily as an administrative body, gathering intelligence information from other governmental agencies and presenting the president with various options on foreign policy problems. However, this role was expanded when Henry Kissinger became head of the NSC in 1968. As Nixon's national security adviser, Kissinger transformed the NSC into a focal point for foreign policy-making that frequently overshadowed the Departments of State and Defense. This pattern largely continued, although to a lesser degree, during the Carter administration, when National Security Adviser Zbigniew Brzezinski at times competed with Secretary of State Cyrus Vance for major influence on foreign policy making.

Some observers have criticized the growing importance of the National Security Council. They insist that it has caused confusion as divergent foreign policy views have sometimes been presented by the NSC and the State Department. They believe that the council should remain largely an administrative tool and that the president and the secretary of state should assume the major responsibility for forging American foreign policy.

As in the past, however, the National Security Council will likely be used differently by each president, depending on his personal preferences and methods of operation. Whereas some presidents will continue to rely heavily on the NSC for advice and policy direction, others will turn more to their personal advisers and department heads in forging American policy.

The State Department

Although the State Department (Figure 14-1) has one of the smallest budgets and staffs of any cabinet department, it is the oldest in the executive branch (1789) and one of the most influential. In addition to advising the president on foreign policy, it represents the United States in the United Nations and in more than fifty other international organizations. It also helps negotiate treaties, administers foreign aid, operates cultural exchange programs, and issues passports and visas. About half of its 30,000 employees—including U.S. Ambassadors, foreign service officers, and country desk officers—are stationed in more than 270 embassies and consulates overseas.

The head of the department, the secretary of state, is the highest-ranking Cabinet member (he is fourth in line to succeed the president) and often serves as the chief adviser to the president on foreign affairs. He may be called upon to act as the president's foreign policy spokesman overseas and before Congress, and to help resolve major policy questions. However, the actual amount of influence wielded by the sec-

Figure 14-1. Department of State

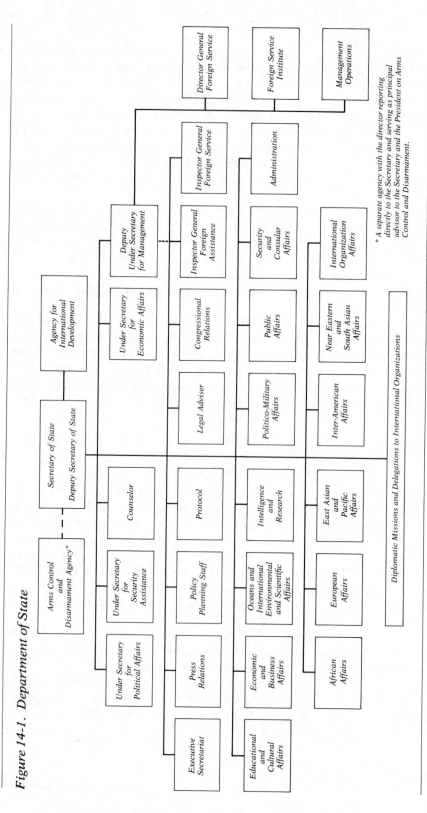

Source: U.S. Government Organization Manual, 1978–1979.

retary of state depends on his relationship with the president. In past administrations his influence has sometimes been eclipsed by the president's national security adviser, the secretary of defense, and other governmental officials.

Because of the State Department's highly visible role, it is frequently the target of criticism when things go wrong. In recent decades, it has been blamed for "failures" ranging from China's "fall" to communism in the late 1940s to the Jonestown, Guyana, mass murder-suicide tragedy in 1978. In countries where political tensions are high, U.S. Ambassadors (who serve as the president's special representatives overseas) often take the brunt of criticism against U.S. policies and, in some instances, even lose their lives. In a world where many perceive the United States as a modern imperial power, U.S. diplomats and embassy personnel are often the closest and most visible symbols of American foreign policy.

The Defense Department

Since the end of World War II, the State Department has had to share much of its influence on foreign policy with the Defense Department. In the National Security Act of 1947, Congress combined the U.S. armed forces under a single Department of Defense, headed by a civilian secretary of defense appointed by the president. The Army, Navy, and Air Force were maintained as separate units within the Defense Department, each headed by its own civilian secretary.

As with the secretary of state, the influence of the secretary of defense largely depends on his relationship with the president. In most administrations, he serves as the president's chief military adviser and plays a central role in shaping American defense policy. He is responsible, among other things, for supervising the military budget, advising the president (and Congress) on new weapons systems, and funneling presidential directives to the military. Carter's defense secretary Harold Brown, for example, played a key role in trying to persuade the Senate to adopt the new SALT II treaty.

Much of the secretary's influence derives from his heading the largest department in the federal bureaucracy. He is boss of about one million civilians and more than two million military personnel. In fact, not only is the Defense Department the government's largest employer, it is also the largest single customer of American business, awarding defense contracts totaling more than $52 billion a year.[8] (For a list of the biggest defense contractors, see Table 14-2). In 1980, the department was re-

Table 14-2. Top Ten Defense Contractors, 1976

Company	Amount of Defense Contracts (in billions of dollars)
McDonnell Douglas	2.5
Lockheed Aircraft	1.5
Northrup	1.5
General Electric	1.3
United Technologies	1.2
Boeing	1.2
General Dynamics	1.1
Grumman	.98
Litton Industries	.97
Rockwell International	.96

Source: U.S. Department of Defense, 1976.

sponsible for a military budget that exceeded $125 billion, or roughly 24 percent of all expenditures by the federal government.

To ensure civilian control over the military, the secretary of defense and the secretaries of the Army, Navy, and Air Force must be civilians by law. However, responsibility for the day-to-day operations of the military rests with the top military officials of the three armed services, plus the commandant of the Marine Corps. They and a chairman comprise the Joint Chiefs of Staff and are appointed by the president with the consent of the Senate. Although the Joint Chiefs officially serve under the secretary of defense, they also directly advise the president and the National Security Council. The president, of course, has to weigh their advice—as well as that of the secretary of defense—against the country's overall foreign policy goals. After all, it is his decisions as commander in chief that history will ultimately judge.

Intelligence and Foreign Policy: The CIA

Like the National Security Council, the Central Intelligence Agency (CIA) was established to coordinate the activities of different government departments and agencies. Created by Congress in 1947, the CIA serves directly under the National Security Council, supplying it with information gathered and analyzed from both covert and open sources. It also acts as a clearing house for information collected by other agencies of the federal government.

The director of the Central Intelligence Agency is appointed by the president, with the consent of the Senate. In addition to advising the president and the National Security Council, the CIA director is responsible for coordinating the activities of the other intelligence agencies, including the National Security Agency (NSA), the Defense Intelligence Agency (DIA), and the State Department's Bureau of Intelligence and Research.

Prior to World War II, the United States had no elaborate intelligence-gathering apparatus. Only after the surprise attack on Pearl Harbor in 1941 was the Office of Strategic Services (OSS) created to gather intelligence and conduct secret operations behind enemy lines. Once the war was over, it was considered vital for the United States to maintain an ongoing intelligence organization, and so the CIA was formed. Without such an organization, the United States would know little about the strengths and weaknesses of other countries or their strategic goals and intentions.

Although many expected the CIA to confine itself to intelligence gathering, it has come under heavy fire for engaging in covert operations to influence the internal affairs of other nations. Among other things, it has helped topple the governments of Iran (1953), Guatemala (1954), and South Vietnam (1963), directed the ill-fated Bay of Pigs invasion of Cuba (1961), maintained a "secret army" in Laos, and aided the overthrow of the constitutional government of Salvador Allende in Chile (1973). It has also plotted the assassination of several foreign leaders, including Cuba's Fidel Castro and the Congo's Patrice Lumumba.[9]

Moreover, despite the provision in its charter stating that the CIA "shall have no police, subpoena, law-enforcement powers, or internal security functions," it has spied extensively on American citizens and infiltrated domestic dissident groups. Newspaper and congressional committee investigations revealed that the CIA and other intelligence agencies had collected dossiers on thousands of Americans involved in antiwar protest activities during the 1960s. It had also engaged in illegal break-ins and wiretapping, intercepted citizens' letters and telegrams, and even administered mind-bending drugs such as LSD to individuals without their knowledge (one subject later committed suicide).[10]

Because many of the CIA's operations have been conducted in secrecy, however, the full extent of its activities has been difficult to determine. The CIA has been unique among governmental agencies in being subject to little congressional oversight. The CIA's budget, for instance, has tended to be distributed throughout the federal budget, making it difficult for most members of Congress to know how much the agency spends and for what purposes. Only in recent years, in fact, has the CIA come in for intense scrutiny and had many of its activities curtailed. In the mid-1970s, various select committees in Congress launched probes of the agency's operations. They confirmed that the CIA had engaged in a variety of unsavory and illegal activities, and recommended expanded congressional oversight and a redefining of its intelligence purposes. In 1976, the Senate established a Select Committee on Intelligence to oversee the CIA and other intelligence agencies. In 1977, the House established a similar committee.

It should be noted that not all members of Congress (or the general public) were sympathetic to the growing criticism of the CIA. Some feared that the CIA would lose much of its effectiveness as a result of the unfavorable publicity and expanded congressional oversight. In their view, so long as the United States had to deal with other nations (many of them hostile), it could not afford to weaken its capacity to gather intelligence and to maintain its awareness.

But whatever one's perspective may be on the CIA's activities and role, the agency has not operated in a political vacuum. As many observers have noted, most of the CIA's operations have been approved or even encouraged by the White House and State Department. Congressional investigations revealed, for example, that the CIA's covert actions in Chile were sanctioned by President Nixon and Secretary of State Kissinger. As a result, some observers argue that efforts to curb the excesses of the CIA without also placing controls on the White House and State Department would leave open the potential for future abuses.

Other Instruments of Foreign Policy

Although most foreign policy decisions are in the hands of the president and the State and Defense Departments, almost every other executive department in the federal government becomes involved at some point in foreign policy. For example, the Agriculture Department plays a role through its distribution of food to other countries, while the Treasury Department becomes involved in its fiscal relations with foreign governments and its efforts to help solve the nation's balance-of-payments problems.

In addition, a number of agencies—some loosely affiliated with the State Department—have played major roles in foreign affairs in recent years. One of these is the Agency for International Development (AID), which helps direct economic and technical assistance to foreign nations. Since its creation in 1961, the AID has distributed tens of billions of dollars in foreign aid, helping to finance local schools, highways, irrigation, and other projects in less developed countries. Another important agency is the International Communication Agency (ICA), formally known as the United States Information Agency. As the main propaganda arm of the U.S. government, it makes documentaries and newsreels for foreign distribution, sponsors shows and exhibitions on American life, and operates the Voice of America radio network. ICA officers often serve in American embassies abroad. There is also the Arms Control and Disarmament Agency (ACDA), which was created in 1961 to conduct disarmament research and oversee American participation in international arms control negotiations. It played major roles in the negotiations of the Nuclear Test Ban Treaty, the Nuclear Nonproliferation Treaty, and the SALT treaty.

Some additional instruments of American diplomacy are found outside the federal government. At times, international organizations have been more useful for implementing U.S. foreign policy than have national ones. Since World War II, the United States has become a member of more than two hundred international organizations, including the United Nations, the World Bank, the Organization of American States (OAS), and NATO.

In recent years, however, the United States has encountered problems in its relations with many of these international organizations, especially the United Nations. The United States was a major sponsor of the United Nations and helped found it in 1945. It was established not as a world government, but as a voluntary association of independent nations aimed at solving international problems and promoting world peace. Since its founding, its membership has grown from fifty-one nations to about one hundred and fifty, with most of the new members coming from the Third World. Many of these countries have been openly critical of U.S. policies (especially its support of Israel) and have used the platform provided by the United Nations to voice their criticisms. Yet, although the United Nations has been too unwieldy and impotent to bring about world peace, it continues to provide a useful forum for confronting problems of international diplomacy, the environment, health, and economic development.[11]

Nor can we exclude the foreign policy role played by the large multinational corporations. These include industrial giants like International Telephone and Telegraph (ITT), Exxon, International Business Machines (IBM), and Texaco, whose plants are scattered around the globe and whose foreign subsidiaries account for major portions of their sales and assets. (As of 1975, U.S. corporate investments abroad totaled more than $350 billion.) These multinational corporations have often worked hand-in-hand with agencies of the federal government to advance America's economic and diplomatic interests abroad. The U.S. government has, at times, subsidized corporate overseas investments and provided military support to protect corporate holdings against threats of nationalization or insurrection.[12] In the early 1970s, for example, ITT—anxious to prevent expropriation of its investments in Chile—tried to persuade the U.S. government to oppose the pro-Marxist government of Salvador Allende and apparently became involved with the CIA in the overthrow of his regime.

At the same time, the policies of these multinational corporations have been known to clash with those of the U.S. government. This has been especially evident in the Middle East, where ties between American oil companies and Arab governments have sometimes been at odds with the government's support of Israel. In fact, some U.S. corporations have been willing to deal with virtually any government—a sheikdom, a dictatorship, or a democracy—so long as it will yield a substantial profit.

But whatever their policies, the multinational corporations have wielded enough economic clout to affect the internal political affairs of many of the countries in which they operate. Lockheed Aircraft's payments to foreign officials as a means of convincing their countries to buy Lockheed planes represents only one example of the kinds of actions in which many of these corporations have engaged.[13] As one French observer noted, the foreign operations of the multinationals have been rapidly turning them into the "third industrial power" after the United States and the Soviet Union, an industrial power few nations can ignore.[14]

The Public and Foreign Policy

While each of us individually may not have much influence on American foreign policy, public opinion in general has had an impact at various times in history. During the course of the Vietnam War, for example, polls registered an increasing public disenchantment with America's participation in that conflict (see Table 14-3). This growing disenchantment, combined with the spread of protest and violent demonstrations, clearly hurt the Johnson administration, and figured prominently in Johnson's decision not to seek a second term. Following the war, greater skepticism about governmental claims and resistance to governmental policies were generally found among the American people.[15] The mood of the country for "no more Vietnams" not only gave impetus to Congress's growing assertiveness in foreign policy making, but also helped keep the United States from becoming actively involved in Angola and other foreign hot spots.

Foreign policy makers themselves disagree about the public's relationship to foreign policy. Some dispute, for example, the wisdom of encouraging active public involvement in foreign policy decision making. They insist that the national security needs of the country require people with special skills and knowledge to conduct foreign affairs. To deal effectively with the growing complexity of international relations, they argue, foreign policy questions must be decided without constant public pressure.

In any event, they point out, a great deal of secrecy necessarily surrounds our relations with other countries. Most Americans do not have access to information that would enable them to make informed judgments about international developments. As a result, most Americans tend to be poorly informed on foreign affairs and only marginally interested in foreign policy issues. One analyst, in fact, compared the majority of Americans to an audience at a theater. "The mass public," he stated, "occupying the many seats in the balcony, is so far removed from the scene of the action that its members can hardly grasp the plot, much less hear all the lines or distinguish between the actors. Thus, they may sit in stony silence or applaud impetuously, if not so vigorously as to shake the foundations of the theater. Usually, however, they get thoroughly bored and leave."[16]

Figure 14-3. Decline in Public Support for the Vietnam War

"In view of developments since we entered the fighting in Vietnam, do you think the U.S. made a mistake sending troops to fight in Vietnam?" (Gallup)

Date	Percent Answering No
August 1965	61
March 1966	59
September 1966	48
May 1967	50
October 1967	44
March 1968	41
August 1968	35
October 1969	32
January 1970	33
May 1970	36
January 1971	31
May 1971	28

At this point, Gallup stopped asking the question.

Source: Adapted from William L. Lunch and Peter W. Sperlich, "American Public Opinion and the War in Vietnam," *Western Political Quarterly*, March 1979, pp. 21–44.

Other policy makers, however, disagree. They contend that, while most Americans may not be privy to sensitive information, they are generally better informed on and more attentive to foreign policy issues than they are given credit for. "Every time we've made a serious mistake in foreign affairs," Jimmy Carter noted during the 1976 presidential debates, "it has been because the American people have been excluded from the process." Moreover, they point out, the goal of any democracy is to allow its citizens to influence governmental policies. Unless the people can have a say on the broad issues that affect them most—war and peace—that goal cannot be fully achieved. When sacrifices in lives and money are at stake, foreign policy decisions do intrude on the public's consciousness and require the public's consent.

Whatever the views of policy makers, groups representing various segments of the public have become actively involved in the policy-making process. Hundreds of special interest groups—labor unions, ethnic groups, veterans' organizations, and others—have established offices in Washington, D.C., to lobby governmental agencies and Congress on specific aspects of American foreign policy. Jewish groups, for example, press for expanded support for Israel, farm organizations lobby for increased grain sales to the Soviet Union and other foreign markets, while business and labor groups lobby for tariff protection or trade contracts.

Among the most interesting of these organizations are the self-styled public interest or educative groups that aim at improving the general climate of international relations. These include such groups as the Women's International League for Peace and Freedom (WILPF), the World Federalists Association, the Institute for World Order, and New Directions. The WILPF, for example, was founded more than fifty years ago to work against what its members regard as the absurdity and immorality of human warfare.[17] With more than 10,000 members in the United States alone and branch offices in more than twenty countries, the organization in recent years has become involved in issues ranging from the plight of political prisoners in South Vietnam to the cancellation of the B-1 bomber project in the United States.

Of more recent vintage is New Directions, founded in 1976. Closely modeled on the citizen's lobby group Common Cause, New Directions relies on a direct mail campaign to obtain new members and contributions. It was founded by a number of prominent figures in government, science, and the arts, including Secretary of State Cyrus Vance, World Bank President (and former Defense Secretary) Robert McNamara, anthropologist Margaret Mead, and publisher Norman Cousins. Its principal policy interests include reducing U.S. arms sales, protecting the environment, safeguarding human rights, halting the development of the breeder reactor, and expanding rural development in poor countries.

Moreover, in a growing number of American cities, organizations of interested citizens have been formed to discuss foreign policy matters and to try to affect the policy-making process. These organizations often provide a sounding board for governmental officials to test policy issues before the public. In 1978, for example, the World Affairs Council in San Francisco sponsored a conference on "United States Policy Toward Africa," attended by more than a dozen high-ranking State Department officials and more than a thousand interested Bay Area residents.

Although these and other interest groups have had varying degrees of success in influencing foreign policy, with many suffering from the same problems afflicting interest groups in general (see Chapter 7), they provide one of the few opportunities for an ordinary citizen to become involved in the policy-making process. Although membership in most of these groups remains small, many Americans are coming to realize that it is important for them to understand and try to participate in the foreign policy decisions that affect their lives. They realize that, to avoid future Vietnams and to encourage policies that reflect more than the interests of large corporations and other powerful groups, they must add their voice to the policy-making process. Indeed, if the United States is to pursue policies suited to the international climate of the 1980s, an informed and active public needs to be encouraged.

Key Terms

Monroe Doctrine	*domino theory*
manifest destiny	*Nixon Doctrine*
cold war	*détente*
containment	*strategic deterrence*
Truman Doctrine	*Third World*
Marshall Plan	

Notes

1. George F. Kennan, "The Sources of Soviet Conduct," *Foreign Affairs*, July 1947, pp. 566–582.

2. U.S. Bureau of the Census, *Statistical Abstract of the United States*, 1978, p. 871.

3. See, for example, Robert F. Kennedy, *Thirteen Days: A Memoir of the Cuban Missile Crisis* (New York: Norton, 1969).

4. See, for example, William Shawcross, *Sideshow: Nixon, Kissinger, and the Destruction of Cambodia* (New York: Simon and Schuster, 1979); Roger Morris, *Uncertain Greatness: Henry Kissinger and American Foreign Policy* (New York: Harper & Row, 1977).

5. Report of the U.S. General Accounting Office (Washington, D.C., June 1976).

6. As of 1979, the OPEC members included: Algeria, Ecuador, Gabon, Indonesia, Iran, Iraq, Kuwait, Libya, Nigeria, Qatar, Saudia Arabia, the United Arab Emirates, and Venezuela.

7. *Gallup Opinion Index*, March 1979.

8. U.S. Bureau of the Census, *Statistical Abstract of the United States*, 1978, p. 377.

9. U.S. Senate Select Committee to Study Governmental Operations with Respect to Intelligence Activities, *Alleged Assassination Plots Involving Foreign Leaders* (Washington, D.C.: U.S. Government Printing Office, 1975).

10. *New York Times*, 22 December 1974; *Report to the President by the Commission on CIA Activities Within the United States* (Washington, D.C.: U.S. Government Printing Office, 1975).

11. See, for example, H. G. Nicholas, *The United Nations as a Political Institution*, 5th ed. (New York: Oxford University Press, 1975); Shirley Hazzard, *Defeat of an Ideal: A Study of the Self-Destruction of the United Nations* (Boston: Little, Brown, 1973).

12. Thomas B. Ross and David Wise, *The Invisible Government* (New York: Random House, 1964).

13. See, for example, Anthony Sampson, ¯*The Arms Bazaar: From Lebanon to Lockheed* (New York: Viking Press, 1977).

14. Jean-Jacques Servan-Schreiber, *The American Challenge* (New York: Avon, 1965).

15. William L. Lunch and Peter W. Sperlich, "American Public Opinion and the War in Vietnam," *Western Political Quarterly*, March 1979, pp. 21–44.

16. James N. Rosenau, ed., *Public Opinion and Foreign Policy* (New York: Random House, 1961), p. 34.

17. For more on the WILPF, see Jeffrey M. Berry, *Lobbying For the People* (Princeton, N.J.: Princeton University Press, 1977), pp. 141–177.

Recommended Reading

ALMOND, GABRIEL. *The American People and Foreign Policy.* New York: Praeger,1960.

BARNET, RICHARD J., and RONALD E. MULLER. *Global Reach: The Power of the Multinational Corporations.* New York: Simon and Schuster, 1974.

HALBERSTAM, DAVID. *The Best and the Brightest.* New York: Random House, 1972.

HALPERIN, MORTON H. *Bureaucratic Politics and Foreign Policy.* Washington, D.C.: Brookings Institution, 1974.

HAMMON, PAUL Y. *Cold War and Detente: The American Foreign Policy Process Since 1942.* New York: Harcourt Brace Jovanovich, 1975.

HILSMAN, ROGER. *The Politics of Policy Making in Defense and Foreign Affairs.* New York: Harper & Row, 1971.

KENNEDY, ROBERT F. *Thirteen Days: A Memoir of the Cuban Missile Crisis.* New York: Norton, 1969.

MORGENTHAU, HANS J. *Politics Among Nations: The Struggle for Power and Peace.* 5th ed. New York: Random House, 1978.

MORRIS, ROGER. *Uncertain Greatness: Henry Kissinger and American Foreign Policy.* New York: Harper & Row, 1977.

NATHAN, JAMES A., and JAMES K. OLIVER. *United States Foreign Policy and World Order.* Boston: Little, Brown, 1976.

SPANIER, JOHN. *American Foreign Policy Since World War II.* 7th ed. New York: Praeger, 1977.

SPANIER, JOHN, and ERIC M. USLANER. *How American Foreign Policy is Made.* 2nd ed. New York: Holt, Rinehart and Winston, 1978.

WALTZ, KENNETH A. *Foreign Policy and Democratic Politics: The American and British Experience.* Boston: Little, Brown, 1967.

PART FIVE

Channels of Citizen Influence

15

Taking on the System:
The Strategies and Pitfalls

As stated at the outset, the question of whether to engage in or retreat from political action is a major concern of our time. In view of the many social and political problems facing American society, the call to action places many of us in a dilemma neither our conscience nor reason alone can resolve. While we may recognize and lament the problems around us, we may either feel too disgusted with politics to become actively involved or doubt whether any effective means exist to permit meaningful participation.

Of course, not everyone perceives such a dilemma. To some, the desire to work within the system as reformers or as full-time politicians requires little reflection. The driving motivation to obtain political power supercedes any concern about effectiveness and outweighs any consideration of costs. Similarly, to those impatient with the slow progress of reform, commitment to revolutionary action seems a necessary response to the problems of society. The willingness to accept personal sacrifice—based on an optimism that radical political surgery can indeed cure society's ills—requires little debate or self-examination.

But to those persons who cannot commit themselves to either extreme, the question of whether to take any kind of political action remains problematic. Even if they are not completely disgusted with the political process, they still may wonder whether any of the common tools and strategies for political influence in this country—the vote, the petition, the media, letters to Congress, interest groups, or direct action (such as demonstrations and strikes)—can be employed effectively to achieve their goals.

Although the endless variety of circumstances in which political action takes place makes it virtually impossible to answer this question satisfactorily, it is possible at least to explore some of the common promises and pitfalls of each strategy. Assuming a person feels strongly about an issue or problem, what can he or she expect from trying to work within the system to influence policy in a limited, pragmatic, and short-range way?

Guidelines for Action

Obviously, any evaluation of action strategies must first take into account the attitude of an individual toward the political system. Deciding whether to participate at all in politics clearly depends on one's faith in the political process. A person who genuinely believes it is *not* possible to affect policy—that the direction of government cannot be altered by political pressure (whatever the form)—is less likely to participate than someone who maintains an optimistic view.

One often hears that this country boasts a viable "democratic" system offering its citizens numerous ways to influence governmental policy and articulate demands. But many different countries and ideologies are described as "democratic" and have adopted the term as their slogan and justification for being. The concept of *democracy* is among the most vague and value-laden in all political thought. One scholar estimates there are as many as two hundred separate definitions of the concept.[1] In this country, for example, many people equate democracy with rule by the majority, that is, an electoral process in which a candidate who garners more than 50 percent of the votes represents all of the people (including those who did not support him). Yet, a problem with this definition is its failure to fit a system with multiparty elections in which the "winning" candidate may not have a clear majority. Was democracy discarded in 1968 when Richard Nixon became president, even though his two opponents, Hubert Humphrey and George Wallace, collectively received more votes?

To many other people, democracy ultimately implies support for liberty and equality, protection of minority rights, respect for the individual, a fundamental written law, and the availability of choice. To still others, it simply suggests rule in the interests of "the people," regardless of the legal and institutional forms. The word itself stems from two Greek roots: *demos* referring broadly to the people and *kratia* connoting rule or authority. Thus, the term implies that rule or authority ultimately is vested in the people.

But definitions should not be our primary concern. The literature on democracy is so exceedingly rich and controversial that we could hardly do full justice to the concept. For the purposes of focusing on citizen action, we might adopt a procedural interpretation of democracy. That is, we might describe a system as democratic if its citizens enjoy a relatively high degree of access to and influence over their government. But *relative* is the key word. In no system is there a total absence of public influence over government, and in no system is the influence complete. Hence, the political system in this country may be more or less democratic than another, depending on one's perception of people's ability to affect policy, and that perception will remain controversial.

It is difficult, in fact, to get an accurate estimate of the number of Americans who try to sway governmental decision making, in part because they tend to exaggerate their involvement. When a sample of Americans were asked in a Harris survey what actions they would take to affect policy, 94 percent reported they would go to the polls, 84 percent said they would contact their representative, 64 percent indicated they would write a letter to a local newspaper, and 72 percent said they would join a citizen-action group.[2] Yet, as shown clearly in Chapter 5, far fewer people resort to any of these political actions. Although 94 percent of the respondents said they would go to the polls, actual voter turnout in the 1978 elections was only 36 percent. Although between 65 and 72 percent said they would write letters to their representative or to newspapers, less than 15 percent have ever done so. In fact, 84 percent of those sampled in one survey said they had never tried to influence congressional policy, while 79 percent said they had never tried to influence local governmental policy.[3]

Moreover, those who participate may do so for reasons other than wanting to influence policy. They may gain expressive as well as instrumental benefits from their actions, such as letting off steam by firing off letters to a local newspaper. Or perhaps they desire the social contacts stemming from their membership in a political club or organization and enjoy rubbing shoulders with prominent civic officials. Sometimes the opportunity to wield power for its own sake provides the major motivation for people to plunge into politics. "To many people in politics," one group of scholars conclude, "the possession of power, in and of itself, is the most desirable goal. It is also a goal which is often underestimated, particularly by those who do not have experience in political affairs, as well as by those at the other extreme who do possess political power but who prefer to disguise their motives in terms of altruism and civic good."[4]

However, despite the different motives and intentions, many do not see any point in becoming politically active. They do not view the system as ultimately democratic in the sense that they can gain access to, and influence over, government. Among a sample of Americans polled in 1976, 64 percent agreed with the proposition, "What you think doesn't count much any more."[5] Indeed, many people feel they do not have any control over the affairs of the country, or even over the policies of the city in which they live. Simply being reminded in school or by bumper stickers that "Our system works if you work at it" and "If you're not part of the solution, you're part of the problem" will not compel them to take action. In their view, the political system cannot be made responsive to public demands, so why bother?

Although many reasons may account for such feelings of political impotency, some people simply feel overwhelmed by the vastness and the remoteness of government. Each has a sense of being only one among millions and feels that those who make policy decisions are distant and unresponsive. In the words of one commentator, "The scale of organization in our society has grown so large that only through large-scale organization does it seem possible to have a significant impact. This impression alone is enough to make individual people feel helplessly overwhelmed by huge impersonal machines indifferent to their uniqueness and humanity."[6]

Obviously, not everyone feels small or impotent. Persons living in relatively small communities, for instance, often voice considerable optimism about affecting local policies.[7] However, negative perceptions of government may produce as much pessimism about participation as do any feelings of personal inefficacy. As pointed out in Chapter 1, there appears to be an erosion of confidence in government at all levels—an erosion that began well before the Watergate scandal broke in the newspapers and on television. For some people, this erosion of confidence becomes immediately translated into political disinterest and inaction. (An intriguing question is why some people who have little faith in the responsiveness of government drop out of all political activity, while others with a similar lack of faith turn to revolutionary action.[8])

Perhaps another factor inhibiting participation is the knowledge that political influence is unequally shared. Whether one adopts the pluralist or ruling-elite view of power distribution, there remains the knowledge that some Americans enjoy considerably more clout than others. As one scholar points out, many people "are not mollified by assurances that the characteristics of the system thwarting them also thwart selfish and extremist interests; it appears to them that only the powerful get attention, and that the already powerful are helped by the system to deny influence to all who now lack it."[9] Because such resources as wealth, expertise, access to communications, and even time are unequally distributed, some individuals have more opportunities than others to achieve their political objectives. Even the vote is not equally shared: although each American has only one vote, some members of society, by virtue of their prestige or access to the media, have additional opportunities to persuade others how to cast theirs.

Thus, even if one accepts the pluralist view that our political system offers citizens a number of viable routes of influence, one must still examine his or her own resources to determine the chances of affecting political decisions. This means evaluating the time one can devote to a political issue, one's access to means of communication, and one's ability to persuade, cajole, or merely reach those who make the appropriate decisions. Information is a particularly vital resource: the lack of it often is a major stumbling block to effective action. Few people are sufficiently knowledgeable about the procedures of decision making even to know whom to contact or how to exert pressure.

Moreover, any decision to take political action must involve some consideration of costs. This means not only the time and money one can devote to an issue but the extent of frustration and conflict one may be willing to bear. Efforts to change existing policies or to persuade others to adopt one's point of view may meet with failure, rejection, and despair. Although a willingness to persevere on a political problem will sometimes yield tangible results, no guarantee of that can ever be made. Perhaps those who seek the greatest changes in policy will court the most frustration. The American political system, while flexible, is not too responsive to calls for sweeping reform. But if an individual feels strongly about an issue and maintains optimism, his or her efforts may be rewarded.

In evaluating some of the traditional means of political influence offered by the system—the vote, litigation, the petition, and so forth—it makes sense to choose a strategy that best fits the goal. Those who want to increase social security benefits, for example, are hardly likely to buttonhole a member of the city council. Their efforts must be focused on the national level, where social security policies are enacted. Moreover, their intensity of participation must be determined by what they expect to accomplish. If they desire to change the federal tax structure, it would hardly be worthwhile simply to dash off a letter to the local newspaper.

It should be understood that the strategies we will examine do not exhaust all existing alternatives. We are excluding, for example, consideration of such long-range strategies as running for public office and engaging full-time in reform activity because of the extraordinary personal commitment they require. Nor are we considering interest-group activity here, since that important means of political action is discussed in Chapter 7. The strategies that follow serve merely to illustrate some of the promises and pitfalls that can be expected from engaging in political action, without covering all of the possible strategies for dealing with different levels and institutions of government.

In fact, political action should not be viewed solely in terms of acting on government. It should also be extended to places we work and live. As one observer has noted, an "essential lesson of the last decades has been that universities, corporations, labor unions, hospitals, and school systems have all been politicized and recognized as 'private' governments and institutions in which one must participate if one wishes to share in the business of societal guidance. Too much of our domestic work is carried out in these polities for participation limited to the governmental level to be sufficiently effective."[10] Thus, a wide variety of activities should be evaluated by those who desire a greater impact on the political and social fortunes of this country.

Into the Voting Booth

Let us turn first to one of the most common forms of political participation in the United States: voting in elections. There is a long-standing belief in this country that elections are important and that each citizen has a duty to be informed about the issues and candidates and to vote. Even adolescents and teenagers are taught to participate in this activity in school, where they may vote for class president or hold mock elections for gubernatorial candidates. Undoubtedly, many would agree with Lyndon Johnson, who proclaimed after signing the 1965 Voting Rights Act, "The vote is the most powerful instrument ever devised by man for breaking down injustice and destroying the terrible walls that imprison men because they are different from other men."

Yet, millions of Americans have not been convinced that casting their ballots is worthwhile. Not only do more than 40 percent of the voting-age population abstain from voting in presidential elections, but anywhere from 50 to 70 percent of the potential voters shy away from the polls in congressional and local elections. As we discussed earlier, there are many reasons people fail to participate, including legal obstacles (such as registration requirements), a dislike of the party candidates, political disinterest, or a sense of political impotency.

But whatever the reasons, some wonder why any sensible person should bother to vote at all. Given the fact that each person is only one of seventy or eighty million voters in the United States, does it make sense to believe his or her participation, his or her one vote, will have any impact on a major election? Simply to raise the question "What if everyone felt the same way?" does not remove the lingering impression that a single person, especially in a national election, is dwarfed by the enormous number of people who do trek to the polls. Indeed, it is likely that the decision of any one of us not to show up would hardly affect the outcome of a major election.

The case for not voting is additionally buttressed by arguments that elections are largely meaningless anyway. As we saw in Chapter 2, supporters of the ruling-elite theory insist that even though voters are given a choice among candidates, their choice is restricted to a narrow range of similar-minded individuals picked by party elites. Elections do not express what most people want or need, nor do they provide guidance for politicians (even if they want it) on what policies to enact. In this view, elections are primarily just rituals that perform a symbolic function for voters. They offer voters a role to play at election time and help tie them to the political system. As one writer scoffs, elections only "quiet resentments and doubts about particular political acts, reaffirm belief in the fundamental rationality and democratic character of the system, and thus fix conforming habits of future behavior."[11]

Still, since most people continue to show their faces at the polls at one time or another, what arguments can be made in favor of voting? One argument is that voting does have significance, if not so much in terms of individual impact, then in putting group pressure on politicians. Because citizens collectively have the power to give or withhold votes, they directly control the tenure of elected officials. Even if the choice is narrowly confined to Tweedledee and Tweedledum, Tweedledee knows that a day of reckoning is fixed by law and that minimally he must strive to avoid displeasing his constituents, or he will lose his job.

There is also the view that an individual can augment his or her impact at the polls by swaying the votes of others. By ringing doorbells, working in a campaign, or just talking to family and friends, one person can turn his or her single vote into many. Such efforts may bring innumerable rewards, considering the number of politicians elected or defeated by razor-thin margins. In 1974, for example, a Senate race in New Hampshire between Louis Wyman and John Durkin was initially decided by a margin of only 2 votes! The vote was so close that a new election had to be held, with Democrat John Durkin finally emerging victorious. Similarly, in 1978, Democrat Tom Daschle beat Republican Leo Thorsness by only 14 votes in a South Dakota congressional race in which more than 128,000 votes were cast.[12] Even some presidential elections have been decided by a small number of votes. Because presidents are officially elected by a majority of the electoral college, a shift of only a few thousand popular votes can change the outcome of a presidential contest. Thus, if just one person per precinct in three states in 1968 had backed Hubert Humphrey instead of Richard Nixon, Humphrey would have fulfilled his ambition to be president. And if just 9,000 people in Ohio and Hawaii had supported Gerald Ford instead of Jimmy Carter in 1976, the Georgia peanut farmer would not have made it to the White House.

A handful of voters can make a difference, particularly at the local level. Although contests for national and state offices attract the largest turnout, the greatest chance for a small number of voters to affect the outcome of an election is in local contests for city council or state legislature. Students at the University of California, for example, played a prominent part in the election of three "radicals" to the Berkeley City Council in 1971 and were influential in electing antiwar critic Ronald Dellums to Congress in 1970. Although they had less success in placing fellow students on the city council, the election of candidates sympathetic to student concerns resulted in the appointments of students to various city boards and commissions.

But perhaps political efficacy in voting is not the only consideration anyway. As ruling-elite theorists suggest, people do not vote only to influence policy. Millions go to the effort to register and vote for a variety of other reasons as well. Some people may participate just to avoid feeling guilty about not voting. They may have been taught that it is their patriotic duty to vote and that they have no right to complain about the outcome if they stay at home. Still others may participate to derive satisfaction from feeling that they are somehow participants, not just spectators, in an exciting electoral contest. One study found that 71 percent of the respondents interviewed said they got a "feeling of satisfaction" out of going to the polls.[13] Even though their one vote may not be crucial, it nevertheless affirms their role in, and support for, the political process. Indeed, if one takes this view, it may be irrelevant whether one's vote is ultimately effective: a person votes not only to influence policy in a personal way but to experience the electoral process itself.

However, voting is only one form of political participation and is confined to fixed intervals. Between elections there are other traditional ways of influencing policy in which the average person can engage at almost any time.

Once Again, There Is Congress

To many who are not satisfied merely with voting as a means of political expression and influence, there is the additional strategy of contacting policy makers directly through letter writing or other activities. Public opinion surveys reveal that most Americans have given thought to making use of the pen to express their concerns, although only about 15 percent have ever done so. While letters may be addressed to practically any official—including the president, the mayor, the governor, a senator, or a bureaucrat—the congressional representative and state legislator are the principal targets of citizen mail.

There are at least two reasons people try to get in touch with their representative: either they wish to influence legislation, or they need assistance with a personal problem. Assuming, first of all, that they want to sway the vote of a member of Congress on a bill, they need to time their letters for the best effect. Probably the best time to write is when a bill is about to reach the House or Senate floor for debate, or when it is pending before a committee. The latter is a particularly crucial time because, as we saw in Chapter 10, the fate of most bills is sealed in committee. This means that potential letter writers must understand the committee process and keep track of the bill at its various stages. One useful source of information on such matters has been offered by the League Action Service (a service of the League of Women Voters), which keeps a watchful eye on the status of legislation and suggests when action should be taken.

Naturally, those who desire to influence policy must also take into account the committee position held and power commanded by their representative. If they desire to influence tax policy, for example, and their representative happens to sit on the Agriculture Committee and is still wet behind the ears, then pressure may have to be directed elsewhere. Indeed, a few letters to the chairman of the Ways and Means Committee may have considerably greater impact than four hundred letters to the young upstart from home. Unfortunately, many people fail to take notice of the position held, talent exhibited, and clout exercised by their representative before taking action. They also fail to consider the difficulties many members face in seeing their bills enacted into law. By expecting immediate returns for their minimal letter-writing efforts, they ignore the special requirements of an effective citizen campaign.

Many people also are unaware of the impersonal way their letters often will be handled. Their carefully composed letters will not likely reach their representative directly, but will be read by an administrative or legislative assistant. Typically, only the most important letters are brought directly to a legislator's attention. In fact, most members of Congress do not compose their own replies to constituent letters; rather, an office assistant types out answers to be signed by the congress member, giving constituents only the appearance of receiving a personal reply.

Moreover, any letter is bound to be only one among many pouring into a legislator's office. In most instances, a letter from a constituent

DOONESBURY　　　　　　　　　　　　　　　　　　　**by Garry Trudeau**

will not determine how a member of Congress votes on a bill. As we discussed earlier, members of Congress often place greater importance on their own opinions of a bill, especially if they feel they have researched the issue more thoroughly than have their constituents. In such an instance, a hapless citizen may simply receive a smug, precomposed reply stating the reasons for the representative's support or rejection of the bill in question.

Occasionally, notice is taken of constituents' views, especially if many people correspond on an issue. Such was the case in early 1974 when members of Congress were stunned by the enormous volume of letters demanding a bill of impeachment against Nixon. In fact, many people believe the only effective way to sway legislators is to trigger a mass letter-writing campaign designed to flood their offices with letters and petitions from home. This strategy is employed to convince legislators that constituents are deeply concerned about an issue and want immediate action.

However, even mass letter-writing campaigns have limitations. An avalanche of correspondence may not be very effective if the letters are not spontaneous and personal. Members of Congress know that in some letter-writing campaigns only a few citizens are behind the effort and that most of the other correspondents have a low commitment to the issue. Such campaigns lose their forcefulness when members learn that letters containing essentially the same information and language are handed to people on the street to sign and mail. "Most experienced Senators and Representatives," Rep. James Wright reflects, "suspect one of these organized campaigns when the first batch of mail begins to hit their desks. The repetition of certain phrases and slogans and the coincidence of several hundred communications in a given day on a certain subject in which little interest previously has been evinced by the constituency almost invariably tip the hand of those who would befuddle the lawmakers with numbers. The design sticks out all over, like a well-developed case of hives."[14] Thus, interest groups often advise their members to state in their own words why they support or reject a bill under debate. Be courteous, they are advised, for more flies can be caught with honey than vinegar.

Most people probably will have more success in asking for help with a personal problem. Although they may not obtain such help directly from their representative (few members of Congress, in fact, personally respond to constituents' requests for aid in most circumstances), they will be assisted by one of the caseworkers in the legislator's office. Each month these caseworkers may accept hundreds of requests for help in retrieving a lost social security check, speeding a relative through immigration, or acquiring information on a bill. Naturally, a person's ability to obtain results depends on the scope of the problem. It is easier to get help from a legislator's office in tracking down a lost social security check, for example, than in trying to stop a new highway from cutting through the neighborhood. Finding a lost social security check may involve little more than a caseworker's convincing an otherwise recalcitrant clerk to thumb through the constituent's records. But halting the invasion of a highway may require cajoling countless high officials into taking appropriate action. In such instances, unless public sentiment runs high against the proposed highway, a simple request for help from a legislator's office probably is doomed to failure.

Furthermore, success often depends on the motivations and talents of the caseworkers. While some respond speedily to a problem and know exactly what strings to pull, others are less committed to constituents and are helpless in cutting through bureaucratic red tape on their behalf.

Still, letters to a legislator's office can have spectacular results. Legislators have, on occasion, responded to a person's misfortune by introducing new legislation to rectify it. In 1972, an elderly woman wrote to California State Senator Nicholas Petris complaining that, under existing law, she would not be eligible for senior citizens' property tax assistance. She had been denied eligibility because she had been unable to meet her tax obligations the previous fiscal year. Her letter inspired Sen. Petris and his caseworker to put together a new bill easing the eligibility requirements. The bill, passed in March 1973, ultimately benefited not only the woman who wrote the letter but countless other citizens who faced a similar problem.

Using Television and Other Media

A more ambitious action strategy is to publicize an issue, with the intention of reaching as many people as possible. Because it is generally assumed (except perhaps among hardened supporters of the ruling-elite theory) that policy makers will be more responsive to an issue due to public awareness and concern, some citizens have turned to the mass media (television, radio, newspapers) to broaden the scope of their influence.

This strategy would seem to be worthwhile because, with the possible exceptions of gossip and rumor, television and newspapers have the greatest capacity to spread information. As stated in Chapter 8, the Roper Organization found in 1976 that 64 percent of American adults said they received most of their political news from watching television. Another large percentage said they received it from reading newspapers. In view of such findings, it might make sense for individuals to find ways to use television, newspapers, and other media to their own advantage.

Firing off a letter to the editor of a newspaper or magazine is, for many people, the first step. Letter writing can provide a variety of satisfactions, ranging from a feeling that one is performing a public service to expanding one's ego. Many people see letters as a way to get their views before an audience, to bend others to their own point of view. One drawback, however, is that writing a letter to the editor does not guarantee publication. Although no one knows what proportion of letters reach print, it is probably fewer than one in twenty in most large cities. Besides, letters to the editor are not very effective in stimulating public interest or in pressuring politicians. Although popular with readers, letters are not likely to compel them to translate what they have read into effective political action, even presuming they know how to do so. At best, a letter may attract a few wavering adherents to a cause or provide an inexpensive way to get something off one's chest.

Breaking into television is another alternative. Television has the advantage over newspapers of potentially reaching larger numbers of people and with more telling effect. If one accepts Marshall McLuhan's thesis, television does not even require as much effort from its audience. Viewers do not have to do something active, such as read, to get the message. (Of course, they may not be mentally attentive to its content, either.) However, getting a message on television is not an easy task. Broadcast time is extraordinarily expensive and beyond most people's financial capabilities. To use television, most people have to find either free or relatively inexpensive means of access.

One way to get a message on the air is through a free speech message or editorial. The Federal Communications Commission's *fairness doctrine*, introduced in 1949, requires broadcasters to "afford reasonable opportunity for the discussion of conflicting views on issues of public importance." This means that if a station carries an editorial on a controversial issue like the death penalty, it must provide air time for "responsible spokesmen" to voice opposing opinions. Although the fairness doctrine does not guarantee equal access for everyone, it can be exploited as a way to obtain free air time, especially if the station has failed to broadcast other points of view.

In fact, rulings by the Supreme Court and federal courts of appeals require stations to allow public access to the airwaves and uphold the citizen's right to challenge the renewal of broadcast licenses. A person who has little money but who can come up with a worthwhile community-oriented message may go to a broadcaster to request use of the airwaves. If a station manager proceeds to throw him into the streets, the individual can write to the Federal Communications Commission and, if the commission agrees with his complaint, make sufficient trouble for the station so that it has to take him seriously.

Assuming a person does succeed in making a brief statement on a local television station, he may reach more than a million people in a large city. Although a thirty-second or one-minute message is unlikely to have tremendous long-term impact on public consciousness, it may attract some support for an issue or publicize a worthwhile event. The impact of such a message can be extended, of course, by supplementing it with other forms of communication in an effort to reach more people.

Some observers note that cable television may provide even greater access to the media than is currently available. In a growing number of communities, people are subscribing to the cable system, which eliminates the "noise" and "ghosts" of over-the-air broadcasts and expands the number of available channels. Some communities that give cable operators a franchise to develop a cable system stipulate certain conditions: that they devote a portion of broadcast time to coverage of city council meetings; that they televise adult education courses; that they provide a channel for use by the schools; and that they offer opportunities for local residents to voice their views on public issues. Most communities, however, have not yet taken full advantage of the opportunities offered by cable television. They have handed out lucrative franchises to cable operators without compelling them to provide maximum service to citizens. But, because of the potential for many channels and two-way response mechanisms, the cable system may eventually provide expanded opportunities for citizen participation and political dialogue.[15]

Doing something newsworthy—something dramatic, new, or of special local interest—is another way to get a message on the air. Television news stations and newspapers will send out eager reporters if an event is sufficiently provocative or unusual. The key, of course, is to know what makes news. Holding an impromptu news conference or staging a demonstration would hardly be gratifying if no one showed up to cover the excitement.

However, one does not necessarily have to stage a dramatic event. Television and radio news stations often will respond to a direct request for coverage if an issue causes some local stir. In April 1974, Mrs. Virginia Kerr of Martinez, California, phoned a local television station asking it to cover an impending neighborhood disaster. The sloping hill behind her home was sliding inexorably into her backyard and threatening to destroy her house, as well as those of her neighbors. With the possibility that leaks in the utility pipes and the housing development on top of the hill were causing the slide, she hoped to use the media to pressure city officials into taking action. Mrs. Kerr was pleased, therefore, when the station sent out a reporter and cameras to film the impending disaster. As a result, her problem reached thousands of viewers in a brief two-minute segment on the 6:30 P.M. news.

Unfortunately, the results of the news coverage were minimal: Mrs. Kerr received no response from city officials or the public. She discovered that publicity alone would not guarantee a solution to her problem. Perhaps if her problem had been presented with more controversy—such as by pointing an accusing finger at city officials—and had broken into the news more than once, the response might have been greater. (The case was finally resolved through the courts.)

What, then, can be expected from using the media? Clearly, bending the ear of the public will not always bring about policy changes. After all, what are viewers likely to do once they become aware of an issue? Even though most people are aware of pollution and crime in the streets, they still feel helpless trying to transform that awareness into political solutions. One answer may be that provoking public indignation is less important than threatening elected officials with adverse publicity. Officials may sense that, even if constituents do not immediately convey their feelings through letters or other means, adverse publicity may threaten their position next time at the polls. In other words, media publicity may still result in policy changes even though it does not stimulate immediate public outcry.

One final question, however, should be considered. If ruling-elite theorists are correct that the media serve as instruments of an entrenched privileged elite, does this mean that few opportunities exist for citizens to present ideas radically opposed to those of the elite? It would seem that if a ruling-elite remains in control, only those who restrict their complaints to sliding hills, poor governmental administration, or occasional social injustices will find the media open avenues for political expression. Those who seriously intend to challenge the existing order, however, will find the same avenues blockaded, that the media resources granted to others will not be made available.

In fact, even if one does not accept the broad tenets of the ruling-elite theory, one may still accuse broadcasters and newspaper editors of not providing an open forum for alternative viewpoints. One only has to recall that, during the Vietnam War, the three major television networks refused to sell time to various citizen groups (including the Democratic National Committee) protesting administration policies on the war.[16] The Supreme Court in 1973 upheld the right of television and radio stations to turn down paid political advertisements on controversial issues.[17] Although stations are licensed by the government, the Court ruled, they are not official organs of the government and thus do not violate First Amendment rights when they refuse to run controversial ads. This means, for example, that an environmental group wishing to counter the political and social implications of Exxon's "Energy for a Strong America" commercials (see Chapter 7) can be denied the right to run their own commercials.

Yet, the extent to which even those who challenge the existing order can gain access to the media depends on the nature of the access. While so-called revolutionary groups might find it difficult to present free speech messages over local television (presuming they would even want to do so), they can and frequently do receive wide television coverage of their acts. In kidnapping Patricia Hearst in 1974, for instance, the Symbionese Liberation Army (SLA) called public attention to themselves far out of proportion to their small numbers.

The Litigation Alternative

In the event that the usual media or legislative channels are closed to pressure, another strategy is to challenge the legality of an action or statute in the courts. Many citizens and interest groups have achieved as much success by taking their causes to the courts as by trying to win public support or to pressure legislative and executive officials into taking action. The National Association for the Advancement of Colored People (NAACP), for example, has for years relied on *litigation* as a tactic to fight school segregation and job discrimination. By persuading the Supreme Court in 1954 to outlaw segregation in the public schools (*Brown* v. *Board of Education*), the NAACP won a legal victory as important as any gained through legislation in Congress. (Of course, as we saw earlier, the Court's inability to enforce its own rulings may retard the full fruition of victory.)

Even when used by an individual, a lawsuit can achieve wide-ranging political reform. In 1959, a registered voter in Tennessee named Charles Baker brought suit against the state's election officials. Baker charged them with violating his constitutional rights by having failed since 1901 to reapportion the legislative districts to reflect changes in population. Their inaction, he insisted, diluted his vote by permitting rural districts—some with fewer than four thousand people—to have the same representation as large urban ones, like his own, with more than seventy thousand people. This meant, for example, that in the Tennessee State Senate, 37 percent of the voters controlled more than 60 percent of the seats. By winning the case in the Supreme Court three years later (*Baker* v. *Carr*, 1962), Baker opened the way for citizens throughout the country to file similar suits demanding reapportionment of their state legislative and congressional districts.

However, despite this and other dramatic cases, legal tactics tend to be unreliable. Often the most one can expect from litigation is to win a delay, such as getting a temporary court injunction to halt construction of a high-rise building or a freeway. Many observers have noted that the courts can be more effectively employed to veto actions than to achieve long-term change. Of course, such delaying tactics can also reap great rewards. As an example of the many freeway construction revolts in recent years, La Raza Unita and the Sierra Club combined forces in the early 1970s to block construction of a controversial freeway through Hayward and Union City on the east side of San Francisco Bay. Taking the issue to court, they won an injunction against the project on grounds of detrimental environmental impact and the potential relocation problems of local residents. Such court actions have been similarly effective in San Antonio, Texas; Beverly Hills, California; Washington, D.C.; and elsewhere.

Litigation has the additional disadvantage, however, of usually involving a great deal of time and expense. After months of preparing a case for court, it may be months—or even years—before it is processed and settled. A typical case reaching the Supreme Court, for instance, may require anywhere from two to three years of hearings and appeals. In addition, litigation costs money—money to cover attorney's fees, research expenses, and court costs. Unless one can proceed *in forma pauperis* ("in the manner of a pauper"; see Chapter 11), a suit may well demand a financial commitment totally beyond the resources of the average person.

One possible exception to this involves a case where a person has suffered job discrimination. Under Title VII of the Civil Rights Act of 1964, the court may appoint a lawyer and assess court expenses and attorney fees against a person or company found guilty of discrimination. This means that a person with little financial support may still bring a legal suit, since a victory will offset all court expenses.

Because of the large financial commitment involved in bringing a lawsuit, some citizens and groups prefer to become involved in court actions by submitting *amicus curiae* ("friend of the court") briefs. As noted in Chapter 7, interested persons who are not direct litigants in a case can try to obtain the court's permission to file written arguments outlining their own legal views on an issue. By submitting amicus briefs, they can try to help one side in a dispute by presenting new information and arguments not provided by those who originally filed the suit. This tactic has been commonly used by the NAACP and the American Civil Liberties Union (ACLU) in civil rights and civil liberties cases.

An additional tactic is to join in a *class action suit.* This is a suit brought by one or more persons with a similar legal complaint who share the costs and other burdens of suing in court. The suit is initiated on behalf of the plaintiff and "all others similarly situated." An example would be a suit brought on behalf of all the women in a large corporation who face sex discrimination in hiring and promotion. The Supreme Court, however, has placed several restrictions on class action suits. The Court has ruled that in order to sue for damages in federal court, each individual in the suit must claim an interest of at least $10,000; individuals in a class cannot pool their claims to reach the $10,000 level.[18] In addition, persons initiating a federal class action suit must notify all other class members at their own expense.[19] This means that the more widespread the injustice, the more difficult it would be to bring a class action suit.

Using the courts is not the only means of taking legal action, however. As we saw in Chapter 12, the regulatory agencies of the federal bureaucracy wield a blend of legislative and judicial powers, and may become the targets of citizen pressure. John Banzhaf, for example, a young attorney from the Bronx, single-handedly compelled the television networks to provide equal time for antismoking commercials by writing a short letter to the Federal Communications Commission in 1967. He argued that, because the surgeon general of the United States had determined cigarette smoking to be hazardous to health, cigarette commercials should be considered legally controversial. Because the FCC fairness doctrine requires radio and television stations to air all sides of controversial issues, he wrote, the networks should be required to present antismoking commercials as well. (As we saw earlier, the Supreme Court in 1973 challenged this notion.) To Banzhaf's surprise, the FCC agreed with him and ordered the networks to provide time for antismoking ads, an action that moved Congress to pass legislation in 1971 banning cigarette commercials.[20]

Initiatives, Referenda, and Recalls

Another legal tactic is to resort to the *initiative.* Although most lawmaking is done by legislators elected specifically for that purpose, voters in at least twenty states have the power to pass laws directly without recourse to the legislature. By means of the initiative process, it is possible for a group to force the enactment of laws that legislators have either refused or failed to consider, as well as to pass state constitutional amendments. After securing a sufficient number of signatures on a petition, a group can place a proposition on the state ballot (as well as on many additional local ballots) to be voted on by the people. In this way, they can bypass both the legislature and the governor, who cannot veto or amend an initiative measure.

The initiative is a formidable tool, for a law passed in this way can have as much impact as any single legislative act. In 1978, for example, voters in California used the state initiative process to slash property taxes (see Chapter 13), while voters in Montana used it to restrict construction of nuclear power plants. Voters in Oregon even used it to allow denture makers, as well as dentists, to fix false teeth (thereby presumably saving themselves some money).

Moreover, voters in at least twenty-two states can employ the *referendum* to prevent laws passed by the legislature and signed by the governor from going into effect. In most of these states, bills do not become law until at least sixty to ninety days after the legislature adjourns. If a group of voters can round up enough signatures on a petition during that sixty- to ninety-day interval, a bill can be held in abeyance until the next election. Then, if a majority votes to kill the bill, it is declared void; otherwise, it goes into effect as planned. In most states and cities, certain measures, such as bond issues and constitutional amendments proposed by the legislature, cannot go into effect until they are submitted to the voters for approval. In Oregon, the legislature passed a sales tax measure half a dozen times, only to have it repeatedly rejected by a referendum vote.

Citizens in many states and cities also have the right to *recall* an elected official before his term officially expires. If enough signatures can be gathered on a petition, a special election must be held to decide whether the official should be booted out and replaced by another candidate. In contrast to initiative and referendum petitions, there usually is no time limit for circulating and filing a recall petition. Nor must the charges be restricted to certain offenses; an official may be removed from office for not parting his hair on the left side. Although successful efforts to recall governors and other state officials have been rare, hundreds of recalls have been effective against mayors and city council members. Voters in Los Angeles, for example, booted out Mayor Frank Shaw in 1938 following charges of corruption. In 1973, Berkeley voters dumped D'Army Bailey, one of three city council members students helped elect in 1971. And, in 1978, Mayor Dennis Kucinich of Cleveland only narrowly avoided being recalled by the voters. He managed to squeak through by only 236 of 120,000 votes cast, hardly a strong vote of confidence in his administration.

All three of these processes—initiative, referendum, and recall—were established as part of the Progressive movement at the turn of the century. In contrast to most of the Founding Fathers, who mistrusted public control over policy making, Progressives in the early 1900s intended the people to exercise more direct control over legislation and thus neutralize the influence of special interests dominating the state legislatures. In the opinion of many Progressives, these procedures represented the best alternative forms of "direct democracy" available in a large territorial system.

However, growing populations and soaring campaign costs have tended to frustrate these ideals. Although any person today may originate an initiative proposal, many people and a lot of money are needed to organize a successful petition campaign at the state level. To place a proposition on the ballot in most states, it is necessary to obtain a sizable number of valid signatures from registered voters. In the state of Washington, for instance, initiative organizers must collect the signatures of voters equal to at least 8 percent of the total votes cast for governor in the preceding election.

Once the proposition appears on the ballot, petition organizers must then face the arduous task of persuading skeptical voters to support it. Usually, doing so requires a well-organized and expensive campaign. Recent history has shown that the most active groups sponsoring or opposing state initiatives have been well-funded special-interest groups, like labor unions and large corporations, served by skilled public relations experts (who may hire professional "petition-pushers" to circulate petitions and collect the required signatures). Relatively few other people have the organization or financial resources to spread word of a proposition and win support for its adoption. Thus, despite the Progressives' hope that the initiative process would reduce control over government by special interests, it has been special interests, not ordinary citizens, who have benefited most from its use at the state level.

Probably an individual's best chance of effectively using the initiative process is at the local level. Cities throughout the country guarantee citizens the right to originate legislation by means of the initiative. Although used less frequently today than in the past, local initiatives still have the advantage of requiring fewer signatures and less expense than state propositions. A handful of people in a small community can win political victories not obtainable through normal legislative channels. Students at Berkeley, for example, resorted to the initiative process to pass a rent control law in 1972, as well as an ordinance in 1973 decriminalizing personal possession and use of marijuana. Neither of these measures was a lasting success, however, since both were invalidated by court action. Although the initiative process in Berkeley and elsewhere has yielded mixed results, it will continue to be used by many groups as one of several alternative electoral strategies.

Resorting to Direct Action

Finally, it has been possible for people to bring about changes in public policy through *direct action*. Direct action embraces a wide variety of both legal and illegal activities, ranging from passive resistance and hunger strikes to mass demonstrations, sit-ins, and boycotts.

Although many people take a negative view of such tactics, several forms of direct action—such as peaceful demonstrations and strikes—have been upheld by the Supreme Court as legitimate expressions of public protest and dissent. As the Court ruled in one important case, the use of the streets and public places "for purposes of assembly, communicating thoughts between citizens, and discussing public questions [is] a part of the privileges, immunities, rights, and liberties of citizens."[21] In fact, even direct action strategies not officially sanctioned by the Supreme Court, such as violent confrontations and seizures of property, have played a prominent role in the history of American politics. Recent studies have made a persuasive case that direct action tactics are very much a part of our political heritage and that virtually every major social movement has resorted to them at one time or another. This heritage has been seen in the efforts of workers to achieve union representation, the early lunch counter sit-ins by civil rights activists in the South, the mass demonstrations against the Vietnam War, the seizure of Alcatraz and other territories by American Indian tribes, and the strikes and boycotts by migrant farm workers organized by Cesar Chavez. It even has been witnessed in nationwide strikes by truckers protesting gasoline shortages and in boycotts by consumers upset over the rising cost of meat.

The reasons for engaging in direct action or protest politics are practically endless. A variety of personal motivations, ideological assumptions, and strategic considerations may underlie a decision to resort to confrontation. The purpose of such action may be to dramatize an injustice, to focus public attention on an issue, or simply to create enough trouble to force a resolution of the problem. "Nonviolent direct action," Martin Luther King, Jr., once wrote, "seeks to create such a crisis and establish such creative tension that a community that has constantly refused to negotiate is forced to confront the issue."[22]

Although well-organized and reasonably confident groups have successfully employed direct action tactics in the past, such tactics continue to have special appeal for groups who are less well organized, less well off financially, and less than optimistic about using conventional political channels to achieve their goals. By resorting to boycotts, strikes, and demonstrations, they hope to call attention to injustice and stimulate others to take action. Inevitably, they expect that by employing such tactics they will achieve an otherwise unattainable solution to their problem. One study suggests that, prior to World War II, challenging groups who resorted to direct action to achieve limited goals enjoyed a higher success rate than similar groups who always "played by the rules."[23]

Direct action may also appeal to those impatient with the sluggishness of conventional political strategies, even to the point of engaging in illegal acts. As Robert Sherrill has noted, "Since it took six years under the Highway Beautification Act to get one billboard removed through official channels, it does seem rather reasonable—whatever the morality of the action—for a band of University of Michigan students to make midnight forays with axe and saw and topple dozens of billboards."[24]

Some doubt whether there is room in a democracy for any form of political action that violates the law. If individuals or groups are willing to play by the rules under most circumstances (and especially when they win), are they justified in defying those rules when it suits them to do so? For those who believe in strictly observing the law, the answer is clearly negative: violations of the law are a threat to the legal system and should be prevented. But for those preoccupied with using the best available strategy to correct an injustice, the question is more difficult to resolve. In their view, willful disobedience to the law may be the only method of changing a "bad" law, and is therefore not inconsistent with democratic principles. More than likely, how one sees direct action tactics will vary, depending on which group is using them. It is easier to be critical of such tactics when one disagrees with the goals being sought, and to be more supportive when one is in sympathy with those goals.

The questionable legality of some direct action tactics does pose problems for many people. Few Americans are aware of the rules covering protest tactics, and probably with good reason. Although the First Amendment guarantees "freedom of speech . . . or the right of the people peaceably to assemble, and to petition the Government for a redress of grievances," there is no automatic constitutional protection for those wishing to dissent or protest at any time or place. State and city officials are given great latitude to restrict almost any public activity they believe might incite violence or disrupt other legitimate interests. As a result, laws dealing even with peaceful demonstrations abound in local variations.

As would be expected, like all other strategies, direct action does have limitations. For one thing, it may be disadvantageous for groups seeking wide-based public support. Strikes, sit-ins, and demonstrations run the risk of alienating potentially sympathetic groups who may agree with the goal but reject the methods used to achieve it. While many in our society welcome the correction of injustice, they tolerate only a narrow range of corrective approaches. They reject the use of any tactic that violates their norm of political conduct.

Nor can one guarantee that, after much effort has been made to organize a meaningful demonstration or boycott, it will accomplish the intended goal. If a protest campaign is designed to persuade other people to join the protest and demand reform, then success would depend on at least gaining television and other media coverage. Tactics and platforms would have to be geared to what those in the media consider newsworthy just to gain publicity for the action. Even then, publicity may not compel the public or decision makers to take appropriate measures. To assume simply that awareness of a problem automatically leads to its solution is to belie the conservatism of the political process.

One often finds it difficult, in fact, to evaluate the gains made through direct action. The domestic protests against the Vietnam War, for example, yielded ambiguous results. Arguably, the wave of protest by students and others succeeded in revealing the deep divisions within the society over the war, in publicizing the war's injustices, and in eventually bringing it to an end. But in the eyes of many, the protests were a failure. Despite pledges to "close down the government" and "stop the war machine," the war dragged on for more than eight years—longer than World War II or the Korean conflict—and killed or maimed millions on both sides.

The civil rights struggle, on the other hand, presents a more convincing case that direct action can bring about tangible results. The sit-ins, freedom rides, and marches in the early 1960s focused national attention on the injustices of segregation and succeeded in winning many local battles against segregation in restaurants, on buses, in churches, hotels, and libraries. They also helped prompt congressional legislation—notably the 1964 Civil Rights Act barring discrimination in public accommodations—and helped force compliance with Supreme Court decisions. Thus, while the effects of direct action tactics are often ambiguous, policy changes can occur. Direct action tactics can modify people's attitudes and pave the way for future reform.

Evaluation: The Measure of Success

Looking at the various strategies we have discussed, we may conclude that an individual working alone will likely have a difficult time achieving many of his or her political goals. It would appear, especially after our discussion of interest groups in Chapter 7, that groups, not single individuals, have become the basic units of influence in our society and that the most promising way to affect public policy is through concerted group action. Membership in an organization enhances the prospects that an individual will be capable of influencing government and will make an effort to do so.

Yet, it is sometimes difficult for people to become part of an effective political organization. Their immediate or long-term needs may not find adequate representation in any established group. Such has generally been true of consumers, the elderly poor, and those generally ignored in the tussle for political favors. Nor is it easy to put together an effective organization from the ground up. Even when people share a common problem or an enthusiasm for similar goals, tremendous efforts and expenditures in time and money are required to give birth to an effective political machine. Of course, this does not exclude temporarily *using* existing organizations for one's purposes. Often a group can be effectively employed by individuals who are not necessarily connected with it. Thousands of people, for example, have benefited from the services of the Legal Aid Society and the American Civil Liberties Union even though they were not members and their own personal resources were meager.

However, many people simply do not feel comfortable or satisfied as part of a larger whole; their basic individualism demands that they alone should be able to bring about sweeping policy changes. Compelled to reject any thought of becoming submerged in a larger collective body, they prefer instead that policy makers respond to their personal expectations and demands. But because they cannot achieve a substantial degree of individual impact, they succumb to frustration and drop out.

In this sense, we might say that the measure of success in influencing policy depends greatly on one's expectations. Those who desire as single individuals to achieve immediate and far-reaching solutions to national or local problems may regard anything short of such solutions as worthless. Moreover, so long as they are concerned only with their own individual potency, they are likely to ignore the potential rewards of working in concerted action. As we have seen in the preceding chapters, ordinary citizens, members of Congress, and even presidents occasionally experience a sense of personal impotency and lack of control over their political environment. Their expectations of personal importance are such that each unrealized goal becomes a testament to the inflexibility of "the system."

On a final note, we should not be so obsessed with the pursuit of power that we measure political actions solely in terms of efficacy and success. In many instances, political acts carry personal and symbolic values separate from the expectation of achieving concrete goals. Participating in a demonstration, voting, or writing a letter to the editor can have expressive as well as instrumental benefits. Persons involved in such activities may care less about influencing other people's behavior than about the positive feelings they enjoy from expressing their views.

Indeed, from a philosophical perspective, political acts may even be seen as expressions of human dignity and morality. In protesting a social injustice or in rebelling against authority, a person may be asserting his or her loyalty to a higher ideal. The fear of failing to achieve a tangible goal may be less important than the need to voice one's commitment to certain values. If a desire exists, for example, to aid the cause of Indian rights or to help ameliorate the deplorable conditions of the elderly poor, then it would be unjust not to become involved simply because one fears failure in the effort. By not participating, we turn the fear of failure into a self-fulfilling prophecy, a submission to expediency.

Key Terms

democracy

fairness doctrine

litigation

amicus curiae brief

class action suit

initiative

referendum

recall

direct action

Notes

1. Massimo Salvadori, *Liberal Democracy* (New York: Doubleday, 1957).

2. U.S. Senate, Committee on Government Operations, "Confidence and Concern: Citizens View American Government, A Survey of Public Attitudes," pt. 1 (Washington, D.C.: U.S. Government Printing Office, 1973).

3. John G. Robinson, Jerrold G. Rush, and Kendran B. Head, *Measurements of Political Attitudes* (Ann Arbor: University of Michigan, Survey Research Center, 1968).

4. James Burkhart et al., *Strategies for Political Participation* (Cambridge, Mass.: Winthrop, 1972), p. 29.

5. Harris Survey, 25 March 1976.

6. Herbert Kaufman, "Administrative Decentralization and Political Power," *Public Administration Review*, January/February 1969, pp. 3–15.

7. For one interesting study of the relationship between participation and community size, see Robert Dahl and Edward Tufte, *Size and Democracy* (Stanford: Stanford University Press, 1973).

8. For one view on this, see David C. Schwartz, *Political Alienation and Political Behavior* (Chicago: Aldine, 1973).

9. Kaufman, "Administrative Decentralization."

10. Amitai Etzioni, *Public Opinion Quarterly*, Winter 1973/74, p. 660.

11. Murray Edelman, *The Symbolic Uses of Politics* (Urbana: University of Illinois Press, 1964), p. 17.

12. *Congressional Quarterly Weekly Report*, 2 December 1978, p. 3369.

13. Gabriel Almond and Sidney Verba, *The Civic Culture* (Princeton: Princeton University Press, 1963), p. 143.

14. Jim Wright, *You and Your Congressman* (New York: Coward-McCann, 1965), pp. 189–190.

15. For a more detailed analysis of the cable system, see Ralph Lee Smith, "The Wired Nation," *The Nation*, 18 May 1970, pp. 582–606.

16. See Robert Cirino, *Don't Blame the People* (New York: Random House, 1971).

17. *Columbia Broadcasting System* v. *Democratic National Committee* (1973).

18. *Zahn* v. *International Paper Co.* (1973).

19. *Eisen* v. *Carlisle & Jacquelin* (1974).

20. See Joseph A. Page, "The Law Professor Behind Ash, Soup, Pump and Crash," in Robert Paul Wolff, ed., *Styles of Political Action in America* (New York: Random House, 1972), pp. 124–134.

21. *Hague* v. *C.I.O.* (1939).

22. Martin Luther King, Jr., "A Letter from Birmingham City Jail," 1963.

23. William A. Gamson, "Violence and Political Power: The Meek Don't Make It," *Psychology Today*, July 1974, pp. 35–41.

24. Robert Sherrill, *Why They Call It Politics*, 2nd ed. (New York: Harcourt Brace Jovanovich, 1974), p. 316.

Recommended Reading

BINSTOCK, ROBERT H. and KATHERINE ELY, eds. *The Politics of the Powerless.* Cambridge, Mass.: Winthrop, 1971.

BURKHART, JAMES, et al. *Strategies for Political Participation.* Cambridge, Mass.: Winthrop, 1972.

CARTER, APRIL. *Direct Action and Liberal Democracy.* New York: Harper & Row, 1973.

GOLEMBIEWSKI, ROBERT T., et al. *Dilemmas of Political Participation.* Englewood Cliffs, N.J.: Prentice-Hall, 1973.

NORRIS, BOB, and KEN ROWE. *How to Take Over Your Local Government.* Berkeley, Calif.: Institute for Self-Government, 1975.

ROUDER, SUSAN. *American Politics: Playing the Game.* Boston: Houghton Mifflin, 1977.

WALZER, MICHAEL. *Political Action.* New York: Quadrangle, 1971.

WOLFF, ROBERT PAUL, ed. *Styles of Political Action in America.* New York: Random House, 1972.

The Constitution of the United States

The Preamble

We the People of the United States, in Order to form a more perfect Union, establish Justice, insure domestic Tranquility, provide for the common defence, promote the general Welfare, and secure the Blessings of Liberty to ourselves and our Posterity, do ordain and establish this Constitution for the United States of America.

Article I

Section 1. All Legislative Powers herein granted shall be vested in a Congress of the United States, which shall consist of a Senate and House of Representatives.

Section 2. The House of Representatives shall be composed of Members chosen every second Year by the People of the several States, and the Electors in each State shall have the Qualifications requisite for Electors of the most numerous Branch of the State Legislature.

No Person shall be a Representative who shall not have attained to the Age of twenty five Years, and been seven Years a Citizen of the United States, and who shall not, when elected, be an Inhabitant of that State in which he shall be chosen.

Representatives and direct Taxes shall be apportioned among the several States which may be included within this Union, according to their respective Numbers, which shall be determined by adding to the whole Number of free Persons, including those bound to Service for a Term of Years, and excluding Indians not taxed, three fifths of all other Persons.

The actual Enumeration shall be made within three Years after the first Meeting of the Congress of the United States, and within every subsequent Term of ten Years, in such Manner as they shall by Law direct. The Number of Representatives shall not exceed one for every thirty Thousand, but each State shall have at Least one Representative; and until such enumeration shall be made, the State of New Hampshire shall be entitled to chuse three, Massachusetts eight, Rhode-Island and Providence Plantations one, Connecticut five, New-York six, New Jersey four, Pennsylvania eight, Delaware one, Maryland six, Virginia ten, North Carolina five, South Carolina five, and Georgia three.

When vacancies happen in the Representation from any State, the Executive Authority thereof shall issue Writs of Election to fill such Vacancies.

The House of Representatives shall chuse their speaker and other Officers; and shall have the sole Power of Impeachment.

Section 3. The Senate of the United States shall be composed of two Senators from each State, chosen by the Legislature thereof, for six Years; and each Senator shall have one Vote.

Immediately after they shall be assembled in Consequence of the first Election, they shall be divided as equally as may be into three Classes. The Seats of the Senators of the first Class shall be vacated at the Expiration of the second Year, of the second Class at the Expiration of the fourth Year, and of the third Class at the Expiration of the sixth Year, so that one third may be chosen every second Year; and if Vacancies happen by Resignation, or otherwise, during the Recess of the Legislature of any State, the Executive thereof may make temporary Appointments until the next Meeting of the Legislature, which shall then fill such Vacancies.

No Person shall be a Senator who shall not have attained to the Age of thirty Years, and been nine Years a Citizen of the United States, and who shall not, when elected, be an Inhabitant of that State for which he shall be chosen.

The Vice President of the United States shall be President of the Senate, but shall have no Vote, unless they be equally divided.

The Senate shall chuse their other Officers, and also a President pro tempore, in the Absence of the Vice President, or when he shall exercise the Office of the President of the United States.

The Senate shall have the sole Power to try all Impeachments. When sitting for that Purpose, they shall be on Oath or Affirmation. When the President of the United States is tried, the Chief Justice shall preside: And no Person shall be convicted without the Concurrence of two thirds of the Members present.

Judgment in Cases of Impeachment shall not extend further than to removal from Office, and disqualification to hold and enjoy any Office of honor, Trust or Profit under the United States: but the Party convicted shall nevertheless be liable and subject to Indictment, Trial, Judgment and Punishment, according to law.

Section 4. The Times, Places and Manner of holding Elections for

Senators and Representatives, shall be prescribed in each State by the legislature thereof; but the Congress may at any time by Law make or alter such Regulations, except as to the Places of chusing Senators.

The Congress shall assemble at least once in every Year, and such Meeting shall be on the first Monday in December, unless they shall by Law appoint a different Day.

Section 5. Each House shall be the Judge of the Elections, Returns and Qualifications of its own Members, and a Majority of each shall constitute a Quorum to do Business; but a smaller Number may adjourn from day to day, and may be authorized to compel the Attendance of absent Members, in such Manner, and under such Penalties as each House may provide.

Each House may determine the Rules of its Proceedings, punish its Members for disorderly Behaviour, and, with the Concurrence of two thirds, expel a Member.

Each House shall keep a Journal of its Proceedings, and from time to time publish the same, excepting such Parts as may in their Judgment require Secrecy; and the Yeas and Nays of the Members of either House on any question shall, at the Desire of one fifth of those Present, be entered on the Journal.

Neither House, during the Session of Congress, shall, without the Consent of the other, adjourn for more than three days, nor to any other Place than that in which the two Houses shall be sitting.

Section 6. The Senators and Representatives shall receive a Compensation for their Services, to be ascer-

tained by Law, and paid out of the Treasury of the United States. They shall in all Cases, except Treason, Felony and Breach of the Peace, be privileged from Arrest during their Attendance at the Session of their respective Houses, and in going to and returning from the same; and for any Speech or Debate in either House, they shall not be questioned in any other Place.

No Senator or Representative shall, during the Time for which he was elected, be appointed to any civil Office under the Authority of the United States, which shall have been created, or the Emoluments whereof shall have been encreased during such time; and no Person holding any Office under the United States, shall be a Member of either House during his Continuance in Office.

Section 7. All Bills for raising Revenue shall originate in the House of Representatives; but the Senate may propose or concur with Amendments as on other Bills.

Every Bill which shall have passed the House of Representatives and the Senate, shall, before it become a Law, be presented to the President of the United States; If he approve he shall sign it, but if not he shall return it, with his Objections to that House in which it shall have originated, who shall enter the Objections at large on their Journal, and proceed to reconsider it. If after such Reconsideration two thirds of that House shall agree to pass the Bill, it shall be sent, together with the Objections, to the other House, by which it shall likewise be reconsidered, and if approved by two thirds of that House, it shall become a

Law. But in all such Cases the Votes of both Houses shall be determined by Yeas and Nays, and the Names of the Persons voting for and against the Bill shall be entered on the Journal of each House respectively. If any Bill shall not be returned by the President within ten Days (Sunday excepted) after it shall have been presented to him, the Same shall be a Law, in like Manner as if he had signed it, unless the Congress by their Adjournment prevent its Return, in which Case it shall not be a Law.

Every Order, Resolution, or Vote to which the Concurrence of the Senate and House of Representatives may be necessary (except on a question of Adjournment) shall be presented to the President of the United States; and before the Same shall take Effect, shall be approved by him, or being disapproved by him, shall be repassed by two thirds of the Senate and House of Representatives, according to the Rules and Limitations prescribed in the Case of a Bill.

Section 8. The Congress shall have Power To lay and collect Taxes, Duties, Imposts and Excises, to pay the Debts and provide for the common Defence and general Welfare of the United States; but all Duties, Imposts and Excises shall be uniform throughout the United States;

To borrow Money on the credit of the United States;

To regulate Commerce with foreign Nations, and among the several States, and with the Indian Tribes;

To establish an uniform Rule of Naturalization, and uniform Laws on the subject of Bankruptcies throughout the United States;

To coin Money, regulate the Value thereof, and of foreign Coin, and fix the Standard of Weights and Measures;

To provide for the Punishment of counterfeiting the Securities and current Coin of the United States;

To establish Post Offices and post Roads;

To promote the Progress of Science and useful Arts, by securing for limited Times to Authors and Inventors the exclusive Right to their respective Writings and Discoveries;

To constitute Tribunals inferior to the supreme Court;

To define and punish Piracies and Felonies committed on the high Seas, and Offences against the Law of Nations;

To declare War, grant Letters of Marque and Reprisal, and make Rules concerning Captures on Land and Water;

To raise and support Armies, but no Appropriation of Money to that Use shall be for a longer Term than two Years;

To provide and maintain a Navy;

To make Rules for the Government and Regulation of the land and naval Forces;

To provide for calling forth the Militia to execute the Laws of the Union, suppress Insurrections and repel Invasions;

To provide for organizing, arming, and disciplining, the Militia, and for governing such Part of them as may be employed in the Service of the United States, reserving to the States respectively, the Appointment of the Officers, and the Authority of training the Militia according to the discipline prescribed by Congress;

To exercise exclusive Legislation in all Cases whatsoever, over such District (not exceeding ten Miles square) as may, by Cession of particular States, and the Acceptance of Congress, become the Seat of the Government of the United States, and to exercise like Authority over all Places purchased by the Consent of the Legislature of the State in which the Same shall be for the Erection of Forts, Magazines, Arsenals, dock-Yards, and other needful Buildings; –And

To make all Laws which shall be necessary and proper for carrying into Execution the foregoing Powers, and all other Powers vested by this Constitution in the Government of the United States, or in any Department or Officer thereof.

Section 9. The Migration or Importation of such Persons as any of the States now existing shall think proper to admit, shall not be prohibited by the Congress prior to the Year one thousand eight hundred and eight, but a Tax or duty may be imposed on such Importation, not exceeding ten dollars for each Person.

The Privilege of the Writ of Habeas Corpus shall not be suspended, unless when in Cases of Rebellion or Invasion the public Safety may require it.

No Bill of Attainder or ex post facto Law shall be passed.

No Capitation, or other direct, Tax shall be laid, unless in Proportion to the Census or Enumeration herein before directed to be taken.

No Tax or Duty shall be laid on Articles exported from any State.

No Preference shall be given by any Regulation of Commerce or Revenue to the Ports of one State over those of another: nor shall Vessels bound to, or from, one State be obliged to enter, clear, or pay Duties in another.

No Money shall be drawn from the Treasury, but in Consequence of Appropriations made by Law; and a regular Statement and Account of the Receipts and Expenditures of all public Money shall be published from time to time.

No Title of Nobility shall be granted by the United States: And no Person holding any Office of Profit or Trust under them, shall, without the Consent of the Congress, accept of any present, Emolument, Office, or Title, of any kind whatever, from any King, Prince, or foreign States.

Section 10. No State shall enter into any Treaty, Alliance, or Confederation; grant Letters of Marque and Reprisal; coin Money; emit Bills of Credit; make any Thing but gold and silver Coin a Tender in Payment of Debts; pass any Bill of Attainder, ex post facto Law, or Law impairing the Obligation of Contracts, or grant any Title of Nobility.

No State shall, without the Consent of the Congress, lay any Imposts or Duties on Imports or Exports, except what may be absolutely necessary for executing its inspection Laws: and the net Produce of all Duties and Imposts, laid by any State on Imports or Exports, shall be for the Use of the Treasury of the United States; and all such Laws shall be subject to the Revision and Controul of the Congress.

No State shall, without the Consent of Congress, lay any Duty of Tonnage, keep Troops, or Ships of War in time of Peace, enter into any Agreement or Compact with another State, or with a foreign Power, or engage in War, unless actually invaded, or in such imminent Danger as will not admit of delay.

Article II

Section 1. The executive Power shall be vested in a President of the United States of America. He shall hold his Office during the Term of four Years, and, together with the Vice President, chosen for the same term, be elected, as follows.

Each State shall appoint, in such Manner as the Legislature thereof may direct, a Number of Electors, Equal to the whole Number of Senators and Representatives to which the State may be entitled in the Congress: but no Senator or Representative, or Person holding an Office of Trust or Profit under the United States, shall be appointed an Elector.

The Electors shall meet in their respective States, and vote by Ballot for two Persons, of whom one at least shall not be an Inhabitant of the same State with themselves. And they shall make a List of all the Persons voted for, and the Number of Votes for each; which List they shall sign and certify, and transmit sealed to the Seat of the Government of the United States, directed to the President of the Senate. The President of the Senate shall, in the Presence of the Senate and House of Representatives, open all the Certificates, and the Votes shall then be counted. The Person having the greatest Number of Votes shall be the President, if such Number be a Majority of the whole Number of Electors appointed; and if there be more than

one who have such Majority, and have an equal Number of Votes, then the House of Representatives shall immediately chuse by Ballot one of them for President: and if no Person have a Majority, then from the five highest on the List the said House shall in like Manner chuse the President. But in chusing the President, the Votes shall be taken by States, the Representation from each State having one Vote; A quorum for this Purpose shall consist of a Member or Members from two thirds of the States, and a Majority of all the States shall be necessary to a Choice. In every Case, after the Choice of the President, the Person having the greatest Number of Votes of the Electors shall be the Vice President. But if there should remain two or more who have equal Votes, the Senate shall chuse from them by Ballot the Vice President.

The Congress may determine the Time of chusing the Electors and the Day on which they shall give their Votes; which Day shall be the same throughout the United States.

No Person except a natural born Citizen, or a Citizen of the United States, at the time of the Adoption of this Constitution, shall be eligible to the Office of President; neither shall any Person be eligible to that Office who shall not have attained to the Age of thirty five Years, and been fourteen Years a Resident within the United States.

In Case of the Removal of the President from Office, or of his Death, Resignation, or Inability to discharge the Powers and Duties of the said Office, the Same shall devolve on the Vice President, and the Congress may by

Law provide for the Case of Removal, Death, Resignation or Inability, both of the President and Vice President, declaring what Officer shall then act as President, and such Officer shall act accordingly, until the Disability be removed, or a President shall be elected.

The President shall, at stated Times, receive for his Services a Compensation, which shall neither be encreased nor diminished during the Period for which he shall have been elected, and he shall not receive within that Period any other Emolument from the United States, or any of them.

Before he enter on the Execution of his Office, he shall take the following Oath or Affirmation:—"I do solemnly swear (or affirm) that I will faithfully execute the Office of President of the United States, and will to the best of my Ability, preserve, protect and defend the Constitution of the United States."

Section 2. The President shall be Commander in Chief of the Army and Navy of the United States, and of the Militia of the several States, when called into the actual Service of the United States; he may require the Opinion, in writing, of the principal Officer in each of the executive Departments, upon any Subject relating to the Duties of their respective Offices, and he shall have power to grant Reprieves and Pardons for Offences against the United States, except in Cases of Impeachment.

He shall have Power, by and with the Advice and Consent of the Senate, to make Treaties, provided two thirds of the Senators present concur; and he shall nominate, and by and with the Advice and Consent of the Senate, shall appoint Ambassadors, other public Ministers and Consuls, Judges of the supreme Court, and all other Officers of the United States, whose Appointments are not herein otherwise provided for, and which shall be established by Law; but the Congress may by Law vest the Appointment of such inferior Officers, as they think proper, in the President alone, in the Courts of Law, or in the Heads of Departments.

The President shall have the Power to fill up all Vacancies that may happen during the Recess of the Senate, by granting Commissions which shall expire at the End of their next Session.

Section 3. He shall from time to time give to the Congress Information of the State of the Union, and recommend to their Consideration such Measures as he shall judge necessary and expedient; he may, on extraordinary Occasions, convene both Houses, or either of them, and in Case of Disagreement between them, with Respect to the Time of Adjournment, he may adjourn them to such Time as he shall think proper; he shall take Care that the Laws be faithfully executed, and shall Commission all the Officers of the United States.

Section 4. The President, Vice President, and all civil Officers of the United States, shall be removed from Office on Impeachment for, and Conviction of, Treason, Bribery, or other High Crimes and Misdemeanors.

Article III

Section 1. The judicial Power of the United States, shall be vested in one supreme Court, and in such inferior

Courts as the Congress may from time to time ordain and establish. The Judges, both of the supreme and inferior Courts, shall hold their Offices during good Behaviour, and shall, at stated Times, receive for their Services, a Compensation, which shall not be diminished during their Continuance in Office.

Section 2. The judicial Power shall extend to all Cases, in Law and Equity, arising under this Constitution, the Laws of the United States, and Treaties made, or which shall be made, under their Authority;–to all Cases affecting Ambassadors, other public Ministers and Consuls;–to all Cases of admiralty and maritime Jurisdiction;–to Controversies to which the United States shall be a Party;–to Controversies between two or more States; between a State and Citizens of another State;–between Citizens of different States;–between Citizens of the same State claiming Lands under Grants of different States, and between a State or the Citizens thereof, and foreign States, Citizens or Subjects.

In all Cases affecting Ambassadors, other public Ministers and Consuls, and those in which a State shall be Party, the supreme Court shall have original Jurisdiction. In all the other Cases before mentioned, the supreme Court shall have appellate Jurisdiction, both as to Law and Fact, with such Exceptions, and under such Regulations as the Congress shall make.

The Trial of all Crimes, except in Cases of Impeachment, shall be by Jury; and such Trial shall be held in the State where the said Crimes shall have been committed; but when not committed within any State, the Trial shall be at such Place or Places as the Congress may by Law have directed.

Section 3. Treason against the United States, shall consist only in levying War against them, or in adhering to their Enemies, giving them Aid and Comfort. No Person shall be convicted of Treason unless on the Testimony of two Witnesses to the same overt Act, or on Confession in open Court.

The Congress shall have Power to declare the Punishment of Treason, but no Attainder of Treason shall work Corruption of Blood, or Forfeiture except during the Life of the Person attainted.

Article IV

Section 1. Full Faith and Credit shall be given in each State to the public Acts, Records, and judicial Proceedings of every other State. And the Congress may by general Laws prescribe the Manner in which such Acts, Records and Proceedings shall be proved, and the Effect thereof.

Section 2. The Citizens of each State shall be entitled to all Privileges and Immunities of Citizens in the several States.

A Person charged in any State with Treason, Felony, or other Crime, who shall flee from Justice, and be found in another State, shall on Demand of the executive Authority of the State from which he fled, be delivered up, to be removed to the State having Jurisdiction of the Crime.

No Person held to Service or Labour in one State, under the Laws thereof, escaping into another, shall, in Consequence of any Law or Regulation therein, be discharged from such Service or Labour, but shall be delivered up on Claim of the Party to whom such Service or Labour may be due.

Section 3. New States may be admitted by the Congress into this Union; but no new State shall be formed or erected within the Jurisdiction of any other State; nor any State be formed by the Junction of two or more States, or Parts of States, without the Consent of the Legislatures of the States concerned as well as of the Congress.

The Congress shall have Power to dispose of and make all needful Rules and Regulations respecting the Territory or other Property belonging to the United States; and nothing in this Constitution shall be so construed as to Prejudice any Claims of the United States, or of any particular State.

Section 4. The United States shall guarantee to every State in this Union a Republican Form of Government, and shall protect each of them against Invasion; and on Application of the Legislature, or of the Executive (when the Legislature cannot be convened) against domestic Violence.

Article V

The Congress, whenever two thirds of both Houses shall deem it necessary, shall propose Amendments to this Constitution, or, on the Application of the Legislatures of two thirds of the several States, shall call a Convention for proposing Amendments, which, in either Case, shall be valid to all Intents and Purposes, as Part of this Constitution, when ratified by the Legislatures of three fourths of the several States, or by Conventions in three fourths thereof as the one or the other Mode of Ratification may be proposed by the Congress; Provided that no Amendment which may be made prior to the Year One thousand eight hundred and eight shall in any Manner affect the first and fourth Clauses in the Ninth Section of the first Article; and that no State, without its Consent, shall be deprived of its equal Suffrage in the Senate.

Article VI

All Debts contracted and Engagements entered into, before the Adoption of this Constitution, shall be as valid against the United States under this Constitution, as under the Confederation.

This Constitution, and the Laws of the United States which shall be made in Pursuance thereof; and all Treaties made, or which shall be made, under the Authority of the United States, shall be the supreme Law of the Land; and the Judges in every State shall be bound thereby, any Thing in the Constitution or Laws of any State to the Contrary notwithstanding.

The Senators and Representatives before mentioned, and the Members of the several State Legislatures, and all executive and judicial Officers, both of the United States and of the several States, shall be bound by Oath or Affirmation, to support this Constitution; but no religious Test shall ever be required as a Qualification to any Office or public Trust under the United States.

Article VII

The Ratification of the Conventions of nine States, shall be sufficient for the Establishment of this Constitution between the States so ratifying the Same.

Done in Convention by the Unanimous Consent of the States present the Seventeenth Day of September in the Year of our Lord one thousand seven hundred and Eighty seven and of the Independence of the United States of America the Twelfth. In witness whereof We have hereunto subscribed our Names.

The Bill of Rights

[The first 10 Amendments were ratified December 15, 1791, and form what is known as the Bill of Rights]

AMENDMENT 1

Congress shall make no law respecting an establishment of religion, or prohibiting the free exercise thereof; or abridging the freedom of speech, or of the press; or the right of the people peaceably to assemble, and to petition the Government for a redress of grievances.

AMENDMENT 2

A well regulated Militia, being necessary to the security of a free State, the right of the people to keep and bear Arms, shall not be infringed.

AMENDMENT 3

No Soldier shall, in time of peace be quartered in any house, without the consent of the Owner, nor in time of war, but in a manner to be prescribed by law.

AMENDMENT 4

The right of the people to be secure in their persons, houses, papers, and effects, against unreasonable searches and seizures, shall not be violated, and no Warrants shall issue, but upon probable cause, supported by Oath or affirmation, and particularly describing the place to be searched and the persons or things to be seized.

AMENDMENT 5

No person shall be held to answer for a capital, or otherwise infamous crime, unless on a presentment or indictment of a Grand Jury, except in cases arising in the land or naval forces, or in the Militia, when in actual service in time of War or public danger, nor shall any person be subject for the same offence to be twice put in jeopardy of life or limb; nor shall be compelled in any criminal case to be a witness against himself, nor be deprived of life, liberty, or property, without due process of law; nor shall private property be taken for public use, without just compensation.

AMENDMENT 6

In all criminal prosecutions, the accused shall enjoy the right to a speedy and public trial, by an impartial jury of the State and district wherein the crime shall have been committed, which district shall have been previously ascertained by law, and to be informed of the nature and cause of the accusation; to be confronted with the witnesses against him; to have compulsory process for obtaining witnesses in his favor, and to have the Assistance of Counsel for his defence.

AMENDMENT 7

In Suits at common law, where the value in controversy shall exceed twenty dollars, the right of trial by jury shall be preserved, and no fact tried by a jury, shall be otherwise reexamined in any Court of the United States, than according to the rules of the common law.

AMENDMENT 8

Excessive bail shall not be required, nor excessive fines imposed, nor cruel and unusual punishments inflicted.

AMENDMENT 9

The enumeration in the Constitution, of certain rights, shall not be construed to deny or disparage others retained by the people.

AMENDMENT 10

The powers not delegated to the United States by the Constitution, nor prohibited by it to the States, are reserved to the States respectively, or to the people.

Pre-Civil War amendments

AMENDMENT 11
[Ratified February 7, 1795]

The Judicial power of the United States shall not be construed to extend to any suit in law or equity, commenced or prosecuted against one of the United States by Citizens of another State, or by Citizens or Subjects of any Foreign State.

AMENDMENT 12
[Ratified July 27, 1804]

The Electors shall meet in their respective states and vote by ballot for President and Vice-President, one of whom, at least, shall not be an inhabitant of the same state with themselves; they shall name in their ballots the person voted for as President, and in distinct ballots the person voted for as Vice-President, and they shall make distinct lists of all persons voted for as President, and of all persons voted for as Vice-President, and of the number of votes for each, which lists they shall sign and certify, and transmit sealed to the seat of the government of the United States, directed to the President of the Senate;–The President of the Senate shall, in the presence of the Senate and House of Representatives, open all the certificates and the votes shall then be counted;–The person having the greatest number of votes for President, shall be the President, if such number be a majority of the whole number of Electors appointed; and if no person have such majority, then from the persons having the highest numbers not exceeding three on the list of those voted for as President, the House of Representatives shall choose immediately, by ballot, the President. But in choosing the President, the votes shall be taken by states, the representation from each state having one vote; a quorum for this purpose shall consist of a member or members from two-thirds of the states, and a majority of all the states shall be necessary to a choice. And if the House of Representatives shall not choose a President whenever the right of the choice shall devolve upon them, before the fourth day of March next following, then the Vice-President shall act as President, as in the case of the death or other constitutional disability of the President.—The person having the greatest number of votes as Vice-President, shall be the Vice-President, if such number be a majority of the whole number of Electors appointed, and if no person have a majority, then from the two highest numbers on the list, the Senate shall choose the Vice-President; a quorum for the purpose shall consist of two-thirds of the whole number of Senators, and a majority of the whole number shall be necessary to a choice. But no person constitutionally ineligible to the office of President shall be eligible to that of Vice-President of the United States.

Civil War amendments

AMENDMENT 13

[Ratified December 6, 1865]

Section 1. Neither slavery nor involuntary servitude, except as a punishment for crime whereof the party shall have been duly convicted, shall exist within the United States, or any place subject to their jurisdiction.

Section 2. Congress shall have power to enforce this article by appropriate legislation.

AMENDMENT 14

[Ratified July 9, 1868]

Section 1. All persons born or naturalized in the United States, and subject to the jurisdiction thereof, are citizens of the United States and of the State wherein they reside. No State shall make or enforce any law which shall abridge the privileges or immunities of citizens of the United States; nor shall any State deprive any person of life, liberty, or property, without due process of law; nor deny to any person within its jurisdiction the equal protection of the laws.

Section 2. Representatives shall be apportioned among the several States according to their respective numbers, counting the whole number of persons in each State, excluding Indians not taxed. But when the right to vote at any election for the choice of electors for President and Vice President of the United States, Representatives in Congress, the Executive and Judicial Officers of a State, or the members of the Legislature thereof, is denied to any of the male inhabitants of such State, being twenty-one years of age, and citizens of the United States, or in any way abridged, except for participation in rebellion, or other crime, the basis of representation therein shall be reduced in the proportion which the number of such male citizens shall bear to the whole number of male citizens twenty-one years of age in such State.

Section 3. No person shall be a Senator or Representative in Congress, or elector of President and Vice President, or hold any office, civil or military, under the United States, or under any State, who having previously taken an oath, as a member of Congress, or as an officer of the United States, or as a member of any State legislature, or as an executive or judicial officer of any State, to support the Constitution of the United States, shall have engaged in insurrection or rebellion against the same, or given aid or comfort to the enemies thereof. But Congress may by a vote of two-thirds of each House, remove such disability.

Section 4. The validity of the public debt of the United States, authorized by law, including debts incurred for payment of pensions and bounties for services in suppressing insurrection or rebellion, shall not be questioned. But neither the United States nor any State shall assume or pay any debt or obligation incurred in aid of insurrection or rebellion against the United States, or any claim for the loss or emancipation of any slave; but all such debts, obligations and claims shall be held illegal and void.

Section 5. The Congress shall have power to enforce, by appropriate legislation, the provisions of this article.

AMENDMENT 15
[Ratified February 3, 1870]

Section 1. The right of citizens of the United States to vote shall not be denied or abridged by the United States or by any State on account of race, color, or previous condition of servitude.

Section 2. The Congress shall have power to enforce this article by appropriate legislation.

AMENDMENT 16
[Ratified February 3, 1913]

The Congress shall have power to lay and collect taxes on incomes, from whatever source derived, without apportionment among the several States, and without regard to any census or enumeration.

AMENDMENT 17
[Ratified April 8, 1913]

The Senate of the United States shall be composed of two Senators from each State, elected by the people thereof for six years; and each Senator shall have one vote. The electors in each State shall have the qualifications requisite for electors of the most numerous branch of the State legislatures.

When vacancies happen in the representation of any State in the Senate, the executive authority of such State shall issue writs of election to fill such vacancies: *Provided,* That the legislature of any State may empower the executive thereof to make temporary appointments until the people fill the vacancies by election as the legislature may direct.

This amendment shall not be so construed as to affect the election or term of any Senator chosen before it becomes valid as part of the Constitution.

AMENDMENT 18

[Ratified January 16, 1919]

Section 1. After one year from the ratification of this article the manufacture, sale, or transportation of intoxicating liquors within, the importation thereof into, or the exportation thereof from the United States and all territory subject to the jurisdiction thereof for beverage purposes is hereby prohibited.

Section 2. The Congress and the several States shall have concurrent power to enforce this article by appropriate legislation.

Section 3. This article shall be inoperative unless it shall have been ratified as an amendment to the Constitution by the legislatures of the several States, as provided in the Constitution, within seven years from the date of the submission hereof to the States by the Congress.

AMENDMENT 19

[Ratified August 18, 1920]

The right of citizens of the United States to vote shall not be denied or abridged by the United States or by any State on account of sex. Congress shall have power to enforce this article by appropriate legislation.

AMENDMENT 20

[Ratified January 23, 1933]

Section 1. The terms of the President and Vice President shall end at noon on the 20th day of January, and the terms of Senators and Representatives at noon on the 3d of January, of the years in which such terms would have ended if this article had not been ratified; and the terms of their successors shall then begin.

Section 2. The Congress shall assemble at least once in every year, and such meeting shall begin at noon on the 3d day of January, unless they shall by law appoint a different day.

Section 3. If, at the time fixed for the beginning of the term of the President, the President elect shall have died, the Vice President elect shall become President. If a President shall not have been chosen before the time fixed for the beginning of his term, or if the President elect shall have failed to qualify, then the Vice President elect shall act as President until a President shall have qualified; and the Congress may by law provide for the case wherein neither a President elect nor a Vice President elect shall have qualified, declaring who shall then act as President, or the manner in which one who is to act shall be selected, and such person shall act accordingly until a President or Vice President shall have qualified.

Section 4. The Congress may by law provide for the case of the death of any of the persons from whom the House of Representatives may choose a President whenever the right of choice shall have devolved upon them, and for the case of the death of any of the persons from whom the Senate may choose a Vice President whenever the right of choice shall have devolved upon them.

Section 5. Sections 1 and 2 shall take effect on the 15th day of October following the ratification of this article.

Section 6. This article shall be inoperative unless it shall have been ratified as an amendment to the Constitution by the legislatures of three-fourths of the several States within seven years from the date of its submission.

AMENDMENT 21

[Ratified December 5, 1933]

Section 1. The eighteenth article of amendment to the Constitution of the United States is hereby repealed.

Section 2. The transportation or importation into any State, Territory, or possession of the United States for delivery or use therein of intoxicating liquors, in violation of the laws thereof, is hereby prohibited.

Section 3. This article shall be inoperative unless it shall have been ratified as an amendment to the Constitution by conventions in the several States, as provided in the Constitution, within seven years from the date of the submission hereof to the States by the Congress.

AMENDMENT 22

[Ratified February 27, 1951]

Section 1. No person shall be elected to the office of the President more than twice, and no person who has held the office of President, or acted as President for more than two years of a term to which some other person was elected President shall be elected to the office of the President more than once. But this Article shall not apply to any person holding the office of President when this Article was proposed by the Congress, and shall not prevent any person who may be holding the office of President, or acting as President, during the term within which this Article becomes operative from holding the office of President or acting as President during the remainder of such term.

Section 2. This article shall be inoperative unless it shall have been ratified as an amendment to the Constitution by the legislatures of three-fourths of the several States within seven years from the date of its submission to the States by the Congress.

AMENDMENT 23

[Ratified March 29, 1961]

Section 1. The District constituting the seat of Government of the United States shall appoint in such manner as the Congress may direct:

A number of electors of President and Vice President equal to the whole number of Senators and Representatives in Congress to which the District would be entitled if it were a State, but in no event more than the least populous State; they shall be in addition to those appointed by the States, but they shall be considered, for the purposes of the election of President and Vice President, to be electors appointed by a State; and they shall meet in the District and perform such duties as provided by the twelfth article of amendment.

Section 2. The Congress shall have power to enforce this article by appropriate legislation.

AMENDMENT 24

[Ratified January 23, 1964]

Section 1. The right of citizens of the United States to vote in any primary or other election for President or Vice President, for electors for President or Vice President, or for Senator or Representative in Congress, shall not be denied or abridged by the United States or any State by reason of failure to pay any poll tax or other tax.

Section 2. The Congress shall have power to enforce this article by appropriate legislation.

AMENDMENT 25
[Ratified February 10, 1967]

Section 1. In case of the removal of the President from office or of his death or resignation, the Vice President shall become President.

Section 2. Whenever there is a vacancy in the office of the Vice President, the President shall nominate a Vice President who shall take office upon confirmation by a majority vote of both Houses of Congress.

Section 3. Whenever the President transmits to the President pro tempore of the Senate and the Speaker of the House of Representatives his written declaration that he is unable to discharge the powers and duties of his office, and until he transmits to them a written declaration to the contrary, such powers and duties shall be discharged by the Vice President as Acting President.

Section 4. Whenever the Vice President and a majority of either the principal officers of the executive departments or of such other body as Congress may by law provide, transmit to the President pro tempore of the Senate and the Speaker of the House of Representatives their written declaration that the President is unable to

discharge the powers and duties of his office, the Vice President shall immediately assume the powers and duties of the office as Acting President.

Thereafter, when the President transmits to the President pro tempore of the Senate and the Speaker of the House of Representatives his written declaration that no inability exists, he shall resume the powers and duties of his office unless the Vice President and a majority of either the principal officers of the executive department or of such other body as Congress may by law provide, transmit within four days to the President pro tempore of the Senate and the Speaker of the House of Representatives their written declaration that the President is unable to discharge the powers and duties of his office. Thereupon Congress shall decide the issue, assembling within forty-eight hours for that purpose if not in session. If the Congress, within twenty-one days after receipt of the latter written declaration, or, if Congress is not in session, within twenty-one days after Congress is required to assemble, determines by two-thirds vote of both Houses that the President is unable to discharge the powers and duties of his office, the Vice President shall continue to discharge the same as Acting President; otherwise, the President shall resume the powers and duties of his office.

AMENDMENT 26
[Ratified June 30, 1971]

Section 1. The right of citizens of the United States, who are eighteen years of age or older, to vote shall not be denied or abridged by the United States or by any State on account of age.

Section 2. The Congress shall have the power to enforce this article by appropriate legislation.

PROPOSED AMENDMENT 27
[Proposed March 22, 1972]
Section 1. Equality of rights under the law shall not be denied or abridged by the United States or by any State on account of sex.

Section 2. The Congress shall have power to enforce, by appropriate legislation, the provisions of this article.

Section 3. This amendment shall take effect two years after date of ratification.

Glossary

advise and consent.   The constitutional power of the Senate to approve presidential treaties and certain presidential appointments.

affirmative action.   The policy of actively recruiting or hiring minority groups and women as a means of remedying past discrimination.

amicus curiae brief.   A "friend of the court" brief or argument filed by an individual or group who is not a direct party to a suit but who seeks to influence the court's decision.

"Anti-Federalists."   The label given to the group of small farmers and others who opposed the ratification of the Constitution.

appeal.   A legal proceeding in which a case is brought from a lower court to a higher court for review. The term also identifies the type of case brought to the U.S. Supreme Court as a matter of right.

appellate jurisdiction.   The authority of a court to try a case on appeal, to review a decision of a lower court.

appropriation.   A bill granting money to carry out a government program authorized by Congress.

Articles of Confederation.   The first constitution of the original thirteen states, adopted in 1781 and replaced by the present Constitution in 1789.

bicameral legislature.   A legislature composed of two houses or chambers.

bill of attainder.   A legislative act that singles out an individual for punishment without benefit of a trial. Such an act is forbidden by the Constitution.

Bill of Rights. The first ten amendments to the U.S. Constitution added shortly after ratification.

bureaucracy. The organization of bureaus, agencies, and departments within the executive branch that administer the laws and services of government. More generally, bureaucracy connotes any administrative system based on a specialization of duties, a hierarchy of command, and formal rules and regulations.

cabinet. An advisory body to the president composed of the heads of the major executive departments, the vice-president, and possibly other high-ranking executive officials.

caucus or *conference.* A meeting of party members in a legislative chamber to select leaders or adopt policy positions. A caucus also can refer to a closed meeting of state or local party leaders to nominate candidates for office.

certiorari, writ of. An order from a higher court to a lower court to send up the records of a case for review.

checks and balances. The practice of providing the executive, legislative, and judicial branches of government with overlapping powers so that each branch can restrain the actions of the others. (See also *separation of powers.*)

"citizens' lobby." See *"public interest group."*

civil service. A system of filling government jobs through competitive examination instead of political favoritism. The term also applies to the body of civilian employees who work for the government.

class action suit. A court suit brought by one or more persons on behalf of a larger number of people with a similar legal complaint.

"closed" primary. A primary election in which only the registered members of a party may vote.

cloture rule. Procedure for shutting off debate on a bill in the Senate. Requires a three-fifths vote of the entire membership to succeed.

cold war. A term used to describe the post-World War II relationship between the United States and the Soviet Union marked by tension and conflict short of a "hot" military war.

concurrent powers. Powers granted by the Constitution to both the national government and the states, such as the power to levy taxes.

confederation. An alliance of independent states, with a central government having only limited authority.

conference committee. A committee composed of members from both the House and the Senate who meet to iron out differences between House and Senate versions of the same bill.

Connecticut Compromise. The compromise adopted at the Constitutional Convention in 1787 that called for a two-house legislature with equal representation of the states in the Senate and representation by population in the House.

conservative. A term usually applied to someone who wishes to maintain the existing order, who values tradition and prefers gradual change. The term also is applied to someone who opposes the expansion of governmental activities.

constituents. Commonly refers to the residents of a legislator's district to whom the legislator is responsible.

constitution. The principal legal statement of a political system, prescribing the powers and procedures of its governmental institutions.

constitutionalism (constitutional government). Implies a government in which there are recognized legal limits on the powers of those who govern.

containment. A policy adopted by the United States after World War II which sought to prevent the expansion of Soviet power and the spread of communism.

convention. A meeting of party delegates to nominate candidates for office and/or adopt a policy platform.

de facto segregation. Segregation caused by residential patterns rather than by law (*de jure*).

delegated powers or *enumerated powers.* Powers specifically granted by the Constitution to the national government, such as Congress' power to tax and to declare war.

democracy. A political system in which citizens enjoy a relatively high degree of access to and influence over their government. In more general terms, it refers to a system in which ultimate political authority rests with the people.

détente. A relaxation of tensions and improvement of relations between two nations.

direct action. A form of political action aimed at achieving an end directly, usually through disruptive or obstructionist means (e.g., boycotts or sit-ins).

direct primary. A preliminary election in which voters select the candidates who will run on the party's ticket in the general election.

domino theory. The theory that if one nation "falls" to communism, then neighboring countries will topple like a row of dominoes.

double jeopardy. Being tried twice for the same offense, a practice forbidden by the Constitution.

due process. Requirement that laws are reasonable and that they are administered in a fair manner. Basically, due process means that an individual has a right to be fairly heard before he or she can be deprived of life, liberty, or property.

electoral college. The body of electors chosen by the states who, following the presidential election in November, formally elect the president and vice-president.

elite. The few who have the most of anything valued in society, such as money or influence. It usually refers to those people who dominate major institutions and who have a major impact on political, economic, and social decision making.

executive agreement. An international agreement between the president and a foreign nation that has the effect of a treaty but does not require formal Senate approval.

executive department. A major agency of the national government headed by a presidential appointee with cabinet rank. Examples include the State Department and the Justice Department.

Executive Office of the President. The group of top staff agencies (such as the Office of Management and Budget, the Council of Economic Advisers, and the White House Office) that report directly to the president and provide him with information and advice.

executive privilege. A presumed right of a president to withhold sensitive information requested by Congress or the courts.

ex post facto law. A law that punishes someone for an act that was not illegal when committed. Such a law is forbidden by the Constitution.

fairness doctrine. Requirement of the Federal Communications Commission that broadcasting stations provide opportunities for conflicting views to be aired on important issues.

federalism. A government system in which power is divided between a central (national) government and regional (state) governments.

Federalist Papers. A series of essays written by James Madison, Alexander Hamilton, and John Jay in 1787–1788 explaining and defending the newly proposed U.S. Constitution.

"Federalists." The label given to those who favored a strong central government and supported the adoption of the Constitution.

filibuster. An obstructionist tactic used in the U.S. Senate whereby a minority of senators try to block action on a bill through endless speeches and debate.

government. The combination of institutions, rules, and policy makers principally involved in settling disputes and distributing benefits. (See also *politics.*)

government corporation. A governmental agency organized like a private corporation to perform a public commercial function. Examples include the U.S. Postal Service and the Federal Deposit Insurance Corporation.

grants-in-aid. Financial aid from the federal government to state and local governments, usually on a matching basis, to be used for specific purposes.

habeas corpus, writ of. A court order requiring an enforcement official to show just cause for holding a person in custody.

impeachment. Formal charges of misconduct voted by the House of Representatives against a president, federal judge, or other high federal official that could lead to his or her removal from office.

implied powers. Powers not specifically granted by the Constitution to Congress but that are "necessary and proper" to carry out those powers that are listed. (See also *"necessary and proper" clause.*)

impoundment. Refusal by a president to spend money appropriated by Congress.

independent agency.   A governmental agency responsible to the president that exists outside a cabinet-level executive department. Examples include the Veterans' Administration and the Central Intelligence Agency.

independent voter.   A voter who claims not to identify with any particular political party.

initiative.   A device allowing citizens, by petition, to propose laws and constitutional amendments which are then accepted or rejected by the voters at the polls.

interest group.   An organized group of people with shared attitudes and goals who band together to influence governmental policy. Sometimes also referred to as a "pressure group" or "lobby."

item veto.   A power possessed by some governors, but not by the president, to strike out sections of a bill while leaving the remainder intact.

judicial review.   The power of a court to determine whether laws or executive actions are in violation of the Constitution.

legislative oversight.   The power of Congress to review the performance of the executive branch, to determine whether the federal bureaucracy is properly administering the laws.

libel.   False or malicious written statement that damages a person's reputation. (If such a statement occurs in speech, it is called *slander*.)

liberal.   A term usually applied to someone who favors political reform and social change, and who supports expanded governmental programs to eliminate poverty and other social ills. Originally, the term referred to someone who opposed governmental restraints on individual liberty.

litigation.   The process of bringing a case before the courts.

lobbyist.   A representative of an interest group who seeks to influence legislation through direct contact with policy makers.

mandamus, writ of.   A court order demanding that a public official perform some duty required by law.

manifest destiny.   The notion held by many Americans in the nineteenth century that it was the destiny of the United States to expand its territories across the North American continent and beyond.

Marshall Plan.   A post-World War II foreign aid program, initiated by Secretary of State George Marshall, to help restore the war-ravaged economies of Western Europe.

mass media.   Means of communication, such as television, radio, books, newspapers, and magazines, designed to reach a majority of people.

military-industrial complex.   The presumed alliance between the military and large corporations (especially defense contractors) who have a mutual interest in keeping military spending at a high level.

Monroe Doctrine.   A unilateral declaration of American foreign policy, first declared by President James Monroe in 1823, opposing any European intervention in the Western Hemisphere and pledging that the United States would not meddle in the internal affairs of Europe.

"necessary and proper" clause. The language of Article 1, Section 8 of the Constitution that grants Congress the power to pass laws "necessary and proper" for carrying out the specific powers granted by the Constitution. Provides the basis for Congress' "implied" powers.

New Jersey Plan. A proposal introduced at the Constitutional Convention in 1787, and backed by the smaller states, that called for a one-house legislature with equal representation of the states.

Nixon Doctrine. The policy proclaimed by President Nixon that while the United States would help protect the security of allied nations, these nations would have to bear the major burden of their own defense.

"open" primary. A primary election in which any registered voter may participate, regardless of his or her party affiliation.

opinion leader. A person who commands respect and who influences the opinions of others.

original jurisdiction. The authority of a court to try a case for the first time (as opposed to appellate jurisdiction).

peers. People of the same general age or social standing with whom one is in contact.

pluralist theory. A theory of government which holds that power is widely dispersed among many separate and competing groups held in check by various social and political forces.

pocket veto. The president's power to kill any bill received within ten days before Congress adjourns by allowing it to remain on his desk unsigned.

political party. An organization that seeks to gain control of government by running candidates for public office.

political socialization. The lifelong learning process by which we acquire our political attitudes and values.

politics. Although the term is vague, it usually refers to the process of settling disputes and distributing benefits, of deciding "who gets what, when, and how."

pork barrel legislation. A slang term for legislation providing federal funds for local government projects that are not always critically needed but that may help politicians look good in the eyes of their constituents.

power. The ability to affect the behavior of others, to influence political outcomes.

pressure group. See *interest group.*

prior restraint. The attempt to prevent certain material from being published by the press.

procedural rights. Rights guaranteeing citizens protection against arbitrary actions by governmental officials. No individual may be deprived of life, liberty, or property except through well-defined procedures prescribed by law. (See also *due process.*)

proportional representation. An electoral system in which parties are assigned seats in the legislature in proportion to their percentages of the popular vote.

"public interest group." An interest group claiming to represent the interests of society as a whole rather than just its own membership.

reapportionment. Redrawing the boundaries of legislative districts to reflect changes in population distribution. To ensure that legislative districts are of equal population, such redistricting is usually carried out every ten years or so following the census.

recall. A procedure by which voters can remove an official from office before the end of his or her term.

referendum. A procedure for referring legislative measures directly to the voters for approval or rejection.

regulatory commission. A governmental agency with legislative, executive, and judicial powers charged with regulating a given sector of the economy. Examples include the Federal Communications Commission and the Federal Trade Commission.

republic. A representative democracy, in which power ultimately rests with the people and is exercised by elected officials responsible to the citizens who elected them. Republican government usually is distinguished from a direct democracy, where political decisions are made by the people directly, and from a monarchy, where power is wielded by a nonelected hereditary ruler such as a king.

reserved powers. Powers reserved by the Constitution to the states.

revenue sharing. The return of federal money to state and local governments with few or no strings attached.

rider. A provision, unlikely to pass on its own, that is added to an important bill in the hope that the president will accept, rather than veto, the entire package.

ruling-elite theory. A theory of government which holds that political and economic resources are concentrated in the hands of a relatively small and cohesive gorup which dominates the major policy-making institutions.

select committee. A congressional committee established for a limited time period and for a specific purpose, such as conducting a special investigation.

"selective benefits." Benefits that are available only to members of a certain group, such as low-cost health insurance or cheap charter flights. According to economist Mancur Olson, selective benefits are sometimes used by interest groups to attract and keep members.

selective exposure/perception. The tendency to pay attention to only those views and opinions with which one already agrees.

senatorial courtesy. The custom that the president, before appointing a federal judge, consult the Senator or Senators of his own party who represent the state in which the appointee is to serve.

seniority system. The practice of assigning a committee chairmanship to the member with the longest continuous service on the committee.

separation of powers. The division of governmental power among the executive, legislative, and judicial branches of the national government. (See also *checks and balances.*)

single-member district system. An electoral system in which only one legislative member may be elected from a district, regardless of how many candidates are running.

spoils system. The practice of awarding government jobs to friends and political supporters.

spot commercial. A short television commercial, usually about one minute in length, that is commonly used in political campaigns to project a favorable image of a candidate or an unfavorable image of an opponent.

standing committee. A permanent committee in the Senate or House of Representatives that considers bills within a given subject area.

strategic deterrence. The notion that the best security against aggression is to maintain military superiority. As a general concept, it assumes that peace can be preserved so long as each side has sufficient nuclear retaliatory capability to deter the other side from attacking.

strict construction. The view that the Constitution should be interpreted in narrow terms, according to the precise meaning of its words.

substantive rights. Rights essential to individual liberty and of value in themselves, such as freedom of speech, assembly, and religion.

sunset laws. Statutes requiring automatic abolition of governmental agencies or programs after a certain period of time unless the legislature acts to reestablish them.

Third World. The group of generally poor nations of Africa, Asia, Latin America, and the Middle East that are not aligned with either the communist or the noncommunist blocs.

ticket-splitting. Voting for candidates of different parties in the same election.

treaty. A formal agreement negotiated between two or more nations. In the United States, it requires approval by a two-thirds vote of the Senate.

Truman Doctrine. The policy declared by President Truman in 1947 calling for U.S. economic and military aid to the governments of Greece and Turkey to prevent them from falling into communist hands.

unicameral legislature. A legislature with a single house or chamber.

unitary system. A political system in which power is concentrated in a central government.

veto. Power of the president to refuse to sign a bill passed by Congress, thus preventing the bill from becoming law. A two-thirds vote of both houses of Congress is required to override a veto. (See also *pocket veto* and *item veto.*)

Virginia Plan. A proposal introduced at the Constitutional Convention in

1787, and favored by the larger states, that called for a strong two-house legislature with state representation based on population.

Watergate. A general term for the abuses committed by the Nixon Administration in the early 1970s. The term was taken from the Watergate apartment and office complex in Washington, D.C. where burglars hired by the Committee to Reelect the President broke into the Democratic party headquarters in 1972.

zero-base budgeting. A type of budgeting that requires governmental agencies to justify every dollar they plan to spend each year, and not just requests for additional funds.

Index

Campbell, Alan, 344
Canada, 402
capital punishment, 90. *See also*
 Death penalty
Carnal Knowledge, 78
Carswell, G. Harold, 253, 329
Carter, Jimmy, 6, 149, 236, 252, 260,
 262, 360, 375
 appointments of, 19–20, 258, 283,
  329
 black voters and, 142–44
 B-1 bomber and, 33
 campaign and election of, 120,
  142–44, 154–55, 163, 166, 167,
  170, 207, 227, 442
 China and, 248, 267
 civil service reform, 343–44
 Congress and 243–44, 248
 debates with Ford, 209, 225–26
 Egyptian-Israeli peace treaty,
  414–15
 electoral college reform and, 165
 energy policies of, 33, 243, 267,
  372–73, 374, 412–13
 foreign policy and, 247, 248, 267,
  409–10, 412–13, 414–17, 419,
  428
 human rights and, 247, 248, 415
 opinion polls on, 413
 Panama Canal treaties and, 248,
  418
 personality of, 238, 246, 254
 as "political outsider," 4, 19, 26,
  138, 161, 163, 243
 and reorganization of
  bureaucracy, 343–44, 362, 364
 ruling-elite theory and, 19–20, 26
 tax policies of, 267, 380–86, 413
 SALT II treaty and, 248, 409–10,
  418, 421
 voting registration proposals of,
  123
Castro, Fidel, 423
Catholics, 82
 party loyalties of, 142, 143
 political officeholders, 285, 328
Caucus system, role of in
  nominating process, 161–62,
  163
Celler, Emanuel, 294
Census Bureau, 360
Center for Auto Safety, 352
Center for Public Financing of
  Elections, 170
Center for the Study of Responsive
  Law, 195
Central Intelligence Agency (CIA),
  283, 348, 416, 418
 assassination plots of, 423
 Chile and, 6, 423, 424, 426
 Congress and, 423–24
 criticisms of, 423–24
 domestic activities of, 40, 423–24
 duties of, 422–23

foreign governments and, 6, 423,
 426
 Nixon and, 56, 424
Certiorari, writ of, 325
Chancellor, John, 217
Chase Manhattan Bank, 18, 22
Chase, Samuel, 320
Chavez, Cesar, 455
Checks and balances, 53–55, 265
Chevron Corp., 182
Chiang Kai-shek, 403
Chicago, Illinois, 34, 164
Chile, 6, 423, 424, 426
China, 319, 403, 408, 421
 Carter and, 248, 267
 Nixon's trip to, 210, 407
 Soviet Union and, 410
 Vietnam and, 406, 416–17
Chisholm, Shirley, 272, 281, 288
Churchill, Winston, 401
"Cinderella effect," 206
"Citizens' lobbies." *See* Interest
 groups
Civil Aeronautics Board (CAB), 180,
 363, 364
Civil Rights Act (1875), 91
Civil Rights Act (1957), 92, 292
Civil Rights Act (1964), 93, 97, 98,
 293, 451, 458
Civil Rights Commission, 92, 363
Civil service, 64, 240, 343–44
 Civil Service Commission, 343,
  344, 364
 Civil Service Reform Act (1978),
  343, 344
Civil War, 91, 154, 314, 321, 342, 343,
 405
Class action suit, 316, 452
Clausen, A. W., 26
Clean Air Act, 180
Cleveland, Grover, 154
Cleveland, Ohio, 453
Closed primary, 162
Cloture, 293
Coca-Cola Corp., 20, 258
Cohen, David, 197
Cold war, 401, 403, 411
Colson, Charles, 260
Columbia Broadcasting System
 (CBS), 22
Commerce Department, 363, 364
"commercial speech," 76
Committee for the Reelection of the
 President (CREEP), 170, 279
Committee on Political Education
 (COPE), 185
Common Cause, 177, 189, 191,
 193–94, 197, 356, 360, 429
Communism, 110
 freedom of speech and American
  communists, 75–76, 99–101
 Karl Marx and, 9–10
 U.S. foreign policy and, 401, 403,
  404, 406, 407

Communist party (U. S.), 75–76, 155,
 156, 159
Congress, 271–302
 advice and consent, 283–84
 budget and, 274, 281–83
 bureaucracy and, 242, 281, 300,
  348–49, 356, 357, 358
 CIA and, 423–24
 committees of, 64, 179, 274,
  286–92, 443–44
 constituents and, 277–79, 443–46
 Constitution and, 47–48, 51–53,
  65–67, 275, 284, 286, 320, 417
 foreign policy and, 247–51, 267,
  409–10, 416, 417–18, 426
 interest groups and, 176, 178–80,
  185, 191, 198–99, 242–43,
  276–77, 291
 investigating by, 279–81
 legislative oversight, 279, 281, 358
 legislative staffs of, 278, 299–301,
  444–46
 membership, 25–26, 95, 284–85
 pluralist theory and, 31–33, 35
 political parties and, 140, 145,
  147–48, 295–99
 power structure of, 272–73, 274,
  286–99
 president and, 243–45, 264–67,
  274, 275, 282–84, 417–18
 public confidence in, 5, 273, 274
 reforms in, 274, 286, 289, 292, 294,
  295, 302
 scandals in, 6, 179, 274
 seniority system, 294–96
 Supreme Court and, 253, 310–11,
  319–20, 328
 Vietnam War and, 406–7, 416, 417
 Women in, 25, 95, 284–85
Congressional Black Caucus, 297
Congress Watch, 195, 199
Connecticut, 34, 157
Connecticut Compromise, 48
Connolly, John, 258
Constitution, United States, 43–70
 amendments to, 62–63, 66–68,
  320
 bureaucracy and, 44, 64, 341–42
 checks and balances, 53–55
 Congress and, 47–48, 51–53,
  65–67, 275, 284, 286, 417
 defined, 43
 economic interpretation of, 45–46
 federalism and, 57–59
 and motives of framers, 44–46,
  49–53, 311–12
 philosophical base of, 49–53
 political parties and, 44, 64, 135,
  159
 president and, 48, 51–54, 236, 239,
  244, 262–65, 416
 ratification of, 60–63
 separation of powers, 52–54
 slavery and, 48–49

Constitution, *(cont.)*
 Supreme Court and, 64, 65,
 308–11, 328, 331
Constitutional Convention,
 compromises, 46–49
 criticisms of, 61
 delegates to, 44–46
Consumer Product Safety
 Commission (CPSC), 354–55,
 359
Consumers' Union, 360
Continental Congress, 44, 46, 47
Conventions, party, 139, 162–65
Coolidge, Calvin, 236, 238, 320
Corporations, government-owned,
 348
 multinational, 425–26
 political power of, 16, 189–90,
 425–26
 ruling-elite theory and, 17–28,
 189–90
 Vietnam War and, 31
Corruption in government, 4–6,
 169–70, 197–98, 216–17, 221,
 274
Corrupt Practices Act (1925), 168,
 169
Council of Economic Advisors, 19,
 240, 382
Courts, federal, appointments to,
 253, 283, 329
 Constitution and, 64, 331
 courts of appeals, 332
 district courts, 330–31
 impeachment and, 56, 320
 special courts, 332
 structure of, 64, 309, 330–32
Courts, state, 332–33, 334
Cousins, Norman, 429
Crosby, Bing, 26
Crouse, Timothy, 228
Cuba, Bay of Pigs, 239, 250, 423
 Cuban missile crisis, 251, 404, 416
 U. S. relations with, 248, 399
Cyprus, 418

Dahl, Robert, 29, 30, 34, 36
Daschle, Tom, 442
Dean, John, 279
Death penalty, 90, 182, 318, 322
Declaration of Independence, 45, 91
Defense Department, 345, 346, 364,
 416, 419, 421–22
Defense Intelligence Agency (DIA),
 423
Dellums, Ronald, 442
Democracy, constitutional law and,
 311–12
 defined, 436–37
 direct, 52, 454
 foreign policy and, 428
 representative, 52
Democratic party, black voters and,
 142–44

differences between Republican
 party and, 21, 25, 141–50
 dominance of, 151–55, 287
 history of, 151–55
 midterm conventions of, 148
 in South, 151, 154, 295
 voters identifying with, 138,
 142–44, 155
Dennis, Eugene, 75–76
Dennis v. *United States* (1951),
 75–76, 315
Detroit, Michigan, 34, 94
Diem, Ngo Dinh, 404–5
Direct action, 92, 455–58
Direct democracy, 52, 454
Direct primary, 138, 160, 161–63
Dole, Robert, 219, 225
Domhoff, G. William, 22, 26
Dominican Republic, 250, 399
Domino theory, 404
Double jeopardy, 85
Douglas, William O., 55, 74, 253,
 319–20
Draft, 58, 416
 draft card burning, 76, 308
Dred Scott decision, 312–13, 314
Due process of law, 72, 84–94, 314,
 315, 317
Duncan, Charles, 20, 258
Durkin, John, 442
Dye, Thomas R., 27

Eagleton, Thomas, 262
Education Department, 364
Edwards, George, 376, 378
Egypt, 414–15
Ehrlichman, John, 259, 260, 331
Eighth Amendment, 88, 90
Eisenhower, Dwight D., 154, 238,
 248, 250, 321, 330, 404
Election campaigns, advertising in,
 167–68, 206–13, 222–24
 debates in, 225–26
 financing of, 167–72
 interest groups and, 184–85, 454
 issues in, 119–20
 participation in, 121–22
 press coverage of, 226–28
 primaries, 138, 160, 161–63
Electoral college, 51–52, 165–67,
 442
Elites. *See also* Pluralist theory and
 Ruling-elite theory
 accountability of, 27–28, 35–36
 competition among, 18, 30–33
 defined, 16, 33
 ✏ interlocking of, 19–20, 22–26
 values of, 22–25, 27, 33–35
Ellsberg, Daniel, 79
Energy, Carter policies, 33, 243, 267,
 372–73, 374, 412–13
 crisis, 397, 411–13, 417, 418
Energy Department, 19–20, 258,
 364, 412, 413

Energy Research and Development
 Administration (ERDA), 364
Energy Security Corporation, 413
Environmental Defense Fund, 193
Environmental Protection Agency
 (EPA), 359, 362, 363
Equal Credit Opportunity Act
 (1974), 96
Equal Rights Amendment (ERA),
 67–68, 96, 376–77
Ervin, Sam, 279, 288
Escobedo v. *Illinois* (1964), 88
Espionage Act (1917), 74–75
Executive agreements, 66, 248–49,
 416, 418
Executive Office of the President,
 240, 241
Executive privilege, 308
Ex post facto laws, 62, 71
Exxon Corp., 20, 184, 412, 425, 450

Fairness doctrine, 80, 447, 452
Family, political influence of,
 109–110, 114
 and politics, 9
Farber, Myron, 80
Farmer-Labor party, 157
Federal Aviation Administration
 (FAA), 348, 363
Federal Bureau of Investigation
 (FBI), 40, 346, 358, 360
Federal Communications
 Commission (FCC), 80, 240,
 348–49, 447–48, 452
Federal Deposit Insurance Corp.
 (FDIC), 348
Federal Election Campaign Acts,
 160, 169–71, 194
Federal Election Commission (FEC),
 170, 171, 184–85, 279, 301
Federal Energy Administration
 (FEA), 364
Federalism, Constitution and, 57–59
 defined, 57
 political parties and, 146
 public policy and, 373
 revenue sharing and, 59–60
 Supreme Court and, 58–59,
 313–14
Federalist, the (The Federalist Papers),
 49–50, 61, 309, 311–12
Federalist party, 136, 151, 310
Federal Power Commission (FPC),
 364
Federal Regulation of Lobbying Act
 (1946), 198
Federal Reserve Board, 240
Federal Trade Commission (FTC),
 359, 362, 363
Fifteenth Amendment, 52, 71, 91
Fifth Amendment, 85, 88
Filibuster, 292–93
Firestone Corp., 26, 352
Firestone, Leonard K., 26

Prohibition party, 139, 155, 156
Proportional representation, 158–59
Proposition 13 (California), 389–93
Protestants, 82
    party loyalties of, 142, 143
    political officeholders, 25, 285, 328
Protests. See Direct action
Proxmire, William, 19, 386
Public Citizen, 177, 193, 194–95
Public interest groups. See Interest
    groups
Public policy, 371–96
    bureaucracy and, 373
    changes in, 376–78, 386
    citizens and, 373, 392, 393–94
    Congress and, 372–73
    consequences of, 375–76
    costs and benefits of, 374–75
    courts and, 373
    defined, 371, 372, 374
    limits on, 378–79
    pluralist theory and, 393
    president and, 372
    ruling-elite theory and, 393
    study of, 371–72, 393
"Publius," 61
Puerto Rico, 399

Randolph, Edmund, 47
Rayburn, Sam, 297
RCA Corp., 22, 214
Reagan, Ronald, 4, 148, 162, 163,
    222
Reapportionment, 321, 450–51
Recall elections, 453–54
Reedy, George, 254
Referendum, 160, 373, 453, 454
Registration requirements (voting),
    122–23
Regulatory commissions, 452
    Congress and, 349, 356
    courts and, 309, 358
    criticisms of, 350, 353–57
    functions of, 348–49, 352–54
    independence of, 240–42, 349–50
    president and, 240–42, 349
Rehabilitation Act (1973), 96
Rehnquist, William H., 317
Reorganization Act (1949), 362
Representative democracy, 52
Republican party, black voters and,
    142
    differences between Democratic
        party and, 21, 25, 141–50
    history of, 151–55
    Jewish voters and, 142
    Nixon and, 130, 247
    in South, 151, 295
    voters identifying with, 137, 138,
        142, 155
Reston, James, 217
Revenue Act (1978), 384–85
Revenue sharing, 59–60
Revolutionary War, 45, 46, 47

Riders, on bills, 244–45
Riesman, David, 115
Rivers, Mendel, 291
Rockefeller, David, 22
Rockefeller, Nelson, 26, 206, 283
Rockwell International Corp., 33
Rodino, Peter, 280
Romney, George, 19
Roosevelt, Franklin D., 154, 236,
    253, 261, 265, 313, 379, 416
    Court-packing scheme of, 314
    New Deal and, 25, 314, 319
    personality of, 238
Roosevelt, Theodore, 149, 157, 236,
    399
Rossiter, Clinton, 242, 246
Roth v. United States (1957), 77
Ruling-elite theory, 15–29, 339, 393
    Congress and, 18, 25–26, 276, 302
    corporations and, 17–28, 189–90
    elections and, 27, 127, 441
    evaluation of, 37–38
    interest groups and, 30, 186,
        189–90
    media and, 18, 28, 34, 214, 216,
        449
    methodology, 37
    political participation and, 16,
        28–29, 36, 38, 438, 441
    president and, 17–21, 258, 266
    Supreme Court and, 301, 311

Sadat, Anwar, 414
Sahl, Mort, 246
SALT. See Strategic Arms
    Limitations Talks
San Francisco, California, 34
San Jose, California, 34
Saudia Arabia, 412
Schenck, Charles, 74
Schenck v. United States (1919),
    74–75
Schlesinger, Arthur M., Jr., 259,
    266
Schlesinger, James, 19–20, 413
Schools, aid to, 82
    busing, 307, 322
    political socialization and, 110–13
    prayers in, 68, 82, 307, 321, 334
    segregation, 92, 321, 322, 450
Schultze, Charles, 19, 282
Schwartz, Charles L., 22
Search and seizure, 62, 73, 86–88
Segregation, and civil rights
    movement, 92–93, 308, 458
    de facto, 94
    school, 92, 321, 322, 450
    in South, 91–92
    Supreme Court rulings on, 91–92,
        313, 321, 322, 450
Seidman, Harold, 362
"Selective benefits," 192–93
Selective exposure/perception, 115,
    209–10, 215–16

Senate, advice and consent, 283–84
    Appropriations Committee, 282,
        290
    Constitution and, 48, 51–54
    filibuster in, 292–93
    Finance Committee, 282, 382
    Foreign Relations Committee,
        283, 288
    v. the House, 48, 51–52, 273,
        282–83, 284, 299
    impeachment trials in, 55
    party leaders in, 299
    president pro tempore, 299
    Select Committee on Intelligence,
        424
    vice-president and, 261, 283, 299
    Watergate hearings, 220, 260, 279,
        289
Seniority system, 294–96
Separation of powers, 52–54, 378
Sevaried, Eric, 228
Seventeenth Amendment, 52
Sharkansky, Ira, 376, 378
Shaw, Frank, 453
Shays' Rebellion, 47, 49
Sherrill, Robert, 295, 456
Sierra Club, 31, 451
Simon, William, 19
Single-member district system,
    157–59
Sirica, John, 308, 330–31, 332
Sixteenth Amendment, 67, 320
Sixth Amendment, 80, 85, 88
Slavery, 48–49, 91, 312–13
Smith Act (1940), 75–76, 315
Socialist party, 157
Socialist Workers party, 155
Social security, 25, 149–50, 314, 342,
    379
Sorauf, Frank, 136, 144
Sorenson, Ted, 283
South, the black registered voters in,
    93–94
    and Constitutional Convention
        compromise, 48–49
    Democratic party in, 151, 154, 295
    Republican party in, 151, 295
    segregation in, 91–92
    seniority tradition and, 295
    voting patterns, 124, 126, 143
South Africa, 397
Southeast Asia Treaty Organization
    (SEATO), 403
Soviet Union, 43, 227, 412, 426, 428
    cold war and, 401, 403, 411
    détente and, 407
    Eastern Europe and, 401
    Nuclear Test Ban Treaty and, 408
    SALT treaties and, 118, 248,
        407–10, 418
    United States and, 376, 401, 403,
        404, 407–10
Spanish-American War, 250, 399,
    400

Photo Acknowledgements

p. xiv, The Bettmann Archive; p. 5, Ken Smorsten; p. 24, Photograph by Win Brookhouse; p. 39, Photograph by Crombie McNeill, Courtesy of NFB Phototeque; pp. 45, 51, 68, 77, 83, 87, 89, United Press International; p. 92, Elliott Erwitt, Magnum Photos; pp. 95, 97, United Press International; pp. 104, 111, © Eileen Christelow/Jeroboam, Inc.; p. 126, © Emilio Mercado/Jeroboam, Inc.; p. 137, from the Wall Street Journal © Dave Gerard; p. 168, Joseph Farris, Time Magazine © Time Inc.; pp. 144, 156, 164, United Press International; p. 196, Photograph by Sam Ashey; p. 208, Charles Harbutt, Magnum Photos; pp. 218, 223, 225, 227, United Press International; p. 232, Wide World Photos; pp. 249, 252, 255, 272, United Press International; p. 278, Christopher W. Morrow, Stock, Boston; p. 280, Owen Franken, Stock, Boston; p. 288, United Press International; p. 300, Ellis Herwig Stock, Boston; p. 312, United Press International; p. 315, Fred Ward, Black Star; p. 317, United Press International; p. 324, Flip Schulker, Black Star; p. 327, Reproduced by special permission of *Playboy*, © 1972 by *Playboy* Magazine; p. 330, Dennis Brack, Black Star; pp. 351, 353, 355, United Press International; p. 363, Pat Oliphant, © 1978, The Washington Star. Reprinted with permission, Los Angeles, Times Syndicate; p. 368, Owen Franken, Stock, Boston; pp. 381, 388, United Press International; p. 391, Copyright, 1978, Los Angeles Times. Reprinted by permission; pp. 402, 406, 408, United Press International; p. 410, © 1979 by Chicago Tribune-New York Times Syndicate; pp. 414, 428, United Press International; p. 432, Mark Godfrey, Magnum Photos; p. 441, Harry Wilks, Stocks, Boston; p. 456, United Press International.